Sustainable Event Management

A Practical Guide

Meegan Jones

publishing for a sustainable future

London • Sterling, VA

First published by Earthscan in the UK and USA in 2010

HB ISBN: 978-1-84407-738-0
PB ISBN: 978-1-84407-739-7

Typeset by Safehouse Creative
Cover design by Susanne Harris

For a full list of publications please contact:

Earthscan
Dunstan House
14a St Cross St
London, EC1N 8XA, UK
Tel: +44 (0)20 7841 1930
Fax: +44 (0)20 7242 1474
Email: earthinfo@earthscan.co.uk
Web: **www.earthscan.co.uk**

22883 Quicksilver Drive, Sterling, VA 20166-2012, USA

Earthscan publishes in association with the International Institute for Environment and Development

A catalogue record for this book is available from the British Library

Library of Congress Cataloging-in-Publication Data

Jones, Meegan.
  Sustainable event management : a practical guide / Meegan Jones.
      p. cm.
  "Publishes in association with the International Institute for Environment and Development."
  Includes index.
  ISBN 978-1-84407-738-0 (hardback) -- ISBN 978-1-84407-739-7 (pbk.) 1. Special events--Management--Handbooks, manuals, etc. 2. Special events--Environmental aspects--Handbooks, manuals, etc. I. International Institute for Environment and Development. II. Title.
  GT3405.J66 2009
  394.2068--dc22
                              2009018116

At Earthscan we strive to minimize our environmental impacts and carbon footprint through reducing waste, recycling and offsetting our CO_2 emissions, including those created through publication of this book. For more details of our environmental policy, see www.earthscan.co.uk.

This book was printed in the UK by CPI Antony Rowe.
The paper used is 100% recycled from post-consumer waste.

The extraordinary rate at which this culture is destroying the planet makes clear the unsustainability and undesirability of this culture. An impressive intellectual critique of civilisation has been building now for many years. Organisations are rising up to fight the destructiveness of the culture, and millions of young people are acting on their knowledge that things just aren't right.

Thomas Berry (9 November 1914–1 June 2009)

Contents

Preface

Across the world each year millions of events of every shape and size are held: community fairs, business functions, religious and cultural celebrations, local sporting competitions and school fairs, through to the world's largest festivals, stadium concerts, conferences, expos and sporting events. These public parties use up resources, send out emissions and generate mountain ranges of waste. They also cause a lot of smiles, community cohesion, celebration, give voice to issues and everyone has a wonderful time.

The idea of creating a temporary city for a massive event, with power, toilets, waste, water, transport, is inherently unsustainable, consuming unnecessary resources, producing masses of waste. It could be said the most environmentally friendly event is no event at all, but that's no fun. Public parties always have and always will be a part of the human story. Those who stage these events have a social and environmental responsibility to reduce their impacts. If all event organizers, from the largest commercial shows to small community fairs, kept sustainability at the core of their planning, the cumulative outcome would be impressive.

But what does running an event sustainably actually mean? Is recycling enough? What about bio-degradable waste? What to do with that? Does being sustainable mean counting up all the emissions and then offsetting them? And if you offset, what projects do you support and how do you know they're effective? If you use biodegradable plates and cups to serve your food and drink on, do you buy those made from genetically modified corn grown in your country or plates that have travelled half way across the world but are made from fallen palm leaves and whose production helps support the sustainable development of India's rural poor? What of the biofuel debate? You want to get away from relying on fossil fuels to power your event, but how can you justify using biodiesel that has been grown from crops which should really have been food? And what to do with all the sewage and waste water? Surely there's a better way to go than full-flush loos with stinky toilet 'blue'?

This book will open up some of these questions and either gives you the outright answers or supplies enough ammunition to go out and ask the right questions of your contractors and suppliers, production staff and venue owners. Hopefully it will also shed light on areas previously left unconsidered.

As we progress through each chapter of the book, we go on a journey towards sustainability with tips, production logistics, projects to undertake and practical solutions to common challenges.
You'll hear from the coalface with real-life examples from event organizers who have tackled challenges and successfully reduced the impacts of their events. There are examples from all around the world, the bulk coming from Australia, the UK, the US and Europe. However the solutions offered can be applied in just about any country and an interpretation of the suggestions can usually be applied to any set of circumstances.

The Science of Sustainability

Scientists, environmental experts, activists and specialists in every field of sustainability, greening, environment, ecology, biodiversity and global warming, have published volumes of books, papers, reports and documents on these subjects. There are thousands of websites, action groups, causes and campaigns online. This book doesn't attempt to recreate or duplicate this work or to teach environmental science. It's written assuming the reader has basic knowledge of the concepts of sustainability and environmental conservation, or at a minimum has the Earth's interest at heart.

When you break it down the base function of sustainable event management is communications, management, marketing and making the right choices. You don't need to be a technical expert. The experts are there to become part of your toolbox of solutions. They are there to bounce your ideas off to ensure you're making the best choices for your event. However these technical experts in environmental science, carbon accounting and the like are not events professionals. It's your role to ensure a healthy marriage between these important functions of sustainability and environmental management with your intimate knowledge of your event, your audience and other particular circumstances surrounding them both.

We are event organizers and our skills are firmly set in this area. We don't need to know the technical details of how to build a reed bed system to recycle water, or the science inside a composting toilet, or how your printing company can clean a printing plate without solvents. All we need to know is what can be done. Learn all you can so you can make informed choices, but don't be afraid to bring in specialists and technical experts when the need arises. In fact ensure you do.

Lead by Example and Create Change

Apart from the obvious improvement environmentally, an attractive by-product of every sustainably produced event is the potential to inspire and motivate others. This includes the supply chain, the media and of course your audience or participants.

Use your event to demonstrate how a sustainable community could work, to show sustainability in action. Every litre of fuel, every flick of the switch, every degree on a thermostat and every bottle or can thrown instead of recycled is directly responsible for using up precious resources, creating waste and inevitably sending up a plume of greenhouse gases adding to climate change. Show how it's possible to do things a better way.

People come in their millions upon millions to our shows and we have the enviable position of a captive and receptive audience. We are in a position to champion causes, highlight issues and inspire changing behaviour. It's a fine line though, as you don't want to hammer people at every turn with your message for a green future. But you could also risk alienating them if you don't consider the environment and take some green steps at your event.

The events industry worldwide – be it the live music scene, outdoor festivals, worldwide sporting competitions, local leagues, community events, agricultural shows or conferences and expos – together make for a huge influencing group. The power of our collective chequebooks has the potential to effect change in the industry and offer a forum for innovators to develop sustainable solutions. There is a need for the events industry to change our production and purchasing habits now.

I hope this book inspires you to adjust the way you produce your event and to use your event in turn to inspire others.

Who Should Read this Book?

- **Event promoters, owners, producers and staff**
  – production coordinators, site managers, festival directors, programmers and crew;
  – music festivals, film and cultural festivals, arena and sports stadium events.

- **Events agencies**
  – professional agencies providing live marketing solutions for corporate clients;
  – product launches, publicity events, sponsorship events and live promotional activities.

- **Conference, seminar, functions and meetings**
  – staff members, promoters or agencies engaged to deliver the event;
  – corporate hospitality, client functions, industry association conferences, specialist seminars, annual meetings.

- **Community**
  – individuals and committees charged with the job of putting on events;
  – community festivals, celebrations and awards, openings, religious celebrations, activist or cause-based events.

- **Schools and universities**
  – teachers, staff, parents and committee members;
  – open days, fairs and fetes, end of year graduation ceremonies, sporting carnivals, excursions, celebrations, entertainment.

- **Sporting clubs, associations, special interest groups**
  – staff, management and committee members;
  – sporting competitions, scouting jamborees and large campouts, social gatherings, ceremonies and graduations, excursions.

- **Event management students**
  – those studying event management, are on internships or work experience, and want to become change agents to move the events industry towards a sustainable future.

Acknowledgements

I would like to thank everyone who has contributed to this book in so many important ways. A special mention must be made of long suffering friends, family, colleagues and mentors who have been sources of inspiration, support, guidance, butt kicks and/or have been kind enough to let me work with them or on their events. Those that must be thanked up front and in name include Esther La Rovere, Jitin John, Ilka Nelson, Lucy Vignola, Matt Grant, Melvin Benn, Zackari Watt and the moz and moon bods... I would especially like to thank carbon guru Catherine Bottrill for her feedback and of course my dad Bob Jones who read through sections and still doesn't get what's wrong with polystyrene or why there aren't enough jokes in my book. Thanks also to India for offering me riverside, beachside and mountainside offices.

I would like to again thank Melvin Benn, Director of Festival Republic for allowing me to put in information on the work I have done for him on Latitude, Reading and Leeds Festivals. Thanks also to the team at Glastonbury Festival including Dick Vernon and Michael and Emily Eavis for allowing me to cover the festival, to Bob Wilson of Greenpeace UK for his guidance and continually being an ethical sounding board. Thanks also to Liz Eliot and Tracey Slough for letting me reproduce photos of the Green Way in the Greenfields at Glasto.

You'll hear from events around the globe in the book and the following experts of event greening must be thanked for allowing me to include their work. Andre L. Jaeger Soares of Ecocentro IPEC/greening Boom Festival; Andy Mead and Ollie Stroud/Firefly Solar, Bill Hauritz and Amanda Jackes/Woodford Folk Festival, Buzz Thompson/Falls Festival, Chloe Wilson and Penny Kemp/Big Green Gathering, Christophe Platel/Paleo, Clare Byrne/Electric Picnic, Gael Leopold/WWF and One Planet Living, Greg Peele/Meredith Music and Golden Plains Festivals, Jaime Nack/Three Squares Inc/2008 Democratic Convention, Jenna Eyrich and Kyle Schember/Global Inheritance/Coachella, Laura Sohn/Bonnaroo, Liam O'Keefe/Creative Environment, Lucy Sheldon, Barbora Patkova and Adam Walker/Magnificent Revolution, Marian Goodall, Tom Price, Travis Miller, Blue and DA/Burning Man, Mat Morris/Global Protection Agency/Splendour In The Grass, National Folk Festival, Paul Sloan/Waverock Weekender, Robert Brewster and Matt Grant/Peats Ridge Festival, Rachel Kemp/Southbound, Shane Collins/GreenSweep, Sarah Haynes/ROTHBURY, Stefano Casalotti/BikeFest, Vickii Cotter/Bluesfest, and of course to Vivian Lees and Susan Forrester/Big Day Out for their words and Julian Smith for the brilliant cover photo of the sun setting over Big Day Out Melbourne.

I need also to thank by name: Angela Richards Donà/Rainforest Alliance, Artur Soares da Silva/Boom, Ben Challis/A Greener Festival, Ben Todd/Arcola Theatre, Bill Eagan/Aggreko, Brenda Platt/Institute for Local Self-Reliance, Christof Huber/Yourope, Claire O'Neil/A Greener Festival and Association of Independent Festivals, Daren Abney/Organic Exchange, David Wick/Spiral Solar Sun Showers, Wilbur and Kate Whittaker/WaterAid, Eamon Pryle and Colin Eade/Workers Beer Company, Ed

Cook/Network Recycling, Ed Warner/One Water, Erica Schuetz and Noelle Ferdon/Food and Water Watch, Gemma Parkhouse/ExCeL London, Greer Allen/TINA, Hamish Skermer/Natural Event, Jeff Horowitz/AD Partners, Harmony Blake/Festival Republic, Lynda Thompson/Ethical Threads, Mark Charman/Dvolve, Mike Lawton and Ben Mayo/Rengentek, Natasha Grainger/London Marathon, Neal Turley/Sustainable Waves, Parasher Baruah and Vinod Shetty/Dharavi Project, Roberto Aponte, Ginger Ridder and Aaron Leventman/Bioneers, Rowena Priess/Philips, Samantha Wright/Terrachoice, Steve Bolton/MBDC.

Thank you to all the organizations and individuals who have supplied information or photos throughout the book. Many are named in the book and you can find their contact information there too.

Rising Tide Newcastle:
I would like to thank my friends and activists in Newcastle NSW Australia, my home, who are kicking up trouble to bring the world's attention to climate chaos which pours out of our city's harbour. As the world's largest coal port even before its capacity was recently doubled, our small city does its part to help along climate change. As a grass roots organization, **Rising Tide Newcastle** does brilliant work in organizing harbour protests, disrupting coal trains, coal loaders, coal mines and the like. This activity brings focus to the issues of coal mining and export is becoming increasingly important as they gain momentum and strength organizing national campaigns on coal and climate issues. I am giving 10 per cent of my author profits to this group and hope that it will help to support their valuable work as I can't often be in Newcastle to get on a blow-up mattress and paddle out to try and stop a coal ship. www.risingtide.org

List of Acronyms and Abbreviations

AD	anaerobic digestion
C2C	Cradle to Cradle
CCBA	Climate, Community and Biodiversity Alliance
CCC	Clean Clothes Campaign
CDM	Clean Development Mechanism
CER	certified emissions reduction
CFL	compact fluorescent lamp
CHP	combined heat and power
CSR	Corporate Social Responsibility
DA	Development Application
Defra	Department for the Environment, Food and Rural Affairs
ECF	elemental chlorine free
EFGLO	environmentally friendly greener living options
EfW	Energy from Waste
EPC	Energy Performance Certificate
EPP	Environmental Preferential Purchasing
EV	electric vehicle
FSC	Forest Stewardship Council
GEK	Gasifier Experimenters Kit
GHG	greenhouse gas
GMO	genetically modified organism
HDPE	high density polyethylene
HSE	health, safety and environment
IEQ	indoor environment quality
IFOAM	International Federation of Organic Agricultural Movements
ILO	International Labour Organization
IPCC	Intercontinental Panel on Climate Change
ISEAL	International Social and Environmental Accreditation and Labelling Alliance
JI	Joint Implementation
KPI	Key Performance Indicator
LCA	life cycle assessment
LDPE	low density polyethylene
LED	light emitting diode
LEED	Leadership in Energy and Environmental Design
LLDPE	linear low density polyethylene
LTL	less than loadfull
MR	Magnificent Revolution

MRF	Materials Recovery Facility
NAPM	National Association of Paper Merchants
NGO	non-governmental organization
OPL	One Planet Living
OPP	oriented polypropylene
PA	public address
PCF	processed chlorine free
PCW	post-consumer wastepaper
PET	polyethylene terephthalate
PLA	polylactic acid
PP	polypropylene
PVC	polyvinyl chloride
RTFO	Renewable Transport Fuel Obligation programme
TCF	totally chlorine free
TINA	This Is Not Art festival
UCEC	Universal Code of Ethical Conduct
UNDP	United Nations Development Programme
VCS	Voluntary Carbon Standard
VER	verified emissions reduction
VOC	volatile organic compound
VPA	vegetation protection area
WEEE	Waste Electrical and Electronic Equipment
WFTO	World Fair Trade Organization
WRAP	Worldwide Responsible Accredited Production
WRAP	Waste and Resources Action Programme
WVO	waste vegetable oil

Figure 1.1 Blending nature and events. Bioneers in San Francisco is a wonderful example of a multi-venue conference, which has minimized its impact

Source: Tim Porter, www.bioneers.org

chapter 1
Sustainability and Events

Rather than being hedonistic, resource gulping and garbage producing, events have the potential to be model examples of a harmonious balance between human activity, resource use and minimal environmental impact. Those producing live events can demonstrate sustainability in action.

Almost every human activity uses up precious resources provided by the planet and results in waste and emissions. To look into the future and see one that is truly sustainable, we simply can't use everything up and discard after a single use. Underscoring all your operations and purchasing decisions with this simple truth will bring your event towards sustainability.

Now is the time to stamp your place as an event sustainability pioneer. Do you want your festival to be a leader, one that others look to for the way forward? If you're organizing a conference, sporting championship, community gathering, scouting jamboree, etc., you have the opportunity to produce the greenest yet. This book will arm you with the skills and knowledge, and most importantly a way of thinking to help make your event truly sustainable.

The chapters of this book will delve into all areas of event planning, showing how each system could have an effect on the environment and suggesting sustainable alternatives. The major areas of impact at events are:

- Energy/power.
- Transport.
- Waste management.
- Waste reduction and resource recovery.
- Materials purchasing and procurement.

Issues such as biodiversity, archaeology, cultural heritage and ethical concerns around procurement should also be considered.

The terms 'sustainability' and 'sustainable development' are understood by a wide and increasingly informed audience. Becoming buzz words, along with terms and concepts like 'climate change' and 'carbon footprint', they are used as brands in media and marketing, and our audiences are listening. These concepts are working as green hooks bringing the great washed masses over to the side of green. And that's a good thing. It gets your audience thinking about the issues and makes your job to tune in your event to sustainability a little easier through engaging an audience already warmed to the idea.

Sustainability – What Is It?

In 1987, the World Commission on Environment and Development created a definition of sustainable development in their report 'Our Common Future';[1]

> *Sustainable development meets the needs of the present without compromising the ability of future generations to meet their own needs.*

How can this be applied to the events industry and how do sustainable events fit into the global picture of sustainable development? In any system, one area affects another, resulting in a cumulative and interlinking effect. Our environment is a system and every person, every business and every industry is part of it and must play their role towards sustainable development on a global scale.

With the sheer size of the events industry across the world and the millions upon millions of people who attend events each year, the industry and all who arrange large public gatherings have a responsibility to ensure sustainable event management.

If the industry continues to ignore this urgent call of nature, we will surely play our part in the continual devastation of the natural environment and its ever diminishing resources.

Areas of Impact

The myriad activities, logistics, production and systems required to put on an event, in the end can be distilled down to just two things: *resource use* or *emissions*. Fleshing that out a little:

- Use of natural and renewable resources.
- Use of non-renewable resources.
- Use of synthetic resources.
- Emissions to air.
- Emissions to water.
- Emissions to land (waste).

Figure 1.2 Stunningly clean Coachella Festival

Source: Global Inheritance, who manage the recycling operations at this event

When you buy 'stuff' to produce your event you may find the products you choose are made from non-renewable resources, from materials produced using unsustainable methods or whose production results in toxic by-products. We're quickly using up the Earth's bounty and poisoning it in the process. Our persistent reliance on non-renewable resources a sustainable future does not make.

Whenever there's a huge gathering of people, they are going to have an impact on the surrounding air, land and water, with knock-on effects on the wider environment. This goes without saying really. At any large event resources will be used, there will be fumes, there will be waste and there will be sewage.

To reduce the impact your event has on the immediate surroundings and the environment at large, we need to address each area of event operations including:

- Purchasing.
- Waste management.
- Energy production.
- Water management.
- Transport.

One area of impact you want to increase is to influence change. Your event's sustainable management and the way you communicate this along with creative ways to involve and inspire your audience and other stakeholders is as important as making the actual changes.

The Power of Change

Moving beyond your actual event, as a result of your sustainability focus you can influence the ongoing behaviour and attitudes of your audience, contractors, suppliers and the events industry. Running your event as sustainably as possible should underlay all operations. Combined across the event industry, the social and worldwide impact of sustainable event management should not be underestimated.

Whatever your event, you have the potential to craft a short-term mini-utopia. You have the power to make change and leave participants and audience with the inspiration to also live more sustainably. This is your legacy and your contribution to a sustainable future for the world at large.

Events such as Boom have a transforming potential in many ways. Firstly, the gathering of thousands of people in a specific place for a limited amount of time is an opportunity for reflection on the communitarian nature of our species: How do we live together? How do we relate? How do we occupy space? What do we leave behind? What is our ecological function in the web of life? How can we satisfy our survival needs in equilibrium with the needs of all other species? These questions can be instigated in any event, even when music and art are the main focus.

Dr André Soares, Ecocentro, Boom Festival

Figure 1.3 Community living at Boom Festival.
Go to the Appendix to read the sustainable
history of this event

Source: Jakob Kolar, Boom

Dollars and Sense

Sustainability is an important aspect of event creation; however in the business world the reality is it must also be balanced with delivering the event on time and on budget. You may come up against those who don't want to change the way they do business. However I encourage you to go forth and blaze trails. Offer opportunities to new and innovative suppliers and contractors who want to move with you to a sustainable future. Work with the old-school boys and coax them into the light.

If you're working on an event with a commercial focus, understand you also need to not bite the hand that feeds you. You may not be able to be as green as you like and some of your ideas may be rejected as the commercial reality wins out. Don't forget to look at the bigger picture. The world is not going to turn miraculously into rainbows and mung beans. There will always be global brands, but with your attention and that of

people like you working for the big brands, they may not always be decimating developing countries through irresponsible business practices.

Everything you do adds to this sustainability soup we're cooking up. Play the corporate game and agitate from the inside. See yourself as a change agent and get in under the corporate skin. The commercial gigs are the ones where great leaps can be made and dollars are available to be spent, which allows the sustainable innovators and suppliers to blossom into profitable going concerns. No matter how much some of us would like to see a change in the current paradigm, in the current model we have business makes the world go around. It probably will continue to do so for some time. (Or at least until we hit 2012 predictions, aliens invade or of course irreversible climate change occurs.)

Corporate Social Responsibility

The Triple Bottom Line

More than just financial goals, a business's end game should include environmental and social responsibility. The crux of the triple bottom line is concern for all three outcomes:

- Economic.
- Environmental.
- Social.

Many events are community minded and created for celebration and demonstration, and are innately social and environmental happenings. However, in the commercial world, to truly

CSR Checklist ☑

Along with the financial health of your event, to be sustainable you need to meet social and environmental responsibilities.

Social

- [ ] Meeting with the local community.
- [ ] Ensuring accessibility to the event for all who wish to attend.
- [ ] Sensitivity to cultural or religious groups.
- [ ] Ensuring everyone who works on your event, including contractors and suppliers' staff, is treated fairly and has a safe working environment.
- [ ] Tracking product supply chains to ensure ethical production and fair trade agreements are in place.
- [ ] Sourcing goods and services locally and employing local people.

Environmental

- [ ] Sustainable land and water use.
- [ ] Reducing and managing emissions to land, air and water.
- [ ] Minimizing non-renewable resource use.
- [ ] Ethical and sustainable product choice and procurement.
- [ ] Considerations for noise pollution.

embrace sustainability, events need to consider not just their financial performance, but also the role the event can play in wider society. Events need to minimize their environmental impacts and maximize any benefits they can offer to the community and the planet. This is particularly relevant when looking at purchasing, and the environmental and social impacts of the decisions you make. We'll cover the things you need to consider to make the best choices in Chapter 6.

The Sustainability Sell-In

So you're organizing an event for a client, a boss or company who's not really interested in sustainability? How do you sell-in sustainability to get your new ideas off the table and into reality? Apart from the environmental benefits, the positives of producing an event sustainably can include:

- Positioning and competitive advantage.
- Public relations opportunities.
- Financial savings.

Positioning and Competitive Advantage

You can appeal to the other green in your client or company – envy (the green monster). If financially motivated and in business for business's sake, they are likely to have a keen competitive streak. This can lead to bouts of professional jealousy when a competitor stakes a claim before they do. Use the green monster to your advantage by demonstrating how your event and

Figure 1.4 Roskilde Festival in Denmark runs for four days with four days of warm up. They share with us plans for getting their massive audience to take Green Footsteps to the festival, later in the book

Source: Roskilde Festival

company becoming a sustainability leader is to its competitive advantage – you could otherwise end up being left behind by your competitors.

Public Relations Benefits

As more people are becoming green at heart, they are voting with their wallets, supporting those companies that are doing the same. The audience is demanding that events be sustainable, be green and be ethical. If your event is not considering sustainability in its operations, could this come back around and bite you? If asked by the media or the audience, can you report on what you're doing to reduce the impact of your event?

Financial Savings

The bottom line (as opposed to triple bottom line) may be a good place to start. Do your budgets and look for savings both on an immediate and long-term basis. There are savings to be had in many green and sustainable choices. Do cost comparisons in all the major areas such as energy, fuel supply, procurement, transport, hire costs, waste disposal, etc. You will be surprised where the sustainable alternative may pan out cheaper than its conventional counterpart.

Waste is an area where a direct financial saving can be easily calculated and communicated. It generally doesn't cost to take recyclable goods to a Materials Recovery Facility[2] (MRF), or you can actually sell your pre-separated plastics and metal directly to the processor. So it makes business sense to reduce the amount of waste you pay to throw.

The Industry, Suppliers and Contractors

The events industry across the world is changing rapidly towards sustainable management. Your audience is becoming more clued into sustainability issues and expects events to toe the line. The government agencies regulating events licences are now placing environmental conditions on them. Your clients may demand that you produce their events sustainably. And so too, those supplying goods and services to the events industry must lift their game and provide the green solutions you need.

Clever suppliers and contractors are developing tailored products and services with event sustainability in mind. Traditional contractors and suppliers would be well advised to look at their systems and what they offer events, to make sure they keep up with the innovators entering the market.

Demand for greener alternatives by events is pulling change up through the supply chain. To achieve event sustainability, managers are requiring suppliers and contractors to change what they offer. Rather than waiting for new green products to appear, demand them of your suppliers or create them yourself.

Very soon however, choices won't be limited, and rather than having to encourage suppliers to investigate greener options, enterprising organizations will be knocking down doors to present their sustainable solution for events. This has increased dramatically even since I started writing this book a year ago.

The soon-to-be abundant availability of sustainable solutions for the events industry will cause competition amongst the suppliers as they look for outlets for their products and services. This will further increase the uptake of sustainability in events management as more options that have been tested and proven in a live situation will be on offer. Event managers who may not have previously considered sustainability could find themselves with sustainable solutions without lifting a finger.

As an event manager you are in a unique position whether organizing a local school fair for 500 people, a conference for 10,000 or a national event for hundreds of thousands, to make a change right now and to help move the industry in the direction it needs to go. The decisions you make will contribute to the burgeoning demand for sustainable solutions for events management.

Help Grow the Market

By making the best purchasing and contracting decisions your contribution to growing the demand for fledgling sustainable products and services for the events industry can help move ideas on to full blown commercial success.

There are pioneering suppliers who have been offering perfect solutions for several years now. They have been knocking on the same doors year in year out and it is only very recently that they have been asked in. Some recently tuned-in event managers are shocked to hear that the solution they have just started to look for has been attempting to present to them for some time. So don't leave the innovators and sustainable designers out in the cold. Give a new contractor a go. This may shake up the old boys and get them thinking green as well.

Greenwashing by those in it for a quick buck will be obvious. As you become more clued up in the issues you'll also become equipped with an arsenal of questions and knowledge from which you can make informed choices. By using your green event know-how you're empowered to keep the contractors honest, talk in green realities and help keep the market innovative and moving in the right direction.

Grants

Governments are under increasing pressure to meet their publicly committed levels of reduction in greenhouse gas (GHG) emissions. As a result, they are offering incentives to individuals, organizations and businesses to consequentially also reduce their emissions. Grants are available to convert to solar power and put in community combined heat and power plants, investing in renewable energy technology and infrastructure. There are also research and development grants. You will also find tax breaks when moving to more sustainable energy sources and operations. Some research into your own area may reveal grants and other projects relevant to your circumstances.

Leaving a Legacy

What you are doing in all this sustainable event management work I hope you take on, is to create a situation where innovators and sustainable designers have a fertile garden in which to grow. In just a few years you will see that the work you do now will be industry changing. The communities, venues and contractors you interact with will all be influenced and changed by your involvement. It's up to you – motivated event managers and those training to enter the industry – to see sustainability in events as a must-take and to make changes happen.

Read in the Appendix how the 2008 Democratic National Convention put sustainability through every aspect of its operations and left a lasting legacy.

To bring this all together, everyone producing your event needs to be heading in the same direction. Although written policies can be tiresome to produce and often then left to go dusty on a shelf, it is a good way to focus your efforts and keep you on the right path.

Read on and you will be pleased to see that the sustainability policy you need to build aligns fairly closely with the layout of this book. As you read through the various sections of the book, you will be able to form a picture of which bits are important to you and your event and from that devise a plan to move towards sustainable event management.

Sustainability Policy

Putting together a sustainability policy for your event will be an important tool to focus your efforts, keeping you on the right path. It is a good document to have to disseminate publicly, give for student enquiries, to new contractors and to new staff. There are many models you could take, and there is no right or wrong way of doing this. You could go into as much detail as you like or make it more of a broad mission statement. It should indicate your commitment to sustainable management and describe your pathways to sustainability.

Included in your sustainability policy should be discussion on the following. You will see that this basically mirrors the flow of the chapters in this book.

- Commitment to sustainability, resourcing and staff.
- Consultation process and training of staff and education of key stakeholders.
- Statement of goals or objectives.
- Description of the Key Sustainability Indicators that performance will be measured against.

It should then have an overview on the key areas of:

- Energy use.
- Transport impact.
- Water conservation and effluent management.
- Resource consumption and purchasing.
- Waste management.

- Other environmental and social impacts such as light and sound pollution, ecological and heritage sensitivity and conservation.

The sustainability policy should then go on to detail how the following will be undertaken:

- Compliance with targets.
- Auditing.
- Monitoring and review.

General observations could also be included such as government or industry policies or protocols which you must meet, aim to exceed or which may make an impact on your operations in the future. Make sure you keep across any policy developments and technological advances which may be relevant to your work.

Be aware also of best practice standards or codes of practice relevant to event management and sustainability. Mention any certifications you are planning to achieve.

A great example of a sustainability policy is by **Bluesfest** in Australia. Read it in the Appendix. On the following page read the overriding principles which direct the **Burning Man** event. These principles have sustainability at their core.

Box 1.2

The Ten Principles of Burning Man

Radical inclusion: Anyone may be a part of Burning Man. We welcome and respect the stranger. No prerequisites exist for participation in our community.

Gifting: Burning Man is devoted to acts of gift giving. The value of a gift is unconditional. Gifting does not contemplate a return or an exchange for something of equal value.

Decommodification: In order to preserve the spirit of gifting, our community seeks to create social environments that are unmediated by commercial sponsorships, transactions or advertising. We stand ready to protect our culture from such exploitation. We resist the substitution of consumption for participatory experience.

Radical self-reliance: Burning Man encourages the individual to discover, exercise and rely on his or her inner resources.

Radical self-expression: Radical self-expression arises from the unique gifts of the individual. No one other than the individual or a collaborating group can determine its content. It is offered as a gift to others. In this spirit, the giver should respect the rights and liberties of the recipient.

Communal effort: Our community values creative cooperation and collaboration. We strive to produce, promote and protect social networks, public spaces, works of art, and methods of communication that support such interaction.

Civic responsibility: We value civil society. Community members who organize events should assume responsibility for public welfare and endeavour to communicate civic responsibilities to participants. They must also assume responsibility for conducting events in accordance with local, state and federal laws.

Leaving no trace: Our community respects the environment. We are committed to leaving no physical trace of our activities wherever we gather. We clean up after ourselves and endeavour, whenever possible, to leave such places in a better state than when we found them.

Participation: Our community is committed to a radically participatory ethic. We believe that transformative change, whether in the individual or in society, can occur only through the medium of deeply personal participation. We achieve being through doing. Everyone is invited to work. Everyone is invited to play. We make the world real through actions that open the heart.

Immediacy: Immediate experience is, in many ways, the most important touchstone of value in our culture. We seek to overcome barriers that stand between us and a recognition of our inner selves, the reality of those around us, participation in society and contact with a natural world exceeding human powers. No idea can substitute for this experience.

www.burningman.com

Box 1.3

Sustainable Event Checklist ☑

Venue Checklist

(Indoors)

☐ What is the public transport access?

☐ Is the venue in the closest location for most participants?

☐ Does venue waste management include recycling and composting?

☐ Are there water conservation and grey water management processes in place?

☐ Do they have programmes to reduce energy consumption?

☐ Does the venue have access to fresh air?

☐ How is the venue heated and cooled?

☐ Do they clean with chemical-free products?

☐ Does the venue have an environmental policy?

☐ Is the venue certified for energy efficiency and sustainable construction?

(Outdoors)

☐ What is the public transport access?

☐ Are there ecologically sensitive areas?

☐ Is there access to water and can grey water be treated and disposed of on site?

☐ How far will sewage and waste need to travel to be treated off site?

☐ Is there access to grid power?

Conference Checklist

☐ Communicate electronically, don't send vast amounts of printed material out by mail.

☐ Supply any handouts on the first day, so there's no chance of being left in hotel rooms and second copies needed.

☐ Provide notes on a thumbdrive, or offer links to download presentations post event.

☐ Any stationery to be from 100 per cent post-consumer recycled paper, and pens to be 'eco' options.

☐ Turn off PA, lights and AC when rooms aren't in use.

☐ Arrange name badges to be handed back in.

☐ Hotel room recycling, bulk dispensing of toiletries, towels not changed every day, newspapers delivered only on request.

Purchasing Checklist

☐ Buy products that are 'eco-labelled'.

☐ Buy locally.

☐ Use local contractors.

☐ Use goods produced under fair labour conditions.

Sound/lights/production Checklist

- ☐ Power your gear on clean green energy (either mains, or by sustainable biofuels, or zero emissions technologies).
- ☐ Use energy saving equipment.
- ☐ Convert lighting to LEDs.
- ☐ If using a lot of low wattage gear, ensure mobile power generators have power factor correction to be able to take advantage of efficiencies.
- ☐ Have a switch-off campaign – turn off everything that's not being used, especially the lights in the daytime.

Sets/staging/décor Checklist

- ☐ Hire, don't buy.
- ☐ Use certified sustainably grown timber (FSC).
- ☐ Construct sets with found, re-used or repurposed materials.
- ☐ Use non toxic paints and varnishes with zero VOC emissions.
- ☐ Use organic cotton and fabric produced under fair labour conditions for curtains, sets and décor.
- ☐ Pack up, store and re-use gear.
- ☐ Mark stage flooring, sets and other construction so that easy reassembly is possible.
- ☐ Donate unused materials, or items salvaged from the de-rig for re-use or repurposing.

Trader/vendor/exhibitor Checklist

- ☐ Produce signs which can be re-used at future shows.
- ☐ Use only energy saving lights.
- ☐ Produce all printed material sustainably.
- ☐ No plastic bags, hand out re-usable bags.
- ☐ No over-packaged single samples.
- ☐ Ethical and environmentally sound product sourcing.
- ☐ Hired materials.
- ☐ Ensure re-use or repurposing is planned for any bespoke construction, set and décor.

Catering Checklist

- ☐ Provide bulk water dispensing and washable cups.
- ☐ No single-serve satchets or individually wrapped meals.
- ☐ Organic, fair trade and locally sourced ingredients.
- ☐ In season food, to avoid unnecessary food miles.
- ☐ Programme for unused food from buffets, such as to a food bank or hostel, or send for composting or to a worm farm.

Transport Checklist

☐ Hold your event close to public transport access.

☐ Provide your audience, participants, delegate, competitors, staff and crew with detailed information about public transport access, timetables and locations.

☐ Put on shuttle buses if you need to 'join the dots' between existing public transport and your event site.

☐ Promote chartered coaches to your event.

☐ Offer incentives to come by public transport, bike or foot.

☐ Offer secure bike parking.

☐ Limit car parking space numbers and charge for parking.

☐ Encourage car pooling.

☐ Ration car spaces for exhibitors, traders and vendors.

Communications Checklist

☐ Tell your audience, delegates, participants and sports competitors what you need them to do to be greener at your event.

☐ Pre-promote things such as public transport and preparatory purchasing recommendations.

☐ Get your staff, crew, contractors, suppliers and service providers on board with your greening goals.

☐ Use the media to promote your greening.

Green your Office

☐ Recycle. Use sustainable office supplies. Put your photocopier to print double sided as default, or collect misprints and print on the clean side.

☐ Sign up to green energy. Put all equipment on power save mode. Make sure battery packs for laptops and phones aren't left on overnight. Have light sensors installed. Open the windows!

Figure 1.5 As you can see above, Roskilde Festival creates a mini-city. This means a massive amount of infrastructure, logistics and organization

Source: Roskilde Festival

Figure 1.6 Artistically converted recycling bins at Coachella Festival by Global Inheritance as part of their TRASHed Art of Recycling programme

Source: Global Inheritance

The Carbon Issue

'Going green' in events must address far more than a carbon footprint and some lightweight action. A wider view must be taken, including sustainability and traditional environmental concerns; resource use is particularly relevant to events.

Coming back to a single issue such as carbon emissions is not appropriate given the complex systems and compounding effects in event management. It's putting the cart before the horse. By concentrating on reducing the overall environmental impact of your event in every possible process, the inevitable result will also be a reduction in carbon emissions.

The issues surrounding global warming are something the events industry must consider very seriously, however, widening the focus from your event's carbon footprint is essential. Climate change science is still a new area and it is being continually developed, reviewed and refined. Carbon auditing is still in development as research continues in the measurement of various activities. Importantly, the relative impact of one activity against another is still being discovered. It is not yet an exact science.

If you want to measure your footprint, you would be well advised to also reflect on the likelihood of a big fat ecological footprint. That includes all the 'stuff' that's needed to produce the event. I'm not suggesting you tackle a comprehensive project to assess your event's ecological footprint (although tools are available to do so as we will discuss later), but I do believe event producers need to consider how much of the Earth's natural resources are swallowed up as a result of their activities.

The following are just some of the broader issues that need to be addressed:

- Greening your supply chain.
- Looking at energy efficiency.
- Waste management and landfill footprint.
- Water conservation and waste water management.
- Fair trade and labour issues.
- Minimizing chemical usage.
- Using sustainable materials and recyclable alternatives.

Looking to sustainability as a whole concept, including traditional environmental issues, is appropriate rather than becoming too focused on the single carbon issue.

Develop a comfortable relationship with the concepts of sustainability and work towards embedding it into the heart of your event and that of your production team, your client, organization or company.

Your role is as a change agent. Knowledge, inspiration and conversation are your most powerful tools.

Figure 1.7 The crowd at Boom Festival. Thousands of people gather in the semi arid lands of Portugal and create a sustainable community
Source: Jakob Kolar, Boom Festival

Event Carbon Footprint

The measurement of an individual's or business's carbon footprint has had a few years to settle into agreed areas of measurement. Transport, travel, energy use, etc., are the key areas in which CO_2 equivalent GHGs are counted. There are hundreds of footprint measurement tools available online and, while the results do vary, simple personal and simple business footprint measurement is possible.

This is not the case currently for events, though in the industry we are working to establish internationally agreed measures. Services are beginning to emerge claiming they can measure an event's footprint, but investigation shows there are wildly varying methods of measurement and indeed they are measuring different things. Until the areas to be measured, methods and emissions factors are determined and agreed, and these accepted by the majority in the industry that work as event footprint auditors, the footprint of an event is not really a valid or robust tool to use, to publicly claim or to use as a performance tool to compare against other events.

Where most of these services fall short is in that they aren't event experts and offer too basic an audit or an inappropriately complex one. Both options ignore the peculiarities of live event production. Auditors can leave a report with a certain figure on the front page, which you should take as your 'footprint'. Perhaps they may also leave you with the promise of a convenient offsetting service, earning a nice commission in the process.

Auditing of emissions is a fantastic management tool, but how you actually use this data to sustainably manage your event going forward is the key. Taking steps to reduce your event's impact is the challenge we all need to take on.

The complex nature of most events makes determining a true carbon footprint a near impossible task. Materials use and freight are big areas of impact but are very difficult to track as you're relying on information from contractors and suppliers. It could become a daunting task where the administration involved could outweigh the eventual benefit gleaned from the data.

Rather than attempting to measure a 'carbon footprint' which infers total emissions, audit the areas where solid robust data can be gathered and actual change can be made as a result of having this information.

The **Greenhouse Gas Protocol**[3] establishes three scopes for measuring GHGs. '**Scope 1**' is direct emissions from on-site operations: power generators and gas used for cooking and heating showers. '**Scope 2**' is emissions from grid power. '**Scope 3**' is indirect emissions, such as transport, waste, water treatment. Scopes 1 and 2 are quite easy to audit. Things get trickier for Scope 3.

The following areas can be measured to assess your performance, set goals for future reductions and, if you choose to, offset the emissions created.

Easy to Measure: Energy and Transport

Calculating CO_2 emissions of energy usage at your event is simple. So is transport of audience if you know the postcode or town where they travelled from (ticket sales info), audience numbers, percentage by transport mode such as coach and shuttle bus figures and car park figures, car occupancy rates, etc. How to do this is explained in Chapters 3 and 4.

Hard to Measure: Food and Beverage

I don't suggest trying to measure the embedded energy in food sold at an event. People would have eaten no matter where they were, and the main way you can reduce the CO_2 impact of food eaten at your event is through ensuring local sourcing of produce to reduce transport impact, offering organic and vegetarian, etc. For an event managed sustainably, these should be part of the plan anyway. Of course having bars and encouraging drinking will add to a person's footprint for the day, but still this is a very complex issue and probably more detail than you need to go into.

Even Harder: Freight and Products

Looking to calculate freight is particularly troublesome. Considerations such as what percentage your load took up on the truck, where it went enroute to your event, what sized truck, open road or city congestion, did it come from the courier's depot, direct from supplier, or did it come from a central warehouse. Before this, were the products you're moving manufactured locally, at the other end of the country or overseas? Where do you stop? And how do you track every delivery? You can of course go with averages, but how accurate is that going to be? The standard measure for freight used by the Department for the Environment, Food and Rural Affairs (Defra) is split into two vehicle sizes and can be done on a tonne of goods per kilometre rate or just per kilometre. But what to do with the info at the end apart from offset? The price of fuel is doing a good part of the job for us, creating efficiencies in transport.

Trying to calculate the embedded energy in products used at your event will be impossible until there is universal carbon emission product labelling.

The Key Sustainability Indicators you're taken through in this book don't include such things as the embedded energy in food and beverages, materials and goods. This is because the methodologies needed to accurately measure this are currently wide and varied. As will be discussed in Chapter 6, the measurement of climate impact of products and materials is becoming more standardized. We are seeing footprint sizes being printed on products, but it will be some time before all products are footprinted and you can easily add up all the CO_2 emissions from your purchasing.

If your event production and purchasing is not too complicated, tools such as that offered by **Best Foot Forward's** 'Event Footprinter' can be used to assess the overall impact of all your purchasing and operations. www.event.footprinter.com

Carbon Offsetting

Unless you demonstrate a rigorous strategy of emissions reduction at your event, you would be well advised to leave carbon offsetting alone. Most of the tips and advice in this book have consequential emissions reduction effect.

It's widely accepted that the best way to reduce carbon emissions is to:

- Reduce energy and transport use.
- Replace fossil fuels with renewable resources and then, and only then,
- Neutralize the remaining unavoidable emissions through carbon offsetting schemes.

Before considering offsetting make sure you have done all you can to reduce emissions from your event including:

- Taking action to reduce power consumption.
- Maximizing public transport use.
- Maximizing car occupancy rates.
- Adjusting to low emissions product purchasing.
- Reducing waste to landfill and incineration volumes.
- Maximizing recycling.
- Capturing biodegradable waste and sending it for composting or biogas production.
- Reducing water consumption.
- Switching to green energy.
- Using sustainable biofuels.
- Using zero emissions power generation.

If you decide to do some offsetting, I recommend you don't refer to it as an offset against your event's carbon footprint as the latter is almost impossible to measure, as we have discussed. I believe the term 'footprint' implies the entire emissions as a result of an event, and with the complexity of event production it is very difficult to measure. Report in terms of carbon emissions for specific activities rather than inferring you have accurately measured every puff of CO_2 associated with producing your event.

Align the offset with a particular element of your event that can be accurately measured, and which can be scrutinized if required, such as energy generation, audience travel or waste volumes.

More details on offsetting options at the end of Chapter 3.

Carbon Neutral

I recommend you don't claim carbon neutrality for your event unless you simultaneously state against which measures you are making this claim. It's difficult for an event to be truly carbon neutral as measurement of all carbon impacts is not possible. For example, the climate impact of purchasing and freight/transport of goods can't be accurately measured in the context of event production. However, you can become carbon or climate neutral against areas you have direct control such as powering your event, waste production, water usage, sewage and crew/artist/participant travel. You may also be able to accurately measure audience transport, which may be one of the largest climate impacts your event has. We discuss how to measure these key indicators of your event's sustainability in the upcoming chapter of the book.

However, simply claiming your event is climate neutral may scream 'greenwash' if you aren't seen to be doing all you can to reduce the impacts – have a robust system in place to accurately measure these impacts, to openly report what you are measuring, and how you are mitigating their impacts, (often through voluntary carbon offsetting).

UNEP has developed the Climate Neutral Network where organizations can sign up to pledge their commitment to reducing their climate impact. Although it may be difficult to truly measure the complete climate impact of live events, by signing onto the Climate Neutral Network, events can show their commitment to reductions and working as hard as they can, towards the ultimate goal of being Climate Neutral. www.unep.org/climateneutral

Measuring Sustainability

To gauge progress in moving your event towards sustainable management, you'll need to measure your results and to set goals for the future. Throughout the book are the tools you'll need to measure the sustainability performance of your event – the Key Sustainability Indicators (summarized in Tables 1.1 to 1.4).

The CO_2 emissions factors used are UK based and sourced from Defra June 2008 unless otherwise indicated. You are advised to check in your country what the agreed measures are.

There are industry benchmarking projects happening at the moment and soon you will be able to place your event against industry standards to see how you have performed.

Setting Goals

Once you have audited your performance you can set goals for future events. As anyone that's done a business or marketing course will know, goals or objectives should be measurable, achievable and have a time frame. Apply this across all your Key Sustainability Indicators. Examples of objectives could be:

- To increase public transport use.
- To decrease landfill and increase recycled and composted waste.
- To reduce total number of mobile generators, fuel volume and consequential carbon emissions.
- To reduce total carbon emissions for the event.
- To reduce water consumption.

Figure 1.8 Glastonbury Festival in the UK is reputed to be the largest music and arts event of its kind. It really is one of a kind though. We hear about what this festival does to reduce its impact throughout the book

Source: Nichola Nichols

Key Sustainability Indicators

The following are the various elements that will indicate your event's sustainability performance and, where relevant, a corresponding greenhouse gas emissions factor.

Table 1.1

Note that for cars, taxis and coaches or shuttle buses scheduled specifically for the event, the emissions are per vehicle, rather than per passenger. For those modes of transport that would be 'running anyway' such as local buses, ferries, trains, flights, a per passenger/mile(km) figure is used from national averages.

TRANSPORT

Cars (average petrol)

Measure:	**Number of cars, occupancy rate, average distance travelled, tonne CO_2**
Emissions factor:	0.3442kg CO_2/mile, or 0.2151kg CO_2/km

Coach (chartered)

Measure:	**Number of coaches, distance travelled, tonne CO_2**
Emissions factor:	1.0790kg CO_2/mile, or 0.6744kg CO_2/km

Source: NAEI Vehicle Speed Emission Factors (Version 02/3). Euro II bus at 96 kph (60 mph)

Shuttle bus

Measure:	**Number of bus runs, distance travelled, tonne CO_2**
Emissions factor:	0.9770kg CO_2/mile or 0.6106kg CO_2/km

Source: NAEI Vehicle Speed Emission Factors (Version 02/3). Euro II bus at 50 kph (30 mph)

Train travel (National Rail)

Measure:	**Number of passengers, average distance, tonne CO_2**
Emissions factor:	0.0963kg CO_2/passenger mile or 0.0602kg CO_2 /passenger km

Taxi

Measure:	**Number of taxis, occupancy rate, average distance, tonne CO_2**
Emissions factor:	0.3567kg CO_2/mile or 0.2229kg CO_2/km (regular taxi)
Emissions factor:	0.4128kg CO_2/mile or 0.2580kg CO_2/km (black cab)

Source: All are Defra 2008 unless otherwise specified (UK)

Table 1.2

FLIGHTS (average cabin class)

Domestic

Measure:	**Number of passengers, average distance, tonne CO_2**
Emissions factor:	0.2805kg CO_2/passenger mile
	0.1753kg CO_2/passenger km

International short haul

Measure:	**Number of passengers, average distance, tonne CO_2**
Emissions factor:	0.1573kg CO_2/passenger mile
	0.0983kg CO_2/passenger km

International long haul

Measure:	**Number of passengers, average distance, tonne CO_2**
Emissions factor:	0.1770kg CO_2/passenger mile
	0.1106kg CO_2/passenger km

ADDITIONAL TRANSPORT FACTORS – LIKELY FOR URBAN EVENTS

Train travel (Underground)

Measure:	**Number of passengers, average distance, tonne CO_2**
Emissions factor:	0.1040kg CO_2/passenger mile
	0.0650kg CO_2/passenger km

Ferry

Measure:	**Number of passengers, average distance, tonne CO_2**
Emissions factor:	0.1152kg CO_2/passenger km

Motorbike

Emissions factor:	0.1707kg CO_2/mile
	0.1067kg CO_2/km

Table 1.3

ENERGY	
Generators	
Measure:	**Total kVA, number generators, litres of fuel, tonne CO$_2$**
Emissions factor:	2.63kg CO$_2$/litre (diesel) or zero emissions (biodiesel)
Renewable onsite power	
Measure:	**Kilowatt hours, tonne CO$_2$**
Emissions factor:	Zero emissions
Mains power	
Measure:	**Kilowatt hours, tonne CO$_2$**
Emissions factor:	0.5619kg CO$_2$/kWh
Mains gas	
Measure:	**Kilowatt hours, tonne CO$_2$**
Emissions factor:	0.206kg CO$_2$/kWh gas
Bottled gas (butane/propane/LPG/CNG)	
Measure:	**kg gas, tonne CO$_2$**
Emissions factor:	1.495kg CO$_2$/kg gas

WASTE	
Landfill	
Measure:	**Tonnage to landfill, kg per person per day, tonne CO$_2$**
Emissions factor:	0.0112kg CH$_4$ (methane) per kilo of landfilled waste × 23*
Recycled waste and composted waste	
Measure:	**Tonnage recycled and composted, kg per person per day, tonne CO$_2$**
Emissions factor:	Zero emissions

Source: Defra, UK Landfill Methane Emissions 2005 and Estimated Emissions of CH$_4$ by IPCC Source Category 2006

Note: * The emissions factor is in methane. As we need to bring this back to CO$_2$ equivalence, the emissions factor is then multiplied by 23 (IPCC, 2001). Please note that this conversion factor includes the fact that many landfill sites are capturing methane to be used as energy from waste.

Table 1.4

WATER

Clean water (water production)

Measure:	**m³ water, tonne CO₂**
Emissions factor:	0.2710kg CO_2/m³

Grey water (salvaged, treated and recycled)

Measure:	**m³ water, tonne CO₂**
Emissions factor:	Zero emissions

Sewage (sewage treatment)

Measure:	**m³ water, tonne CO₂**
Emissions factor:	0.476kg CO_2/m³

Source: Water UK Sustainability Indicators 2006–07. Note there are 1000 litres in a cubic metre.

Depending on how easy and relevant it is to collect, you may also wish to calculate the impact of freight transport and hotel accommodation. Also the transport impact of moving waste and sewage off site.

FREIGHT

Measure:	**Distance travelled, tonne of goods, tonne CO₂**
Emissions factor:	0.2660kg CO_2/vehicle km (average van, light commercial up to 3.5t)
	0.2830kg CO_2/tonne km
Emissions factor:	0.9060kg CO_2/vehicle km (UK average all HGVs)
	0.1320kg CO_2/tonne km

HOTELS (average UK hotel)

Measure:	**Number of guests, number of nights, tonne CO₂**
Emissions factor:	34.32kg CO_2 per person per night

Source: Defra 2007, CIBSE 2004, IEA 2006

Certification and Best Practice

As the sustainability at events becomes more sophisticated and many more events take on the concepts outlined in this book and other guides that are being published, certifications and standards will also be developed. The following are some of the certifications, standards and awards that are currently in play:

A Greener Festival

The **A Greener Festival** website has established a system in the UK to assess the sustainability performance of festivals. They have a checklist which they measure events against. If they meet their standards, the festival is awarded the 'Greener Festival Award'. The website is also an excellent forum for those in the industry wishing to share ideas around making their events more sustainable.

www.agreenerfestival.com

EcoLogo Certification

The **EcoLogo**™ programme certifies events that have a reduced impact on the environment. Events are evaluated and audited to ensure compliance with EcoLogo™ criteria. These criteria reflect environmental leadership in terms of making an event environmentally sustainable,

and encourage reduced environmental impacts. www.ecologo.org

Yourope Green'n'Clean Award

In 2006/7, **Yourope**, the European Festival Association, launched environmental guidelines for music festivals. The original printed booklet *Green'n'Clean* has been supplemented by a new online tool, providing festival organizers with customized environmental advice plus a Green'n'Clean Award for festivals that achieve a defined number of criteria in terms of environmental measures.

www.yourope.org

Tiger Marked ECO-OK

In India a new system has been developed to certify events as sustainably managed. www.tigermarked.com

Live Earth Green Event Guidelines

In 2007 Live Earth produced one of the first guides on how to produce events sustainably. These guidelines are available to download from their website liveearth.org. See the appendix for a case study on Live Earth.

To finish off this chapter and before we launch into the details of sustainable event management, to get you in the mood for what is possible, I have written a couple of little stories for a fictional conference and then a fictional festival – to illustrate what could be possible. Many of the examples from events in this book are very close to being model events and I hope you enjoy reading about what's happening in reality as well.

The BS:8901

In November 2007, after consultation with industry in the UK, the British Standard **BS8901:2007 Specification for a Sustainable Event Management System** was released. It offers a framework from within which an event manager can gauge the sustainable progress of their event. The standard comes under BS8900:2006 Guidance For Managing Sustainable Development. www.bsigroup.com.

Box 1.4

A Model Event: The Conference

What experience can you give a conference delegate which will have the potential to motivate them to action in their business and their everyday lives? Below is an example of what could happen …

The delegate confirms their participation in your conference and receives their info pack via pdf into their inbox. Included in their pack are the environmental credentials of the venue, public transport options and the timetable for the conveniently planned shuttle buses.

Delegates arrive at the conference and are given their welcome pack, which includes all printed material on 100 per cent post-consumer recycled paper. Pens supplied are made from recycled plastic, newspapers or old CD cases. The conference timetable is printed and displayed in the foyer, rather than printed and dropped into 1000 sample bags. Any bags that are given out are made from hemp or other sustainable material, and are designed in a way to encourage re-use.

At break time, the tea, coffee and sugar are all fair trade. Milk is organic and from the local dairy co-op. Water is dispensed through a filter and glasses are provided, rather than plastic bottles or cups. Catering is from organic produce and sourced from the local farmers' market by a catering contractor based in the same city as your conference. Compost bins are on hand to scrape unused food into. Recycling is available for newspapers and other things the delegates have brought in.

The hotel rooms have bulk dispensers for bathroom products and there are signs up to encourage re-use of towels rather than new ones each day. The hotel's power is provided by a green energy supplier.

All conference notes and presentations are available to be downloaded after the conference. A list of suppliers of everything available at the conference is emailed to all participants after the event so if they wish to use the same in their businesses, the process is simple.

The delegates will leave the conference inspired to initiate action in their own workplaces. They may not have in-office recycling at work, let alone thought of composting their food waste. They may return to work and encourage a change to sustainable stationery alternatives for the whole office. They may need to organize a seminar or large meeting within their own organization and can take back tips and ideas that they have seen in action at your conference. Allowing the supplier contacts and ideas to be freely disseminated to delegates after the conference will further help towards building sustainability across the industry.

Box 1.5

A Model Event: The Festival

If you're putting on a multi-day event and building a community for your audience to live within, what can you do to not only make the event more sustainable but also to really get under the audience's skin. Let's go on a journey to a festival together.

Now imagine you are a going to a music festival, camping out in the sun for a few days with 50,000 others. The festival is announced and you purchase your tickets online. Upon arrival you swipe your credit card, or show ID and a booking reference. Your wristband, made from recyclable materials that can also be recycled, is placed on your wrist. No paper has been used to print tickets and nothing sent out in the mail.

Prior to arriving at the festival you've been encouraged to think about how to get there. Although you usually don't take buses or trains, the organizers have made a pretty good case for why you should leave your car at home. As tickets to the festival are hard to snag, you've snapped up one of the pre-allocated Rail & Ride tickets, signing up to go on the train; the tickets are a little cheaper and you don't have to pay a car parking fee. You are amazed at how smoothly it went getting to the festival. No long queues on the roads leading up to the festival. No mammoth trek to haul all your camping gear to the campsite. The train was packed with others going to the festival and it had a fantastic vibe. The shuttle bus was waiting for you at the station and drives you right up close to your campground instead of having to walk for ages from the car park with all your gear.

All that gear you would usually have to carry in on your back though, has been reduced because you've worked out (through helpful advice from the festival organizers on their website) that there are much better ways to live at the festival than in a throw away tent you would normally have bought from a supermarket chain.

With your small backpack on, you stroll over to your pre-booked solar powered cardboard tent, bunkhouse, tent hotel or teepee. Or you rock up to the Festival Survival Kit stall where you pick up the gear you ordered online, which is reclaimed gear from festivals last season, and they've all had a bit of bling added, so your kit's looking really cool. In the survival kits is also a raincoat made from last year's left-over damaged tents, plus a funky water bottle holder and a waterproof tote bag. There's even a pair of recycled wellington boots with a one-off handcrafted design on them.

Strolling to your campground you pass the lockers, where you drop off your mobile phone to get charged at the solar charging station.

Past the recycling stations and compost bins, you find the perfect spot to pitch your pre-loved tent.

Nature calls and you're off to use the purpose built compost toilets. On your way back you spot the solar showers and note they have been thoughtfully stocked with environmentally sound body wash.

Although you plan to, you haven't quite kicked the habit and you light up a ciggie for your stroll back to camp. You notice a sign about cigarette butts and have a fleeting thought about flicking the butt. Then you go past the supermarket and see a stall selling personal butt bins and think to yourself 'Yeah, I really shouldn't drop my cigarette butts here, everything else is just so green' and pick up a butt bin for a buck.

The tummy starts to rumble and you go back down to where the food stalls are. You can tell something's different. Everything seems a little bit calmer and it smells a whole lot better. Then you clock the little wind turbines stuck up above all the food stalls and see the solar panels. Your eyes follow the shine of the panels and you see signs on the fence leading to the back of the stalls. The sign explains how they get their power. All the lights in the food stalls are LED, it says, and that draws very little power. The solar and wind give enough power to run the stall, but if it goes cloudy or still, a generator is ready to pump into action.

Aha! That's why it's quiet, there's no diesel powered machine grunting and groaning and pumping out exhaust. But there is a generator though. What's that? It's fuelled using reclaimed vege oil?

Looking at the sign you read all about Waste Vegetable Oil biodiesel and the penny drops that they don't have to chop down rainforests and plant palm oil to run biodiesel in generators. You didn't know that, but now you do. You wonder if it'll smell like chips if they turn it on.

You do a three-sixty to check out what's on offer to eat. There seems to be some kind of sign in the front of all the stalls. You get dragged towards the pizza stall and see the sign says they are serving 80 per cent of their menu from organic produce. There's also a note there that all their fresh veggies have come from the local farmers' market.

You wander to find a place to sit and realize you can find a spot no trouble, you're not wading through knee high rubbish. At the same time as you take a seat on the grass you read something written around the plate your pizza is on. 'This plate is made from beer cups recycled at last year's festivals.' What the??? You remember handing in your beer cups last year for a refund. They've made this year's plates out of those cups? Awesome!

Because the ground's so clear you'd better not leave your rubbish there, and with a quick glance around you see a set of bins with signs on them. As you get nearer you realize there's a volunteer standing there and they show you where to put your plate. 'In the composting? Wow, it's gonna be composted?' you ask. 'Yep' comes the reply. 'Just over that back fence there is a huge allotment and community gardens. Some of the stuff is going there to be composted. The rest is going just down the road into a big commercial composter. The compost makes its way to the local farmers who grow the veggies that are sold to those food stalls. Cool hey?'

Not quite ready for a beer, you head over to the coffee shop. There's a band playing in the little tent but you'd prefer to go for a wander with your cuppa. You're given a mug but say to them you wanted a takeaway. 'No that's fine, take that mug' they say. 'The mug jugglers are working this year. See where you go to put your plates in for composting? Well there's a collection point there. The mug jugglers take all the cups back to get washed and then bring them back to us. It's an extra couple of bucks for the coffee, and you can get that back when you bring your cup back. They're cool cups though, so you can keep it if you want.'

You hand in your coffee mug and it's time to check out the merch stand. There's a great range of t-shirts and hoodies, but this year there looks like there's something different about the display. You read the sign and see that all the shirts are fair trade. There's a big display board with all sorts of photos and stuff about how the cotton used is organic, or how you can choose a hemp version, and how all the people who make the shirts, from growing the cotton, to printing the design on the front, are all treated ethically and have fair wages. The shirts are only a bit more expensive than last year, but you feel really good buying the shirt this year. Last year you didn't even think about where the shirt was made.

You grab a programme too, and later when you read it from cover to cover you read the bit about it being printed using soy ink. It turns out the ink usually used to print programmes and stuff is toxic, and that this ink made from veggies and soy is much kinder to the environment. More than that, the paper it's printed on is what's called post-consumer recycled paper. They say that means it has been some paper product before and then gone to be recycled, rather than just being the bit they cut off the edges of brand new paper when they make it and then call that recycled. Didn't know they did that. So 100 per cent post-consumer paper is the way to go.

With the programme in hand and the t-shirt on, phone picked up from the solar charger and thrown into the waterproof tote bag along with the camera and rain poncho, it's off to the arena and straight to the bar. Yep there's the deposit thing on beer cups again. Excellent, you'll be able to make a bit of extra cash by snagging some cups people have left laying about. Oh yeah, look at that, they're saying the cups from this year are going to make next year's plates. Hilarious.

You notice the food stalls all have those bin stations outside them and people are putting their plates in the composting bins like nothing else. No more wading through other people's crap to go get a hamburger.

The three days pass in a haze. In between boozing and bands, you go to the compost loo, take a solar shower, eat some organic chow, compost your plates, do a bit of mug juggling and score ten bucks by picking up cups at the end of the night.

Time to go home and you wonder to yourself whether you can be arsed carrying your new camping gear back on the train. As you crawl out of your tent, an over-enthusiastic volunteer makes a deal with you.

If you pack your tent down and take it just 50 metres over there to where those big bags are, they'll make sure your gear gets either re-used again next year, or sent to a really good cause. Result!

You look around and you realize everyone's packing up and you can see the grass!!! This is unheard of. There are usually thousands of plastic shopping bags blowing around like tumble weeds in some kind of post-apocalyptic landscape with a sea of trash knee deep. That bribe thing they did for the rubbish must have really worked. Bring back a bagful and you get a free beer. You didn't do any cooking at camp so you didn't make much mess. But you saw other people taking shopping bags full of rubbish over to that caravan and coming back with a smile. Someone said they were getting beer vouchers for three bags of rubbish. Have to remember that one next year.

Usually there's also a sea of aluminium cans from all the beer that's been drunk. You wonder where those cans went to that you had in a pile outside your tent. Then you glance back over to the caravan and realize there is a MOUNTAIN of aluminium cans there. Were they there before? You have no idea. Then someone walks past you with a big bag of cans and you ask what's going on. You find out they're from a local charity and they've been given the rights to all the aluminium cans in the campground and that they get A LOT of money from what they collect through Cash For Cans. He tells you that recycling aluminium is so much more environmentally friendly than mining it up.

You stroll with your backpack towards the shuttle bus, conveniently located at the gate. You've got your rubber boots on for the first time because the ground got a bit muddy overnight, but when you get to the bus stop you realize you can't really wear the boots on the bus. You say a fond farewell to the boots you wore only once and drop them off at the donation point. You wonder where they'll end up next year.

And so our happy festival goer returns to the real world with some first hand experience of what a bit of thought and planning can do. They've composted (never before), travelled there on the train (usually drive), eaten organic food for the first time, actively recycled, donated their camping gear back for re-use and learnt a few other things along the way.

By putting in place some simple programmes such as those described above, the community you create at a festival can become a fantastic example of a closed loop system. The compost from the plates and food waste makes its way back to nature. The aluminium recycling gives much needed funds to local charities, reduces the environmental impact of mining, and reduces the landfill footprint of the festival. The beer cups made from recycled paper get turned into paper plates. And one more thing that didn't really get explained: the compost that's created from the toilets, after six months, is put back out onto the land to fertilize the newly planted trees along the riverbank offering more shade and a windbreak to campers. They'll find about that when they return next year.

The projects put in place in the example above have caused a change in normal behaviour for this festival goer. The cumulative impact of similar experiences, at other events and in everyday life, could well affect this person to such a degree that they may change the way they act at home and at work.

Watch | Read | Visit

Sustainable Events Planner

The Sustainable Living Foundation is a community-based not-for-profit organization committed to creating major platforms to help accelerate the uptake of sustainable living.

They have developed the Sustainable Event Planner. The Sustainable Event Planner aims to assist event organizers and their visitors make sustainability the main event.
www.slf.org.au/eventplanner

GreenBase

'The intersection of music and climate change.' Visit this site to read blogs, reports, postings and news on greening of music events.
green-base.blogspot.com

A Greener Festival

Network with other events professionals looking to green their shows.
www.agreenerfestival.com

Sustainable Event mamagement System

SEMS is a sustainability tool designed for the production of events. It measures sustainability results by event type and industry. Mention you heard about it in this book for a discount on your subscription.
www.sustainableeventsolutions.com.au

Julie's Bicycle

Julie's Bicycle is a not-for-profit company in the UK helping the music industry cut its GHG emissions and create a low carbon creative future.
www.juliesbicycle.com

Notes

1   World Commission on Environment and Development (1987) *Our Common Future*, Oxford University Press, Oxford, www.un-documents.net/ocf-ov.htm#1.2, accessed September 2008.

2   Materials Recovery Facility (MRF) – A facility that processes collected mixed recyclables and sorts them into their separate waste streams such as paper, cardboard, plastics, glass, aluminium, steel. Some facilities are 'dirty' MRFs where recycling is mixed in with general waste and 'recyclate' is picked out. Others are clean MRFs where source-separated (at home, business, factory, festival) recyclate is delivered, and contaminants are picked out.

3   Greenhouse Gas Protocol, www.ghgprotocol.org.

chapter 2
Marketing and Communications

The way you communicate your sustainability goals will impact on the image of your event and the effectiveness of your initiatives. Strategies are needed to engage those people vital to the success of your greening plans and thought must be put into the way you present your new green credentials.

There are several aspects to be considered in marketing and communicating the sustainability strategies of your event. These include:

- **Green positioning.**
- **Stakeholder engagement.**
- **Audience communications.**

In the following pages we'll discuss options for positioning your event with its new green flavour. That is, how you want the audience and the wider community to see your event and its sustainability intent.

We'll also walk through all the potential stakeholders for your event and look at tools and techniques to engage them and their active participation.

One of the major stakeholder groups is of course your audience. If you're putting together projects to green your event and you need the audience to get involved, there are many ways to get the message out to them. We'll look at options to send the green message in the lead-up, and also how to influence their behaviour and involvement once at your show.

Green Positioning

Think through how you want your event to be perceived now that it will have its new green-ness at heart. How you place your sustainability credentials and green initiatives in relation to the overall image will impact how the event is seen in the minds of your audience.

You may decide to give the event an overt 'greening' with sustainability being pushed to the front of all activities. This could be appropriate if it's the first time you're introducing sustainability, and pushing it out the front can give the focus it needs to gain traction.

However, just because you run an event sustainably it isn't necessary for you to wave your 'green-ness' in the audience's face at every turn. You may decide it isn't right for your event and may not want to confuse the positioning, branding or image by overemphasizing this. Events don't need to position themselves as 'Green-with-a-capital G' in order to be environmentally responsible.

It's also possible in your audience's day-to-day life that things such as recycling, re-using shopping bags, having a green energy supplier, composting, etc. are second nature to them. They may not see themselves as 'greenies', but as responsible members of society, caring for the Earth and thinking about the well-being of future generations. Likewise it's probable they will expect you to be as they are and take on minimizing the environmental impact of your event as a matter of course, as part of your everyday operations, rather than a special 'theme'. If you want to wave the green flag or use your event

for eco-education, or even expanding to eco-edu-tainment (!), that's fantastic, but it doesn't need to be the case.

Brand your Greening

If you decide to go down the green-theme road, a great way to get your audience's attention is to brand your greening projects under the one banner.

'Ecobound' is **Southbound Festival's** programme to brand all their sustainability activities. Their full suite of initiatives, including green tickets, composting, biodiesel, recycling incentives, cigarette butt campaign, etc., come under the Ecobound name.

At **Roskilde Festival**, they have introduced the 'Green Footsteps' programme. This asks the audience to participate in various greening activities, taking Green Footsteps, and they give rewards in return. See the boxed text in the upcoming pages for details on this programme.

Greenwash/Green Sheen

People can be cynical about companies hiding behind green ideals, their radars finely tuned to detect a greenwash. If they feel they are being misled regarding environmental practices or benefits, they may react against you. Make sure you walk the talk, rather than just talk it. Be prepared to be scrutinized. Don't overstretch the truth of what you are doing.

The green sheen is where only a token nod to improving the sustainability of the event is given, with just the appearance of adopting new products and procedures, rather than actually following through. Don't claim anything that isn't strictly the case, and if things fall apart in the middle of your event, be prepared to admit it if asked, and commit to learning from your experiences.

Think about whether more effort is put into promoting the green in your event than is actually committed to resourcing new products and practices.

Partner with an NGO

Partnering with environment or social justice non-governmental organizations (NGOs) is a great way not only to learn more about sustainability but also to raise the profile and credibility of your projects. By partnering with an NGO you can also potentially bring their volunteers on board and have them take charge of some of

your greening action. The NGO can also have an info booth or their own creative activity to engage the audience in their message.

At **Glastonbury Festival**, **Greenpeace**, **WaterAid** and **Oxfam** are the main charitable causes for the event. Greenpeace have an entire field which they programme and run. They have eco-showers, a kid's play area, gardens, café and bar, FSC timber skate ramp (!), a Carbon Dating activity, and lots of other good Greenpeace information. Bob Wilson and his team do an extraordinary job.

At the 2008 festival, WaterAid encouraged revellers to 'Love their Loo' to highlight the 2.5 billion people worldwide who don't have access to a toilet. The charity has also put in pit latrines similar to those they install in their projects across Africa and Asia.

Oxfam supply hundreds of volunteers to help in the campgrounds and pedestrian zones. Those people that wish to both support Oxfam and attend the festival volunteer their time.

All three NGOs are recipients of a proportion of the profits earned at the festival. They also work together to come up with the overall key campaign for the festival each year.

Figure 2.2 WaterAid's African pit latrines at Glastonbury Festival, UK

Source: Glastonbury Festival

Key Campaigns and Green Themes

Earlier we talked about branding your greening under a common name so that you can give focus to your activities. You can go one step further than this by creating a green theme or a key campaign around greening.

If you're kick-starting your greening operations for the first time, a green theme through all operations as well as within the event's programming content is an option to take up. Have all contributors take on green themes in their area of operations. Ask content programmers and activity organizers to bring sustainability into their programmes.

Each year at Glastonbury Festival the three 'Worthy Causes', Greenpeace, WaterAid and Oxfam, propose a key campaign to overarch the event's messaging. Due to the nature of these three organizations, this invariably has an environmental theme. In 2007 the event ran with the 'Stop Climate Chaos – I Count' campaign where they asked festival goers to sign up and commit to changing their behaviour in certain ways. During the course of the event, the festival goers were told, via announcements on stage and on screen, how many people had made the pledge. In 2008, the festival turned its focus closer to home, taking on the 'think globally, act locally' ethos. The mountains of rubbish and discarded gear left at the show in 2007 inspired the 'Love the Farm, Leave No Trace' theme. This was messaged through all the communications channels, with the overall objective of getting people to think about their personal impact on the creation of rubbish and disposal of stuff. Taking the Leave No Trace ethic the organizers hoped this would strike a chord with the audience and encourage them to a more responsible attitude to consumption and disposal.

At the 2007 **Burning Man** event in the US, they had the 'The Green Man' as their art theme and also started in parallel the 'Cooling Man' project, where they encouraged the participants to consider their personal contribution to the environmental impact of the event. Read about that in Box 2.2.

Box 2.1

Energy FACTory

The Energy FACTory at Coachella Festival is a conglomeration of alternative energy exhibits designed to teach people about everything from solar and wind power to biodiesel and kinetic energy.

Set up by enviro activators and educators Global Inheritance, the Energy FACTory includes eight pedal powered energy generators plus a how-to-make-biodiesel exhibit, a solar powered DJ station, a 45-foot high wind powered clock, and a screen printing area where people could design Energy FACTory t-shirts on eco-friendly materials.

The Energy FACTory offers an interactive forum for people to learn about and experience alternative energy first hand.

www.coachella.com
www.globalinheritance.org

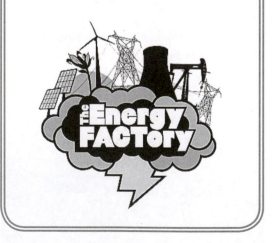

Box 2.2

The Green Man, Burning Man, US

'This year our art theme will express the immanence of nature in our lives in a variety of ways. The Burning Man will stand atop a structure that resembles a green mountain peak. Nestled at its base will be the Green Man Pavilion, 30,000 square feet of shaded exhibition space for the display of interactive artistic, scientific and educational models, a "World's Fair" of emerging technologies. Artists and inventors are invited to contribute. This pavilion will be surrounded by the "Mangrove" made from simulated "trees" fashioned from recycled industrial materials. These artificial trees will not be burned: they will survive to subdivide the blue of other skies.

But we will do much more than this. In 2007, we will calculate the amount of climate changing gases that are released into the air by the construction and the burning of the Man and its pedestal. This is called a carbon footprint. Then we'll sponsor projects in the outside world that will efface this imprint. Such actions might include the planting of trees or the development of non-polluting energy resources. Having played with fire, we'll take care to cleanse its atmospheric playground.

This represents a first symbolic step aimed at redressing nature's balance. In its sum, this maiden effort may seem small. Widespread cheatgrass and sagebrush fires annually sweep the Nevada landscape, releasing far more carbon dioxide than the entire infrastructure of Black Rock City. Yet our endeavour constitutes a kind of contemplation of our place within the natural world. Thousands of Burning Man participants, who carefully inspect their campsites for any lingering trace of litter, inevitably enhance their everyday awareness of the impact of their actions on the world. It's difficult, upon returning home, to thoughtlessly discard one's refuse in the street. In this spirit, we'll encourage everyone to calculate the carbon footprint of their campsite and make efforts to redress it.

Apart from and beyond such practical concerns, we encourage every artist to elicit nature's power from a much more personal and primal source of consciousness. Natural variation will ensure that each such vision is unique and unpredictable, producing artwork as diverse as all the different gifts that people bring to Burning Man. Hidden behind the masks of convention, there is surely a Green Woman or Green Man in every one of us.'

www.burnerswithoutborders.org
www.coolingman.org
www.burningman.com

Source: Information in this box reproduced with the permission of Burning Man

Box 2.3

Marketing and Communications Checklist ☑

Green positioning

☐ Establish where the green profile of your event sits. Will you push sustainability goals out front, or have them as a matter of course in operations?

☐ Brand your greening. Place all your sustainability initiatives under a theme or brand, so that you can easily communicate your intent.

☐ Don't green wash. Make sure you do what you say you will. Don't pay lip service make token greening gestures. Green it like you mean it.

☐ Partner with an NGO. Get green cred by having a well respected NGO on board with your event.

☐ Choose a key campaign or overall sustainability theme to support.

Identify and engage stakeholders

☐ Work out who will influence the success of your sustainability initiatives.

☐ Empower those who make purchasing and production decisions with the knowledge they need to make the best choices.

☐ Attract sponsors to your event that can add value and support to your sustainability projects.

☐ Encourage all traders to be as sustainable as possible.

☐ Put into supplier and contractor agreements your expectations to meet sustainability goals including materials choice, product use and waste management.

☐ Work with regulating authorities, industry associations, interest groups and associations to be part of your green campaigns.

☐ Choose inspiring performers, speakers, artists and other participants who can champion your green goals.

☐ Use a variety of techniques to communicate with stakeholders including face-to-face meetings, newsletters and emails, resource websites, summary sheets and info packs.

Audience communications

☐ Establish what your audience's level of 'green' is. This will direct the tone and how 'in their face' your sustainability messaging needs to be.

☐ Think about the energy level at your event, whether it will be congested or relaxed. This will direct your at-event communications methods.

☐ Pre-promote all of the key issues that people need to think about before coming to your event such as transport decisions and preparatory purchasing.

☐ Tag your green messaging onto all standard promotional material produced pre-event, including publicity campaigns.

☐ Use signage, installations, announcements, programmes, information stalls, video screen clips, etc. at your event to promote any sustainability activities you need your audience to participate in.

☐ Set up an 'eco village' precinct full of great sustainability projects, green traders and the like.

☐ Make your recycling stations highly visible, easy to understand and staff them with volunteers to talk to people about what waste goes where.

☐ Use art installations and performance artists to create environment themed art.

Communicate results

☐ Don't forget to let all the stakeholders know how you went, whether goals were achieved or not, and what the plans are for the future.

Box 2.4

Green Footsteps, Roskilde Festival, Denmark

Roskilde Festival in Denmark's 'Green Footsteps' programme is their response to how the festival can shoulder their part of the responsibility for solving the potential climate catastrophe. Of course, the audience is also invited to be part of the campaign so that together they can send a message to the world.

The festival takes many green footsteps to take the event towards sustainability. This includes waste management, recycling and composting, container deposits for beer cups and energy management to source renewable energy options. To encourage a greener footprint by their audience, the Green Footsteps programme has been implemented. It neatly communicates how the audience can be involved. The ultimate reward is to be allowed to camp in the newly created 'Climate Community' camp. This encourages purchasing an offset and, importantly, travelling by public transport.

At Roskilde '09 a 'Climate Community' was created. It is a centrally located camping quarter primarily running on CO_2 neutral energy. The energy was generated thanks to the festival-goers' efforts, for example through the use of energy-producing bicycles and dance floors – as well as from renewable energy sources. The audience can reserve a spot at Climate Community – before the camping area opens – by contributing by leaving green footsteps in the shape of environment-friendly actions at home and on the way to the festival. The audience has to leave three green footsteps to reserve a spot at Climate Community at the camping area. The first green footstep can be left by supporting windmills in Malawi when buying a ticket through purchasing an offset. Another green footstep can be left by using public transportation to the festival.

At Roskilde Festival the guests can also participate in refund collection competitions where they get cold beer in return, they can donate tents and sleeping bags to charity, and they are introduced to an extensive sale of organic and fair trade goods as well as a refund arrangement that makes sure that about 97 per cent of all sold plastic cups are recycled.

Information in this case study has been supplied by Thomas Niebuhr, Environmental Manager for Roskilde Festival. www.roskilde-festival.dk

Figure 2.3 Campsite Crew at Glastonbury Festival are vital to get the message out to the audience about any changes happening at the event

Source: Glastonbury Festival

Stakeholders

If you have been charged with the role of making your event or organization more sustainable (by self-appointment or otherwise), you will need to kit yourself up with an arsenal of techniques to help get all those people that can make a positive impact, doing just that.

Moving an event towards sustainable management will only work if all stakeholders and decision makers are actively engaged, participating in change-making behaviour and committed to reaching your greening goals. There are many individuals and organizations you need to convince to come on the journey with you. You'll need strategies to get people within your organization, and those that contract to you or provide products and services, into the idea of sustainability, and to enlist their commitment.

Once you have finished going through this book, you will be armed with information, ideas and strategies to move your event towards sustainable management. As you read through the book keep in mind who the important people or groups are that will need to be on board. Not only that, you'll need to think about who could buck the system, and what sneaky methods you're going to use to get them thinking the way you want them. You may be looking at a long-term strategy here, or may just need to gently guide people towards the right decision.

It's marketing really. You have a product – 'sustainable event management' – and you need to sell it to them. If you don't sell it to those people that can influence your final success, meeting your goals may be all the harder. Communication is the key. You want to get to a situation where the person involved in impacting your event's sustainability, without any prompt or direction by you, makes the most sustainable decision.

Before you think about the best way forward for each person or group, you'll need to both identify who your stakeholders are and indicate whether they are going to be an easy nut to crack or are going to take a bit of work. In the next few pages we'll look at the different stakeholder groups.

You may need to use some hard core psychological techniques to get people to embrace change. Especially those old timers stuck in their own way of doing things, or worse, those that have 'tried it before and it didn't work'. Very likely that was previously the case, but the playing field is drastically different today than it was even five years ago. Sustainability as a topic is ripe for the picking and you should find fertile ground now to grow your ideas and your projects to fruition.

Depending on your style of delivery and powers of persuasion, you may find that completely empowering people to make their own discoveries is the way to go. Rev them up, point them in the right direction and let them go for it. Drop in vital information at the right moment, to keep them on the right track, but back out and don't get too in their face. This will work where you

have highly experienced events professionals that are making daily decisions on operations and purchasing, and don't really need your help to do so. Get them inspired and interested in the issues and they should then take this knowledge on board when going about their job.

One of the best influencers we have right now is the fact that at every turn in daily life, the topic of greening is in your face. Just about everyone has seen, or at least heard of, Al Gore's film *An Inconvenient Truth*.[1] If you haven't seen it yet, do so. Every mainstream newspaper has pages on green living and environmental issues. The television is full of documentaries on environmental issues, or they are staging green-a-thons. Supermarket shelves are flooded with new green/organic/eco products. And so on. Sometimes a single television show or report on a current affairs programme can switch people on. If people are being influenced only by mainstream media the info they are getting may be a little simplified or biased. Nonetheless it is a fantastically rewarding experience to have people come to you with their new-found knowledge. You can then adjust this to align with your event's sustainability goals and send them on their way to help you meet your goals.

Internal Stakeholders

You want to get to the point with the team working on your event where the green penny drops. When the eco light bulb switches on. I was working in India in a production company where I got what we called 'the green smile' when we talked about 'the environment'. This was an eyes-glazed-over slightly perplexed and weak-cheeked smile that conveys 'that sounds good but I have absolutely no idea what you are talking about'. Then one morning one of the main guys doing the purchasing and contracting came to me with: 'Meegan, I was watching the television last night and I was so shocked to find out that it takes FOUR HUNDRED YEARS for a plastic bottle to break down.' Even though I'd been talking to him about recycling every day for a month, the penny had finally dropped for him and we went on to make some great waste plans. India's greening is taking hold.

Depending on your event, internal stakeholders may just be one person, you, the person diligently reading this book. On larger festivals, sporting events and expos, there will likely be a separation of roles with numerous people having either decision making and purchasing power, or being involved in producing the various aspects of the event.

Some of these roles may be contracted out and some may stay internally staffed. Some events may also separate into theme areas, with many roles repeated in each precinct, several site managers, production coordinators, stage managers, etc. For smaller sporting and community events you are likely to have an organizing committee with responsibilities shared across various areas, supported by a large volunteer base.

Figure 2.4 Your site manager and production manager are very important cogs in the sustainability wheel. They need to have it under their skin so that every decision they make has the environment and logistics on an equal footing. Lucy Vignola's the greenest one I know

Whichever way the roles and responsibilities are allocated for your event, people are the common denominator. Working out the best way to get the ideas of sustainability into their hearts and minds will be one of your biggest challenges.

Facilitating Change

Your fantastic networking skills will come to the fore when facilitating change. This is where you will stick your nose, ever so gently, into matters that others think perhaps don't concern you. If left to their own devices, people will likely do what they have always done. You can connect these decision makers with new options, or contractors. You could also place a new topic on the table for discussion between contractors and event production staff.

For example, have your sponsorship manager and your food service provider talk through organic, fair trade and local supply issues and identify ways to change suppliers and potentially leverage sponsorship or product placement into the event.

Get your waste manager and recycling industry bodies such as the aluminium recycling association or plastics recycling group together and look at ways to not only improve recycling separation and treatment, but also to use your event to promote the recycling organization's aims.

A new green printer and your graphic designer, marketing or advertising staff could get together to discuss green printing practices, paper and ink choices.

Put yourself between the green issues and the contractors and decision makers, and get the key parties discussing the issues and moving solutions forward.

A lot of your work will be done through one-on-one conversation, facilitating change by helping new processes get off the ground, and through constantly, yet subtly pressuring change.

More formal ways of communicating with internal stakeholders can include:

- E-newsletters.
- Resource website.
- Workshops.
- Meetings.
- Presentations.
- Reports.

We will look at these tools in more details in the upcoming pages. A list of likely internal stakeholders and division of roles is included in Box 2.6.

Let's now look outside your organization and go through the different groups of external stakeholders that will help you move your event towards sustainability along with ways to help influence them towards the green light.

 ## External Stakeholders

Apart from your team of staff and crew involved with producing the event, you will also have many external people and organizations that can influence the success of your sustainability initiatives. These external stakeholders need to be identified and strategies put in place to bring them on board.

Sponsors

Sponsors have the potential to dramatically affect the appearance if not the actual sustainability of an event. Choosing sponsors whose product or company ethic aligns with your sustainability goals is essential.

Image transfer is one of the prime benefits in a sponsorship relationship (apart from money and exposure). This is where the event benefits from the brand image or reputation of the sponsor, or the reverse. Your event may be such that an association with it is hugely beneficial for the image and credibility of the brand. It's an important part of the sponsorship offer and something you can leverage where greening themes come in.

If you are OK to have commercial product alignment, getting sponsors on board which have an environmental ethic is an excellent way to extend your green offer. A company that wants to demonstrate their commitment to sustainability could sponsor your recycling, or grey water management, or subsidize the shuttle bus transport from the train station encouraging public transport use. Other sponsorship alignment ideas include the following:

- Paying for and branding recycling volunteers' uniforms.
- Product logo on recycling bin signage.
- The sponsor constructing a venue, bar or installation from found and salvaged objects. The venue could be run on renewable energy, and offer mobile phone charging, for example.
- Bathroom homewares, range of cleaning products, or personal products, to sponsor showers.
- Offer free product in return for audience participating in green initiatives such as recycling, car pooling or taking public transport.
- Bike shop to sponsor a pedal power cinema or stage, and audience bike parking station.
- Organic food brand to sponsor the creation of a permaculture garden on site including the composting programme for the event's wet waste which will be used to 'feed' the garden.
- 'Eco' paint company to supply all paints for the event's décor, in exchange for exposure. Activation on-site could include a painting activity.
- Solar power provider such as solar showers for domestic use, to set up temporary solar heated showers at the event.

Good examples of companies and products to align with include:

- Green energy suppliers.
- Solar power/product companies.
- Organic food range.
- Organic beverages.
- Environmentally sound cleaning products.
- Eco media/magazines.
- Ethical investment.
- Green retailers.
- Hybrid or electric car companies.
- Ethical clothing range.
- Other eco products such as energy saving lightbulbs.

Product placement would be naturally part of the partnership. Apart from food and beverage products that can be sold or given away at the show, look to partner with companies that can offer you products to use in the production of your event. Preferably choose those that also have a consumer line, for example, a brand of commercial cleaning products which can be used on bathrooms at the event, but also promoted for use by your audience at home.

Figure 2.5 Reva Electric Cars sponsored the Climate Solutions Roadshow run by the India Youth Climate Network. www.iycn.in

Sponsors' participation needs to be managed and guided to ensure they also add to the event's sustainability credentials. Make sure the sponsor includes sustainable practices in their logistical operations at your event, as well as through the message they are presenting to your audience. Encourage creative interpretation of sustainability ideas in their on-site activity. Their involvement should underscore your greening goals.

Figure 2.6 Neco is an on-line (and now real-life) store for sustainable living solutions. They sponsored Peats Ridge Festival, including supply of two of these biodiesel-run vans for festival transport. On-site activation also included supply of a water tank to dispense bulk drinking water and supply of CFL light bulbs. They also produced a hand-held site map of the festival which doubled as a fan. www.neco.com.au

Source: Meegan Jones

Box 2.5

Sponsor Checklist ☑

☐ Invite local sponsors to participate, not just national brands.

☐ Ensure any activity at your event has considered sustainability and environmental conservation. No overindulgent and excessive use of resources and waste creation!

☐ Contract 'green' requirements into their agreements, including materials use and waste management.

☐ Flying people around the world to participate in your event as part of a sponsor competition prize is not advised.

☐ Provide an info sheet to sponsors on all of the sustainability initiatives for your event along with any 'musttakes' they need to be aware of.

Traders

If it's for sale at your event, it reflects on your sustainability claims. You must get those selling goods at your event involved in greening up their act. The resources used in producing the goods on sale, and the ethical nature of this production are key concerns.

Following closely after audience transport, one of the largest areas impacting on the sustainability of an event is the cradle-to-grave impact of purchasing to put on the event. If the audience makes lots of purchases to gear up for your event as well as at the show, the impacts are compounding. This is not only the embedded energy in the production of the products (many researchers are keen to look at the resulting CO_2

outcome of product production), but the use of resources for production, and of course the ultimate disposal of the product. We will discuss the impact of consumption and the social and environmental concerns which must be taken into account in Chapter 6. We also look at the climate impact of waste, the by-product of all this purchasing in Chapter 7.

Working with your food stalls and non-food traders on the 'greening' of their offer is essential. Your traders are also likely to be one of the largest areas of waste creation and you must work closely with them on waste management. This is not only in managing how they deal with waste generated as a result of their sales, but also putting controls on what they are allowed to bring in the first place – product packaging, plastic bags, take away food packaging, etc.

This also applies to the merchandise produced for your event. You may control what branded products you produce for your event or you may license out the rights for merchandise. Either way, sustainable procurement needs to be considered.

Glastonbury Festival encourages good practice by their stalls through their 'Green Trader Award'. During the event they judge vendors at the festival on a variety of areas from waste management through to product sourcing. Each year traders are awarded Gold, Silver and Bronze awards.

Figure 2.7 Green Trader Award at Glastonbury Festival

Source: Glastonbury Festival

Contractors and Suppliers

Every contractor and supplier of products to your event will have areas that could be more sustainable. Waste management contractors, amenities suppliers, power contractors and plumbers: these are all main service providers whose work methods will have a direct impact on reaching your sustainability goals. Work with each of them to create solutions that will reduce their environmental impact. Contractors and suppliers include: staging, marquees, sound and lighting production, portable building hire, fencing, roadways, barriers, signage, décor, furniture hire, security, welfare, medical, first aid, caterers, consumable suppliers, IT, phones, two way radios, trucks, machinery, golf carts, transport, grounds workers.

The list goes on. Every single one of these companies could green their offices, switch to a green energy supplier, put B20 biodiesel in their trucks, and other general greening changes. They can then go a step further and actively change the way they source materials, manage waste, products they use, etc. Simply requesting to see their business's environmental policy and a list of their sustainability initiatives could motivate them to review their current systems.

Figure 2.8 It's important to get contractors involved in your goals, especially if the work they do has a direct environmental impact such as with plumbers.

Source: Peats Ridge Festival

Regulating Authorities

Authorities who regulate your activities or grant licences for your event are very important stakeholders. These include Local Government, Police, Fire, Ambulance, Environment Agency, etc. The local council and environment agencies may even be a step ahead and have tools or resources to help you. Work with them to seek out their targets for various environmental measures, and aim to better them. For example, your local authority may already have a very active recycling and composting campaign. Seek out those in the council responsible for rolling out these campaigns and enquire how your event can take on the concepts they are promoting. They may have created a recycling 'brand' or bin tops or signs you can use. They may even have mobile recycling displays and staff that can come and set up at your show.

Participants/Artists/Speakers

Those participating in the event through performing, speaking, hosting a workshop or panel, etc., must also be part of the sustainability process. They are prime talking heads who can promote the new sustainability initiatives both pre-event and on show day. Make sure they know what's what before the event and brief them accurately during it. Pre-briefing may spark interest in a participant over a particular element of sustainability, and they could become an ambassador or spokesperson for that project.

Artists and performers are role models and are really effective as spokespeople for causes. History has shown this to be the case. Through song, performance, theatre and art potent statements can be made on environmental and social justice issues. They can entice and inspire crowds of people to take on issues, and with collective action invoke change.

- Target particular performers who align with your philosophy.
- Engage installation artists to produce thought provoking artwork.
- Ask performance artists and roving performers to tackle green issues in their work.
- Set up a one-page info sheet, pdf'd and emailed, that summarizes all the green things you have going at your event.
- Ask programmers and artist relations people in your team to make sure they get the word out that your event is a green one.

Figure 2.9 Ask performers who have environment and social justice issues at the heart of their work to perform at your event. Goldie Feather is one such artist.

Source: Dr Ed

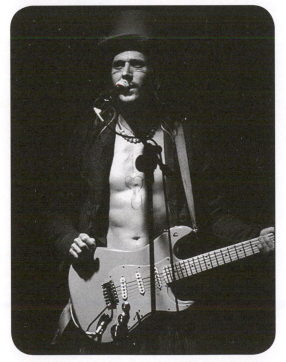

Competitors

If you're organizing a big sporting event your competitors are a slightly different category than the spectators. Talk to them as a separate group, informing them how they can minimize their impact on the environment through their participation in the competition. Of course coach travel for sporting groups is an obvious way to reduce the transport impact. Ensure that this is promoted to clubs so that you don't have hundreds of individual competitors driving separately from all over the region to compete.

Venue Owner

Whether indoors or out, if you're hiring a venue, enlisting the venue owner's commitment to sustainability is vital. Working with them to make major infrastructure changes or smaller operational changes will leave a lasting sustainability legacy from which future users of the venue can benefit.

Media

Tag your green initiatives on all media communication. But also set up a separate all-inclusive media release detailing all your projects to reduce the event's environmental impact, on the one page. Target green media outlets along with those that you would traditionally try to get to cover your event.

Clients

If you're contracted to output an event on behalf of a client, engaging them in sustainability is absolutely necessary. It's possible that your client

Figure 2.10 Building Universal Sustainability BUS at Peats Ridge Festival. Performance artists ran this bus around the festival site transporting the audience from one place to another in a bus that is a truly sustainable way of getting about. Installation by Bella & Dan of the Lovelorn Living Party

Source: Peats Ridge Festival

has actually asked for the event to run sustainably. However, if you have to sell-in sustainability, the triple bottom line angle will do you some good. Depending on where your client is at, if they care about or understand sustainability issues, you should have enough in your toolbox to convince them going green is good.

Local Community

The local community can have a massive impact on the success of your event. If you're bringing in a large number of people, the day-to-day life in the local area is likely to be disrupted. Traffic and public transport, noise and waste are potential areas of contention. By consulting with the local community on greening your event and your sustainability policies, you will be able to pre-empt any potential environment-based complaints.

Industry Sector Organizations

If there are industry associations connected to your suppliers and contractors that can help effect change across an entire industry, this is a good place to start. Waste is an obvious area which will have a lot of support and initiatives happening through industry associations on the various recyclable materials and also composting.

Volunteers and Stewards

Your volunteer stewards are often on the front line, dealing directly with your audience. These are people who direct traffic in the car parks, who run information booths, direct foot traffic, manage campsite hubs, direct people to seats, stand sentry over recycling bins, check wristbands and tickets, etc. Ensuring 'green' messages that flow to the audience through them are clear and correct is really important. Engaging and motivating the stewards over various schemes on site, will flow through to the audience. Make sure you have a really thorough and continuous communications programme in place to get the word out to the audience through your coalface volunteers.

Community Organizations, Interest Groups and Associations

Regardless of the topic of your event, there are likely to be community, special interest or activist groups working in the area of sustainability you're focusing on. Engaging them in the development of your sustainability projects will not only expand your workforce, but also increase the likelihood of your making the best decisions. Groups exist to promote issues such as climate change, water conservation, biofuels, renewable energy, recycling, re-use, etc.

Look for local groups who may wish to participate in your green schemes. For example, there may be action groups whose objectives are to rejuvenate a stream, or wetlands. There may be community gardens that are well established or a group trying to create one. They could be an action group promoting organic vegetables or a local farmers' market. There may be an

upcoming 'Clean Up' campaign, or an activist group campaign for non-GMO foods. By inviting groups who are working these issues locally into your event, you get the benefit of their passion for environmental issues, probably some very motivated volunteers, and also a chance to offer their causes some vital exposure to the audience at your event.

Box 2.6

Identify Stakeholders

Identify who can have an influence on the sustainable management of your event.

To identify stakeholders, ask the following questions:

- Do they make purchase decisions?
- Do they make operational decisions either pre-festival or on show days?
- Do they interact with the audience and therefore have the potential to influence their behaviour?

Below are examples of positions, people or organizations that may be part of your event's production. Identify this person and indicate whether they have influence over purchasing decisions or operations, or interact with or influence the audience.

Internal stakeholders

Event director	Artist liaison
Event manager	Backstage manager
Programming manager	Guest and VIP manager
Production manager	Stage managers
Site manager	Sound and lighting production
Event assistant	Site crew
Infrastructure manager	Signage
Marshalls and stewards	Race officials
Licensing manager	Marketing, advertising, publicity
Website	Sponsorship
Safety, medical, welfare, security	Community liaison
Traffic management	

External stakeholders

Sponsors	Market stalls
Media	Contractors and suppliers
Regulating authorities	Audience
Local community	Volunteers and stewards
Clients	Participants/artists/speakers/performers
Venue owner	Industry sector organizations
Relevant community organizations	Interest groups and associations

Box 2.7

Influence Stakeholders

Before you think about the best way forward for each person or group, you'll need to think about categorizing them. I know, to some of you, lists are boring. But if you're a Virgo or Capricorn start categorizing your victims, something along these lines:

Categorize Stakeholders

- Name.
- Role.
- Area of Influence.
- Level of importance to having them onside.
- Current state of mind towards sustainability.

Communications is the key to engaging stakeholders. You must come up with the best way, or combination of ways, to communicate, engage and ultimately encourage participation in your sustainability goals. You want anyone that impacts on the production of the event to think of most sustainable option when making a purchasing or production decision. Options for communicating with stakeholders are listed below.

Devise the best ways to communicate with, engage and influence your stakeholders:

- Face-to-face meetings and casual influencing discussions.
- Formal or scheduled meetings to discuss sustainability.
- Sustainability issues tabled at existing meetings.
- Ad hoc information and ideas exchanged through email.
- Creation of an online toolkit resource website for stakeholders to access information on sustainability issues.
- PDF or printed information guides relevant to each stakeholder group based around their participation in your event, for example a crew handbook.
- Briefing documents and face-to-face briefings with those who interact with the audience.
- Targeted publicity in trade journals or other publications read by your stakeholder groups.
- Weekly reports to update internal stakeholders on developments of certain initiatives or fledgling projects.
- Presentations at industry associations or other interest group gatherings.

Communication Tools

Talking to your various stakeholders, in meetings, on the phone, via email, etc. will continually reinforce your commitment to sustainability. You'll need to have discussions with major contractors and product suppliers about greener options and creating new solutions. However, more formal communications tools can also be used to reinforce your goals, highlight issues, promote new ideas and successes, and to showcase results.

Newsletters

A newsletter can be sent out to those whose operations and purchase decisions have an environmental impact on the event. The newsletters could include good news stories, tips and ideas, resources, contacts and concepts:

- Profile contractors that have 'gone green'.
- Introduce new initiatives which will be at your event.
- Include 'how to green your business' info.
- Information on how event activities can impact on the environment.
- Set out your goals.
- Explain your expectations for their participation in your sustainability plans.

You may wish to tailor the newsletter to suit each stakeholder group. For your infrastructure and equipment contractors you could put out a newsletter that not only speaks about your sustainability initiatives but also offers resources and information on how companies can green their business, such as switching to green energy, tax relief or funding sources for environmental initiatives, etc. For those staff heavy contractors, tailor the information so it can be forwarded out to their team, with information on how they can personally be involved in greening their participation at your event.

Resource Website

For larger organizations with ongoing events throughout the year or with a major annual event with year-round pre-production, setting up a website full of resources, which the event's production staff and key stakeholders can access, may be a good way to go.

This becomes an archive of resources, and also makes it a one stop-shop for those needing to find out a quick piece of information on a particular issue. For example, you may remind people in your newsletter that if they are having any printing done for your event, they need to follow your guidelines for sustainable printing. These guidelines, along with contacts for approved printers, can be placed on the resource website. This would be really useful for those kind of city-wide events like fringe festivals or multi-arts festivals where many individual promoters put on shows across many venues. National 'days' for charities and NGOs where events are coordinated in every city and town across a country can also benefit from such a website. **Festival Republic** has a resource website called 'Green Republic' for staff, crew and major contractors to access contacts, requirements and green must-takes for their events.

Green Info Summary Sheets

Set up a strategically timed information sheet that summarizes the green initiatives both for the event and its audience, but also your expectations for the involvement of the staff, crew, volunteers, sponsors and contractors. This could include information on staff travel options, expectations around their HQ waste management, letting them know the food from catering will be organic and local, explaining the benefits of the compost loos in their compounds, etc.

On-site Communications for Staff

Apart from pre-event communication, your volunteers and staff that only have show day work will likely also have team briefings and possibly volunteer handbooks or info kits handed out to them. Hijack these tools and make sure the green messages also get in there. Get the green initiatives onto the agenda for pre-event and morning briefings. If any staff or crew's daily activities will come into contact with sustainability projects, they need to be reminded of how they can influence their success. Pull together a summary of your initiatives, tailored to each group of staff and volunteers, and supply the copy to the person responsible for handling communication with these teams.

Another good option is to summarize the key messages and things you want your audience to know and projects you want them to participate in, and create a laminated lanyard to hang around volunteers' and staff's necks. They then have constant access to the right information and will hopefully tell your audience the correct info too. If your volunteers have an HQ, put up a sign, reminders and messages about the green initiatives and what you want them to communicate

Figure 2.11 Garbage Goalies at ROTHBURY Festival in the US wear bright 'One Person Who Cares' RVL7 shirts, made of organic cotton and recycled PET bottles. Five hundred enthusiastic and committed volunteers staff hundreds of Waste Reclamation Stations throughout the festival grounds, 24 hours a day. They also re-sort trash, conduct line sweeps and educate the public as to 'What Goes Where'

Source: The Spitfire Agency, which manages the green initiatives at ROTHBURY Festival

out to your audience. If the key messages change each day, put someone on the job of updating these messages.

Figure 2.12 The crowd at Reading Festival

Source: Festival Republic

Audience Communications

An event planner has good control over influencing back of house and internal operational activities such as reducing energy demand, using renewable resources, responsible purchasing, re-use of materials and resource recovery. However, influencing the way the audience behaves, particularly at a crowded event, is another story altogether.

When considering a new audience-dependent sustainability initiative, understanding the state of mind of your audience prior to and during the event will lead you to the best decisions and devices to motivate them to action. Bribery is a common and effective strategy!!

Communication is the key here. The way you explain your ideas before the event, and the way you convince people to act in a certain way at it, is all influenced by the way you communicate with them and how convincing you turn out to be. You really are applying basic marketing theory here, with a dash of psychology. A crash course in marketing might come in handy, or enlist your marketing team in ways to sell your call to action at your event.

Things to think about in your strategies to get your audience involved are:

- Audience profile and pre-disposition to engaging with a green theme.
- Event practicalities such as site layout, foot fall, congestion etc..
- Pre-event communications opportunities.
- At-event communications.

Audience Personality

Before you kick off into any ideas for reducing the environmental impact you need to have a good hard think about the overall personality of your audience. Are they the type likely to respond enthusiastically to your greening efforts or will you need to coax them into participating?

Some questions to ask yourself:

- Is the audience likely to respond to your on-site messaging of sustainability issues and requests to act in a certain way?
- Do they have the time/headspace/clarity of mind/aptitude to take on the messages you are trying to impart?
- Will your audience object to being told how to behave (teenagers/old people)?
- Are you preaching to the converted, thus making your job relatively simple?
- Is the audience likely to actively participate in initiatives where they must change their normal behaviour?
- If not given a choice and they must participate, will they take it on easily, or try and buck the system?
- Are you making it easy for them?
- Will behaviour-changing initiatives have a positive or negative effect on the audience's vibe?
  – And do you care?
- Do they need to be enticed or bribed into action? Will there be a penalty if they don't do it? Carrot or Stick?
- Do you want to avoid a preaching tone? (The answer to this one should be yes.)

Once you have the answers to these questions you will then have a good perspective on the style of initiatives that are going to work, and what your likely hurdles will be. Importantly, they will also inform you of the tone of communications needed to get them to tune into your ideas. Obviously any communications should be similar in style to the overall event's; however, the subtleties of the language and imagery you choose will definitely impact on how effective your campaigns are.

And so what do you have on hand to forecast how your audience might react? The front-line crew: those happy, hard working, outdoorsy types running around in waterproofs, two way radios in hand, shod with sturdy boot, are the number one tool. Ask the people on the front line, those that interact with the crowds and talk to the people to predict how your audience will react to the initiatives you propose to spring on them. At festivals, outdoor entertainment and sporting events, the site manager, traffic manager, security chief, campground managers, volunteer coordinators, waste managers and toilet cleaning crew will have an arsenal of experience you can draw on. They know traffic flow, pinch points, audience habits and regular occurrences like the backs of their hands.

For conferences, expos and indoor sporting events the venue's head of security, the front of house manager, the ticket office and info desk staff, as well as floor manager and production team, will all know the ebbs and flows of their venue and how people respond within it.

There is no use reinventing the wheel; however, a fresh viewpoint from a green perspective can also lead to wonderful innovations and sustainability achievements. So don't be scared to put some left field suggestions on the table.

If you feel you have a bit of a challenge on your hands and getting your audience involved may be very difficult, it may turn out that you could also be pleasantly surprised by the uptake of some of your ideas. When dealing with the huge volumes of discarded camping gear at UK festivals (a shock as an Australian I can tell you), I was charged with the job of trying to get the audience to actively pack up and hand in their camping gear for donation. We ended up with more than 10,000 items of camping gear donated, and were actually quite overwhelmed by it all. It seemed the more people that took their camping gear to the donation points, the more visual the donating option became, and that encouraged more to make the effort to pack up their gear and donate it. I would prefer them to take their gear home and re-use it, but we are talking about kids that tend to prefer to blow tents up (yes, like a bomb, not an air mattress) at the end of the festival, so handing them in is quite a massive achievement.

Remember, by the time show day comes, the horse has bolted. It's in the planning phase that you will be able to make the biggest changes. So do your homework. Talk to your people, and maybe, if you are up to it, talk to your audience too.

Focus Groups and Discussion Forums

Getting feedback and ideas from your audience is of course an obvious way to get an idea on what could work and also what they'd like to see happen. If you don't have it already on your website, set up a feedback and ideas thread on the discussion forum. Just remember to have someone go into the forum to answer questions, comment back, and glean the pearls of wisdom to bring back to the event planning staff for further consideration. (Do remember though, that sometimes those that get onto these forums with a bit too much enthusiasm are sometime 'forum botherers', rather than a balanced representation of your entire audience.) Nonetheless, it is a great tool.

If you feel it's appropriate, and won't end up in too much of a free-for-all, look at having a gathering of audience representatives, to try out new ideas for discussion. This would be for more than just the greening ideas, depending on the content of your event. Talking face to face with your audience is a great way to bounce ideas around to see what could be successful. You could also present a problem or challenge and see what solutions they come up with.

Footfall, Congestion and Event Layout

You will be familiar with the sheep mentality, people blindly following the crowd at large events. You've probably been one of them at an event when you're not working. When people are in a crowd moving around an event, you need to put strategies in place to influence their behaviour and guide them to where you want them to

Figure 2.13 'Andy's Handy Hoops' as used by UK waste contractor Leisure Support Services. These handy hoops work where there is a lot of crowd congestion leading to difficulty of access to bins, and roving litter picking staff are necessary

Source: LSS

Figure 2.14 Southbound Festival in Western Australia hands out bin bags to patrons, who fill them up, return them to the recycling centres and are rewarded with Green Money to be redeemed at stalls at the festival

Source: Sunset Events

be and what you want them to do. This needs to be considered when planning greening schemes that you need your audience to take part in.

For example, all your best plans may come undone if you have beautifully presented sets of bins for rubbish separation, but the crowd density is such that either you couldn't possibly keep up with the volume of rubbish produced, or that your audience just can't see the bins because of the human tide and everything ends up on the ground anyway. In this case, one solution could be to have a team of roving litter pickers rather than stationary bins. Kit them out with

bin bag hoops so that that they become mobile bin stations, and set them off into the crowd. The separation of recycling from general waste may go out the window, and you would then need to have a mini sorting centre to go back through the rubbish. Or you could send them out in teams of two, with separation happening there and then. More on waste ideas in Chapter 7.

Remember to be ready to react to change also, as sometimes you can't predict how a crowd will flow.

If you have things such as starting lines, entry gates, meeting points, eating zones, bars or other areas that have specific purposes which will gather a crowd, you need to think through how your proposed initiatives will play out in that circumstance. What you have in mind may work where people have the time and space to think things through, but in the excitement of the particular activities it all may come unstuck.

Put yourself in the audience's shoes and think through the journey they will go on while attending your event, from arrival, through to getting settled in, purchasing stuff, getting to where they need to be at your event, eating and drinking, disposing of rubbish, participating and anything you can think of.

 ## Pre-Event Communication

In the lead-up to your event, there will be many opportunities to communicate with your audience or those considering attending. You can start seeding your greening ideas from the very first opportunities to speak to your audience. Your communications strategy may already be in place through your marketing team and if that's so, integrate the green messages into their content, or work with them on creating a specific campaign around your sustainability initiatives.

The key areas which will be common to most events and good topics for pre-promotion are:

- Audience travel.
- Purchasing and preparation.
- At-event participation.

Communications methods can include:

- Publicity and media releases.
- Website.
- Emailed newsletters.
- Posters and promotional flyers.
- Pre-event printed programmes or literature.
- Letters and invitations.
- Printed material accompanying tickets.
- Advertising.

Audience Travel

As audience travel is the largest impact at many events, getting the timing right on promoting sustainable travel options is really important. Audience transport research I have undertaken has shown that travel decisions were made either upon purchase of the ticket (if travel is bundled with the ticket) or generally no sooner than one month before the event. This escalates from two weeks out, with many people starting to get organized and working out how they'll get there.

Your event may have all the great plans in place to provide buses, charge for parking, offer a link to a lift share service on your website, etc., but if people aren't reminded about it, don't get the right information at the right stage of their decision making, and aren't motivated to change their usual travel habits, then the whole thing is likely to fall over.

If you're putting any restrictions on how people can get to your event these must be pre-promoted effectively. Get the audience thinking, from the outset, about their travel options. As will be discussed in Chapter 4, you will need to put strategies in place to dampen enthusiasm for driving and to encourage public transport or car pooling, and these need to be pre-promoted.

Your audience needs to know about these options up front, and you should increase the frequency of communications and details of options as the event gets closer.

Audience Participation

Getting the audience involved in your green schemes is going to be a major part of your work. One of the main areas you need to get them in on is active waste separation — getting them to put their recyclable and compostable waste into the right bin. We'll look at ways to do this in Chapter 7.

Audience Purchasing

Asking people to consider their purchases and actions they need to undertake in preparing themselves to attend your event should be a big part of the green message you send out. You don't want to reduce people's enjoyment and enthusiasm by bah-humbugging buying stuff, but understanding the impact of their recreation, entertainment, sporting activities, business networking or what-have-you, should be put under focus.

Think through what 'stuff' the audience needs to get together to come to your event. Get them to consider goods made with environmental sensitivity, and ensure they get the message to pack up their gear and take it all home with them again.

Tell people what will be available to purchase or hire at your event, so that they don't end up double purchasing, or overbuying, thinking they will be caught short if they don't prepare.

List your preferences for suppliers that tick all your purchasing policy boxes. Remind the audience about environmentally and socially responsible purchasing. Get them to buy locally to support the community that is hosting your event and to reduce product miles. (But remember to pre-warn those shops close to your event so they also don't get caught out.)

Now let's look at how to get the message out to them.

Figure 2.15 Punters bringing barrow loads of 'stuff' to festivals

Source: Meegan Jones

Newsletters

Most events would have a newsletter or an email news update that is sent out to ticket holders or those that have registered interest in the event. Include a section in the newsletter to highlight your green initiatives. Work out a plan to drop in the right information at the right time. People don't need to know the details of your recycling operations months in advance, but they would need to know information about transport and accommodation. Work out when people would be purchasing stuff and getting kitted up to attend your event, and time the info on sustainable purchasing accordingly.

Publicity and Media Releases

If you decide to position your event as 'green', a good way of doing this is seeding stories into the media. Your media team will know the tricks of the trade on how to successfully secure editorial space (as opposed to paying for advertising). I won't take you on a publicity and media relations lesson, as either you won't need to know as you already have someone else doing this job for you, or if you're responsible for the PR, then you'd know how to do it.

What you do need to think about is what the key messages are that you want to get out into the public domain through the media. If you are innovating a new solution, or implementing a 'first' this is more likely to get coverage than something as mundane as 'we're recycling'. There has been a green rush on reporting sustainability in events and festivals over the past couple of years, so you will really need to have some good stories to tell in order to successfully secure a stand-alone piece.

Promotional Material

Your printed material that is distributed pre-event can include:

- Programmes, letters and invitations.
- Printed material accompanying tickets.
- Posters and flyers/leaflets.

It should go without saying that your printing is on sustainably produced paper stock and using sustainable print processes. Make sure you include a note on the environmental printing credentials on all your printed material. More info on sustainable printing in Chapter 6. Use your pre-event printed communications material to promote your greening activities. If brochures are produced to be sent to potential audience members, include details on transport options and minimizing their attendance's impact.

Website

The event's website is one of the most powerful tools you have. It allows you to explain your plans in detail, to use photos, put in context the way you will reduce the impact of your event, and show the audience how they can take part. The 'green pages' on your website can also be used to educate on various issues and offer links to further information.

If you have a news feature, you can use this to strategically drop in stories on various issues, particularly those that have relevance to decision making timing by your audience.

Don't bury the 'green' information within the menu hierarchy. If possible put it at the top level so that it stands alone. You may need to duplicate some information and drop in 'green' info into other areas such as travel, merchandise, toilets, showers, etc.

In the Appendix is an example of a sample hierarchy which could be used for a music festival. You can subtract or add as many topics as are appropriate to this example to suit your event.

At-Event Messaging

Now we look to communicating your green messages on site at your event and techniques to encourage participation. These tools will reinforce the messages you have promoted to your audience in the lead-up to the event. Tools include:

- Key campaigns and green themes.
- Signage.
- Waste stations and eco booths.
- Volunteer stewards.
- Green zones.
- Art installations.

You can also hijack existing communications to include your green messages:

- Printed material and info kits.
- Information stalls.
- Video screen clips.
- On-stage announcements.

Figure 2.16 Eco Wall at Peats Ridge Festival explains all the sustainability initiatives and was built by Ilka Nelson. See close up photos throughout the book

Source: Peats Ridge Festival

Get together copy to place into existing communications options and to supply for stage announcements and screen grabs. Produce a summary info sheet and a poster to place on the wall of your information stalls so that staff in these kiosks know what you have going on.

Signage

Creative use of signage can be a great way of conveying environmental messages and information about sustainability activities at your event. Depending on the tone you decide to take with the green messaging on site, you can be subtle, or take a bolder stand and include it as part of your creative décor and display.

Bonnaroo Festival in the US has created structures which are placed around the site letting people know what the recycling and composting successes have been and what they will be trying to achieve.

Glastonbury Festival in the UK has an entire side of the event called 'Green Fields', where green crafts, alternative therapies, green futures, Greenpeace, the permaculture garden, etc. are placed. There is a roadway called the 'Old Railway Track' which divides the festival in two. It acts as a natural barrier between the Green Fields and the 'other side'. Along this road, they have created 'The Green Way', several photos of which have been sprinkled throughout this book with the kind permission of the creator of the installation, Tracey Shough. www.wildatart.info. As people walk along this roadway some fantastic use of signage has been created. The signs and images are mini installations, with an overall theme of climate change, but they also have relevance to the activities that are evident at the festival such as recycling, green energy, buying 'stuff' and use of waste vegetable oil biodiesel.

At **Peats Ridge Festival** the sustainability activities have been summarized and communicated via an info wall, created using old bread crates and items from the scrap store **Reverse Garbage** in Sydney. Sunflower seeds were planted in cones and attached to the installation during the site build, timed so they would break through the soil and grow during the festival. Close up photos of the panels are also throughout this book and reproduced with the kind permission of the installation artist and sustainability guru Ilka Nelson of The Last Tree. www.thelasttree.net

Figure 2.17 The Green Way at Glastonbury Festival

Source: Courtesy of Tracy Shough

Waste Stations and Eco Booths

A lot of the activities you're going to need your audience to get involved in will be ultimately based around rubbish. As we will see in Chapter 7, the way you set up your waste stations and the bin signage you use will be part of the equation on how effective your waste separation projects are. Make an event out of the waste stations, so that you really can't miss them, and so that they become mini eco-education centres.

If you have campgrounds, set up recycling points where campers can bring back sorted rubbish. Use these recycle centres as info points on recycling and composting at home.

Another option is to set up an eco booth, like an info booth but one which summarizes all the greening initiatives you have at the event. **Paleo Festival** in Nyon, Switzerland does this with their 'Environmental Information Centre'.

Figure 2.18 Interactive eco zone at Paleo Festival in Switzerland. In this area the audience can participate in interactive eco-entertainment while also learning about the greening initiatives at the festival

Waste in their Face

At big events that produce a lot of waste, don't hide away the rubbish. Put the waste processing area in a visible location (though not in a place that's going to make your event look ugly and smelly!).

If you have waste separation happening in a sorting area at the event, have this in a spot that the audience can see it, and invite them to come and have a look. Put up signage and use it as a way of demonstrating what waste is being produced and how it is being dealt with. It's all too easy for everyone, every day of their lives, to throw things in a bin and forget about what happens next.

Unless it has been burnt, every piece of plastic you have ever thrown out in your life still exists. By showing the audience what has to happen to the stuff they throw away, you are making a potent statement.

Figure 2.19 Splore Festival in New Zealand has the Trash Palace as their waste sorting centre. The audience can see what happens to their rubbish and see the sorting in action
Source: Splore

Volunteer Stewards

Face-to-face communication is probably going to be your most effective tool. Having people talk to your audience about the green initiatives will cut through the clutter and get the message through. Recruit motivated people who have environmental issues under their skin.

Of course, the free ticket to the event will be one of your main enticements, but you want to make sure you have motivated people who really believe in the issues and also are outgoing, friendly and OK to talk to strangers!

Give them a task to do, such as handing out bin bags, or directing people around the site. Station

Figure 2.20 Green Team volunteers at Southbound Festival. Kit them up in t-shirts, tabards/vests, or get them to dress up

them at sets of bins. Get them to walk around and hand out butt bins, or to help people set up camp. All the while, they should be charged with the role of promoting the environmental messages you want conveyed to the audience.

Box 2.8

At your Event:
On-site Messaging

- Set up prominent recycle points.
- Include information and ideas about recycling and composting at home.
- Set up a garden at your event and use the compost created to fertilize it.
- Use theatrics to get your message across.
- Dress up your eco stewards and have fun promoting greening.
- Set up a green zone.
- Have art-from-waste sculptures.
- Use performance and interaction.
- Set up hands-on activities.
- Don't hide your waste separation out of site, showcase what you do.
- Hand out bin bags to campers upon entry.
- Offer incentives and rewards for them to bring them back full of recycling and composting.

The Green Zone

If you're serious about using your event to promote sustainable living and giving a voice to environmental issues, set up a green zone. Cluster activities, info booths, demonstrations, discussion forums, films and the like in one area.

The type of event you're producing will direct the content and this may not be appropriate at all events. But if you have large numbers of people and opportunities within your programme to fit such a space, it really is an opportunity not to be missed. Get creative with your content and come up with ways to demonstrate and promote environmental conservation, sustainable living and the big issues that are affecting the Earth today. Create activities that people can be involved in, be it hands on, participating in discussions or watching films and listening to presentations. Invite NGOs, community groups, activist associations, single issue campaigns and everything in between.

Installations and Interaction

Team up visual artists and performance artists with various issues and see the creative sparks fly. By twinning these natural bedfellows, environmental issues and the arts, you can creatively, humorously and inspirationally communicate key messages and provoke thought and action in your audience.

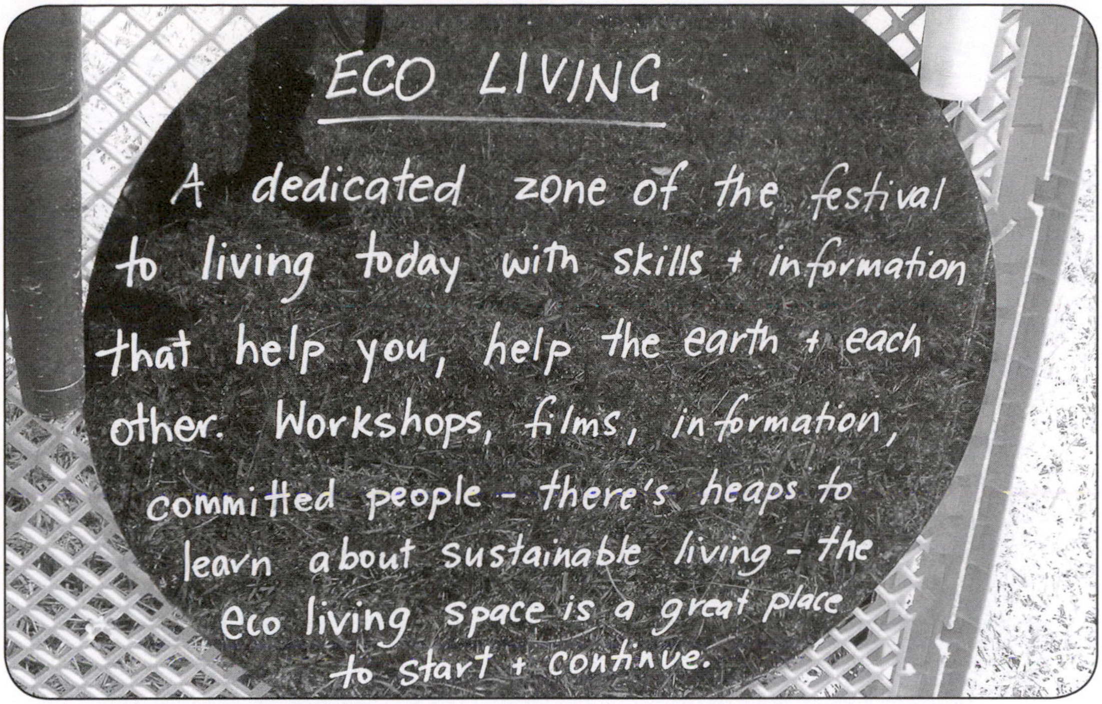

ECO LIVING

A dedicated zone of the festival to living today with skills + information that help you, help the earth + each other. Workshops, films, information, committed people – there's heaps to learn about sustainable living – the eco living space is a great place to start + continue.

Figure 2.21 Many events use the eco village concept to showcase environmental issues

Source: Peats Ridge Festival

Figure 2.22 Glastonbury Festival's Green Police are a fun and creative way of getting the environmental message across to festival-goers.

Source: Dominic Search

Box 2.9

Global Green, Electric Picnic, Ireland

The Electric Picnic has always had a strong environmental focus but in 2008 the gloves came off to tackle the festival's impact on climate change. A new area, the 'Global Green', was launched at the 2008 festival, aimed at being a place to relax and reflect on critical issues.

The Global Green features Cultivate's 'Re-Think Tank', Amnesty's tea and bingo tent, sustainable fashion with Re-dress, the Science Gallery, Trocaire's flower garden, Friends of the Earth, green crafts, EmissionZero, Stop Climate Chaos, Change and others creatively communicating a positive message and encouraging the audience to get active.

Cultivate, the Sustainable Living and Learning Centre in Dublin's Temple Bar, hosts the Re-Think Tank, at the hub of the Global Green. Re-Think Tank is a packed schedule of films, talks and discussions. On the agenda, the very hot issues of energy and food security, ethical fashion, our shifting climate and what it means to be a global citizen in the 21st century.

Cultivate and the Change Campaign created the 'Changing Room' in the Global Green. The audience can calculate their carbon number and confess carbon sins in this carbon confession box.

'Re-dress' set up an area for punters to get active and make their own slogan 'T'. Fashion designers were also on hand turning last year's tents into this year's fashion. They also have an area to up-cycle clothes with LEDs (light emitting diodes) at the Science Gallery stand.

Also present were local and international NGOs covering the full spectrum from climate change to global injustice.

www.electricpicnic.ie

ElectricPicnic

Box 2.10

TRASHED Art Of Recycling, Global Inheritance, US

TRASHed Art of Recycling is an initiative that Global Inheritance has organized at various festivals and events for the past five years. It premiered at Coachella 2002 with 100 painted recycling bins on display as an interactive art walk and recycling programme.

TRASHed is a programme that promotes both art and recycling. Recycling bins are transformed into works of art by different artists across the country. This provides the venue with usable recycling bins that stand out and remind people to recycle. They also serve as interactive art pieces, which complement the festivals' aesthetic goals nicely.

This campaign is an ongoing recycling education programme that redefines the way people view recycling and trash collection. Global Inheritance arranges the artistic redesign of recycling bins, and then integrates the bins at events to encourage recycling and provide additional ways to view the artwork.

Live paintings often occur at events, while bins designed and created by artists beforehand are also featured. Through a network of over 7000 artists, TRASHed appoints the right talent to match each event's aesthetic. Canvasses are not limited, as TRASHed Art of Recycling artists also design bottles, compost bins, and oversized recycling containers in addition to recycling bins.

www.globalinheritance.org

Figure 2.23

Source: Information and photo supplied by Global Inheritance

Watch | Read | Visit

Hot Box Events

If you need stewards at your event and you are in the UK, you can't go past Hot Box Events for effective steward recruitment and management. They are a highly experienced team and have lots of repeat-stewards who have built up some great skills in dealing with the audience. www.hotboxevents.com

Note

1   *An Inconvenient Truth*, www.climatecrisis.net.

Mobile or portable solar power set-ups are a great way to power your event with zero emissions and are a visible show of your commitment to producing the event sustainably.
Souce: Firefly Solar UK

chapter 3

Energy and Emissions

Sustainable energy production is a controversial topic; however, the solutions to minimizing the impact of energy use at events are relatively simple. Reducing power consumption and looking for alternative ways to provide power to your event are the pathways to sustainability. Innovation in new ways of powering our lives is moving rapidly and events can take advantage of this burgeoning field.

The use of non-renewable resources to produce energy and the resulting emissions are the main issues we need to consider. We can reduce the amount of energy used at events through energy efficient equipment, smart power planning, switch-off campaigns, careful planning and distribution of mobile generators, and through powering them with sustainable biofuels. You could also take the next step and use zero emissions energy production.

The following pages look at what you can do right now to power and light your event, as well as where we may be headed in the future. We also look at ways various events have taken on the challenge of reducing their energy use and emissions impact.

Traditional dirty methods of mass power production use coal, gas and uranium. The result is energy, along with alarming volumes of greenhouse gases (GHGs) pluming into the air or hazardous waste which we hide away and hope will do no harm for the next few thousand years. There are also the compounding effects of mining the natural resources and the full range of environmental impacts, along with transportation of the raw materials.

At coal and gas fired power stations, carbon dioxide (CO_2) is the most famous of the GHGs emitted, and is a major player in the energy production controversy.

CO_2 is naturally found in the Earth's atmosphere in small amounts. It also has the neat function of acting as an insulator for the Earth's atmosphere, allowing it to keep the heat from the sun at a temperature we've become accustomed to – the greenhouse effect. Because of human activity the amount of CO_2 and other GHGs being released into the atmosphere has risen dramatically since the beginning of the industrial age. It's now reaching artificially high levels because of the burning of fossil fuels needed to power all the stuff we are building and producing. These artificially high levels of CO_2 consequently produce the even more famous effects of global warming and climate change. The **Intercontinental Panel on Climate Change** (IPCC) in early 2007 announced that irrefutable evidence exists that human activity is the main driver behind the big G W.[1]

So now we have that cheery news where do we go from here and how can we become part of the solution? Entwining energy efficiency, renewable energy and shining a light on the issues surrounding climate change in the context of your event and perhaps influencing the audience to consider doing the same is a good place to start.

Although an extremely important element in the sustainability formula for your event, we should reflect on the fact that rather than powering your event, it's likely most of the CO_2 emissions are puffed out of the exhausts of planes, trains and automobiles used to transport people and players to and from the show. Nonetheless, plugging in and powering up is a big part of any event and ensuring the most sustainable plans are in place for power consumption is your responsibility.

A huge opportunity exists for your event to demonstrate what alternatives to traditional power production are possible. Powering your event through sustainable biofuels, solar, wind,

hydrogen fuel cell and even pedal power is possible. We'll discuss the options and how to apply them at your event later in this chapter.

To put things in perspective, let's look at the state of solar and wind power capacity as it stands today. According to estimates by **WorldWatch Institute**, more than 2935 megawatts of solar modules were installed in 2007, bringing cumulative global installations of photovoltaic cells since 1996 to more than 9740 megawatts – enough to meet the annual electricity demand of more than 3 million homes in Europe. Global installed wind power capacity passed the 100,000 megawatt mark by early 2008. This is enough to provide power to 150 million people.[2]

CO_2 is of course not the only GHG. There is a great long list of gases, and we'll look at a couple of others that occur as a result of your activities in putting on an event – methane, and volatile organic compounds (VOCs). How the impacts of these can be reduced through purchasing and operational decisions will be discussed in the upcoming pages.

Lighting is also in focus in this chapter as it deserves some treatment of its own. As you'd know, the incandescent bulb has been around for some time and isn't a favourite amongst those trying to reduce emissions. We'll look at how to adjust your lighting to a greener level.

The following box is a checklist of ways to reduce energy and emissions. After this we will look separately at energy use for indoor and outdoor events, then move onto sustainable energy production and finally at options to offset those unavoidable emissions.

Box 3.1

Energy and Emissions Checklist ☑

Below is an overall summary of ways to reduce energy use and emissions at your event.

Lead by example

☐ Use your event as a showcase for sustainable energy production and energy efficiency.

Choose a sustainable building for indoor events

☐ What is the venue's energy rating?

☐ Choose an energy efficient building as your event venue.

☐ Do they have techniques such as insulation, passive solar, energy saving bulbs, low energy appliances, lighting timers, sleep mode, etc?

☐ Make sure your venue is signed up to green energy if on the grid.

☐ Do they have off grid microgeneration including combined heat and power?

Plan power consumption efficiencies at outdoor events

☐ Reduce demand for generators through planning for placement, distribution, usage patterns.

☐ Use sustainable biofuels.

☐ Install permanent distribution.

☐ Use alternative energy and zero emissions technology such as solar, wind, hydrogen fuel cell, battery packs and pedal power.

Reduce demand for power through technology and usage

☐ Conduct a switch-off campaign.

☐ Put quotas on users or financial incentives or penalties for power use.

☐ Encourage low wattage equipment and use low wattage lighting including compact fluorescent lamps (CFLs) and light emitting diodes (LEDs) in their lighting displays.

☐ Put your show on an energy diet.

Audit and usage patterns

☐ Audit power usage during the show to assess consumption patterns for future planning.

☐ Audit third party users to make sure they are using what they said they would.

Reduce other greenhouse gas emissions

☐ Reduce VOCs from printing, paints, cleaning and solvents by using low or zero VOC alternatives.

☐ Don't send biodegradable waste to landfill or incineration. Compost it!

Figure 3.1 Bioneers Conference is an excellent example of an event produced sustainably. The conference itself discusses practical solutions for sustainable living and therefore has many tools at hand to produce the event appropriately

Source: Jennifer Esperanza

Indoor Events

Most indoor events will use mains power provided by the venue. However the power coming down the line isn't the only consideration in reducing energy consumption at indoor venues. Improvements to your event's sustainability can be achieved through:

- Choosing a certified sustainable venue.
- Reducing demand for power.
- Renewable energy supply.

In the following pages we look at the benefits of choosing a venue for your event that has met sustainability certification. We'll also cover techniques to put in place to reduce power demand, and look at green energy supply to buildings.

 ## Use a Sustainable Building

A building's sustainability is more than being energy efficient. Sustainability as a broader concept has been included in regulations and ratings systems for buildings, particularly new constructions. By choosing a sustainable building you'll benefit from reduced energy consumption and emissions, along with other broader benefits.

Features of sustainable buildings include:

- Use of alternative and sustainable materials.
- Design and operation responsive to the local climate.
- Water management, including rainwater capture and recycling, and grey water recycling and re-use.
- Waste management and minimization.
- Consideration for the natural environmental and sensitivity to biodiversity.
- Consideration of indoor environment quality (IEQ) issues such as ventilation, clean air, low VOCs, natural light, etc.

Energy efficiency is a major element contributing to a building's sustainability; heating and cooling systems, insulation, passive solar, energy saving light bulbs, low energy appliances and equipment, lighting timers, sleep mode on equipment, etc., are all ways of reducing energy consumption.

When looking for a venue, you don't have to do your own inspection with a clipboard and pen in hand to identify the venue's sustainability. As demand for energy rating information grows, more venues have this information available, and are actively making changes to their facilities to ensure efficiency and they promote themselves as such. It's likely they have been certified by your country's sustainable building codes and you can use that somewhat like an 'eco-label' for buildings. Don't forget to tell your audience why you've chosen the venue.

Sustainable Building Codes

Government agencies and industry associations in many countries have introduced buildings ratings programmes. Buildings must either meet the various minimum standards set or they may be assessed and given a rating that's publicly available.

The **Green Building Council Australia** has implemented the 'Green Star' rating scheme, a great tool to measure a building's sustainability. There are three levels of certified ratings: 4 Star Green Star for 'Best Practice'; 5 Star Green Star for 'Australian Excellence' and 6 Star Green Star for 'World Leadership'. The **US Green Building Council** has developed the Leadership in Energy and Environmental Design (LEED) Green Building Rating System™. In the UK and Europe, the Energy Performance Certificate (EPC) for commercial buildings is being introduced. An EPC will tell you how energy efficient a building is on a scale from A to G. The most efficient buildings are in band A. The EPC is a result of the European Building Performance Directive and each country in Europe is developing an EPC system using the A to G ratings.

Figure 3.2 Part of the 'Greenway' installation at Glastonbury Festival by installation artist Tracey Shough

Source: Meegan Jones

Reduce Power Demand

Reducing the demand for power at events can be accomplished through technology and changes in energy usage habits. At many indoor events, such as trade shows and exhibitions, stallholders will be plugging in en masse. To get everyone to kick the power-board habit, communicating the reasons why reductions are important, along with rewards and penalties, should work.

Encouraging the production team to consider power reducing behaviour is also necessary. They are the ones likely to leave PAs humming, unnecessary lighting on, fans blowing, etc.

Efficiency products

Low energy equipment and lighting is available off the shelf and continually being developed. Request that participants use low wattage alternatives such as CFLs or LEDs. You may need to make it a matter of policy and contract it in.

Switch-off campaign

Through developing on-site messaging along with pre-show communication, encourage people to switch off and unplug when equipment is not in use. Encourage power boards with on/off switches so people don't have crawl under tables or unplug in order to switch off. Make sure motion sensors and timer switches are used where they will be effective in reducing power demands.

Quotas and Penalties

Venues may have financial incentives for reducing energy use. They could offer discounts if you achieve preset minimum goals, and if not, then flow excess usage charges back to you. Even if the venue doesn't offer this, you can implement this system to dampen enthusiasm for plugging in by participants.

Just because you're hooked up to the grid doesn't mean you have to use it. Offer incentives to those who can do without power.

The **Carbon Trust** in the UK has a toolkit of posters and stickers you can obtain free of charge, with 'Switch It Off' and 'Turn It Off' messages. Go to www.carbontrust.co.uk to order a free set or to download the logos. (A sample is below, reproduced with kind permission from the Carbon Trust.) They also have a suite of posters you can put around your offices.

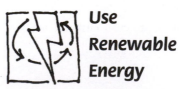

Use Renewable Energy

Power producers supply electricity to national grids across the world through coal, gas, nuclear, large-scale hydro and incineration – leaving a legacy of GHG emissions and hazardous waste, and using up precious non-renewable resources. The alternative is nice clean green renewable and non-polluting energy such as wind, solar, geothermal and biogas. Which makes sense to you?

Large-scale green energy producers along with myriad small producers send their excess energy to the grid. On the grid the lovely clean green electrons get mixed up with the dirty polluting ones. Power retailers in many countries offer a 'green energy' option. They buy the green energy delivered to the grid from the producers, or are in fact green energy producers and retailers themselves.

Through switching to green energy you're supporting the development of renewable energy production. By adding to this development and also to the overall demand, governments will be encouraged to increase their targets for total renewable energy reaching the grid. Producing green energy results in measurable benefits through reduction in GHG emissions and air pollutants. Of course there is also the added benefit of the reduction in use of non-renewable resources and the reduction in the production of hazardous waste by-products.

If you own your venue, or are advising your event's venue to switch to green energy, check for an accreditation scheme for renewable energy in your country to make sure you're switching to a good green energy source. Most venues should be able to sign straight up or choose the green energy option from a conventional power company. It's as simple as that. You'll need to check if your country actually has green energy options available for purchase as it's not available everywhere.

Micro-Power Generation

The ultimate would be for the venue to be powered through microgeneration, completely off the grid, with wind, solar, biogas or a combination as part of the building infrastructure.

Another option for microgeneration is a 'combined heat and power' (CHP) system. Here, as the name states, both heat and power are produced from a single process. Losses of energy through unused heat and transmitting electricity out to the customer via the grid make traditional centralized power plants inefficient in comparison to CHP. In a CHP system the recovered heat is distributed to the immediate surrounding areas and used for hot water or space heating, or the steam can be used for industrial purposes.

Box 3.2

At your Event: Powering indoor events

Choose a sustainable building

What is your venue of choice's Green Star rating, LEED certification, EPC or similar?

If the venue doesn't have a rating, or your country doesn't have such a programme, and you wish to go through a checklist yourself, consider the following:

- Is the venue constructed of alternative and sustainable materials?
- Is it designed and operated to be responsive to the local climate?
- Are energy efficiency considerations evident including things such as passive solar, insulation, natural light, etc.?
- Does the venue undertake sustainable water management such as rainwater capture and recycling, and/or grey water recycling?
- What waste management and minimization procedures are in place?
- Is the venue considerate to the natural environmental and sensitive to biodiversity?
- Have indoor environment quality issues been addressed?

Renewable energy

- Is the venue hooked up to a green energy supplier? If not, can you get the venue to switch?
- Does the venue have its own microgeneration or CHP plant?

Reduce demand for power

- Put energy usage quotas in place for participants.
- Ensure energy efficient equipment is used.
- Have financial incentives or penalties relating to energy consumption.
- Conduct a 'Switch Off' campaign.
- Make it a policy that all lighting by exhibitors is low wattage and no urns or other high energy consuming equipment is used.

Report results (Key Sustainability Indicators)

- Audit all power consumption.
- Ensure you receive energy consumption readings from the event.
- Analyse usage patterns and set goals for future events.

Figure 3.3 All fuel used in generators by Greenpeace at Glastonbury Festival is biodiesel made from waste vegetable oil

Source: Meegan Jones

Powering Outdoor Events

Many outdoor events in greenfield sites will use mobile generators to supply power. The majority of generators today run on mineral diesel, a non-renewable and polluting fuel. By moving to sustainable fuels or zero emissions technology you'll also move to a more sustainable event.

Keep emissions reductions and minimizing fuel use in mind when planning your distribution of power, through using energy efficient equipment, and in fact deciding on the way you produce the power in the first place. You are able to reduce the environmental impact of mobile generated power through:

- Reducing demand for power.
- Using sustainable biofuels.
- Using alternative/renewable energy.

Reduce Demand for Generators

There's no substitute for cutting emissions at the source. By reducing the number of generators you need, and using fewer more efficiently, you can reduce fuel volume and resulting emissions, no matter if they are from mineral diesel or a sustainable biofuel. Undertake a thorough assessment of likely power requirements for your event in collaboration with production staff and the power contractor.

Plan, plan, plan, plan, plan ... for:

- Placement of generators.
- Loads and usage patterns.
- Distribution of cabling.
- Usage peaks and troughs.

Before we delve into these topics, let's look at who we're dealing with when trying to put these measures in place.

Generator Contractors

Your power contractors are experts and it's often better to leave it to them to plan efficiencies and alternatives. However a fresh set of eyes (yours) that aren't too narrowly focused may come up with options to reduce demand for generators and other innovative solutions to reduce energy consumption. Your power contractor may have a vested interest in providing as many generators and as much fuel as possible. Coaxing them to efficiencies while also reassuring them of their nice fat invoice at the end of the show is something you need to balance. Perhaps working a bonus into their contract to reduce

kVA (generator sizes) or fuel volume would be an incentive. Using a contractor who isn't also the owner of the generators but hires kit from multiple sources may be your best bet. Consider striking a deal that includes you paying for the fuel bill separately, so that they are not getting a kick-back for every litre of fuel that goes through the generators.

You need to educate yourself so you can talk turkey with the sparkies. You don't need an electrician's qualification, but if you can demonstrate a basic understanding of the principles behind supplying power to your event, you can have a decent conversation about options and solutions. If you're starting from scratch, there's no one better than your friendly power contractor to ask for this education. Get them talking amps and kilowatts, kVA and loadings, and although you may start losing to will to live, you'll become more equipped to investigate some energy saving options.

As an example of some straightforward but beneficial information to know, there's a load range, where a generator runs at optimum efficiency. Below this and fuel is burnt off. Above it and the generator is in danger of cutting out. You may remember seeing huffing and puffing generators at events. This is often not a sick piece of machinery; it's your money going up in smoke as the gear is underutilized and fuel burns off. You need to allow for spikes in demand to ensure no power cut-outs, but consistently running a generator at well below the optimum range will lead to burn-off of fuel which is wasteful financially, a waste of resources and causes unnecessary emissions.

Also something to look out for is the generator hire company supplying kit that's well above the size needed for the specific job. Get an assurance that the requested kVA for the generator ordered would be the kVA supplied. One power contractor has confessed to me that sometimes up to 50 per cent of fuel goes up in smoke, a lot of which is due to oversized generators delivered because of planning issues on behalf of the hiring company.

Plan for Efficiencies

The event site manager or production manager and the power contractor will work together to plan numbers and placement of generators. Often power distribution planning has to come after site layout factors such as footfall patterns, creative production and aesthetics, access routes, and lay of the land, etc. are considered. With careful planning of generator placement, efficiencies can be made.

Usually generators will be sited as the centre of a 'hub' with distribution fanning out from it. If you don't have the benefit of a power contractor based on site to do your planning and it's up to you, the following need to be considered:

- Number of outlets requiring power.
- Maximum load for each outlet.
- Estimate of peak usage times.
- Distribution and cabling planning.

Production staff not worried about minimizing the energy used will do rough estimates and then throw a generator at it a couple of sizes up, to make sure there are no power cut-outs. If you want to be diligent in your energy planning, you need to gather as much information about potential power pull and usage patterns as possible. Overlay this onto your site plan, do some calculations and you should come up with a good estimate on power required in each area.

Look for areas where a generator is used for a single purpose and if there are other ways to power that piece of equipment. In remote locations at large events, oversized generators are often sited for a single use, which leads to wastage, the reasoning being that a small generator, which could do the job, is vulnerable to theft.

You may have generator powered tower lights in car parks, remote entry points and any areas that need security lighting at night. Ensure these are switched off during the day. A simple thing, but often overlooked. Mobile solar powered lights could be an alternative solution. If they don't exist in your region, talk to a solar power supplier and see if they are interested in putting together a prototype, trialling it at your event with a view to future development.

Also be aware of possible overstating of power requirements by production staff on music stages for sound, and particularly for lighting. There tends to be a snowball effect, with more power added as the word passes from band to tour manager, to production manager, to site manager, to power contractor.

Energy Efficient Equipment

There has recently been a noticeable increase in the amount of energy efficient gear coming onto stages. Any efficiency presented by equipment has generally not accumulated to make enough of an impact in reducing the size of generators. However the amount of new energy efficient gear is now having an impact and it's time we took advantage of this to make sure it's translated to reductions in generator sizes and fuel consumption and resulting emissions.

Power factor correction is something which needs consideration. It becomes an issue when energy efficient equipment causes the load to become unbalanced. In order to take advantage of the reduction in wattage offered through energy efficient equipment, power factor correction devices have to be installed onto generators. If power factor correction isn't addressed production staff and power contractors will keep using larger generators than are really required, leading to wasted fuel and increased emissions.

Install Permanent Cabling

If your event is on a permanent site and has a fairly stable site plan, you'll find terrific savings by putting in permanent distribution. Often stand-alone generators are required in the far reaches of your site as running temporary cabling isn't possible or efficient. Installing permanent underground cabling to these key areas will mean a reduction in the number of generator units you need and therefore create efficiencies.

Power Usage Monitoring and Show Day Auditing

Asking how much the end users require is all well and good, but if you don't put quotas on them up front and actually police usage, then you could end up with some problems. Ensure continual monitoring during the event so that the pledges made by end users are kept or if increases are needed, you know what to expect next time around.

An audit of load and usage patterns will give you solid data for future planning. Most generators will produce readouts, which can be tracked manually or automatically. Monitors can be attached to the generators and the data then transferred to computer. This is similar to doing an energy audit at home. By measuring your power consumption over the time of your event you will see if you're oversupplying an area or where other savings could be made.

Oversupply of generators, in terms of kVA size, is common, and you should see whether what was planned was actually delivered, so that all your planning doesn't go out the window because of an administrative or booking challenge at the generator hire company's depot.

The results may highlight potential efficiencies where you could:

- Reduce the generator size.
- Have secondary generators connected to switch on only at peak times.
- Reduce generator numbers by extending distribution.

Natural Gas

Compressed gas such as butane, propane or liquid petroleum gas (LPG) is used for cooking or heating. This will either be supplied bottled, or via the mains. There are also compressed natural gas mobile power generators available. Include gas in your emissions calculations so you can see what impact gas usage is having.

Use Sustainable Biofuels

Biofuels are made from raw materials such as oilseeds, wheat and sugar, resulting in ethanol (alcohol) and biodiesel. The feedstock can be seen as carbon neutral as it releases the same amount of carbon dioxide as it takes out during the recent growth cycle as opposed to unlocking ancient carbon through burning fossil fuels. However, the use of fertilizers and other chemicals to grow fuel crops such as corn/maize, and the transport and energy needed to convert to biofuels does bring them back from being carbon neutral.

There is much campaigning against using arable land for production of crops for fuel not food. It's believed that only so much land can be set aside to grow biofuels before food supplies and biodiversity are threatened. Also the insatiable demand for fuel crops can push up grain prices. There has been a strong backlash against biofuel crops grown in Malaysia and Indonesia where palm oil plantations and the consequential destruction of forests is happening on a grand scale.

Organizations such as UK-based **Renewable Fuels Agency** and international **Global BioEnergy Partnership** (GBEP) are researching the effects of growing fuel. They are developing best practice and sustainable development policies.[3]

However, it can be seen that the current crop (pardon the pun) of biofuels is a transition solution. They are a bridge to get to where we need to be without cutting us off from our existing technology. Using biofuels builds demand for renewable fuels, encouraging a market for

---

Box 3.3

GreenPower Events

All types of public events in Australia can now become more environmentally friendly by becoming a GreenPower event.

Even if the show is off grid and using mobile generators running on mineral diesel, by purchasing 'GreenPower Credits' the event can ensure that an equal amount of renewable energy is fed back onto the grid. This is achieved through the purchase of Renewable Energy Certificates and means that when events buy GreenPower, although they still take their physical electricity from the mobile generators, the event is ensuring that renewable energy is being fed into the grid on their behalf.

www.greenpower.gov.au

GreenPower™
Accredited Renewable Energy

and making potentially viable advancement in second and third generation biofuel technologies. These next generation biofuels include biohydrogen diesel, biomethanol and algae oils. Non-food oils are the way ahead and without a proven market, bringing these new technologies to commercial viability may not be possible. Next generation biofuels could be more sustainable in production, cheaper, have greater environmental benefits and, significantly, not upset world food production and price stability or threaten biodiversity.

The **Energy Biosciences Institute** (EBI) is a joint partnership between the **University of California Berkeley** and **BP**. BP has committed US$500 million to the project over the next ten years. The Institute will 'perform groundbreaking research aimed at probing the emerging secrets of bioscience and applying them to the production of new and cleaner energy, principally fuels for road transport'.[4]

Looking to the past as a way to a bright green future … Henry Ford's first car was run on pure alcohol and the man diesel technology is named after, Rudolf Diesel, ran his first engine on peanut oil. But it was soon discovered that getting oil from the ground was a cheaper and more effective fuel source. But we are no longer in this position. We are moving towards Peak Oil and the environmental costs of continued fossil fuel use are manifest. If we are going to delve further into cropped fuels, the only way really to ensure that fuel doesn't threaten food security is to take food crops out of the picture completely and to look to growing non-food oil crops.

We are lucky in the events industry to be using a piece of machinery (the mobile power generator) that's well suited to a fuel available at a commercial scale right now. It has no ethical dilemmas to consider: waste vegetable oil (WVO) biodiesel.

Waste Vegetable Oil Biodiesel

WVO biodiesel is in ready supply in many countries, and at a competitive price. WVO biodiesel isn't only a renewable resource, thus eliminating fossil fuel use; it has already been used once before. It's the ultimate in up-cycling – closing the loop by taking a waste product and transforming it into a fuel with so many excellent benefits.

Suppliers of WVO biodiesel source their raw material from commercial cooking operations, such as frozen food factories. Some use tallow from abattoirs. **Southbound Festival** in Western Australia uses a biodiesel blend of 80 per cent tallow and 20 per cent waste vegetable oil to run their generators.

There are backyard producers and boutique commercial operators who source their WVO from local takeaway shops and businesses. There's word on the street in the US that Mc-Who-Shall-Not-Be-Named are using their WVO to turn into biodiesel to fuel their trucks. There you have it.

At the time of writing it was more cost effective to use high grade WVO biodiesel than mineral diesel. However things quickly change. World oil prices fluctuate, and in some countries there may be levies, taxes, exemptions, etc., which can alter the prices one way or the other. Governments continue to flip-flop on the issue and with rising anti-biofuels opinion, we must be ready to lobby on behalf of this great sustainable solution for our industry's mobile power supply.

Little has to be done to a standard generator, except for a tank clean and filter changes, to run on biodiesel. There is no reduction in performance and no reliability problems with using generators fuelled by biodiesel – assuming high grade ISO/EN 14214 is used. This is the international

Figure 3.4 Part of the 'Greenway' installation at Glastonbury Festival. Image printed with the permission of the artist Tracey Shough

Source: Meegan Jones

Figure 3.5 WVO biodiesel being delivered to Peats Ridge Festival in NSW, Australia. They brokered a partnership with generator hire company PremiAir to run kit on WVO biodiesel. PremiAir has committed their entire fleet to run only on WVO biodiesel, benefiting all their other customers as well as the environment

Pure Plant Oil

Rather than converting oil produced from crops into biodiesel, it's possible to use straight oil. Pure Plant Oil is the term and there are mobile generators which run on this fuel. Conventional diesel kit can also be converted to run on pure plant oil. The benefit of using this over biodiesel is less energy is used in its manufacture. Large chemical processing facilities and associated environmental and financial overheads are not needed. The use of pure plant oil comes with the same concerns for all cropped biofuels – that land is being used for fuel not food. The pure plant oil business is taking this head on and sustainably sourcing its fuel feedstock. One of the major things to look for is that no palm oil is used by your pure plant oil supplier and that any rapeseed or soya seed oil is sourced from certified sustainable producers.

standard that sets the minimum requirements for biodiesel. To avoid filter changes and tank cleans, generator suppliers need to switch and commit their fleet or part of it to permanently running on biodiesel. If your supplier resists your request seek out a supplier with biodiesel kit available and an eye on the future.

Apart from hesitation by contractors, the availability of supply of good quality sustainably produced biodiesel will be your main hurdle. If there is an ongoing supply of WVO biodiesel, do all you can to coax your generator provider into committing their kit to it full time.

Regenatec in the UK is a leading supplier of pure plant oil fuels along with the conversion technology needed for vehicles, machinery and mobile power generators. It currently sources sustainable pure plant oils but it's also actively supporting the development of next generation non-food oil stocks. Regenatec is working closely with award winning **CleanStar Energy** of India to develop a form of 'FairTrade Fuels'. It's the intention to grow Jatropha on waste land – the poorest areas of the country – and then bulk ship the oil back to the UK to displace mineral diesel. Already large plantations of Jatropha (an arid loving, desert type tree) are being planted on scrub land – no food crops or people are being displaced. The production of environmentally friendly biofuels creates new jobs in some of the poorest regions of Asia. This can both offset the carbon emissions of Europe and fuel Europe's appetite for renewable energy.
www.regenatec.com

DIY Energy

The people at All Power Labs have developed an old technology into new, and offer Gasifier Experimenters Kits (GEKs). Taking the technology from WWII when over a million cars in Europe ran from on-board gasifiers, this brilliant team of DIY energy geeks have come up with an amazing solution for small-scale, and almost immediate, energy production. Any biodegradable waste, coffee grounds, food scraps, garden waste, etc., can be put in one of their GEKs to produce biogas.

allpowerlabs.org

Box 3.4

At Your Event: Biofuel Checklist ☑

☐ Promote WVO versus cropped fuel.

☐ Broker partnerships
Between WVO biodiesel suppliers and your generator hire company.

☐ Use pure plant oil
Demonstrate pioneering (yet old) technology and run your generators on pure vegetable oil.

Algae Oil

Let's now look to the future potential of algae oils. Algae grows in waste water, it's high yielding and can be used to create oil or processed into ethanol. Companies such as **GreenFuel** in the US are producing algae and algae oils. They recycle CO_2 from smokestacks, fermentation and geothermal gases in the process. The algae can then be converted into fuels for transport or as a combustion source for power generation. They are on their way from development to commercialization and it's a very bright green future we are looking at if this becomes commercially viable. The benefits of algae as a feedstock for oils include not needing potable water or using land to grow. They also take CO_2 from industrial and other power generating processes. Keep an eye on the future of algae oils.

www.greenfuelonline.com

At your Event: Powering Outdoor Events

Plan generator placement and distribution
- Reduce the generator size (kVA).
- Establish the number of outlets requiring power.
- Work out the maximum load each outlet will require.
- Estimate the peak usage times.
- Plan distribution and cabling.
- Install permanent distribution if you have a permanent event site.

Put quotas and restrictions on users
- Supply one 10amp power point as standard, and charge participants such as stallholders, demonstrators, exhibitors, etc. for power, along with any extra they want.
- Ban electric kettles and electric urns from stalls, as these are big users and often the cause of power cut-outs!
- Audit stallholders to ensure they use only what they said they would.

Supply all generators and ban any small petrol ones
- Supply all generators. If you allow small generators to be used by individuals, you won't only be unable to keep a handle on fuel volume, but may also have noise problems.

Measure usage and set goals
- Work with your power contractor and production staff to assess where savings and efficiencies can be made and set goals for fuel consumption, kVA and total kW hours for the next event.

Sponsor and Partner Opportunities

- Broker a deal with a WVO or pure vegetable oil supplier to promote the fuel's use in conjunction with your event.
- Invite solar power providers that sell domestic solar power solutions to sponsor or provide the solar power. Often the same contractor will supply wind turbines as well.
- Look for companies that market zero energy products such as solar power phone chargers, hand pump torches, dynamo chargers to put on bikes, etc., that can be used at your event and by the audience at home.
- Invite an energy saving light bulb supplier to sponsor, as well as supply, lighting solutions.
- Invite eco-paint suppliers to sponsor your event, promoting their zero VOC products.
- Invite cleaning product brands that are solvent free to sponsor your event.
- If you're offering an option for carbon offsetting to your audience, bring in examples of the technology they will be funding with their offsetting dollars.

Figure 3.6 Firefly Solar's power rig on site at Shambala Festival in the UK

Source: Firefly

Zero Emissions Energy

Relying solely on fossil fuels is not a sustainable long-term solution to energy supply. Look for alternatives to power your event and mimic developments in zero emissions solutions to not only power your event but also to demonstrate what is possible.

Zero emissions energy is growing rapidly with large-scale investment and development of big wind and big solar. Apart from the need for global emissions reductions being at crisis point, no one can predict with certainty what will happen to global oil and coal supplies and the relative costs to extract them. There isn't just one solution to low-impact energy production. The answer is in variety and harnessing the natural resources in the immediate geographic area – wind, sun, tidal, river, etc. The current reality is that green energy isn't the solution to 100 per cent of the world's energy needs, but maximizing every alternative energy and zero emissions option is surely the best and most immediate action we can take. Scientific advancements in solar technology, energy efficiency, hydrogen fuel cells and yet undiscovered solutions will bring us closer to a sustainable and stable energy future.

Rather than simply replacing mineral with WVO biodiesel or other sustainable fuels, it's possible to do without diesel generators at all. This is where we move to truly green energy sources for your event.

Use Solar Power

Mobile solar set-ups are available to power events – proven and reliable, assuming you have some sun. There is no need to take you on a detailed lesson on the science of converting solar energy into electricity. A crash course is going to be best. Here goes …

There's the sun.

It shines on solar panels (photovoltaic cells).

This is captured and goes through a technical process beyond most of us, but includes batteries, inverters and the like.

It comes out the other end as a steady stream of electricity.

A distribution board is set up.

You plug your things in and they work.

But … you must put your event on an energy diet in order to achieve reliable results. What you need to know in order to successfully run solar is the following:

- What power various equipment pulls.
- How long you'll be running the equipment for, and what time of day … which leads to:
- Wattage and amp hours.
- Is there a spot, facing north in the southern hemisphere, and south in the northern hemisphere, where the solar panels can be set up, without shade being cast on them?
- Do you have a backup if the sun doesn't shine?
- Do you have a plan in place to stop someone from plugging in and using up all the allocated power?

Solar power providers are emerging who provide mobile kit specifically for the events industry. Mobile solar panels pop up out of trailers, or swing out from the sides of trucks. Some are stand-alone units, others form part of the staging infrastructure and display. Have a look at the wonderful rig by **Southwest Solar Solutions** from the UK on their website www.mobilesolarstage.co.uk. They come with their own staging, PA, lighting, backline, etc. and it is often better as they know exactly how much power everything uses rather than having a separate company supply sound and lights.

If one person sees a solar array for the first time, understands how it works, and then goes home and installs one, then we've succeeded.

Tom Price, Environmental Manager Burning Man, and Executive Director Black Rock Solar.

If you have a one-day show, solar power is a hassle free option. If you're running a multi-day show, things will become a little trickier. You need the sun to shine so the batteries are topped up ready for the next day. If the sun doesn't shine, then you need a backup – such as a WVO biodiesel fuelled generator on standby to recharge batteries.

Demonstrating what it is possible to power using the sun is a big benefit. If you've powered your show resulting in no emissions and your audience leaves inspired then you've won.

There are other solar power solutions for events that are not based around performance stages – solar powered ice cream carts being a lovely example. What could be greener than getting an ice cream which has been frozen using energy from the sun? Brilliant. Installations are also a great way to combine energy production with décor, art and eco-education.

At **Boom Festival** in Portugal they have set up a solar cooker, similar to the kind that are used in offsetting programmes in Africa and India. This is a great way of showing the audience the power of the sun. At **Glastonbury Festival** all the power in the Green Fields comes from microgeneration. Individual stalls bring their own solar set-ups. It's a splendid vision, walking through the fields and seeing the colourful trucks and rigs and stalls festooned with solar arrays and strung with LED lights.

The Green Man theme at the 2007 **Burning Man** event spurred solar power projects and the money-free environment has spilled out into the real world as a result. **Black Rock Solar**, a non-profit organization builds low or no-cost solar power in unlikely places. They install in schools, hospitals and public places and buildings that would not otherwise be able to afford it. They teach the communities how to do DIY solar. www.blackrocksolar.org
www.burningman.com

Figure 3.7 Sustainable Waves in the US specializes in sustainable energy solutions for the entertainment industry. They provide solar powered stages, sound systems, lighting www.sustainable-waves.com

Source: Sustainable Waves

Figure 3.8 Installation and solar panel structure. Big Green Gathering, UK, 2007

Source: Meegan Jones

Figure 3.9 Solar cooker being used at Boom Festival

Source: Boom

Figure 3.10 Solar powered ice cream cart at Peats Ridge Festival

Source: Meegan Jones

Box 3.6

Zero Emissions Checklist ☑

Use solar and wind power

☐ for stages, installations, lighting, stalls.

Use pedal power

☐ Get your audience involved with powering their entertainment. This can include stages, cinema or mobile phone charging.

Use hydrogen fuel cell power

☐ Team up with a group pioneering this technology to power a part of your event.

Produce your own biogas

☐ Use a biogas unit to produce gas and/or electricity in real-time.

The team at UK-based **Croissant Neuf** have developed a solar power system to run PA and lights in their own circus tent. The venue is hired into festivals, either programmed or as a dry hire. It comes complete with seating, carpets, staging, lighting (solar powered) and a studio quality, 10Kw, 16-channel, solar/wind powered PA. They have also put together the 'Green Roadshow', a unique variety of fascinating exhibits, combined with a continuous programme of environmentally themed entertainment.
www.greenroadshow.co.uk

Box 3.7

Firefly Solar Stage

Firefly Solar started life in the summer of 2007. They were approached by a local councillor and asked if it would be possible to produce a live stage on renewable power. Not one to say 'no' to anyone, they set about finding a renewable solution and Firefly Solar was born. Here's the story of how a request from an event organizer has encouraged the creation of a purpose built sustainable solution to the events industry.

At the time the company was two guys with backgrounds in event production, business and electronics, who owned a small amount of PA and some staging and backline, and produced events in Brighton and Hove in the UK. With their brief to provide renewable energy for the stage, the more research they did, the more it became evident that there was no one in the vicinity that had anything suitable, and in fact very few systems existed anywhere in the UK that could do the job.

The need (and market) for a renewable stage was identified. With an outside investment from an individual inspired by the project, Firefly purchased their first set of batteries and panels. After working out exactly what batteries and panels would best suit a live set-up, they produced their first stage powered solely by the sun. It was a one-day community event held on a beautifully sunny day in Brighton. The equipment worked exactly as planned and the council was very happy with the result. From then on the phone was ringing and another event producer was on the end of it, very interested in a solar solution for their outdoor event.

The first major hurdle that Firefly needed to overcome was transportation. Deep cycle lead acid batteries are heavy – very heavy. It was not practical to carry these batteries across fields and wire them up each and every time they were used. They designed a trailer system that could house batteries and panels in the same unit.

The next step was to expand their set-up to produce enough power for a stage at large events. They packaged their offer to be attractive to the mainstream events market, bringing together the power they supply, a 'saddlespan' stage, lighting, sound, backline gear and staff. A complete plug-n-play package. By controlling all gear that's used, they can carefully monitor and predict power consumption.

In 2008 they had back-to-back bookings throughout the UK season. By offering a full solution to the industry covering all areas of production, from supplying and erecting the structure right through to managing the stage over the event, Firefly had found a format that was instantly sellable to event producers. That it was powered on renewable technology using cutting edge lighting and PA made it incredibly desirable also.

The company is still in development in these early years and all employees are shareholders in the company, which allows this innovative contractor to survive through heavy capital investment. Firefly Solar has so far concreted its reputation as the premier supplier of mobile solar power solutions in the UK and is looking to expand its business to Europe, India and South Africa.
www. www.fireflysolar.co.uk

Source: Information in this case study supplied by Ollie Stroud of Firefly Solar

Figure 3.11 Solar Power Music Tree at Southbound Festival in Australia. Created by local industrial design and electronics creatives Vince Austin and Katie Cochrane, and powered by clean renewable energy, the music tree is an interactive electronic sculpture on which multiple punters can play music

Source: Southbound Festival

Microgeneration

Solar, wind, combined heat and power, methane or biogas digesters, and micro hydro are all examples of microgeneration; permanent energy supply that's off the grid. If you have a permanent outdoor site, you could consider permanent microgeneration that can not only power your event, but also offer value to your surrounding community. Businesses and local government are leading the way in microgeneration. You should be able to find grants and subsidies to underwrite some infrastructure costs. A wonderful example in the spirit of microgeneration is the Brothers Cider Company in Somerset, UK. The heat generated from their factory is used to heat the local town's swimming pool.

Wind Power

Wind power is another alternative. It's obviously going to work best if you have a windy area on your site. The same thing goes for the crash course previously on how solar power works, except this time it's the wind blowing, rather than the sun shining. It's worth investigating whether there are boutique providers of wind power in your region and matching them with small users of electricity. For example, an info kiosk that just needs some lights on for four hours at night could be perfect. A little LED light set-up, a stash of batteries, and you're good to go. The additional benefit of this kind of power option is showing the audience microgeneration in action. Get the wind turbine provider to leverage promotion from their participation to increase awareness about the availability and ease of use of this excellent zero emission technology on every day homes.

Hydrogen Fuel Cell

The commercial viability of power supplied by a hydrogen fuel cell generator is increasing quickly. A hydrogen fuel cell is an efficient form of power supply with no emissions and only water vapour from the exhaust. It's a clean and efficient alternative to diesel generators. A fuel cell is an electrochemical device that converts hydrogen and oxygen into water, and produces electricity in the process. A battery is also an electrochemical device. It has the chemicals stored inside it and converts those chemicals to electricity, but the charge eventually dies out. With a fuel cell, the chemicals are constantly flowing into the cell so it never runs flat. As long as there's a flow of chemicals into the cell, out comes the electricity. The technology is being developed to power motor vehicles; however it has also been set up

Figure 3.12 Hydrogen fuel cells used at Latitude Festival, UK

Source: Festival Republic

to provide electricity. Keep your eyes out for this option becoming available.

 ## Pedal Power

Figure 3.13 Bike-powered juice blender at Big Green Gathering, UK

Source: Meegan Jones

Pedal power is something that's making a bit of a splash, especially in the festival environment. Operators are emerging that have bike powered set-ups. The audience, or dedicated volunteers, sit on stationary bikes and pedal their hearts out to produce power. Ten bikes daisy-chained can power a PA big enough for around 200 people.

There are also novelty set-ups where the pedalling is directly attached to a sound system using vinyl records. I have also seen a pedal powered washing machine. My personal favourite is a pedal powered Juice Bar, where a mechanical set-up attaches bikes, through a series of cogs and wheels, to food blenders. This juice stall has staff pedalling, which powers the blenders.

Micro Hydro Power

We all know about massive dam based hydroelectric schemes. Micro hydro or run-of-river hydro is an alternative for small power requirements. If you happen to have a permanent location and also have a reliable running water course near it, a run-of-river hydro power set-up could be for you.

Figure 3.14 Pedal power by Magnificent Revolution

Source: Lucy Sheldon

Box 3.8

Pedal Power Cinema and Sound

Magnificent Revolution (MR) is a not-for-profit collective, based in London, UK, established in 2007 to build The Magnificent Revolutionary Cycling Cinema. The cinema had its premiere as part of The Arts Trail at the 2007 Big Chill festival. The collective consists of artists, musicians, designers, eco-builders, ecologists and engineers.

Since the summer of 2007, MR has progressed beyond just pedal powered cinema and flourished into a cross-disciplinary organization, bringing together education, ecology, engineering, design, art, music and film.

MR's generation system uses up to ten bikes, and therefore 20 legs, to power up to 600W of DC or AC mains power. This gives them the ability to power a projector, laptop, sound systems and a mini recording studio completely off grid. MR are always researching and showcasing new and old technologies which complement the use of bicycle power including LED lighting and LED projectors. They've developed a real-time generator, without energy storage, so if you stop pedalling, the electricity stops. It uses real bicycles and can be transported easily.

The beauty of pedal power lies in its participatory nature and its dependence on human effort. No cyclists means no power, no music and no film. This creates a unique experience for DJs, bands and their public due to the co-dependent relationship between the performers and their audiences. At MR events people power everything from the lighting to the bands themselves, creating a unique collaborative experience.

MR do not see themselves as just energy suppliers to music and film festivals. They are aware of the shortcoming of pedal power as a practical solution to current unsustainable energy options, especially in the case of large-scale festivals with stages accommodating thousands of people. They have powered small stages and cinemas at festivals in the past but the ultimate aim is to strengthen and reinforce commitment towards social and ecological change and foster respect for energy and sustainable technologies.

As MR's system uses the same components as home renewable systems it's a great introduction to renewable energy. Their goal is to catalyse critical thinking and nurture an understanding of environmental values and positive visions of a sustainable future. MR

Magnificent Revolution

aims to inspire people to re-examine their individual choices and develop creative ways of living with less impact on our planet. Their work generates a dialogue about environmental concerns and how personal actions can be linked to greater global problems such as climate change.

> *This applies not just to the individual and the choices that they can make, but also relates to the role of the music industry including its performing artists. Musicians and the music industry have the power and responsibility to set a leading example, motivating and inspiring audiences to take action to tackle climate change and create opportunities to promote the use of sustainable technologies. Through our work we hope to align musicians and the music industry with the environmental movement and help create new role models and sources of inspiration for their audiences.*
>
> *Lucy, Magnificent Revolution*

Read more about the credo that underlines all the work this magnificent organization does in the Appendix.

www.magnificentrevolution.org

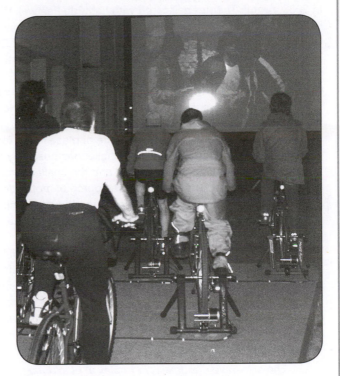

Figure 3.15 Cycle power cinema in Greece

Source: Orhan Tsolak

Source: Information in this case study provided by Lucy Sheldon and Barbora Patkova from Magnificent Revolution

Box 3.9

Innovation in sustainability through the arts

Arcola Theatre is a Hackney-based off-West End theatre, founded in 2000, and widely recognized as one of the most significant and successful fringe theatres in the country. Trailblazing sustainability projects as part of its core business, Arcola Theatre aims to be the world's first carbon neutral theatre.

Arcola's commitment to the responsibility for making environmentally sustainable art was declared with the launch of Arcola Energy in 2007. With scarce resources but enthusiasm and passion plentiful, Arcola has built a strong reputation for taking innovative steps within the field of sustainability. By partnering with representatives of London's theatre industry, equipment manufacturers, the Mayor of London's Office and central government, Arcola has been a crucial catalyst in mobilizing the entire industry, establishing a position of global leader, despite working within the constraints of being a cash-strapped charity.

In 2008, Arcola Theatre partnered with Latitude Festival. With environmental issues at its core, Latitude welcomed Arcola and its fuel cell to power the Theatre Arena lighting. Deploying state-of-the-art low energy lighting including LEDs, energy consumption and thus CO_2 emissions were cut by approximately 50 per cent in the theatre arena.

Back at their permanent location, Arcola's 'greening' goes from the stage to the box office. The installation of Arcola's fuel cell in February 2008 made the venue the first theatre in the world to power its main house shows and bar/café on hydrogen. The 5kW IdaTech ElectraGen™ fuel cell system takes pride of place in the foyer of the theatre accompanied by displays describing the benefits and challenges posed by this groundbreaking technology. The prominent location of the fuel cell and the challenge of relying entirely upon it provide both a powerful educational tool and a source of motivation for reducing energy use.* This approach has attracted the support of internationally acclaimed lighting designers and cutting edge equipment manufacturers, creating a test bed for future best practice.

Thus Arcola Theatre has demonstrated that marrying artistic excellence with sustainable practice is both achievable and advantageous for a growing business. Widening its remit to include the full sustainability agenda has been a natural step for the organization.

Dr Ben Todd, the theatre's Executive Director, who also works as a consultant in the fuel cell industry, comments on Arcola's role as a leader in sustainability and the arts:

> The arts have a crucial role to play in elucidating and motivating the changes in lifestyle necessary to deliver an equitable future for all humankind. Through Arcola Energy, Arcola Theatre is demonstrating that bold changes can be made and that making them offers exciting opportunities for new creative partnerships ...

Arcola Theatre – Fuel Cell

Working with Friends of the Earth and Live Nation, Arcola plans to take the fuel cell and low energy lighting system to numerous high profile events in 2009, motivating further positive change and delivering CO_2 savings. Arcola's achievements have been recognized by the British Renewable Energy Association, naming it a Renewable Energy Pioneer alongside recognition in the Charity Awards, Clarion Awards, CBI Growing Business Awards, London's Green Tourism Awards and the TMA Awards.

www.arcolatheatre.com

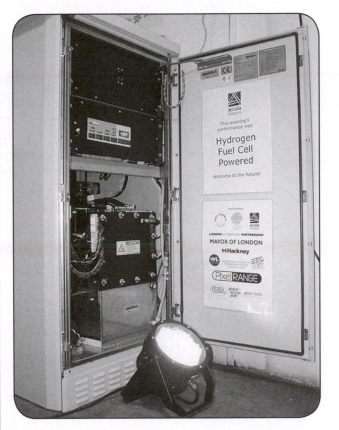

Figure 3.16

* Arcola's fuel cell system was supplied by London Hydrogen Partnership with additional funding from the UK Department for Culture, Media and Sport, Arts Council England, the London Borough of Hackney and the Mayor of London's Greening Theatre Plan.

Source: Information in this case study supplied by Ben Todd, Executive Director of Arcola Theatre

Key Sustainability Indicators

The key sustainability indicators in measuring energy performance are:

- Energy Conservation.
- Fuel Usage.
- Generator Numbers.
- Greenhouse Gas Emissions.

To measure your performance (how much energy you're taking from the grid and how much fuel you are burning in power generators), you'll need to do some auditing. Apart from emissions, we also measure fuel consumption, numbers of mobile generators and their capacities. The **Greenhouse Gas Protocol** establishes three scopes for measuring GHGs.[5] For powering events these are:

Scope 1: Direct emissions from on-site operations: power generators and gas used for cooking and heating showers. Key Sustainability Indicators to measure are:

- Total number of power generators.
- Total kVA for power generators.
- Fuel volume consumed by generators.
- Total mains or bottled gas.
- Resulting CO_2 emissions.

Scope 2: Emissions from grid connected electricity. The KSIs are:

- Grid power in kilowatts.
- Resulting CO_2 emissions.

Scope 3: Indirect emissions, such as transport, waste, water treatment.

We discuss these in Chapter 4, Transport, Chapter 5, Water, and Chapter 7, Waste.

Generators

By stating the number of generators and total kVA, you can track whether your strategies and power efficiency planning are having an effect in reducing them.

Fuel Volume

Gather this information from your fuel supplier or generator contractor. On one-day shows, generators usually come with a full tank and will be enough to run the day. To get an accurate measure, you'll need to ensure they do a tank top-up in order to assess the actual amount of fuel used at your show. The same thing applies on multi-day shows really. It's like when you hire a car, you get it with a full tank of fuel, and you return it full.

Grid Power

You will be able to gather the total kWH by simply referring to your invoice. If at an indoor event, make sure you tell the venue you would like a power reading so that they put this in play before your event commences.

CO_2 Emissions

It's a relatively simple process to calculate CO_2 emissions from power generation. Take the figures (kWh, litres fuel, kg gas) and multiply them by the emissions factor.

The following table shows you the emissions factors used in the UK for diesel fuel, for mains electricity, and bottled gas. Use these emissions factors (or those of your own country if they differ) to establish the Key Sustainability Indicators.

Box 3.10

Energy Emission Factors

The following are the emissions factors for various energy production methods.

Fuel usage for power generators:

Diesel   2.63kg CO_2 per litre diesel

Biodiesel   0kg CO_2 per litre biodiesel
(Factored as 0 as CO_2 was absorbed during recent growing cycle.)

Other power generation sources:

Mains electricity   0.53702kg CO_2 per kWh electricity
On-site renewable electricity   0kg CO_2

Gas use for heating and cooking:

Mains gas   0.2060kg CO_2 per kWh gas
Bottled gas   1.4950kg CO_2 per kg butane (LPG)
Bottled gas   1.4950kg CO_2 per kg propane (LPG)

Source: Defra June 2008 (UK)

Figure 3.17 Philips light up the National Theatre in London with LED

Source: Philips Electronics UK Limited

Lighting

Efficient lighting is a way of illuminating your sustainability. Lights left on in the day, use of old technology, grunting and puffing lighting towers … Are these the best way to shine a light on your green credentials? Let's now look at energy efficient bulbs, stage lighting and LEDs.

Old-fashioned incandescent light bulbs waste as much as 95 per cent of the energy they use. CFLs have been put forward as the answer and have been enthusiastically taken up across the world.

I am proud to say that Australia was the first country to put an outright ban on incandescent light bulbs. In order to reduce greenhouse emissions by approximately 800,000 tonnes, incandescent light bulbs are being phased out by 2010. From November 2009 the retail sale of non-compliant lighting is banned. (I am not so proud that my home town of Newcastle is the world's largest coal port and that the NSW government a couple of years ago agreed to double its capacity. Kind of takes the sting out of the bulb announcement.)

In the UK it's calculated if only energy efficient light bulbs were sold, over 5 million tonnes of CO_2 emissions could be saved across a year.[6] Most of the countries with new laws ban the sale and production, but not the use of incandescent bulbs.

In tandem with the laws come tight controls on the disposal of CFL bulbs. Mercury is in every CFL and is an issue of contention; however, the burning of coal in power plants also releases mercury, so there you go.

The use of CFLs in the home and at work is becoming standard practice and your outdoor event may feel some pressure to do the same. However, the technology that currently exists for CFLs limits their practicality at outdoor and temporary events. Those events that string miles of festoon lighting around their sites will need in the short term to justify their continued use of incandescent bulbs, as without explanation, this may seem irresponsible. The use of CFLs in an outdoor event is discussed coming up, as is the other brilliant solution for low energy lighting, LEDs. But before we do, let's focus on a simple truth your dad has been telling you since childhood. Turn the lights off!

Turn the Lights Off!

No matter which light bulb you choose, you should ensure they are not left on during the day, to demonstrate a responsible attitude to power conservation. You must be aware, however, that if powered by mobile generators, turning them off will most likely not actually save power, fuel and resulting emissions. This is a broad statement and may not apply to every set-up as it depends on what you have plugged in to each generator. Generally though, where a generator is running stuff such as market stalls, stage sound and lighting, plus strands of festoon lighting, turning the lights off isn't going to make much of a drop in overall load. The generator needs to run at the optimal load range in order to run efficiently anyway.

All of this may be too difficult to explain to your audience and it's best just to make sure you remember to turn the lights off!

There is a complicating factor with turning lights off though, and that's the rain. If it rains during the day when the lights are off, you may experience failures when switching them back on, especially if your festoon has twisted and the bulbs are upside down. If it rains and the lights are on during the day, then the heat from the bulbs should evaporate off any water. So maybe turn them off in the day, but if it rains, flick them back on.

It also may not be a simple case of turning a switch on or off given how the distribution may be set up. If it's impossible to turn the lights off, then you have some messaging you need to roll out to explain the whys and wherefores to your audience about the lights being left on.

Energy Efficient Bulbs

Using energy efficient light bulbs (CFLs and LEDs) is a popular way of reducing energy consumption in the home and office. However, at an outdoor event using mobile power generators, there are not the same savings when using CFLs. Bear with me, as I try and explain some technicalities as described to me by those in the know …

CFLs, while having less wattage (11 watts versus 60 for example), have a poor power factor. This means the current is not reduced proportionately with the power. CFLs are heavily 'inductive' in their power use and thus need power factor correcting or they can cause damage to a generator or at the very least, lead to poor efficiency. The current is the determining factor in sizing a generator. Therefore by replacing large numbers of incandescent bulbs with CFLs, a reduction in generator size isn't necessarily going to occur. As generator engines are normally sized to match the maximum output of the alternators, this poor power factor may lead to inefficient running of the engine and therefore higher CO_2 emissions per kW generated. Phew.

This information is included (courtesy of the lovely Bill Egan from Aggreko who does the power at Glasto) so you don't automatically assume changing to CFLs when powered by mobile generators is a beneficial step.

The expectation of your audience and the opportunity to spread the message about switching to CFLs and low energy lighting in their everyday lives may justify the use of CFLS and any additional costs and labour incurred.

CFLs are designed for long-term use, and the financial returns come back through the reduction in energy bills along with the fact that they last longer and therefore you don't need to outlay for new bulbs every year or so. These savings don't translate at a temporary event.

CFLs are also difficult to handle. Not a problem when you only have to change them once in five or ten years in your home or office, but once a week for lighting and power contractors is a different story. They're fragile, not really suited to handling in bulk, and not designed for outdoor use. The kind of bulbs that look like little curled tubes are particularly unsuitable, but there are bulbs that come with a traditional outer casing, which are probably more practical. Nonetheless, your crew must be committed to minimizing breakages. Each bulb contains mercury and if broken it's recommended you don't breathe in the dust. In fact it's recommended you open windows and leave a room for 15 minutes before clearing up a broken bulb. Broken bulbs also can't be placed in landfill because of their mercury content. They must go to an authorized

Figure 3.18 LED lighting used by Firefly Solar on their solar stage

Source: Firefly Solar

WEEE recycling facility. This will add to the inconvenience of using CFLs at a temporary event. It's unlikely your crew will adhere to these warnings due to the realities and pressures of event logistics. So unless you're a boutique event with time and space for careful handling, CFLs probably aren't for you.

Developments in LEDs are coming thick and fast. **Philips** seem to be leading in innovation and commercial viability, with some of their large scale LED lighting projects being absolutely stunning, and their range of domestic and office solutions attractive and functional. The fast growth in development of LED lighting is being fuelled by both environmental concerns for energy efficiency and the technological advances around the lighting effects that can now be achieved. The reliability and maintenance costs are also considerations, with life cycle costs of the product now being competitive. LED lighting is particularly useful when using zero emission energy supply. The low loads pulled by LED set-ups make it the perfect partner to solar, wind or hydrogen fuel cell power. The development of technology and application of LED is moving quickly, and you're encouraged to keep your eye on it as this excellent lighting solution gains traction.

Box 3.11

At your Event: Lighting

Use energy efficient bulbs

- Plan for the phasing out of incandescent bulbs.
- Promote the use of CFLs and LEDs to your audience.
- Look to move to LED lighting for your event both on stages and throughout your site.

Switch off the lights!

- Remember to switch lights off in the day, or to communicate why they aren't.

Box 3.12

LED Lighting by Philips

A word on LED lighting

My absolute mission as the Creative Director at Philips is to address the long standing problem of lifetime of LEDs and efficiency by supporting our technical information with actual proof, and showing the effects possible in a creative and innovative way for everyone to enjoy and learn from.

Sometimes an LED solution is not the best solution and a mix of technologies is always worth considering. This is the reason for our involvement with the National Theatre in London which we have partnered with in order to show the industry the mix of solutions available in a simple way so that change can be driven by experience and documented benefits.

The National Theatre is fitted with energy meters and an array of solutions, from lamp technology, efficient gear technology, new Philips LED screens and LED luminaries. The energy benefits are huge and the visual effects are often enhanced.

However one noticeable effect of elements such as dynamic lighting by LED technology is that it opens a lot of doors in the aspect of control and the impact it has in the cityscape. For example the complete exterior lighting solution which wraps around the Theatre can be completely interactive and can follow you by colour as you walk around the building. It can also be controlled by web interaction allowing us to explore ideas such as designing your own lighting scheme online, saving it and then visiting the site to experience it in reality.

So whilst the main agenda may well be to save energy this approach can inspire our younger generations to go out and really experience the environment in a new and fun way, and hopefully they will come to value the environment and look after it!

Rowena Priess
Creative Director, Philips Electronics UK Limited
www.asimpleswitch.com

Figure 3.19 Biodigesters at Thames Water's Reading sewage treatment plant capture methane. It's a CHP plant, with the methane created from the sewage processing burnt to create energy. This electricity is enough to power almost half of the treatment plant's requirements. The exhaust heat from the electricity generation is also used in the sewage sludge treatment process

Source: Thames Water

VOCs and Waste Emissions

CO_2 from energy and transport are not the only GHG emissions to be concerned with. Other event activities cause the creation of GHG emissions such as methane and VOCs which also contribute to global warming.

Sources of VOCs at events include paint, printer's ink, solvents, degreasers and cleaning supplies. VOCs are harmful to humans if inhaled excessively or trapped indoors. Events cause the emission of VOCs on site and through production of materials purchased. Many emission sources are outside the control of organizers, but you can take direct action through sustainable procurement policies.

Methane (CH_4) and carbon dioxide (CO_2) are created in landfills by the rubbish we throw away that isn't captured in the recycling and re-use loop, or sent for composting, as it decomposes in landfill. About half of landfill gas is methane and half CO_2. Waste around the world is dumped in landfill and gases generated are emitted into the atmosphere. The **Environment Protection Agency** estimates that municipal solid waste landfills are the second largest source of human-related methane in the US. Defra reports that in the UK methane from landfills accounts for 40 per cent of the country's methane emissions.[7]

We discuss landfill gas and incineration emissions in further detail when discussing waste and climate change in Chapter 7.

Sewage

Of course every event is going to have the ultimate by-product of all that eating and drinking ... sewage. The by-product of this by-product is indeed a GHG – methane. Luckily the science heads have knocked together on this one and at newer sewage treatment plants, methane is harvested, rather than bubbling, gurgling and fluffing off into the atmosphere.

Treatment of sewage also consumes energy and the emissions factors included in Chapter 7 take into account both the methane emissions of the sewage and the electricity needed to run the treatment plants.

Paint

Paint has the potential to be harmful to the environment through toxic substances being washed into water and through releasing VOCs. You know that new paint smell that lingers? That's the paint 'off-gassing'. VOC fumes are making their way up your nostrils or up into the atmosphere to play their role in global warming.

Use zero VOC paint, or at least one from the 'minimal' VOC content level. Many 'eco' paints are available on the market at competitive prices. Not only are some of these at zero VOC levels, they are also non-toxic to the environment, which is particularly relevant in the wash-up process.

In the UK, coatings suppliers have adopted a VOC labelling scheme for all decorative coatings to inform customers about the levels of solvents and other volatile materials present. A five-band classification shows the VOC content as Minimal, Low, Medium, High or Very High. In the European Union all member states are required to label coatings and in 2010 further restrictions will come into place further reducing maximum VOC levels allowed. Look for a labelling scheme in your country.

Cleaning Supplies

Products used to treat or clean toilets, showers, offices, catering kitchens and service areas are all likely to include solvents and produce VOCs.

Environmentally sound commercial alternatives are available and their use should be mandatory. Strike a deal with a brand of eco-cleaning products that has both commercial and consumer brands. Use the product at your event and promote its use and sale to your audience.

Printer's Ink

Traditional printing methods use solvent-based products which are a potent source of VOCs. The clean-up process needed when using traditional mineral inks also needs solvents. Printing for events can include the programme, tickets, vehicle passes, on-site newspapers or leaflets, various forms and documents, along with promotional material such as posters and flyers. Many participating organizations may print materials in association with your event. Ensuring the use of environmentally friendly printing processes is essential. Sustainable printing solutions are easily available and it's as simple as choosing a printer that works hard to ensure their environmental impact is minimized. In relation to VOC emissions, the following should be considered. (Paper choice is discussed in Chapter 6.)

- Is your printer BS EN ISO 14001 accredited?
- Insist on soy or vegetable ink.
- Does your printer use solvents in clean-up process?

Measuring Emissions

The GHG emissions resulting from processing waste to landfill and sewage treatment can be measured in CO_2 equivalence. These measures are included in Chapter 5, Water, and Chapter 7, Waste.

It's not practical to attempt to measure emissions that result from printing, paints, cleaning products and the like. By reducing the use of the offending products you'll be reducing the VOCs as a result, though it would be virtually impossible to accurately record.

If your waste goes to an incinerator, then you may wish to measure the emissions as a result of this treatment method. More on waste, climate change and incinerators in Chapter 7.

Let's now look at a summary of the ways to reduce VOC and methane emissions as a result of your event activities. Following this will be a discussion on offsetting the unavoidable emissions generated at your event.

Box 3.12

At your Event: Reduce Other GHG Emissions

Printing

Is your printer BS EN ISO 14001 accredited?

- Choosing a printer with BS EN ISO 14001 will ensure that every means is taken to minimize the environmental impact of the printing you order, including most of the issues outlined below.

Insist on soy or vegetable ink

- Traditional inks are solvent based, a major cause of VOC emissions, along with being toxic to both land and water.
- Vegetable or soy-based inks produce high quality printing without being harmful to the environment.

Does your printer use solvents in clean-up process?

- Printers have access to a range of zero VOC solvents for clean-up; ask if yours uses this environmentally friendly alternative.

Not strictly a VOC concern but nonetheless …

Does your printer use sustainable waste ink disposal methods?

- In the clean-up process from printing, waste ink sullage is the by-product.
- Non-sustainable printing practices would see toxic ink waste being put in landfill.
- Ensure your printer uses appropriate disposal methods, which may include composting waste ink.

Other VOC emissions

- Choose zero or low VOC paints.
- Work with cleaning contractors, market stall coordinators and catering companies to ensure all cleaning products used are environmentally sound.
- Consider also putting environmentally sound handwash or hand sanitizer in the amenities for your audience.

Sewage

If you're using traditional portable toilet facilities at events, such as trailer cabins or the dreaded portaloo, you're going to be at the mercy of the technology available at your nearest sewage treatment facility. Here's how to reduce GHG emissions from your loos!

Use composting toilets

- If you own a greenfield site, or have an agreeable landowner, you may wish to consider moving to composting toilets … which are aerobic and do not produce methane at all. More on that in the section on loos in Chapter 5.

Send sewage for methane extraction

- Investigate whether the local sewage treatment facility has methane digesters. If so, then you've not got too many worries with the disposal of your sewage effluent.

Waste

Ensure your event's waste is not contributing to GHG production

- Prevent biodegradable waste from making its way to landfill by restricting production of this waste stream through on-site regulations and procedures.
- Carry out on-site separation of waste with audience participation and send biodegradable waste to composting facilities.
- Alternatively, send your compostable waste to a landfill site with technology in place to capture and convert landfill gas to energy.
- Keep abreast of technological advances in waste treatment in your region and adjust the waste generating aspects of your event to suit the processing available.
- Send your recyclables for recycling not for incineration.

Figure 3.20 Gadhia Solar's parabolic sun concentrators in Ladakh
Source: Gadhia Solar

Carbon Offsetting

Measuring carbon emissions and then carbon offsetting is the final way to deal with unavoidable emissions from your event. Footprinting measures the total GHG emissions of a particular activity, reported as CO_2 in kg or tonnes. When offsetting, an equivalent tonne of CO_2 is removed elsewhere through practices including renewable energy production, supply of energy saving light bulbs, or sequestered through reforestation.

The way offsetting works, in simple terms, is 'carbon credits' are awarded to projects that have been certified to be carbon reducing, and those organizations that are required to, or who voluntarily wish to offset their own emissions purchase these credits, thus supplying funding to support the reduction projects. A carbon credit represents the removal of one tonne of CO_2 or its GHG equivalent from the environment. Carbon offset schemes set a price on the amount it costs to mitigate the harm from emissions, and this does vary from scheme to scheme as the carbon credits are traded and supply and demand economics come into play.

Many companies and projects have sprung up to jump on this bandwagon. Many fantastic projects are being developed and retailers of offsets are setting up even faster. These retailers are the websites and companies which sit between the buyers and sellers – the projects and the offsetters.

Whilst a great tool to get funds flowing to renewable energy and other carbon reducing projects, voluntary offsetting is the final option an individual, business, organization and certainly an event, should look at.

Voluntary carbon offsetting isn't a cure for climate change but it can be seen as a tool to help raise awareness of the issues and reduce the impact of our actions on the environment.

In the early days of offsetting schemes there was little regulation, codes of practice or controls in place. Many projects happen outside the country where the emissions are created and the offset paid, and it's with a leap of faith that voluntary offsets are purchased by consumers. However as we will discuss shortly, regulation is now entering the voluntary offsetting market.

There is still some discussion being held on the appropriateness of carbon offsetting as a concept. At one end of the debate is the view that buying offsets is like paying for the right to pollute, on the other side is the view that through funnelling money to support development of solutions, new zero carbon and carbon reducing technologies will be more quickly developed.

The projects I love are the ones that use leapfrog technology. Solar power, solar lighting, biogas, wind power, solar cookers, micro hydro, etc. Funnily enough, a lot of these options can also be used at events for power generation and waste management.

Also beginning to emerge are projects that simultaneously reduce carbon while protecting biodiversity and community. More on these projects coming up.

To tackle climate change we need to cut our present emissions and to help developing nations to cut theirs too. Offsetting can help redistribute wealth, gained by exploiting the Earth's resources and polluting it in the process, to emerging nations to make sure they don't become a carbon copy of the West.

To put things in context and a quick and basic brush up on the offsetting market, let's walk you through both types of offsetting: voluntary and mandatory.

Mandatory offsetting is where the big carbon emitters – oil, power and car manufacturers, etc. – offset the emissions resulting from their operations to meet their country's obligations to the **Kyoto Protocol.**[8] Those countries that have ratified the Kyoto Protocol and agreed to meet certain GHG reductions goals pass this requirement along to their country's big emitters. Regulation has swiftly entered the mandatory offsetting market as those organizations required to reduce emissions can only have their reductions count if they purchase carbon credits from certified projects.

Under the Kyoto Protocol there are two programmes emissions reductions projects can be certified through – the **Clean Development Mechanism** (CDM) and **Joint Implementation** (JI). Once projects meet these standards they are certified through various schemes. The Gold Standard is one of the optimal certifications and more information on this can be found on their website if you're inclined to dive in further: www.cdmgoldstandard.org.

The projects that meet the standards have the carbon credits or certified emissions reductions (CERs) awarded to them which are then sold to companies whose governments have mandated that they must reduce their emissions. CERs are registered and issued by the **Executive Board of the Clean Development Mechanism** of the **United Nations Framework Convention on Climate Change**.[9]

The Outcome of COP15 and new agreements and deals made will impact on mandatory offsetting along with the 'price of carbon'.

Let's now look at voluntary offsetting as it applies to events, how the offsetting market is regulated and what project options there are that your offsetting dollars can support.

 ## Voluntary Offsetting

Businesses and individuals can offset their emissions on a voluntary basis. This is done through verified projects rather than certified projects. Verified emissions reductions (VERs) are the cornerstone of the voluntary carbon offsetting market.

The largest contributor to CO_2 emissions at many events is the travel impact of the audience. Having a voluntary offset or 'green ticket' is an option you can offer your audience to allow them to offset their personal GHG emissions from attending. You could also calculate various emissions impacts of your event such as power usage, transport of participants, waste tonnage, etc., and offset these. More on how to calculate an event's GHG emissions in Chapter 1 and in 'Measuring Performance' in other chapters.

As compared with the big solar and big wind projects supported by CERs, the voluntary offsetting market mostly supports projects with strong sustainable development benefits, improving the quality of life for local communities as well as reducing emissions. They have climate, community and biodiversity in mind.

This thinking has lead to the development of projects which meet the trio of community, biodiversity and climate change mitigation goals. 'Social Carbon' is a methodology developed by the **Instituto Ecológica** in Brazil. This evaluation methodology ensures high quality projects which meet more than just climate mitigation goals are available to the voluntary carbon market. Importantly these projects ensure that the economic and social benefits of the carbon emissions reductions projects are transferred to the communities involved in these projects. More information on how they have monitored, adjusted and evaluated the approach to Social Carbon and its verification and certification can be found on their websites.
www.ecologica.org.br,
www.socialcarbon.org

Climate Change Adaptation Projects

Just starting to be developed are climate change adaptation projects. These are projects that help communities at risk from, or those already experiencing, the effects of climate change to adapt to its impacts.

Supporting climate change adaptation projects gives businesses and individuals a way to take responsibility for the part they have already played in climate change impacts. Keep your eye on these projects as an option to support as they develop.

Offsetting Regulation

The voluntary offsetting market is not yet regulated by law, so it's still a case of buyer beware. However, there are many certification systems that do ensure rigorous auditing of projects selling voluntary offsets. This allows transparency, and those purchasing voluntary offsets can be confident their money is going to a project that will have an effect. The projects are generally smaller scale and it's likely you'll find community projects that tick all your boxes.

I believe that with thorough investigation into the offsetting programme you're considering, you should be able to make an informed choice and support a scheme that is beneficial to conservation and biodiversity, sequesters carbon, encourages development of new technologies, and does not displace people or damage ecosystems.

Above all else it should have one of the voluntary certification standards such as the Voluntary Carbon Standard (VCS) and one of the certifications based around sustainable development.

Go to one of the websites in Box 3.14 to check up the status of the project you propose to support.

CCB Alliance

The **Climate, Community and Biodiversity Alliance** (CCBA) recognizes that there is an urgent need to simultaneously protect biodiversity, support sustainable development and mitigate climate change. CCBA has developed voluntary standards to encourage land management projects to additionally meet goals of conserving biodiversity and protecting and developing communities. Carbon project developers are can strive for this triple agenda so that community and biodiversity impacts are included in their carbon mitigation projects. The CCBA is a partnership between leading companies, NGOs and research institutes.
www.climate-standards.org

Box 3.13

Offset Checklist ☑

Report abatement initiatives first
☐ **Report what you've done to reduce emissions before offsetting.**

Offset emissions not a 'footprint'
☐ **Don't call your audit of carbon emissions a 'carbon footprint'.**

Publish your process
☐ **Report what you're measuring and the process.**

Box 3.14

Check your offset

- Voluntary Carbon Standard: www.v-c-s.org
- Climate, Community and Biodiversity Alliance: www.climate-standards.org
- Green-e certification: www.green-e.org
- California Climate Action Registry's Climate Action Reserve: climatregistry.org/offsets.html
- Carbon Offset Guide Australia: carbonoffsetguide.com.au
- Social Carbon: www.socialcarbon.org

Box 3.15

Green Ticket – Audience Offsetting

Splendour in the Grass is an annual music, arts and youth culture event, which has taken place on the outskirts of Byron Bay on the north coast of NSW, Australia each July/August since 2001. The two-day event accommodates 17,500 people and has sold out in advance in each year of its existence, often within hours of going on sale.

The challenge

Splendour is committed to combating emissions associated with its artists, crew, production, suppliers and even the punters who attend the event, through energy efficiency measures and carbon offsetting. In 2008 Splendour partnered with Climate Friendly (recently ranked by Choice Magazine as Australia's No.1 carbon offset service provider) to calculate and offset those unavoidable carbon emissions. www.climatefriendly.com

Objectives

To completely offset all emissions associated with the hosting of the event.
To encourage the audience to voluntarily sign up to offset their personal average daily emissions while attending the event.

About the project

The Green Ticket allows punters to neutralize their average carbon emissions over a 48-hour period (not just travel emissions). Australians generate on average a total of 28 tonnes of GHG emissions a year, or 77kg a day. Purchasing a $7 Green Ticket will neutralize 144kg of carbon (i.e. covering two days) making them climate neutral for the duration of the show. Funds raised from the Green Ticket and Splendour are invested in renewable energy generation (wind farms), providing a meaningful and long-term solution to our reliance on fossil fuels. If punters decided to purchase a Green Ticket from the Climate Friendly stall (rather than when they originally purchased their event tickets) they were given an organic cloth badge to show that they are serious about tackling climate change.

Results

Given climate change is such a massive issue the organizers were delighted to see so many audience members putting their hard earned money where their mouth is by purchasing a Green Ticket to neutralize their average daily carbon emissions over the two days.

Splendour in the Grass

A total of 4091 Green Tickets were sold which resulted in the following amazing statistics:

- Over 23 per cent of the Splendour audience purchased a Green Ticket.
- Together Splendour and their Green Ticket buyers neutralized over 1000 tonnes of CO_2.
- A total of $28,637 was invested in renewable clean wind farm energy both in Australia and overseas.
- Emissions neutralized are equivalent to taking 248 cars off the road for an entire year or powering over 130 homes for a year.

The land the festival is on is owned by a campground operator and is around 47 acres. Splendour in the Grass, in conjunction with a core group of event professionals, has just bought a property just out of Byron Bay that's 660 acres and will allow them to fulfil their dreams of total self-sufficiency (such as on-site waste water treatment using bioremediation techniques).

Figure 3.21 Aerial shot of the site

Source: Marc Grimwade

Keep your eyes on Splendour in the Grass to see what amazing initiatives unfold in the years to come.

Decided to Offset?

If Not a Full 'Footprint' then What?

Some consultants and auditors like you to measure everything that has a whiff of CO_2 about it, but this may be just creating an excuse for work, rather than actually benefiting the event and its possibility for sustainable management. Rather than try to calculate a complete carbon footprint for your event, which is likely to be inaccurate, it's recommended you concentrate on measuring those areas where you can gain robust and accurate data. These include:

- Power from mains.
- Generator power (fuel volume).
- Audience transport.
- Waste to landfill and waste transport.
- Sewage treatment and transport.
- Water usage.

Depending on your resources, you may also wish to measure:

- On-site and office vehicles (fuel or total distance travelled).
- Crew/stewards/artist transport.
- Transport of deliveries.
- Contractor and supplier transport.
- Hotel accommodation.

Each of these area's emissions factors and methods for measurement are included in the relevant chapters. All of these are Key Sustainability Indicators and can be found in Tables 1.1 to 1.4 in Chapter 1.

If you're keen on offsetting, you'll need to ensure you have some robust ways to measure your various emissions, look at your conversion factors, and how and what emissions data is gathered so that you're able to show your methodology if asked.

Offsetting Projects

You'll need to decide which projects you want your offset money channelled to. It goes without saying the project is certified and that it's audited so you know the project is doing what it says it will. It's also worth doing your own research to see exactly what the offsetting money is supporting, and how the projects are rolled out to make sure this resonates with your event's ideals. Ask questions of your retailer and look at how much money is held by them for administration as compared to the percentage that makes it to the project.

You'll also need to decide whether you want your project to happen in your own country or offshore, most likely in developing countries such as India, Africa and South America. There are usually myriad projects under each offsetting scheme or offered by offsetting retailers. You may not get to choose which of the schemes your money goes to, but if you do, you'll have a choice of projects such as supplying solar cookers, water pumps, solar and wind power microgeneration projects in schools or villages, or longer-term sequestration projects through planting trees.

As a barometer of the state of play on carbon offsetting and various projects they feed money into, it's a good idea to keep abreast of what organizations such as Greenpeace and Friends of the Earth are saying about offsetting schemes.

Here's a quick review of a couple of popular offsetting projects.

Planting Trees/Reforestation

The tree planting solution has been debated from every angle and the upshot is that opinion is still divided. In the early tree planting days the carbon cowboys had more of a tree 'farm' with wide-scale planting of a single species with no regard for biodiversity issues, appropriateness of the species for the area, and no ongoing maintenance to ensure the trees actually grew to maturity and therefore sequestered the carbon that was claimed they would.

Things have moved on from that now with considerations such as the local population who live in or depend on forests being involved in projects to ensure they are not displaced. Land that has been farmed but is no longer viable is being converted into managed forests and the farmers who originally worked the land are paid to protect and nurture the newly established forests, offering them a much needed income. Biodiversity issues and conservation concerns are embedded into greening projects, so that the restoration of forests and habitats and the flow-on benefits of this are just as important as the sequestration of carbon.

In Australia, clearing land has lead to erosion and loss of topsoil, soil salinity and the destruction of biodiversity. Massive areas of land have been clear felled and as a result after a very short time these lands are sucked dry of fertility. There are some planting schemes such as those run by **Greening Australia** that are carefully managed and offer the dual benefit of revegetation alongside carbon sequestration. **Southbound Festival** in Western Australia sends its offsetting funds to support Greening Australia planting projects.

More on that in the case study on Southbound's green ticket programme.

Avoided Deforestation

A cousin of the tree planting option is 'avoided deforestation' which is being worked up as an option for offsetting schemes. According to the **Stern Review on the Economics of Climate Change**, deforestation causes 24 per cent of CO_2 emissions and 18 per cent of GHG emissions globally:[10] 'The loss of natural forests around the world contributes more to global emissions each year than the transport sector. Curbing deforestation is a highly cost-effective way to reduce emissions; large-scale international pilot programmes to explore the best ways to do this could get underway very quickly.' Millions of people live in and depend on forests around the world and avoided deforestation projects must not happen without indigenous people who are linked to target areas being involved in the process. Most of us would see this as going without saying, but as centuries of displacement and disenfranchisement have shown, this is always not the case. By empowering and involving people who live in the forests, sustainable solutions to forest conservation rather than anti-people models could be implemented. If this one appeals to you as an option, keep an eye on **Avoided Deforestation Partners** (www.adpartners.org) to see what progresses.

Giving financial incentives to communities to keep their forests intact is not, however, accepted by the **IPCC** as a certifiable project as there are many areas for subjective measurement of a project's effect.[11] As with tree planting schemes, there's controversy over this solution and the area will need work from groups such as Avoided Deforestation Partners to bring this option to certification.

Stoves

In many developing countries the main source of fuel is wood, which is used for cooking on an open fire. Apart from the CO_2 emissions from burning wood, if used inside, the kitchen fills with smoke and creates health problems. Cooking with an open fire is inefficient, with much of the heat lost meaning more wood is used than needed. In areas where firewood is scarce, deforestation becomes an issue.

Many options have been developed to combat this problem and are the targets of offset programmes. The 'rocket elbow' stove is one such design, and it reduces wood use by 50 per cent or more, and eliminates smoke from indoor areas.

Moving to zero emissions cookers, **Scheffler Solar Concentrators** have been developed for domestic and large-scale use. Large-scale adaptations include where big volumes of rice need to be cooked such as in hospitals and schools.

Light Bulbs

Supplying energy efficient light bulbs to houses was one of the original ways to reduce carbon emissions. Where dirty energy production is predominant and not going away in a hurry the best way to reduce emissions is from reduced consumption. Enter energy efficient light bulbs. By consuming less energy over the life of the bulb, fewer emissions are caused as demand for power production is reduced. In Australia a switch to energy efficient bulbs project was effectively carried out by companies such as **NECO**. They went into homes and businesses in Australia and changed all their bulbs over to CFLs, getting a pledge that they would continue

to be used. Offsetting funds were channelled into paying for this project.

Supplying energy efficient light bulbs is still a popular offsetting option and can also be seen in a clutch of developing nations from Kazakhstan to Kenya.

Foot Power Water Pumps

International Development Enterprises India (www.ide-india.org) has developed the treadle pump, a foot operated water lifting device that can irrigate small plots of land of smallholders in regions that have a high water table. A low cost system, simple in design and easily manageable, it's perfect as an irrigation solution for small farmers. Getting water to the fields from streams, lakes and wells means the farmers don't need to hire a diesel generator in the dry season. With the installation of treadle pumps come environmental, financial and social benefits. Crops can be grown in the dry season, increasing income for families. The farmer's production isn't tied to their ability to pay the rent on generators and to purchase diesel. The knock-on effect of this is that families can also afford to send their children to school and fathers don't need to migrate to the cities to look for work. Women are also participating in the treadle pump work. Tribal women have shifted their roles from being wage labourers to independent farmers with keen and vigorous farming interests and increased time flexibilities.

Biomass

Agricultural waste such as husks, stalks and sugar cane waste are collected from farmers and burnt to create electricity, rather than using coal or gas.

Although still emitting CO_2 when burnt, it's seen as a carbon reducing option. I would prefer to see sugar cane waste (bagasse) made into paper and compostable waste made into fertilizer than be burnt for electricity. It's up to you to make your own mind up on this one. If the farmers are going to scoop up their waste and burn it anyway, we may as well make it into electricity.

Solar Technology

Solar offsetting projects range from providing lighting, and solar cookers as described earlier, to solar hot water and electricity for homes and business. A wonderful application of solar is for portable lighting. These mainly replace kerosene lamps in uses such as for street hawker stalls, solar head-torches for midwives and agricultural workers, and allowing work after dark for migrant workers who live in temporary shanty accommodation and have no access to electricity. **TERI's** Light a Billion Lives campaign is a great example. They provide a solar charging station for villages, and lamps for all the homes. labl.teriin.org

Selco India provides sustainable energy solutions and services to underserved households and businesses in India. Their projects are also recipients of offset funding. www.selco-india.com

Gadhia Solar Energy Systems is the world's biggest producer of solar steam production systems. More than 15 years of experience in the application of parabolic sun concentrators makes Gadhia Solar the world leader in this technology. Various applications, such as cooking, food processing, space heating and cooling for institutions and industries are possible. www.gadhia-solar.com

Wind

Wind generated energy is growing very fast; however, building and installing turbines is expensive. Carbon offsetting funding offers the added finance needed to make these projects viable. Wind projects are generally profit making ventures and sell electricity into the national grid. They are often the recipient of the compliance offsetting market purchasing carbon credits, but wind power projects are also available to those wishing to voluntarily offset. Here's a quick review of a couple of popular offsetting projects.

Figure 3.22 Treadle pump in use in Asha Devi, UP, India

Source: IDE India

Biogas

Anaerobic digestion is a commonly used treatment for waste. This is taking green waste, agricultural waste, food scraps, animal manure or sewage, and processing it in the absence of oxygen to produce biogas (methane). This is then burnt to generate electricity or used as a fuel for cooking, etc. Its capture and use as a cooking fuel or source of electricity prevents methane from being naturally produced and expelled into the atmosphere and also prevents other sources of fuel and electricity from being used such as burning wood or coal. Methane digestion projects are available to support.

Compost

There are measurable GHG reductions from using compost over chemical fertilizers. The use of energy and fuel in mining and transport of the non-renewable raw ingredients for chemical fertilizers (petroleum and minerals), along with the manufacture of the final product all add up to a much weightier carbon debt than the natural alternative – compost. An example is the project based in the Sharkia region of Egypt. The Libra/Sekem project receives offset funding to support the collection of biodegradable waste from the streets of Cairo, such as coffee grinds, raw food scraps, etc. The resulting compost is used to enrich the desert soil locally, increasing agricultural productivity.

Micro Hydro

Remote regions that can't be connected to a central grid but where electricity is an important element in a villager's life are receiving the benefits of micro hydro, or 'run-of-river' hydro.

Rather than running diesel generators to provide electricity, the naturally produced power, using the force of a running river, provides light and power. Having reliable power in these regions improves villagers' livelihoods.

 Instead of Offsetting

If you're baulking at offsetting against your event as a whole, I still encourage you not to ignore all the wonderful projects around the world innovating ways to reduce carbon emissions. This is particularly important in developing countries where the benefits are also social and economic, and are empowering to local people and the rural poor, improving standards of living and reducing the need to move to cities to earn an income.

Social Responsibility

View your financial support of the projects as part of your triple bottom line, financial, environmental and social responsibilities, and not a way to excuse yourself for CO_2 your event has chugged up into the atmosphere.

Seek out the project that fits your ideology, and actively support it. If you choose to go down the carbon offsetting route be careful about calling it an offset against a footprint unless you have played out every possible emissions reduction solution. Otherwise your offsetting may scream of a greenwash.

Calculate your GHG emissions, as best you can, and qualify your calculations. Then pick a programme that suits you and support the hell out of it.

Internal Offset

Rather than sending money offshore to projects you are not convinced are sound solutions to emissions reductions, you can turn back to your own event and reinvest in projects that will either result in reductions in your emissions or, through educating the audience, will in turn help them in reducing theirs.

Consider investing in, funding or supporting an area where the audience can learn about the consequences of GHG emissions and global warming, their personal contribution to creating emissions, and the best ways for them to reduce their impact. This is a way of leveraging the power you have in putting on the event to talk to the people about these issues. If you feel it inappropriate to have such an area at your event due to its nature, look at other ways you can include these ideas.

Perhaps you could invite activist groups to manage recycling points or property lock-up tents, where they can also promote their messages in a less intrusive way.

If there are extra costs involved with hiring in solar kit, composting toilets, running a dual or triple waste management programme, to purchase biodiesel, or to have all your signs hand painted – look at these extra costs as an internal offset.

Calculate energy, waste, sewage and transport impacts in CO_2 equivalence. Then cost that out at standard offsetting rates for purchasing voluntary emissions reduction certificates. There is your budget for up-scaling and funding your sustainability initiatives.

Box 3.16

Green Fee and Trees

Southbound Festival is held in Western Australia in a rural, greenfield site with a capacity for 20,000 people. As transporting all the audience to the event is a major part of the GHG emissions, they have put in two programmes to offset carbon emissions.

Optional green fee

For an additional $3 on the normal ticket price, an optional green fee is the basic peace of mind that patrons have more than covered their own carbon footprint. In 2009 almost 40 per cent of patrons who purchased tickets for Southbound took the opportunity to offset their own travel emissions to and from the festival by taking up an optional green fee.

Patrons can also donate the green fee on site at the Eco Village if they forgot to take it up when they purchased their ticket. In 2009, 7915 patrons took up the offer to offset their travel emissions to and from the festival, up from 5945 people in 2008.

Tree per ticket

Greening Australia implements the tree per ticket policy for Southbound where for every ticket sold the festival purchases a tree. They expect to plant 20,000 per year. In 2008 the tree per ticket activity focused on restoration in the Gondwana Link project, a large-scale revegetation project in an internationally recognized 'biodiversity hotspot' that's helping to restore the ecological link stretching from Kalgoorlie to the Karri in Western Australia. In 2009 they will plant an additional 100 hectares of biodiverse revegetation on its Peniup property.

A MUSIC, CAMPING AND ARTS FESTIVAL

www.sunsetevents.com.au

Green Fees at Southbound

Box 3.17

Carbon Free Day – Green Tickets

Australia's biggest music festival, the Big Day Out offers the audience a chance to offset their carbon emissions while at the festival, with the creation of a Carbon Free Day. Along with enjoying a day of spectacular music, patrons can do their bit to slow the pace of climate change and be clean and green. The Big Day Out is an iconic music festival which tours to Gold Coast, Sydney, Melbourne, Adelaide and Perth in Australia and Auckland, New Zealand in January/February each year.

By calculating Australian greenhouse emissions for one year* and dividing by the population and then by the days in a year they have determined the emissions for a person for a day. The audience have the opportunity to opt in when buying a Big Day Out ticket online costing A\$1.34 per person per day. This covers the cost of offsetting carbon through Mallee Eucalyptus tree plantations over the life of the trees. In 2009, 33,863 people opted in on the Carbon Free Day, offsetting a total of 2641 tonnes of CO_2.

Why planting trees?
Although a controversial offsetting option, in Australia it's a valid and well managed one. The Big Day Out has chosen tree plantation for creating carbon credits because it creates jobs, has sound conservation benefits, reduces soil salinity and improves farm viability in marginal areas as well as converting GHG CO_2 to oxygen for us to breathe. The credits recouped over a 30-year life span of the trees and management is consistent with the technical guidelines provided by the Australian Greenhouse Office.

What Big Day Out also does
The Carbon Free Day follows the Big Day Out's other environmental initiatives including reduced energy usage, proactive recycling on all sites, and energy audits of the show. Prior to the 2007 show, Big Day Out conducted two energy audits of the show to understand the GHG emissions caused by their energy usage.

In calculating the energy audit, Big Day Out considers the usage and expenditure levels across various production, venue and site management areas. This includes analysing domestic and international air travel and freight movements, trucking and ground transport, generator usage and recycling levels.

They made a commitment to carbon offset the show and as a consequence in 2007 planted 6735 Eucalyptus Polybractea (Blue Leaved Mallee) on approximately 4.5 hectares of land at Narromine in central NSW and planted another 9248 at a property 10km outside Fifield in central west NSW in 2008. An energy audit of the 2009 show is to be carried out and the Big Day Out's commitment to carbon offset remains steadfast.

Big Day Out

Figure 3.23 Big Day Out

Source: Julian Smith

www.bigdayout.com

*Australian emissions per year = 576 MtCO$_2$-e (*Source*: AGO, *National Greenhouse Gas Inventory 2006*, published in 2008.)

Source: Information in this case study provided by Vivien Lees, Director Big Day Out and Susan Forrester, Event Manager, Big Day Out Melbourne.

Notes

1   IPCC (2007) *Climate Change 2007: Synthesis Report*, www.ipcc.ch/pdf/assessment-report/ar4/syr/ar4_syr_spm.pdf, accessed February 2008.

2   Information from WorldWatch 'Vital Statistics VS2008' www.worldwatch.org, accessed February 2008.
    The WorldWatch Institute is an independent research organization recognized by opinion leaders around the world for its accessible, fact-based analysis of critical global issues. Its mission is to generate and promote insights and ideas that empower decision makers to build an ecologically sustainable society that meets human needs.

3   Global BioEnergy Partnership, www.global-bioenergy.org, accessed February 2008.

4   Energy Bioscience Institute, www.energybiosciencesinstitute.org, accessed February 2009.

5   Greenhouse Gas Protocol, www.ghgprotocol.org, accessed February 2008.

6   Greenpeace UK, www.greenpeace.org.uk/blog/climate/how-many-retailers-does-it-take-to-change-a-lightbulb, accessed September 2008.

7   Defra, May 2007, Waste Strategy Factsheets, www.defra.gov.uk/environment/waste/factsheets/landfillban.htm, accessed February 2008.

8   Kyoto Protocol, unfccc.int/kyoto_protocol/items/2830.php, www.kyotoprotocol.com.

9   Executive Board of the Clean Development Mechanism of United Nations Framework Convention on Climate Change, unfccc.int.

10 Stern, N. (2007) *The Stern Review*, www.hm-treasury.gov.uk/sternreview_index.htm, accessed October 2008.

11 IPCC, www.ipcc.ch, accessed February 2008.

Opposite. The Big Red Bus is a great way to shuttle people from central points such as train stations or drop off points to your event gates. www.thebigredbus.com
Souce: Sunrise Celebration

chapter 4

Transport

Transport is the largest CO_2 contributor for live events. Moving people, goods and equipment are all necessary, as without these you have no event. The cost of fuel and pressures of climate change impact are helping to realize freight efficiencies. However, convenience rather than cost still largely influences audience travel decisions and strategies are needed to dampen enthusiasm for driving.

Unless we all stop throwing public parties, people still need to get to and from our events. The equipment, food, infrastructure, participants, staff, goods and crew do too. The waste has to be transported away, as does sewage, and everything else you took to the party.

This chapter looks at immediate steps to reduce the transport impact of your event given the current transport practices in place today. We then discuss innovations, strategies and programmes to progress solutions in the not too distant future.

Mass transport is fossil fuel reliant. It functions through sucking up oil or gas and belching out toxic emissions, getting us where we need to be in the process. The result of our reliance on this transport technology is obvious. Oil prices are fluctuating and we are moving towards (or have even passed) Peak Oil.[1] The knock-on economic, social and environmental effects of this are well documented. We plant fuel crops, growing while people starve. We rip out the Earth's lungs to have space to plant these crops. We have ever-present global warming as we keep pumping out greenhouse gases (GHGs) and sabotaging what was a really clever natural air-conditioning system for the planet. We have countries invading and bombing and killing in the name of oil, and we of course also have pollution and consequential health problems.

Transport is, however, a necessary part of the current model of modern living and economic growth. Following the assumption that for the foreseeable future the way we currently live will be the status quo, our ultimate goal should be a model where transport has a minimum or even zero impact on the environment. A truly sustainable transport system.

Concerns over the ongoing availability of fuel supply are driving our need to find alternatives to the nearly full dependence of the transport sector on fossil fuels. Innovations in sustainable transport solutions are revving up around the corner and we will hopefully soon see technology offering drastic emissions reductions, fuel efficiency improvements and sustainable solutions for alternative fuels. Advances in vehicle technology such as hybrids, electric vehicles and hydrogen fuel cells are all part of the picture.

While we wait for these innovations to present we need to look to the here and now. That includes looking at ways of changing people's transportation behaviour to be more sustainable.

From a social or economic perspective, motivators to reduce the amount of time people spend behind the wheel are important. Towns and cities need to be geared towards the use of public transport, bike riding and walking. As we see technological, social and community aspects of sustainable transport develop, events will be able to contribute to this growth. Keep your eye on developments as you delve into creative ways of influencing the travel habit of your audience, and importantly, as you order another prime mover to get goods to your event. Agriculture, mining, manufacturing, retail and construction are transport super-users and they are the main players in encouraging sustainable transport development. The events industry really is a small part of the market, but as we are creative and experimental types, maybe we can push some greener alternatives into the limelight.

Promote electric vehicles in conjunction with your event. Recharge them using sustainable biofuelled generators. The US government has committed US$2.4 billion to development grants for electric vehicle research. They have a target of getting 1 million EVs on the road by 2015. Let's hope they get it right this time. To see what went around last time, watch the excellent documentary *Who Killed the Electric Car?*

Figure 4.1 Electric vehicle (EV) charging in London

Source: New Ride

Box 4.1

Transport checklist ☑

Encourage public transport use
☐ Make using public transport easy.
☐ Provide incentives to use public transport.
☐ Provide maps, timetables and other information on local scheduled public transport.

Leg power
☐ Encourage cycling and walking.
☐ Team up with cycling groups to create bike buses to your event and supply a support vehicle for riders' gear.
☐ Offer rewards for cycling or walking to your event such as ticket upgrades or freebies.
☐ Put on a cycle festival in coordination with your event.

Reduce car travel impact
☐ Limit availability of car spaces.
☐ Charge parking fees.
☐ Reward those that arrive with every seat full in their cars.
☐ Set up lift share schemes.

Offset travel
☐ Offer the audience the opportunity to offset their travel to your event.
☐ Consider offsetting year-round staff transport and event-specific staff transport.

Sustainable freight and site transport
☐ Plan your freighting and encourage load sharing by contractors.
☐ Work with existing programmes in your city/region to promote sustainable transport.
☐ Keep an eye on sustainable transport technological and infrastructure developments including electric vehicles and sustainable fuel.
☐ Use sustainable on-site transport.
☐ Communicate the CO_2 impact of extra deliveries, runner's trips to pick up forgotten supplies etc.

Audit audience transport
☐ Analyse your audience's transport habits in order to create the best transport plan.

Key Sustainability Indicators
☐ Percentage arriving by each mode of transport for audience and staff/crew.
☐ Car occupancy rates.
☐ Average distance travelled.
☐ On-site transport fuel use.
☐ CO_2 impact.

Figure 4.2 TNT is developing a fleet of electric vehicles, for urban couriering. They transported runners' gear from the start line to the finish at the London Marathon
Souce: London Marathon

Freight

Achieving efficient and yet sustainable distribution for goods and equipment is a challenge facing the events industry. Events are reliant on the efficient movement of stuff in order to deliver the event on time and on budget.

Equipment and purchases may be moved by contracted freight, shipping or couriering companies, or through supplier-owned transport. Contractors bringing in big infrastructure items such as staging, generators, fencing, etc., have their own transport, or they may use freighting companies. If you're a small event it's

possible many runs to and fro in privately owned vehicles will fill your transport needs.

There are several ways to reduce freight impact including procurement policies and encouraging sustainable choices by staff, contractors and suppliers when freighting and purchasing decisions are made. Some simple steps to look at include:

- Using sustainable transport companies.
- Reducing transport mileage.
- Encouraging contractors to use sustainable transport solutions.

Sustainable Road Transport

Road transport is the most convenient, most popular, largest sector and most polluting surface transport mode. It's also popular in the events industry because of convenience and accessibility.

Road freight companies looking to be more sustainable reduce their environmental impact through planning, technology and fuel choices. It won't be long before we see an international standard or country equivalent to which transport and freighting companies should comply. This will make the choice of transport contractors all the easier.

Transport Research

Emissions control is being researched and regulated by government and this will benefit all freight users as the findings make their way into production. Freighting industries are working with government and industry associations to make sustainable trucking a reality. Truck manufacturers are working at a fast pace to minimize their vehicles' emissions and maximize fuel efficiency. CO_2 emissions are top of the list for those researching sustainable transport. However, sustainable solutions for fuel and fleet technology are coming at us at a cracking pace.

Wider government controls, scientific research and infrastructure development are the answers to sustainable transport, but while waiting for these to gain traction, immediate action is being taken by local authorities.

Local Government Intervention

Local councils are managing freight in their local areas by implementing transport sustainability directives which impact on vehicle movement, development approvals and public transport systems.

In areas where local councils have taken matters into their own hands, event organizers will need to entwine transport restrictions, levies or other activities into their traffic and freighting plans.

Looking at the here and now, transport companies can provide sustainable solutions through alternative fuel choice, engine efficiency and planning logistics.

Efficiency and Planning

So while we're waiting for these new sustainable solutions, a transport company interested in sustainability delves into efficiency and planning in fleet operations to reduce their impact.

You may be surprised at the number of trucks running around roads empty, having failed to secure return trip loads. It's an obvious place to start and one that's being tackled as an immediate solution. With a commitment to change and the implementation of systems including load sharing and minimizing 'less than loadfull' (LTL) freighting, the road transport industry could make a genuine move towards increased sustainability.

You can work your magic by networking your suppliers and contractors to see if freight and load sharing is a viable option.

TNT's Electric Fleet at London Marathon

As you could imagine, with a 26-mile long event site, getting things from A to B is a logistical challenge. The London Marathon has enlisted the help of TNT for event freight logistics.

The competitors' offloaded gear they arrive with needs to be safely transported to the finish line. At the 2008 event two of the trucks used by TNT were zero emissions vehicles, and this will quadruple at the 2009 event.

TNT is the London Marathon's transport partner and they are expanding their fleet to 100 zero emissions vehicles across the UK, Australia and London. Fingers crossed it grows even larger.

www.london-marathon.co.uk

Biofuels

Alternative fuels are one solution currently sweeping the transport industry. More companies are moving to biodiesel or ethanol as these fuels become readily available, widely distributed and financially competitive to mineral diesel.

Biofuels such biodiesel and cellulose ethanol are made from cropped oil plants, from reclaimed oils or from waste products from agriculture such as bagasse (crushed stalks left after the juice is extracted from sugar cane). There are also exciting movements in algae-based oils and even

a recent discovery in a South American rainforest of a fungus that reacts under certain conditions to produce diesel compounds – a fuel potential they are calling myco-diesel.[3] Stay tuned. The current range of biofuels available is a stepping stone to other innovative solutions and a sustainable future for fuel.

Crop-grown biofuels, however, come with social and environmental concerns such as destruction of rainforests, pushing up food prices due to land shortages, land clearing, and biodiversity concerns of mono-crop agriculture. With agitation from NGOs, progress is being made into sustainable solutions such as certification for sustainable cultivation of palm oil with the assurance of no new forest clearings for plantations, the use of set-aside land in the UK for growing non-food oil crops and the use of arid and non-viable land for production of hardy oilseed crops.

Rather than crop-grown oil, some countries have access to large quantities of waste vegetable oil as a feedstock for biodiesel. Tallow from abattoirs (animal fat) is also used. But there is not enough volume available for an entire country's fuel needs from these two sources.

A small-scale alternative can be where a company who has waste oil as a by-product of their operations and also owns a fleet of trucks could quite easily produce their own biodiesel. This micro-solution may be worth considering as a recommendation to your food concession contractor who collects waste oil from all the food stalls at events.

The best solution to sustainable biofuel production differs from country to country. For example, in India there is no excess supply of used cooking oil as it has an eager secondary market, through street food stalls and as lamp oil in homes and temples. Australia, along with many other countries, is looking to Jatropha and Pongamia as a cropped oil solution. These are trees which grow in arid or marginal lands unviable for agricultural cultivation. Look to the work **CleanStar** and **Regenatec** in India are doing to develop this solution.[4]

In the UK the government has stepped in to fuel biofuel demand as it were, through the implementation of the Renewable Transport Fuel Obligation programme (RTFO).[5] From April 2008 the RTFO required 5 per cent of all fuel sold on UK forecourts to come from a renewable source by 2014. Originally set for 2010, they have extended this to 2014 and committed research funds to UK's **Carbon Trust** for the development of sustainable biofuels. The concern over the original 2010 target was that it created a headlong rush into adding demand for unsustainable biofuels. The RTFO has been heavily protested by NGOs such as **Friends of the Earth** and **Greenpeace** and it seems their pressure has added to the decision to extend the target date to

2014 to allow time for sustainable sourcing and development of biofuels. This continued agitation and pressure being felt against cropped fuel may force change. Waiting it out to see where the next stage of development and innovation in fuel and engines takes us into an exciting time.

On-site 4WDs, Plant and Machinery

If your event hires vehicles and plant to use on-site, consider having vehicles that can run on either 100 per cent WVO biodiesel or a diesel/biodiesel blend. Any vehicles that can run on mineral diesel will be able to run on this fuel. Note that you will probably need to use biodiesel that meets the EN 14214 standard in order to maintain vehicle warranties.

Plant and machinery such as telehandlers, forklifts, trucks, tractors, diggers, etc., should all be able to run on a biodiesel blend.

Electric golf carts are easily available to hire and are a wonderful silent and calming alternative to petrol ones. They do of course need recharging by electricity, but if you are hooked up to green power on your mains or running generators on sustainable biofuels, then you are on a winner.

An excellent sustainable option for on-site transport is bikes. Supply site bikes to crew so they can get around quickly without being tempted to jump in a vehicle or cart.

If you have an office car, consider using a hybrid or an electric vehicle.

Figure 4.3 Glastonbury Festival uses 100 per cent WVO biodiesel in its on-site tractors provided by New Holland
Source: Glastonbury Festival

Reducing Transport Miles

Trailing behind the transport of raw materials and manufactured products is a significant CO_2 legacy. Food, goods and materials criss-cross the planet in a never ending journey from farm gate to plate, from mine to manufacturer, from ship to shop. Product miles are a common consideration when people are looking at the environmental impact of their purchases. The same concept applies for freighting kit and goods to your event. By reducing the distance travelled of everything you need at your event, you will also reduce CO_2 emissions. Also consider where your contractors are based.

Include local sourcing as part of your procurement policy and you should experience an immediate reduction in event-related CO_2 emissions. Require the sourcing of all products and hiring of contractors locally as a first choice.

Not only should goods be purchased from suppliers as close to the event as possible, you should also consider where these products originated. Were they manufactured in your country using raw materials also from your country? This concept is discussed in more detail in Chapter 6.

Sponsor and Partner Opportunities

- Align with a sustainable freighting or courier company. This could be a business that uses sustainable vehicles, a bike courier or other green transporter.

- Match up branded biodiesel suppliers with plant and machinery suppliers to have a high profile roll-out of the fleet in conjunction with your show (generators, tractors etc.).
- Get a bike brand to supply site bikes for your crew to move about on.
- Approach 'green' vehicle manufacturers – of hybrid cars, electric vehicles or biofuel vehicles – to sponsor your event. Use their vehicles in conjunction with the event, to move participants and staff, or for on-site movement.
- Create a brand around public transport to your event.
- Align a sponsor with your public transport and car pool activities and use their products as incentives or rewards.
- Align with a coach company and big-up your coach travel.
- Establish a partnership with one car pool scheme, and invite them to be part of your on-site activities.
- Have a special ticket upgrade or other exclusive offers for those that come by sustainable means, and offer the whole shebang to a company to sponsor.
- Schedule a special train to your event: align a sponsor, and include on-board brand activation.
- Align with an offsetting project and have an example of the project in action at your event so your audience understands where their money is going. Set up a booth to allow people to offset their emissions then and there.

Contractor Compliance

Contractors and suppliers should be encouraged to also have a sustainable transport policy. If they own their own fleet, this should include the areas discussed earlier: efficiency and planning, alternative fuels and choosing low-emissions vehicles.

Unnecessary Transport

The many small trips off site to pick up forgotten supplies can lead to a significant CO_2 legacy. Planning of course is the key. Schedule one trip off site a day for your 'runner' and have all in the event team know when they must put their requests in by. Or take it a step further and follow Oya festival in Norway's lead. They give their runners a carbon calculator so when a request comes in for an off-site purchasing trip, the runner can let the person requesting the goods know what the carbon impact of that run will be. Fantastic. It is in your face carbon intervention at its finest. Oya are leaders in unique sustainability solutions and have produced a wonderful guide. www.oyafestivalen.com www.environmental-handbook.com

Box 4.3

Sustainable Freighting Checklist ☑

Use sustainable transport companies that:

☐ Use sustainable biofuels.
☐ Have efficiency training for drivers.
☐ Use low emission and fuel efficient vehicles.

Reduce transportation miles by:
☐ Using local contractors.
☐ Hiring local kit.
☐ Buying local supplies.

Encourage contractors to use sustainable transport solutions.
☐ Communicate the environmental impact of transport.
☐ Assist in coordinating load sharing.

Figure 4.4 Local cycling initiative Rebycycle provided site bikes at Peats Ridge Festival in Australia so crew could get around the site quickly. This saves emissions and keeps vehicle tracks off the grass
Souce: Peats Ridge Festival

Crew and Participant Transport

The GHG emissions produced as a result of transporting performers, participants and crew for your event are likely to tally to a considerable figure. As you have some control over these groups and how they get to your event, you have the opportunity to streamline their travel impact.

Provide performers, participants, crew and volunteers information on transport options and comparisons on the various impacts.

The contractors that supply large numbers of staff such as security, bars, volunteers, etc., should be encouraged to transport their crews to your event by bus. Ask these operators provide you with transport impact statements of their involvement in your event.

The following looks at ways to influence the transport of crew and participants to your event.

Performers

Performers are probably the most difficult to manage in terms of sustainable transport. Appeal to their conscience and ask them to consider how they get to your event. If you arrange ground transport, transferring from airports or hotels to the event, consider the most sustainable solution. Look at people movers, low emission vehicles, electric vehicles, etc. Ensure someone within your team has the responsibility of co-ordinating ground transport for artists so there are no unnecessary trips with half-full vehicles.

Volunteer Stewards

Volunteers are often sourced from charities and community organizations. Encourage them to promote lift share. Put on coaches or shuttle buses specifically for stewards, or require the volunteer organizations to do the same. Pre-allocate car spaces to volunteer groups, rationing out how many each can have.

Crew

Crew and staff are generally working hard and long hours. Interruption to their work plan to include sustainable transport may not be so welcome. Rather than annoy individual crew members, work with major contractors who bring in large numbers of crew to devise the best transport solutions for their people, including buses if appropriate. Crew includes production, security, medical, welfare, etc. Place limits on the number of car spaces allocated to each team to encourage car pooling.

Participants

This can include market stallholders, caterers, bars and their staff. Participants can also be speakers, workshop leaders and competitors in sporting competitions. Put together information for participants so they can understand the transport impacts of their attendance. Place limits on the number of car spaces allocated to each group of participants.

Measuring Performance

To assess how well your programmes worked to get them on public transport and into car pooling, you will need to measure their mode of transport similar to the way it is measured for the audience. Gather the following:

- Numbers of crew, participants, performers, and volunteers.
- Point of origin for each participant (or averages).
- Mode of transport.
- Car occupancy rates.

Use the methodology in the Audience Transport example starting on p169 to determine the measures above and assess the CO_2 emissions for each transport mode per the.

Box 4.4

Crew Transport Checklist ☑

- ☐ Place car parking quotas on each group of participants.
- ☐ Put on shuttle buses for crew arriving early from key transport hubs linking public transport to your event.
- ☐ Promote the impacts of transport and promote alternatives.
- ☐ Set up lift share schemes specifically for crew, staff and volunteer stewards.
- ☐ Ensure ground transport for performers, participants and VIPs is well coordinated to maximize occupancy rates in vehicles and minimize unnecessary runs.
- ☐ Put on shuttle buses to event locations for participants to avoid taxi use.
- ☐ Supply site bikes to get crew around the event.
- ☐ Use electric vehicles, hybrid, or vehicles running on biofuels rather than petrol or diesel.

Box 4.5

Green Delegates, 2008 Democratic Convention

The 'Green Delegate Challenge' was an effort to involve delegates in making the 2008 Democratic National Convention in the US one of the most sustainably produced events of its kind.

Delegates were able to offset their carbon from air and ground travel to Denver. With nearly 2900 delegates and alternates from every state in the country participating, the programme was a clear success. A total of 31 states and territories offset 100 per cent of their Convention-related travel.

Delegations with 100 per cent of their members participating in the programme were recognized in their seating section on the Convention floor with a Green Delegate Challenge icon atop their delegation placard. Each participating delegate and alternate received a limited edition 'green' lanyard for their Convention credentials and an invitation to a special event during Convention week. Through the Convention Committee's partnership with Native Energy, delegates obtained carbon offsets from a number of domestic community-based clean energy projects.

www.demconvention.com

Figure 4.5 Leave your car at home! More messaging from the Green Way at Glastonbury Festival
Source: Reproduced with the permission of artist Tracey Shough and Glastonbury Festival

Audience Transport

The common ingredient of most events is the presence of large numbers of people. Getting them to and from the event sustainably will prove one of your biggest challenges. The options you have right now are to turn your audience onto using public transport, getting them to walk or cycle, or to fill up every seat in their cars.

Events exist to attract people and the transport impact of the audience is generally the largest contributor to CO_2 emissions. When choosing a venue, access to public transport is essential for the event's sustainability to minimize emissions from audience transport.

In the long term the biggest reductions in audience transport impact will be achieved through vehicle and fuel technology innovations and through city and country-wide transport infrastructure developments. While we wait it out for these to come, we have the following options available to us to reduce audience travel impact:

- Get more people on mass transport.
- Encourage walking and cycling.
- Increase car occupancy rates.

Traffic Management and Congestion

When preparing the event licence, application or approval document to hold a one-off event of significant size, you'll need to have addressed transport impact in the traditional sense. Licensing, traffic and police authorities are interested in congestion, parking, road closures, etc.

As your assigned team member is analysing the traffic impact and developing the traffic plan, they can also be given the responsibility of considering the environmental impact of transporting your audience and of coming up with sustainable audience transport solutions and programmes.

In many situations congestion and car parking space will be a problem, and therefore public transport will be part of your overall traffic plan. This may be to use existing public transport services, or putting on extra coaches and shuttle buses. Whether indoor or out, you need to analyse the most efficient and sustainable way to transport your audience.

For planning permission approval, many councils are now giving preference to − or in fact insisting on − developments that encourage travel by walking, cycling and public transport. To meet their sustainable transport goals, some councils don't grant planning permission for developments or initiatives that would be dependent on travel by private motor vehicles. This is relevant for new events where development applications and licence approvals must be sought.

Depending on where your event is located, you may find your city, town or region is actively promoting sustainable transport for its citizens. Rather than going from a standing start, it would be wise to work with these existing programmes and leverage the exposure they already have, along with resources and knowledge.

The 'Connected Cities' programme across the European Union is an investigation into how unrestricted sustainable transport and mobility can be provided to cities and regions in such a way that 'will strengthen their territorial cohesion and improve the quality of life of its citizens'.[6] One project of the Connected Cities programme is 'Clear Zones'. This is a project between several London councils to reduce congestion, air and noise pollution and improve the urban realm. It does this by reducing the impact of road transport and promoting integrated transport. Tied in with the Mayor of London's Transport Strategy, it aims to encourage a shift to walking, cycling, public transport and other more sustainable vehicles. It plans to make London one of the most walking-friendly cities by 2015.

Seville, amongst other European cities, has banks of identical bikes parked around the city, available for hire. They work on a credit card and passcode system. These have been implemented in coordination with the city's transport plan to make cycle ways around the city, special bike lanes on roads and shared bike and pedestrian zones. There are 2500 bikes available and 250 parking stations distributed in all city districts.

With more cities moving towards sustainable transport you will find your audience may become less car dependent. You can then leverage these sustainable transport trends into your event.

Influencing Audience Transport

Understanding the practical reasons why people prefer to take their car must be understood if you're to come up with strategies to influence them otherwise. These include:

- Inflexible departure times of buses and trains.
- Inflexible routes;
- Pre-planning or booking of tickets necessary for long distance locations.
- Possibly cheaper in a full car with fuel shared amongst all passengers.
- Difficult to coordinate a group of friends to travel together and depart at the same time.
- Walking or cycling is too far, too difficult or will take too long.

However, there are also some great benefits to travelling by public transport, walking, cycling or car pooling, including:

- Skip traffic jams and congestion at car park entrances.
- Delivered right to the event doors rather than to outer car parks.
- Environmentally friendly.
- Can be cheaper than driving alone.

Overarching all of this is the need to achieve a change in travel behaviour by the audience so that they will consider car pooling, coming by public transport, cycling or walking to your show.

It may be your current plan makes it easy for your audience to drive to the event, with plenty of parking and no penalties in place if they do. If this is the case you'll need to create situations to encourage them to use public transport and discourage driving. A car parking fee could be charged, with a price point chosen to discourage driving or single occupancy. If doing this, make sure it doesn't backfire. Your audience could buck the system by parking in the surrounding streets outside the car park which will cause neighbourhood complaints.

Other tactics to consider are pre-purchased car passes and limiting the number of cars that can park up, even if you have the space.

Packaged coach or train travel with event tickets can be bundled at a lower price than if purchased separately. If your event sells out quickly, allocating these bundled tickets may be effective.

If you discourage driving, you need to ensure you have capacity available on public transport to cater for demand. You'll need to meet with public transport providers to assess likely volume of trains and public buses, to see whether more services need to be added. If you're considerably increasing the number of coaches arriving

Figure 4.6 People lined up in a car park unpacking gear for a multi-day camping event
Souce: Meegan Jones

at your event, of course you need also to have capacity for drop-off and pick-up points and well thought through and laid out bus lanes and bus stops on your site. This will be all part of your traffic plan.

When encouraging your audience to travel by public transport you need to meet their requirements for timing, accessibility, reliability and, most importantly, to have a successfully functioning system so as not to discourage its use in future years. If public transport hubs are more than a quick walk away from your venue, shuttle buses will be needed to make using public transport a seamless ride from home all the way to the event.

To reduce audience transport impact you could also encourage carbon offsetting by your audience against their travel emissions. More on how other events have rolled out Green Tickets in Chapter 3.

Car Travel

Travelling by car will be necessary for some of your audience. Encouraging them to fill up all the seats in their car is the best option for those that have to drive. Provide information on the transport impact of travelling solo to your event by car, to encourage single drivers to bring friends along for the ride. If your event is prone to causing traffic congestion and delays in entering the car parks, promote quick entry and easing of congestion through reduced car numbers.

If driving an average sized petrol car, four people in it will bring the impact down to less than travelling by train. Offering information such as that below can be quite effective.

Box 4.6

Promote Public Transport Benefits

Promote the benefits of travelling by public transport:

- Drop off close to the entry gate.
- Avoid car park congestion, traffic jams.
- Environmentally friendly.
- Possibly cheaper than driving alone.
- Fun of the travel.
- Don't have to carry gear a long way from the car park.

Box 4.7

Car Travel Checklist ☑

- ☐ Charge for car parking.
- ☐ Reward those that arrive in full cars.
- ☐ Charge a green tax to all cars to those that arrive less than full.
- ☐ Offer premium parking spots to full cars, including fast tracked exit at the end of the event.
- ☐ Promote lift share schemes.

CO_2 emissions per passenger mile, based on UK figures are:

40 people per coach	26.97g
4 people per car	86.00g
Train travel	96.30g
3 people per car	114.7g
2 people per car	172.2g
1 person per car	344.2g

Incentives such as free parking, vouchers to use on site, discounts or other rewards can be put in place to encourage your audience to fill up every seat in their car. Alternatively you can put in penalties for those that drive with only one or two people in their car. Charge a green tax, of a significant amount, for those that arrive less than full. A single driver should be charged double the tax levied on two people. Free for three or more.

The **Big Green Gathering in** the UK charges £30 for car parking. This reduces the potential car numbers. They also have convenient shuttle buses running to and from the closest town, so people jump on that if they need to get cash, top up mobiles, pick up supplies, etc., rather than starting up their car.

Download Festival in the UK has a programme to encourage people filling up every seat. Car park attendants identify those cars that arrive full and give them an entry form to win an upgrade to VIP passes which gets them into the special guest area. A winner is drawn every day.

And as we'll soon hear from **Coachella**, they have a long-standing programme to get people car pooling.

Car Pooling and Lift Share

Lift share is a concept which can be promoted if you have a destination-based event where driving will be convenient for your audience. Lift share programmes match drivers with those needing a lift. It works particularly well for multi-day festivals where the audience are used to making friends with strangers during the event, and so that spirit translates into camaraderie en route.

www.liftshare.com is a popular service.

Look online for a programme near you and form a partnership with them. Drivers and passengers put in their details of where they want to go (which event or festival) and they then use the search tool on the website to match lifts. It is best to align with just one programme so that a critical mass forms rather than offers and requests scattered across many programmes and unlikely to be matched up.

There has been some concern over safety issues with matching with drivers and passengers you previously don't know. As an event organizer, you should put together tips for safe lift sharing on your website. Look at the tips on www.agreener-festival.com for a list of tips you can use.

Figure 4.7 Festival goers arriving at Coachella Festival having car pooled to the event
Source: Coachella Festival

Box 4.8

Carpoolchella

Coachella Valley Music and Arts Festival is a three-day annual music festival held at the Empire Polo Fields in Indio, CA. The event features music from rock to pop to hip-hop on several outdoor stages. Its capacity is 100,000 people, and it is held in an urban area. Up to 50,000 cars drive to the event each day. In order to alleviate traffic congestion around the venue and cut down emissions from the transport of their audience, Coachella has put together two campaigns:

Carpoolchella is a car pooling initiative that rewards people for driving to the venue with four or more people in a car. Festival attendees that do this put a sign on their windshield that says 'Carpoolchella'. Attendees often decorate their cars more elaborately to make theirs stand out. A few times a day, a representative walks around the parking lot and chooses a car at random to reward with special prizes. Some of these prizes include VIP wristbands, tickets to the next year's Coachella Festival, and Coachella tickets for life. Apart from congestion and emissions reductions, Carpoolchella creates excitement about the festival before people even enter the grounds.

The **Coachella Express** is the first train ever chartered for the sole purpose of transporting passengers to a festival in the US. Over 500 people showed up to ride the free train to Indio in 2008. Cars on the train were outfitted with DJ equipment and popular DJs spun during the ride, preparing passengers for the weekend of music to come. During the two-hour train ride, passengers were allowed to dance, drink and socialize with their friends. Passengers were rewarded on the train with free VIP tickets for the entire Coachella weekend and free ice cream!

The train arrives in Indio in the afternoon at the temporary train station constructed specifically for the Coachella Express. Passengers are picked up by shuttle buses and transported a mile to the festival. Coachella Express kept hundreds of cars off the road while introducing people to the underused public transportation system. By providing rewards on the train and creating a fun atmosphere before the music festival even began, Coachella makes people feel good about the steps they are taking to preserve the environment without hitting people over the head with that message.

Carpoolchella and the Coachella Express are coordinated with the assistance of the team at Global Inheritance who provided the information for this case study.

www.coachella.com, www.globalinheritance.org

Coachella Festival

Coach and Train Travel

Coach travel has the lowest CO_2 impact per person, followed by rail and then car (depending on how full the car is). Setting up convenient coach or train travel from handy geographical centres, and bundling it with ticket sales is essential to reducing the audience transport impact of your event. You should promote coach and train travel to your audience as enjoyable and convenient, as well as appealing to their inner greenness by promoting its positive environmental aspects.

There may be perceived and real barriers to getting people into buses and trains rather than the convenience of a car. Coach and train travel tickets will usually need to be booked in advance. In research I have done for music festivals, people don't start thinking about the way they'll travel until one month before the event, whereas they may purchase the ticket to the festival more than six months before.

You need to make public transport easy to do, easy to commit to, and more convenient than driving. Think through the departure times from various locations if you are scheduling coaches. Make sure people can get to the coach without having to take too much time off work. Consider when they would need to get back in order to start work after your show.

Put the bus stop close to the event gates. This is a major selling point for coming by coach or shuttle bus. Having to walk a long way from the car parks can be a deterrent to driving. Keeping buses out of the car parks also means they won't get caught up in traffic jams.

My research has also shown that the cost of transport isn't a major factor in transport decisions. Of course this is research for music festivals with a certain demographic and based in the UK. But it is worth noting in case you feel it may be a similar situation for your audience. The respondents in the research preferred the flexibility and convenience of their chosen transport mode (even if it was coach or train) as compared with concerns over cost.

If the cost of coming by train or coach is considerably more than say two or three people in a car for a similar distance, it's not going to stack up. Make sure you consider fuel versus coach or train ticket costs when planning public transport services. The ultimate solution could be to have the public transport free, and charge heavily for car parking. **Peats Ridge Festival** in Australia is

---

Box 4.9

MrBusDriver

'Bringing fans and music together'
MrBusDriver is a coach service set up in the US to service events, particularly music festivals and concerts.

They team up with events to set up coach travel to the show. Their coach trips include travel guides on board so the fun starts as soon as people get on the coach.

The intricacies of the coach transport network across the US don't need to be negotiated as the coaches go door to door, arriving straight at the event gates.

They understand the needs of festival goers and make sure they stop for food and grocery shopping along the way.

www.mrbusdriver.com

moving this way, aiming to have all coach travel to the event free, with car parking fees to cover this cost.

To encourage taking public transport, walking or cycling to your event, offer incentives, bonuses or rewards. Ticket upgrades, special camping, free drinks, etc. are all ways to promote sustainable travel.

Rothbury Festival has a special 'car-free camp'. It's reserved camping for those that come by public transport. The campers get special privileges and rewards, and it's located in the best pick of the campgrounds. **Roskilde Festival**'s 'Green Footsteps' programme includes setting up an all-green camp called 'Climate Community' specifically for those people that have taken green footsteps to get to the festival (public transport being one of the steps they need to take). **Peats Ridge Festival** has a dedicated campsite for people that have ridden their bikes to the show. The campground is the pick of the bunch, right on the edge of the river and nice and close to the arena. Importantly, it is in the car-free campground where no cars are allowed.

The **Coachella Express**, as described in Box 4.7, is a fantastic example of a commitment to public transport. Chartering an actual train which comes right to the door is really something quite special.

Glastonbury Festival commits a significant percentage of available tickets bundled with coach travel. With the sheer size of this event, every step must be taken to encourage people to come by bus and train to reduce congestion on the small countryside roads leading into the event site.

Air Travel

Air travel has increased remarkably in recent years and shows no signs of slowing. Public demand is rising exponentially and the aviation industry is quickly standing to attention and servicing our demands. The aviation industry and government are working towards solutions to make air travel more sustainable.[7] In the UK, for example, the goal is 'limiting climate change impact by improving fuel efficiency and CO_2 emissions by 50 per cent per seat kilometre by 2020 compared with 2000 levels'.[8]

Assuming we are all going to keep flying around the world, fuel efficiency and alternative fuels are where progress towards sustainability will be made. **Virgin** has made a public show of testing biofuels in one of its aircraft. They say they understand that crop-based fuels are not a viable alternative given the size of demand for fuel the aviation industry currently uses, and predicts for

---

Box 4.10

Air Travel Checklist

Right now the options you have to reduce the impact of flying to your event are:

- [ ] **Change location of your event closer to your audience base.**
- [ ] **Look to offer video conference hubs.**
- [ ] **Encourage offsetting by all participants who fly, possibly building it into the ticketing.**
- [ ] **Not holding the event at all!**

the future. Virgin and Boeing are investigating algae biofuels, which could be the solution the industry is looking for.

Short haul domestic flights are where you could appeal to your audience's climate conscience, encouraging train travel over flying.

Events such as specialist conferences, international sport and destination event tourism are all likely to need air travel. So too will destination locations such as Singapore and Hong Kong for business conferences, and island resorts around the world for professional conferences. Without air travel, these events couldn't take place. Perhaps we should stop holding them? I imagine the conference organizers and venue owners in these destinations would not see this as a sustainable future.

Seminar-based events may be able to grow their audience through offering online real-time video conferencing or holding several smaller events in various geographical markets, to reduce air travel. This would need to be judged against other efforts needed to replicate the event.

Whether the biggest steps towards a sustainable future for air travel happen in the technology of aircraft, the fuels they run on, or the choices we make in needing to travel, remains to be seen. The challenge of sustainable air travel faces us all: the events industry, tourism, business and the airline industry. We will need to look at multiple solutions to combat the environmental effects of air travel.

Box 4.11

Beaming Bioneers Video Conference

Each year the Bioneers Conference is held in California. It convenes leading social and scientific innovators to share stories, present model solutions and network with each other.

They also have the 'Beaming Bioneers' programme. Beaming Bioneers' satellite partners receive a simultaneous broadcast of the conference plenary talks and complement them with locally produced workshops, tours and activities tailored to the needs of specific bioregions.

Beaming all across the US this enables the conference to expand its horizons without expanding its footprint unnecessarily.

BIONEERS

Revolution from the Heart of Nature

www.bioneers.com

Cycling

Riding bikes to your event is probably the ultimate in sustainable transport. If your event is located in an area with safe bike routes, and if bike riding is popular, you should really push bike riding to your show.

If there are organizations promoting cycling in your region, bring them on board to help increase the number of people that come to your event by bike. This group can be a transport partner. Also look at setting up a partnership with a bike shop or bike brand to sponsor your cycling activities on site. Support cyclists by having a bike repair shop at your event which the bike shop or brand can host.

Peats Ridge Festival organizes a bike bus to their event. Cyclists arrive at one of two railway stations which are about 40km away from the festival. Bikes and gear can be easily taken on trains in the area. A support vehicle then takes the cyclists, camping gear to the festival site. The group then rides together in what is known as a 'bike bus' to the festival. A special cyclist camping zone is set up in the nicest area of the campground.

Figure 4.8 On the road from Gosford to Peats Ridge Festival

Source: Supplied by Peats Ridge Festival and Rebycycle

Box 4.12

Bike Library at TINA

This Is Not Art festival (TINA) is a new media festival held across numerous venues in the city centre of Newcastle, Australia. Its cutting edge programme includes Electrofringe, Sound Summit, National Young Writers Festival, Critical Animals and a massive Zine Fair. People from around the country and across the world attend.

Although the festival venues are all quite close, the programme is packed full and getting from one venue to the other is sometimes a rush. As a response to this, innovative volunteers have come up with a couple of sustainable transport concepts.

In 2005 a number of 'White Bikes' were released on to the streets of Newcastle during the festival, branded with stickers that read 'free for your use'. A mysterious man, only known as 'the White Rider' was believed to be behind them. The bikes became communal property and were left outside venues. If a bike was outside a venue the audience was free to take it to ride to another venue. The theory was there would always be bikes outside all venues. The project was not repeated, perhaps because none of the bikes were returned, or because the organizers moved onto other projects.

In 2008, the White Bike project was given a tune up and morphed into the 'TINA Bike Library' coordinated by bike activists from the Newcastle Bike Ecology Centre, an organization run by volunteers to train the community in building and maintaining bikes, as well as environmental and sustainable transport education. This time, more and better bikes were pulled together and the audience could borrow them for the duration of the festival. This ensured that the bikes made it back at the end and also gave those who wanted to ride the guarantee that they would have a bike always available.

The Bike Library is promoted on the TINA website and offers people the opportunity to 'book a bike' before the festival starts to ensure that one will be available. This booking includes a $30 refundable deposit as well as the use of a bike lock and helmet. All the bikes are made up of salvaged and donated bike parts, which gives each bike a sometimes wacky, always organic edge.

The TINA Bike Library also offers workshops for fixing and mending bikes from other festival attendees, run by volunteers from the Newcastle Bike Ecology Centre.

In 2008, over 60 bikes were booked before the festival began. All the bikes were decked out with 'licence plates' that gave the bikes individualized names and identities. While 'Wayne' ended up hanging from a lamp post at the end of the festival, most of the bikes were returned to the TINA Bike Library on the last day. This is attributed to the $30 deposit, which was an increase on the previous year and is a way of encouraging the bikes' return. Still, it is an important philosophy to keep when running a bike library that a lost bike from the library means more bikes (and fewer cars) on the road.

Source: Information in this case study supplied by TINA Bike Library coordinators Greer Allen and Daniel Endicott

THIS IS NOT ART

Figure 4.9 Biking is popular at TINA Festival in Newcastle, Australia
www.thisisnotart.org

Source: TINA

Box 4.13

Bikefest

Camden Green Fair and Bikefest is a celebration of local and regional sustainability projects and an educational event for the public. It takes place annually and for the last three years it has been located at Regent's Park in the heart of London, UK. Camden Green Fair and Bikefest has attracted on average 20,000 visitors and runs 1.00pm to 6.00pm on a Sunday.

Bikefest was initially a stand-alone event organized by the Camden Cycling Campaign, part of the London Cycling Campaign. After two years it was decided to combine this event with the Camden Green Fair and Bikefest is now an integral part of this event.

One of the constant features of Bikefest has been the possibility to try out a variety of bicycles on a traffic-free road. Bicycles that have been available have included regular bikes, recumbents, tandems and tricycles. Visitors have been able to try out these bicycles at no cost, thanks to the cycle shops that have provided them: www.bikefix.co.uk and www.velorution.biz.

There is also an information stall where they give out information on local cycling facilities and training opportunities, and listen to the comments of the public. They also try to recruit new members for the London Cycling Campaign.

A service that Bikefest provides which is of increasing popularity is 'Dr Bike'. This is an opportunity for owners of bicycles to have them checked and for simple repairs to be carried out. For the last three years Bikefest has had eight mechanics working non-stop for six hours servicing bicycles. There are also other activities: a cycling obstacle course for children, Rollapaluza (a 'pedalling' competition with bicycles on frames (www.rollapaluza.com) and home-made rope-pulled go-carts.

Overall objectives of the Camden Green Fair are to promote all forms of sustainable living and to celebrate sustainability projects.

Objectives of Bikefest

- Celebrate the pleasure of cycling (hence the idea of trying out unusual bicycles).
- Encourage more people to cycle.
- Promote membership to the cycling campaign.

Stakeholders
Enthusiastic individuals: Each section of the fair is led by one or two volunteers that invest a considerable amount of their time to ensure the success of the fair.

CAMDEN GREEN FAIR

Community groups: They are critical to the success of the fair. In addition to the Camden Cycling Campaign the involvement of local chapters of Friends of the Earth, Greenpeace, faith groups, sports group, art groups, music groups, etc. are also included.

Camden Council: It has been very helpful in the past but it is important that the organization can become more independent and this is now happening.

Local business: Bikefest would not have been possible without the support of Bikefix with whom it was originally conceived.

Environmental Guidelines

The Camden Green Fair and Bikefest have very strict self-imposed environmental guidelines. These include:

- no generators allowed on site;
- no electricity used;
- caterers must use recyclable materials;
- music stages powered by renewable energy;
- manage own recycling on site;
- no parking, and encourage stall-holders to minimize use of motor vehicles;
- construct temporary cycle parking.

Figure 4.10 Bike parking at BikeFest

Source: BikeFest

Source: Information in this case study provided by Stefano Casalotti

Box 4.14

Black Rock Pedal Transportation, Burning Man

Burning Man occurs in the desert near Reno, Nevada, US. To read more about the core principles of this unique gathering, see the entry in Chapter 1. Biking around the temporary city at Burning Man – Black Rock City – is the main mode of transport.

There's a thriving bike culture at Burning Man. The Blackrock Pedal Transportation group manage cycling at and to the event, host the 'bike camp', operate a lost and found bikes service and run a repair shop.

So, how do you move 47,000 people around a city where driving is prohibited? The answer is bicycles, bicycles and more bicycles! In 2006 Black Label Bike Club launched the pilot programme for the Yellow Bike Project with plans to slowly grow the number of bikes each year. The Yellow Bikes are community property at Burning Man, and are designated to be shared within the community and available for all to enjoy.

Gifting is part of the philosophy of the event and in 2007 the programme got an unexpected boost when an anonymous donor gifted 1000 bikes to the Yellow Bike project. The shipment of unassembled bikes hit Black Rock Station just a couple of weeks before the event. After a mammoth assembly operation, the bikes were transported to Black Rock City by truck, except the last load, which came via a pedal powered armada of bike enthusiasts riding from the ranch to the playa on a historical ride that's now repeated each year.

Like all new programmes in Black Rock City, it takes a couple of years to educate everyone about community bike etiquette. Bike volunteers inspected parked bikes to ensure that community bikes were not being locked or hoarded.

Bolt cutters helped educate a couple of participants that community bikes are owned by, well, the community. About 80 per cent of the yellow bikes were recovered after the event, meaning that about 20 per cent were taken from the playa either as outright theft or perhaps because people thought they were MOOP (Matter Out Of Place) and were trying to do their part to Leave No Trace.

Since 2006 the Yellow Bike project has had a staggering 2000 per cent growth. One of the most important aspects of the cycling projects at Burning Man is the community gifting that happens each year after the event. Approximately 1000 bikes are left/lost/abandoned/donated and these make their way to charity and community projects. The team are currently raising funds to send a shipping container of 500 bikes to Ghana.

Volunteer cycling groups such as the Bike Guild and the Black Label Bike Club have supported the bicycle metropolis in numerous ways over the years. The Bike Guild taught participants how to maintain bikes, and in 2003 it began matching lost bikes with happy riders. In 2007, the Reno-based Black Label Bike Club took over lost and found duties and also created the pilot Yellow Bike programme. There's also a great bike shop onsite called 'Bike Rock City'.

Box 4.15

At your Event: Reduce Audience Travel Impact

To reduce audience transport impact, you need more bums on seats in all vehicles travelling to the event. That means bus and coach travel, train travel and full cars. Of course cycling and walking should be promoted if appropriate for your event.

- Traffic Manager to devise audience travel impact reduction strategies.
- Create a project to encourage or reward public transport use.
- Link public transport hubs with shuttle buses to your event.
- Take advantage of existing sustainable transport initiatives.
- Hold your event close to transport networks.
- Communicate examples of CO_2 impact from different types of travel.

Ask the following questions and consider the following points when devising your audience transport strategies:

Public transport access

- What public transport options are available adjacent to the venue?
- Identify the modes of transport, routes, timetables and bus stops.
- Assess capacity if your event adds significantly to occupancy. Could it cope?
- Meet with local public transport authorities to establish a plan.
- Will you need to put on additional public transport such as shuttle buses, in order to 'join the dots' between transport hubs and your event's location?

Discourage driving and reward full cars

- Charge for car parking, with a price chosen to dampen demand, but not alienate.
- Sell pre-purchased car passes.
- Limit the number of car spots, even if you have the space.
- Reward those that arrive in full cars.
- Charge a green tax to all cars or those cars that arrive less than full.
- Offer premium parking spots to full cars, including fast tracked exit at the end of the event.

Encourage coach and train travel

- Promote public transport access before tickets go on sale and ensure all options to get to the event are available on your website so people can plan before they purchase.
- If you have group registration, work with group organizers to ensure coach travel is also arranged.
- Bundle ticket sales with coach or rail travel.
- Promote the convenience and environmental benefits of coach travel.

Encourage cycling and walking

- Forge partnerships with walking and cycling clubs.
- Organize a 'bike bus' with support vehicle for gear.
- Have secure bike parking, bike workshop for puncture repairs and tune ups.
- If camping is permitted, offer premium camping to those that cycle or walk.
- Offer incentives or rewards for those that cycle or walk.
- Put together a special walk or cycle campaign to promote this to your audience.
- Get a bike sponsor involved.
- Release free bikes across your event to get people around.
- For multi-venue events, have a bike library so people can borrow a bike during the event, discouraging taxi use.

Encourage carbon offsetting for audience travel

- Identify the best carbon offsetting scheme for your event and develop a partnership with them.
- Promote it online and make the purchase of it an add-on to ticket sales.
- Alternatively add it into all tickets as a green tax. Compulsory for car and air, optional for coach and train.
- Put a carbon calculator on your website, so the audience can calculate their emissions based on their mode of transport and the distance they travel.
- If you expect your audience to offset their transport emissions, you should look to also offset your staff's transport emissions.

 **Key Sustainability Indicators**

The Key Sustainability Indicators for travel are:

- Percentage of travel by each mode of transport.
- Occupancy rates.
- Average distance travelled per person.
- Tonnes of CO_2.
- CO_2 emissions per person for each mode of transport.

Assess Mode of Transport

To establish the success of your public transport campaigns, you will need to measure the percentage of your audience who have travelled to your event by coach, occupancy rates and the overall CO_2 impact. Ways to do this include:

- Receive a report on coach numbers and occupancy rate, to get total passengers by coach.
- Get similar information from your shuttle buses. Ensure you have told the driver or company organizing it in advance that you want these data captured. You'll need daily data so you can analyse usage patterns for future years, along with uptake of the service.
- If you have a certain entry gate that feeds from car parks versus from bus stops or train stations, put people counters on these gates if you have no other way of counting people.
- Get car parking figures and cross tab that with your occupancy rate survey figures to gain estimated number of people in total number of cars.

- Have manual counters at bus stops and train stations.
- Include bundle ticket sales.
- Ask your participants when arriving or registering how they travelled.
- Ask your local train station if they have automatic traffic counters on gates and ask if they can provide figures for the day your event is on.
- Count the number of bikes in your bike parking station.

Use all of this information to come up with the total percentage of people that have travelled by public transport versus car, foot or bike. This information will then feed into the key sustainability indicator – Audience Transport Emissions.

Go through the steps in the following pages to establish Key Sustainability Indicators for audience (and crew) transport.

UK DEFRA June 2008 emissions factors are used in this book along with data from the UK's National Atmospheric Emissions Inventory. A full list of this can be found in Chapter 1.

Train Travel

The Key Sustainability Indicators for train travel are:

- Number of passengers.
- Average distance per passenger.
- Tonnes CO_2.
- Percentage of total audience travelling by train.

Passenger miles are the standard way to measure train travel emissions. As trains used by your audience are likely to be regular scheduled services, this is the only option for measurement.

Because the trains used by your audience are likely to be regular services it may be difficult to accurately assess the actual numbers of your audience coming by train, unless you have pre-sold bundled tickets.

If the venue is within walking distance of the train station, ask the train station to do a door count, which they can then compare against their usual average traffic figures.

If you put on a shuttle bus from the station to your event, then it is very easy to estimate the number of people that came by train as you just need to use the shuttle bus figures to estimate train travellers.

Use the total passenger numbers gleaned from whichever method you have at your disposal.

Track through the following for an example on how to calculate impacts:

(A) Train passengers:	21,000
(B) Average return distance:	109.4 miles
(C) Total passenger miles:	2,297,400
	(A × B)
(D) Total CO_2 kg:	221,239.6kg
	(C × 0.0963kg)
(D) Total tonnes CO_2:	221.24
	(C / 1000)
Total CO_2 per person:	10.53kg
	(D / A)

Shuttle Buses

It is likely your shuttle buses are moving people from major transport hubs. If you can split your reporting between those that are connecting with train stations and those that are 'locals' or from other departure points, that is useful data.

Here is an example to follow through to calculate shuttle bus impact. Don't forget return trips, so if you want to work out total number of people that travelled by shuttle bus, you'll need to halve passenger numbers.

(A) Total shuttle bus runs:	420
(B) Distance from station:	2 miles
(C) Total shuttle bus miles:	1680 miles
	(A × B × 2)
(D) Total kg CO_2 shuttle bus:	1812.72kg
	(C × 1.079kg)
(E) Total tonnes CO_2:	1.81
	(D / 1000)
Total CO_2 per person:	0.86kg
Total CO_2 train & shuttle:	223.05 tonnes
Total CO_2 per person:	11.39kg

Coach Travel

The Key Sustainability Indicators for coach travel are:

- Number of coaches.
- Total distance travelled.
- Tonnes CO_2.
- Occupancy rate.
- Number of passengers.
- Percentage of total audience travelling by coach.

The per passenger mile CO_2 emissions factor works for car and train transport but not so much for coaches. The DEFRA per passenger figure for coaches is from a national average of 9.2 people per bus/coach. If coaches are chartered specifically for your event, you should look to measure total distance travelled by all the coaches regardless of whether they were full or not. The coach would not have run if you didn't hold your event, so the actual CO_2 emissions, rather than per passenger mile should be used.

If there is mainly urban bus transport rather than chartered coaches, use the per passenger mile figure. Get the departure information for each coach and use Google Maps from the point of origin to your event's location to get a total distance. Double it for the return trip!

Follow the example to see how to calculate impacts:

(A) Total coach miles: 16,410

(B) Total passengers:	6000
(C) Total kg CO_2 emissions:	17706.39kg
	(A × 1.079)
(D) Total tonnes CO_2:	17.70
	(C / 1000)
Total CO_2 per person:	2.95kg
	(C / B)

Flights

If you are likely to have people taking flights to attend, then you need to gather the following info:

- Number of people flying.
- Percentage of total audience travelling by plane.
- Point of origin and return.
- CO_2 emissions.

You should also try and discover if the flight/travel is specifically for your event or if they are travelling for other purposes.

Car Travel

When measuring the impact of car travel to your event, you will need to measure the following.

- Number of cars.
- Occupancy rate.
- Average distance travelled.
- Tonnes CO_2.
- Percentage of total audience travelling by car.
- Liftshare/carshare uptake.

Use your ticket sales data to establish average distance travelled.

Car Numbers and Occupancy Rates

In order to assess just how well your audience is packing people into their cars to conserve CO_2 emissions, and whether there's room to improve this, you will need to measure car occupancy rates. The best way to do this is through an entry or exit survey at the car parks. Have people stationed at key entry points around your car park where you can do a quick visual count of the number of people per car. A simple survey like this will give you a wealth of information. In the end you will get percentages per occupancy size and an overall occupancy rate. Make a mention of motor cycles, minibuses and campervans.

From these data you'll be able to see the most common actual number of people per car, and if there is any practical room to increase this. Here is an example of a table reporting occupancy rates.

1 passenger	12%
2 passengers	45%
3 passengers	30%
4 passengers	7%
5 passengers	6%

Average occupancy rate of 2.5.

Average Distance Travelled

Even without going into the intricate analysis of how people travelled, how many per car, what percentage went by coach or train etc, knowing how far afield they came from will be illuminating.

Figure 4.11 Communicating transport impacts and initiatives is part of the plan at Peats Ridge Festival
Souce: Meegan Jones

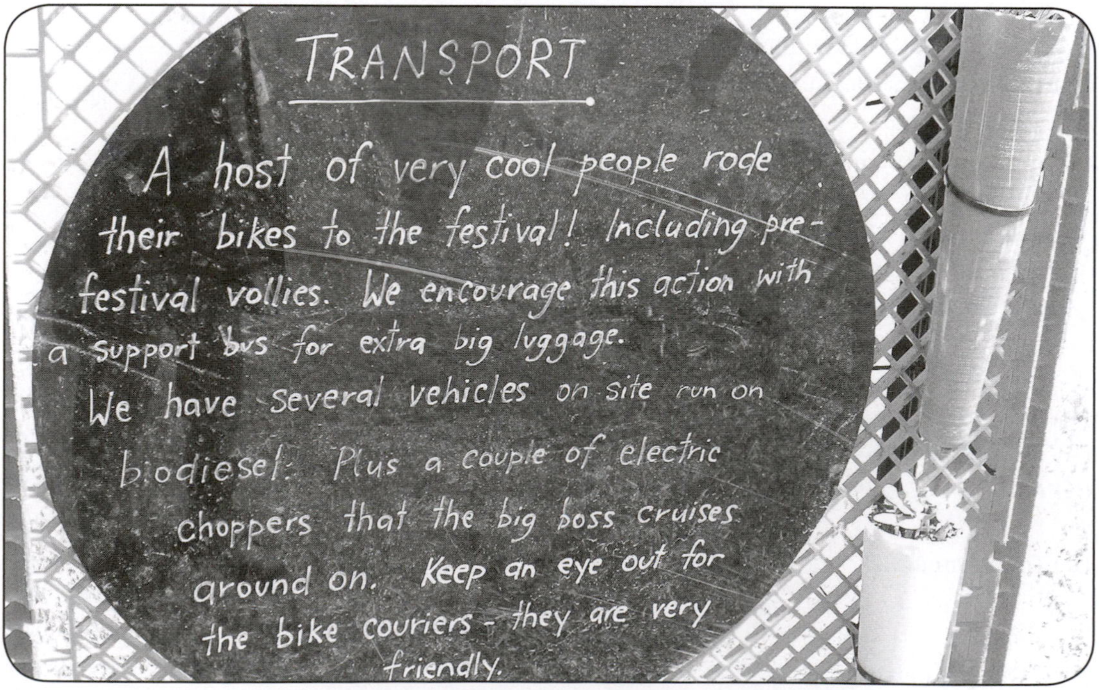

Collect Point of Origin Information

Get postcode, suburb, city or town information from your ticket sales data. If you don't have ticket sales, but register participants, gather details at registration. If you don't do any registration, then you will need to do a manual survey of at least 10 per cent, preferably 20 per cent, of your audience to get a good solid sample of where your people came from. (If you have to do that, you may as well add in mode of transport, how many in the car etc.)

Percentage from Each Point of Origin

You may have a sophisticated data crunching software program to do this for you, or a market research company. But if you want to do it yourself, below is a guide to doing so.

Enter the postcode or suburb data, into a spreadsheet. Hopefully ticketing department can supply you a spreadsheet file so you don't need to manually type in each ticket's info. Calculate percentages for each postcode, suburb, town, city etc against total audience figure.

Town	Number	Percentage
Reading	19,500	39
London	15,500	31
Bath	7000	14
Manchester	8000	16
Total	50,000	

Enter Distance Data

Next you'll need to do some data wrangling to input the distance travelled. My favourite manual way is to get a spreadsheet on one half of the computer screen, and Google Maps on the other. Enter the location of the event, and then click the 'from here' button. Then you go on a meditative

day of copying and pasting new suburb or postcodes into the 'from here' bit and copying and pasting the total distance back into your spreadsheet. It is quite a therapeutic process though with a cup of tea and a nice view if you have the time as you start to form a picture in your mind of where your audience is coming from. Your marketing people may also want these data to do their advertising and promotion planning.

Town	No.	%	Miles
Reading	19,500	39	1
London	15,500	31	41
Bath	7000	14	74.2
Manchester	8000	16	195

Calculate Total Mileage

Take the percentage for each suburb/postcode and multiply it by the total audience size to get total distance and average distance per person.

Add all the totals up for each town/postcode to get the grand total miles/km travelled by all your audience.

Town	No.	%	Miles	Total
Reading	19,500	39	1	19,500
London	15,500	31	41	635,500
Bath	7000	14	74.2	519,400
Manchester	8000	16	195	1,560,000
Total	50,000			2,734,400

Average Distance Per Person

Divide total distance by your total audience number, and you have the per person distance. (Remember to double it for the return trip.)

Total miles: **2,734,400**
Average one way: **54.7 miles**

Next is the simple matter of calculating CO_2 emissions.

Total event audience:	50,000
(A) Total cars:	8200
(B) Occupancy rate:	2.6
(C) Total people by car:	21,320 (A × B)
(D) Average return:	109.4 miles
(E) Total distance:	897,080
	(A × D)
(F) Total kg CO_2:	308,774.9kg
	(0.3442 × E)
Total tonnes CO_2:	308.77
	(F / 1000)
Total CO_2 per person:	14.48kg
	(F / C)

Transport Emissions Summary

The following is a summary of all the workings in this example.

	%	Tonne CO_2	CO_2/person
Car	42.6	308.77	14.48kg
Coach	12	17.7	2.95kg
Train/ shuttle	42	223.05	11.39kg
Cycle	3.4	0	0

Total: 549.52 tonne CO_2

Freight

If you choose to include freight as part of your GHG emissions and Key Sustainability Indicators calculation, you will need to put in place a mechanism to record deliveries. Delivery dockets can be kept and an admin project put together to estimate and log distances for deliveries. However as previously discussed, this is fraught with the potential for inaccuracies and assumptions. What will you do with the figure as a result apart from report them and possibly offset?

The Key Sustainability Indicators as they apply to freight are:

- Total distance transported.
- Tonnage transported (goods).
- CO_2 emissions.

Interpreting Results

From the summary we can see that 54 per cent travelled by public transport, 3.4 per cent cycled and 42.6 per cent came by car.

Coach travel has the least CO_2 impact per person after cycling.

Occupancy rates are quite high at 2.6 people per car, bringing the per person transport impact in cars not too far off that of train travel. Adding one more person per car on average (up to an occupancy rate of 3.66) would reduce per person impact to around 18kg, just less than travel by train.

So you can see this type of analysis can give insight into where there is room for change in your audience transport habits. In the example above, increasing from three to four people could be effective, as could from two to three. A campaign could be built around 'double up and cut down' encouraging the most common number of passengers per car – two – to turn up with another couple, bringing their occupancy up to four.

If your event is a camping one, such as a multi-day music festival, you may wish to also survey whether people seem to have enough room in their cars to actually fit more people and their gear in. It may be that in your country the trend is for tiny cars, and there just may be no more space for more than two people and their gear. Or you may have large numbers of SUV/4WD cars that can fit loads more. If you think either of these could be an issue, include capturing those data in your entry/exit survey.

Watch | Read | Surf

Eco-Passenger

A great website that calculates emissions impacts of various modes of travel. It shows you how to get from A to B by train.
www.ecopassenger.com

Ethical Transport Association

The Ethical Transport Association is Britain's largest charity focused on transport and the environment. Its aim is to raise awareness of the impact of excessive car use and help individuals and organizations to make positive changes in their travel habits.
www.eta.co.uk

Loco2

Low carbon travel adventures. A website that connects people to low carbon travel.
www.loco2travel.com

Who Killed the Electric Car?

Writer/Director Chris Paine, Papercut Films:

> It was among the fastest, most efficient production cars ever built. It ran on electricity, produced no emissions and catapulted American technology to the forefront of the automotive industry. The lucky few who drove it never wanted to give it up. So why did General Motors crush its fleet of EV-1 electric vehicles in the Arizona desert?
>
> Who Killed the Electric Car? chronicles the life and mysterious death of the EV-1; examining the cultural and economic ripple effects caused by its conception and how they reverberated through the halls of government and big business.

Writer/Director Chris Paine's documentary feature film premiered at the Sundance Film Festival in 2006 before its release by Sony Pictures. It was often shown in tandem with An Inconvenient Truth.
www.whokilledtheelectriccar.com

NewRide

NewRide is a website for users and buyers of electric vehicles (EVs) in London. It promotes on and off-street charging facilities in the Clear Zone for electric scooters, bikes and cars. There is no congestion charge payable in the city of London if you drive an electric car. The NewRide website includes everything you need to know about EVs including the location of all electrical charging points – via an interactive Google map that shows all the public recharging points in London city and surrounding boroughs.

www.newride.org.uk

As I write this chapter I am actually on a 24-hour train journey from Delhi to Mumbai. While I am encouraging travelling by train, I have to admit we had a five-hour delay and I did get to spend a bit more time on the platform in the fog with 100 army soldiers than I had planned. On trains in India there's a power point and, with my mobile internet, I was hooked in and got a good 20 hours' work done straight. So train travel does have its benefits.

Figure 4.12

Notes

1 Peak Oil is the point in time when the maximum rate of global petroleum extraction is reached, after which the rate of production enters decline. Oil becomes more difficult and expensive to extract after we reach Peak Oil.

2 TNT Express, www.tnt.com/express/en_ca/data/news/tnt_builds_up_its.html, accessed August 2008.

3 Environmental News Service Newswire, www.ens-newswire.com/ens/nov2008/2008-11-04-02.asp, accessed November 2008.

4 **RegenaStar BioFuel Solution.** CleanStar and Regenatec are working together to take the world's most advanced diesel-to-plant-oil engine conversion technology to the world's biggest diesel markets. The two companies are launching an integrated technology plus biofuel solution that provides heavy diesel engine operators an alternative that's cheaper, greener and simpler than biodiesel. www.cleanstar.in

5 Renewable Transport Fuel Obligation programme, www.dft.gov.uk/pgr/roads/environment/rtfo, accessed January 2009.

6 Connected Cities, www.connectedcities.eu, accessed January 2008.

7 International Air Transport Association, www.iata.org/whatwedo/environment, accessed December 2008.

8 Sustainable Aviation, www.sustainableaviation.co.uk, accessed December 2008.

Opposite: Jakob Kolar, Boom Festival, Portugal

chapter 5

Water

Water is the new oil, a valuable, scarce, necessary, highly sought after and protected commodity. It's been estimated that by 2025 1.8 billion people will live in water scarce areas.[1] Including water conservation and waste water management into your event will be an integral part of its sustainability, now and in the future.

Whether your event's in an indoor venue, a park, school, club grounds or on a greenfield site, it will use clean water and produce waste water. To be sustainable, you must put practices in place to reduce the demand on dams and the strain on sewer systems.

If you live in a dry region the reality of water scarcity will be part of your everyday life. Water restrictions are commonplace. Even in seemingly wet countries such as the UK where you imagine water supply not to be a problem, they are experiencing the direct impact of water shortages and it's being felt in the hip pocket. Water charges have increased significantly in recent years and are forecast to continue to climb.

There's also a direct climate change impact on water production, as pumping, delivery and waste water treatment consumes a significant amount of energy and therefore production of greenhouse gas (GHG) emissions.

Sensitivity to water scarcity and conservation in the local area that your event's held in is of utmost importance. Make sure you respect local water conservation protocols. This is especially important if your event is in a rural area where the livelihood of the local population depends on adequate water supply.

The big three when looking at sustainable water management at your event are:

- Water conservation.
- Emissions to water.
- Waste water management.

The following pages go through innovative examples of what events around the world have done to conserve, use and manage water. To put things in perspective, let's first look at the issues surrounding water scarcity to understand why we need to conserve water.

Water Scarcity

Water's necessary for securing livelihoods, for social and economic welfare and for protecting ecosystems. It allows food to grow to support the human population, and is essential for ongoing development and improvement in standards of living.

As the planet's population continues to grow, demand on ground and surface water grows with increased domestic, agricultural and industrial use. It's predicted that the next round of global conflict may come off the back of water rights, access and allocation.

Of course arid regions are affected by water scarcity; however, with unpredictable climate patterns, more regions are finding themselves in drought.

The way forward to ensure water for all is through:

- Increasing productivity of the water we use (using it more efficiently, recycling grey water, etc.).

- Protection of ecosystems which naturally capture, filter, store and release water (rivers, lakes, forest watersheds, wetlands).
- International and governmental cooperation (all water sectors working together to agree on equitable allocation and management of water globally).

The **Food and Agriculture Organization** of the United Nations reports that one in five people in the developing world lacks access to sufficient clean water, with a suggested minimum of 20 litres per day. The average water use in the West across all activities to support their lifestyles ranges between 200 and 600 litres per day.[2]

The rural poor in developing countries are impacted most by water scarcity. As dams and canals are built, those living downstream are affected. As groundwater is taken for industrial and commercial use, those who have previously accessed this reserve through pumps and wells find lowering water tables taking water out of their reach. Sanitation issues and water quality are of biggest concern to those living in poverty and are the focus of many NGOs as the lack of such a basic human requirement causes such compounding problems.

So you can see, water conservation and protection is vitally important to ongoing sustainability and needs to be considered as an important part of your event. To promote worldwide water issues, invite one of the many water NGOs to participate in your water conservation operations and to have a presence at your event to promote their messages of water conservation and sanitation issues.

To read some statistics on the state of worldwide water compiled by **WaterAid**, please refer to the Appendix.

Let's now have a quick run down different types of water that need to be managed.

Types of Water

Management of various stages of water at your event is needed all the way from fresh drinking water supply to handling sewage. Here are the different categories of water:

Clear water

For drinking only, supplied from standpipes if water is 'potable' (drinkable) or from bulk dispensing tanks.

Blue water

For washing, showering and other human contact activities. This can be bore water, from a dam, river, tanks or other supply. Not suitable for drinking.

Grey water

Used water from showers or other washing operations. The water doesn't have any organic contamination. This grey water can be recycled to toilet flushing once filtered, used for non-contact activities, or stored on site and then used for irrigation.

Brown/Black Water

Effluent from toilets and sullage from food stall washing up. This usually goes straight down the sewer drain, into a septic tank or, for temporary events, kept in tanks and then taken by 'suck trucks' which dispose of it into the sewer system.

Health and Safety Regulations

Safety and hygiene are paramount to any decision an event makes about water supply, management and treatment. Each country and indeed each local council will have regulations on what can and can't be done. The Environment Agency in your country will also direct you.

At some events 'recirc' toilets are allowed. (This is where the urine, mixed with chemical, is used to reflush the toilet. Yuck!) No matter how seemingly effective the chemical is in a recirc toilet, I don't want any splashback from that concoction.

At other events I've wanted to redirect the waste water from showers to flush the toilets but haven't been allowed by regulations for fear of 'splashback'. They required the water to be filtered before going back through the toilets. Fair enough.

Sometimes it's a simple process to manage a water bottle refill station. At other events a convoluted system is needed to ensure there's no cross contamination between the tap nozzle and the top of the bottle that people put their mouths on. Spit transfer. So do check with your local council and environment agency on what's appropriate in your local area.

Let's now look at a quick checklist for water management at your event.

Box 5.1

Water Management Checklist

Water conservation

☐ Reduce water use through water saving devices on taps, hoses, showers and drinking water standpipes.

☐ Reduce water use through 'water wise' grounds preparation and gardening.

☐ Use dust suppressant additives to reduce water volume used to dampen dust.

☐ Capture water and store in rainwater tanks.

☐ Use waterless urinals and toilets.

Waste water management

☐ Capture and treat grey water.

☐ Use soakaways, a reed bed or mechanical filtering.

☐ Re-use grey water for non-contact uses.

Emissions to water

☐ Use chemical-free cleaning products.

☐ Use biological toilet treatment products rather than chemical.

☐ Use non-toxic paints so wash-up water is not full of toxic pigments.

Land protection

☐ If disposing of grey water through run-off or soakaways, ensure it's chemical free and 100m from a waterway.

☐ Protect the riparian zone, the region between land and a waterway, from any activity or impact.

☐ Prevent excessive urination direct to the land or waterways.

Audience messaging

☐ Conduct a water conservation campaign at your event to encourage water savings by your audience.

☐ Conduct a waterways protection campaign at an outdoor event to protect the riparian zone from urination and emissions to waterways.

☐ Include free water bottle refill stations.

Box 5.2

WaterAid

WaterAid is an international charity whose mission is to overcome poverty by enabling the world's poorest people to gain access to safe water, sanitation and hygiene education.

WaterAid's vision is of a world where everyone has access to safe water and sanitation. They aim to help 1 million people gain access to water and 1 million gain access to sanitation every year. To date WaterAid has helped over 12 million people gain access to these essential services.

WaterAid and its partners use practical solutions to provide safe water, effective sanitation and hygiene education to the world's poorest people. They also seek to influence policy at national and international levels.

They are one of the main charities involved with the UK's Glastonbury Festival. They run the 'love your loo' campaign, along with messaging water conservation and sanitation issues.

Figure 5.1

Source: WaterAid / Marco Betti

www.wateraid.org

Figure 5.2 Water tanks are used to store water captured on rooftops of the shower blocks at Golden Plains Festival in Victoria, Australia

Source: Mik la Vage

Water Use and Conservation

Clean water may be supplied to your event by tankers, through the mains water supply, or you may harvest it off roofs and store it in tanks.

Whichever method you choose, water conservation should be the goal. Water is used and waste water produced at events through:

- Catering and food stalls.
- Cleaning.
- Toilets and showers.

- Handwash facilities.
- Standpipes and free drinking taps.
- Misting stations at hot and dry events.
- Dust settling.
- Grounds preparation and gardens.

If you have chosen a sustainably built venue for your indoor event, water conservation techniques should already be in place. You will have little control over implementing anything at an existing building; however, choosing the right venue in the first place is something you can control. You can also implement your own water saving campaign at your event by layering a messaging programme over existing infrastructure to encourage water saving by your attendees.

One way of ensuring you conserve water is through mechanical intervention. The right technology exists now and it's just a matter of getting your plumbing contractors and suppliers to understand your requirements and to supply the right gear. They should always be using water saving devices, so it's probably just a case of double checking with them.

Ways to reduce water consumption include:

- Reduced water pressure.
- Using low-flow showerheads and taps.
- Using tap fittings that have an automatic stop mechanism.
- Using water-free toilets and urinals.
- Supplying water-free hand sanitizer.
- Water conservation messaging.

Aside from using low-flow technology you can manipulate the amount of water used, by not having it on tap, so to say. Not literally of course, but by not having a free flowing and limitless source available at everyone's beck and call.

Such measures could include opening showers for public use only at certain times (and not having hot water!) and requiring food vendors to decant and transport water.

The following are techniques to use to encourage water conservation.

Cleaning

High pressure hoses encourage excessive water to be used by cleaners. Require cleaners to use a mop and bucket, rather than hoses attached to taps. This will discourage overly zealous hosing as a cleaning technique, rather than using elbow grease.

Catering and Food Stalls

Supply water at central standpipes so that physical transport of water in containers is necessary to get water to market stalls. Vendors that do events are always set up to transport water, usually having a neat little system with a barrel on wheels that pulls along, so you won't be inconveniencing them too much. Don't allow hoses to run from standpipes to market stalls.

Dust Settling

A major use for water at some outdoor events is as a dust settling agent. Thousands of litres of water are sprayed on roads and tracks to prevent dust rising during the course of a hot and dry event. As the ground dries and footfall and vehicle movements increase over the course of your show, along with wind gusts, dusty conditions can occur.

You will often see water tankers drive up and down dusty tracks to dampen down the ground. Within a short space of time it evaporates off, and the whole process needs to be repeated.

Dust settling products have been developed for the mining industry and equestrian industry and are also a perfect solution for events with a dust problem. Using a non-hazardous organic dust settling agent mixed in with the water drastically increases the effectiveness of spraying and therefore reduces the volume of water and number of repeat applications needed. Most will claim that you only need to apply it once. These products cause the dust particles to cling to each other which prevents them from floating up into the air.

Ensure a non-toxic product is used. There are chemical heavy products on the market. Track down a dust settling product that is approved to be non-toxic to the environment.

Recycled water (grey water) can also be used in the water trucks rather than potable water, if your health regulations allow. You may need to put your grey water through a filtration process before being allowed to spray it, as who really wants to get caught in the drift of someone else's shower water?

Grounds Preparation and Gardens

Events held in beautiful parks, gardens or landscaped rural locations should also consider the volume of water needed to keep the grounds in pristine green and shiny condition. Enquire about the water conservation and recycling techniques used. Make sure they don't use sprayers and sprinklers in the heat of the day. Drip irrigation, mulching and a range of other water saving techniques are commonplace. Enquire what's used on your grounds.

If you have gardens at an outdoor event, or the opportunity to create them, consider bringing in a permaculture group to set up waterwise gardens. They can create grey water recycling systems, use the compost created from your event's waste, even from the toilet waste (see composting toilets coming up). **Boom Festival** in Portugal and **Electric Picnic** in Ireland have done just that.

If you are unaware of permaculture principles, I encourage you to do some research into this marvellous gardening technique. It's a whole new (old!) way of looking at self-sufficiency and the cycles of nature.

Water Tanks and Harvesting

If you have a permanent site, set up water tanks to capture and store water. This may need to be investment heavy, industrial sized tanks, placed underground and out of view, with serious plumbing, piping and pumping. However at a minimum you can have a domestic-scale water tank set up to demonstrate to the audience what may be possible in their own homes. By capturing your own water, you are reducing reliance on mains water, or more importantly, water that needs to be delivered by tanker.

Standpipes and Handwash

Having standpipes, free drinking taps and handwashing facilities is essential for your audience's convenience, comfort and hygiene. It's also a way to reduce plastic bottle waste. However unless you have good drainage, grey water capture, and taps which automatically shut off, you are likely to see a quagmire develop around standpipes and sinks. Make sure the taps have a spring release so that they have to be held open when being used and automatically shut off when released. This will save water and also prevent a muddy pit forming.

Figure 5.4 Hand sanitizing stations set up at the toilets to reduce unnecessary water use to wash hands

Source: Glastonbury Festival

Figure 5.3 Free drinking water at ROTHBURY Festival. Note the pile of straw to prevent muddy footing

Source: The Spitfire Agency

Hand Sanitizing Stations

Set up hand sanitizing stations near your toilets, similar to that pictured in Figure 5.4. This will provide a necessary sanitation service, but will also prevent the unnecessary use of water. There are some wonderful solvent-free options available on the market made from all natural ingredients, and alcohol free. Not that your audience is likely to drink the sanitizer, but we have seen it being used as a propellant to start fires. Also alcohol free means VOC free.

There's no need to use a chemical heavy product when great all natural products are available such as Quash, Citrofresh and Zapp-It. Set up these hand sanitizing stations back of house also, for food service staff, near the toilets.

Misting Stations

At hot and dry events nothing can be better than walking through a misting station. This is where overhead sprinklers spray mist down on hot and bothered patrons. It's truly a wonderful experience – however, quite a water wasteful one. The alternative could be to have volunteers with hand-held water sprays (scented with lovely oils) roving the crowd or set up in a central spot. They could also supply and apply sunblock.

Water Messaging and Promotion

Apart from putting in mechanical or logistical barriers to inhibit water consumption, convincing users that conserving water is important is your next challenge. Just like convincing them to use public transport or to recycle their bottles, getting the message across and having them actually conserve water will require psychology and a dash of marketing.

If your event is in a country or region where water scarcity is an everyday concern, your job will be easier. Tools will be at hand from water conservation groups, the language you use will be established and the techniques to cut water use familiar.

If you're attracting people from outside the area who may not be used to water conservation techniques, getting the message across will be especially important. Contact your local water board and see what water conservation materials they have.

Consider partnering with a water bottle brand or NGO that supports water conservation and equitable distribution such as One Water. See Box 5.3.

Figure 5.5 Hunter Water from Newcastle, Australia is an active contributor to events in the region. They promote grey water re-use in homes and rainwater capture

Source: Hunter Water

Figure 5.6 Water tanks are used at Golden Plains and Meredith Festival to harvest water during the year. That a water tank is visible to the audience and they are in an area experiencing drought encourages conservative water use

Source: Mik la Vage

Sponsor and Partner Opportunities

- Align with a water conservation organization or water NGO/charity to co-promote your water conservation message.
- Approach a brand of hand sanitizer and offer a product placement opportunity. Free product can be available in bulk at the toilets and the brand can also retail their product at your event.
- Get a sunblock range to do promo around patron welfare. They can apply and simultaneously promote their products, along with offering the 'misting' service. There are some lovely all natural, chemical-free sunblocks out there. Alternatively, get an essential oil or skin care brand to do the same.
- You could also invite health organizations that promote sun protection such as the Cancer Council to run this activity.
- Invite a cleaning product range to supply product to your event for cleaning and for showers and handwash in bathrooms.
- Align with a range of bathroom accessories that promotes low-flow taps and shower heads.
- Partner with a spring water brand and have them supply water in bulk, stored in a tank with re-usable bottle refills.
- Partner with a water tank company to supply permanent or loaned water tanks to dispense water.

Box 5.3

Water promotion, One Water

One Water was launched at Live8 in the UK and donates all its profits to essential water projects around the world. So far the money they have raised has brought drinking water to thousands of people in need.

Simply purchasing a bottle of One Water gets the money to water projects – all profits, every last drop, fund essential clean water projects, such as PlayPump® water systems and SkyHydrant® community water filters, in Asia and Africa.

One Water is available in the UK, Australia, Ireland and the US.

www.onedifference.org

Box 5.4

Water Conservation Checklist ☑

- ☐ Use water saving taps, nozzles and shower heads.
- ☐ Reduce water pressure.
- ☐ Use auto shut taps.
- ☐ Have central standpipes and require water to be carried to food stalls.
- ☐ Use a dust settling agent.
- ☐ Ensure sustainable irrigation practices are used for grounds preparation.
- ☐ Use hand-held misting sprays not constantly running misting stations.
- ☐ Supply hand sanitizer.
- ☐ Carry out water conservation messaging to your audience, participants and crew.

Figure 5.7 One Water's play pump
Souce: One Water

Box 5.5

Take Back the Tap – water bottle-free event

Slow Food Nation, held in three venues in San Francisco, is a celebration of American food in history. More than 85,000 people attended. The range of activities at the event highlighted the connection between plate and planet. They held a water bottle-free event.

Slow Food Nation connected community and cuisine at a farmers' market, urban garden and 'soap box' stage. The Taste Pavilions showcased good, clean and fair food from America's best food artisans. Inspired by the self-sufficiency campaigns of World War II America, the 'Slow Food Nation Victory Garden' was a living testament – right in front of City Hall – to a healthy community's ability to feed and support itself. At the 'Food for Thought' sessions, leaders in food, health, environmentalism and social justice convened for teaching, discussion and calls to action. To top it all off was a music festival.

Slow Food Nation partnered with Food and Water Watch's 'Take Back the Tap' campaign to produce an entirely water bottle-free event, also teaming up with the San Francisco Public Utilities Commission. Along with their work on food and fish issues, Food and Water Watch's Take Back the Tap campaign works towards the goal of clean, safe and affordable water for all by encouraging Americans to switch back from bottled to tap water, fighting to prevent the privatization of water utilities, and lobbying for public funding for water infrastructure. The campaign educates consumers about the marketing myths created by the bottled water industry, and the environmental and economic benefits of reducing plastic bottle production and waste by taking back the tap.

One component of the campaign aims to provide information for event producers, conference organizers and caterers to help them transition back to serving only tap water at their events and functions. They encourage organizers to differentiate their event from others by kicking the bottled water habit and going back to the tap. They have produced a guide to going water bottle free at events.

Embracing the philosophy of a bottled water-free event, Slow Food Nation set up water stations and smaller satellite stations at each of the three event locations. The outdoor stations were connected to potable water lines on site and the indoor water stations were connected to water lines in the site kitchen and main pavilion. A water truck supplied water to one outdoor site. US Pure Water, a local filtration company, provided the filtration/distribution machines in exchange for company recognition.

Slow Food Nation

Figure 5.8 Water refill station at Slow Food Nation

Source: Food and Water Watch

Food and Water Watch sold 4000 co-branded Take Back the Tap and Slow Food Nation 'Kleen Kanteen' water bottles. Branded compostable cups were also provided by the San Francisco Public Utilities Commission for attendees. According to Food and Water Watch, a person at an event drinks on average between one and one and a half litres of water per day, depending on whether the event is held indoors or outdoors. Events that serve tap water therefore have the potential to save between two and three plastic bottles per attendee, based on a 500ml bottle. So estimates for Slow Food Nation with 80,000 people are the potential to save 200,000 plastic water bottles in one day!

Slow Food Nation advertised the event in advance as bottled water free. Food and Water Watch and Slow Food Nation also developed a collaborative media strategy to bring attention to this aspect through radio, web and print media.
www.slowfoodnation.org,
www.foodandwaterwatch.org

Source: Information in this case study reproduced with the kind permission of Noelle Ferdon and Food and Water Watch.

as grey water and any solid matter caught from the straining, composted. Black water is sewage and catering sullage. Sewage is discussed in the following section on toilets.

Whichever method of waste water disposal is applicable to your event, cleaning products and other chemicals that end up in the waste water have the potential to have a hazardous environmental impact. Chemical-free waste water should be your event's goal.

In looking for a sustainable solution for waste water management, you should address the following areas:

- Emissions to water.
- Waste water management.
- Grey water re-use.

In the following pages we will look at different types of waste water created at your event. We then discuss waste water treatment options. We'll also hear from a couple of events on the mechanisms they have put in place to manage and recycle grey water.

Figure 5.9 Handwash stations at Golden Plains Festival

Source: Mik la Vage

Waste Water

Waste water may disappear down the sink into a sewer system or it may be in-your-face with 'suck trucks' carting grey water and sewage away. Some grey water can make its way straight into the groundwater using soakaways. How you manage waste water is a primary environmental concern.

Waste water can be classified as grey or black. Grey water is the waste water from showers or other washing operations. It's free of organic matter, and can be used for non-contact purposes such as toilet flushing and irrigation. If strained and filtered, catering waste water can also be treated

Emissions to Water

It may sound obvious to not use chemicals which will end up in your waste water. But why do we want to prevent this? What will it actually do? When water is disposed of directly onto land, if any chemicals are present in the grey water toxic residue will remain on the land and in the soil. Soil is a fantastic natural filter. It's not a problem to dispose of grey water that has no chemicals present into a soakaway or run-off as long as it's not within about 100m of a water course. However, grey water polluted with chemicals will leave these chemicals in the land. Eventually the chemicals could make their way into waterways through run-off and groundwater. Residue left on the grass can also be taken in by animals, domestic or otherwise. Of course, any grey water disposed of down the drain can make its way directly to waterways and oceans, depending on the drainage system of the area.

Chemicals commonly used in toilets will disturb the natural processes in sewage treatment plants, where biological not chemical treatment is used. The better option is to use biological treatment products or odour eaters, or to go to a waterless loo. Toilets are discussed coming up.

Sources of potential emissions to water at events include:

- Personal products in showers and handwash.
- Cleaning products.
- Paint wash-up water.
- Catering waste water.
- Urination.
- Toilet treatment products.

Personal Products in Showers

If your event includes staying overnight, either through accommodation or camping, you should encourage the use of environmentally sound personal products: shampoo, body wash and handwash. You can provide the products for use, perhaps leveraging a sponsorship with a retail brand.

Cleaning Products

Products used to clean bathrooms, floors, kitchens and any other surface or material need to be environmentally sound. There are two issues to contend with when looking at these products' impact on the environment through resulting emissions to water:

- Raw materials used to make the product.
- Biodegradability of the resulting effluent.

Another happy by-product of using environmentally sound products is not exposing your

Figure 5.10 Paint washup. If you are doing a lot of painting at your event site, firstly use water based paint – but importantly, set up a system for cleaning brushes so that the paint waste water doesn't contaminate the land as in this photo
Source: Meegan Jones

staff or your audience to unhealthy and toxic chemicals. More details on choosing the right cleaning products are in Chapter 6.

Paint Sullage

If there's a lot of painting done during the event build, you may wish to consider the impact of large amounts of paint being washed down the drain or poured onto the land. To minimize potential problems use environmentally friendly paints free of toxic pigments. There are many brands available. What to look for in an environmentally friendly paint includes:

- VOC (solvent) free.
- Water clean-up.
- Non-toxic pigments.
- Petrochemical free (if possible).

Catering Sullage

Encourage caterers and food vendors to use environmentally sound, chemical-free cleaning products.

There will be health and safety issues for products used to clean public amenities governed by your local council and may be to the exclusion of environmentally sound products. However many brands are meeting the rigorous standards. Investigate the contents of the products you choose. Just because there's a picture of a lovely whale, or the product has the word 'eco' does not mean it's the best choice.

Figure 5.12 'Don't Take the Piss' campaign hopes to discourage urination anywhere but in the loo

Source: Glastonbury Festival

Figure 5.11 1000-litre pallet tanks are used to temporarily store grey water at Peats Ridge Festival. This is a great option for catering waste water. The opening has mesh on it, so any solid matter will be caught and only liquids make their way into the tank for onward grey water treatment. Organic solids are composted

Source: Peats Ridge Festival

Urination

Excessive amounts of urine can quickly make its way into waterways. Men at events with crowded toilets are often tempted to take a leak in any dark nook or cranny they can find. These dark corners quickly become stinky fly-ridden places. If it rains, the urine makes its way to the water table, especially at those muddy events you often get in the UK. One thing's for sure, you don't want to get any splashback from mud near main stages at these shows.

Increased urine levels in waterways can be extremely harmful to the delicately balanced ecosystems. Think about how easy it is to get the balance of a tropical fish tank out of whack. Thousands of people peeing in a stream will do the same thing.

In order to deter urination on the ground, you need to:

- Provide enough loos.
- Provide urinals for men.
- Site them close to places where large numbers of people will be gathered for a long time.
- Light any dark corners to prevent weeing there.

Glastonbury Festival has a campaign 'Don't Take the Piss' to discourage people urinating on the ground, in bushes and in the streams. The festival also tests the streams three times a day to ensure that no damage is being done and unacceptable amounts of urine hitting them. Over the years they have identified likely spots for renegade weeing, and have either lit these spots, placed installations in them, put signs all over them or put in urinals. The 'Green Police' also stage theatrical arrests, approaching the offender mid-stream, and giving them a cup to finish into, and then escorting them to the nearest toilet, which is usually very close.

Waste Water Management

Waste water can either be disposed of through a sewage treatment plant or directly onto the land. Events that are not connected to municipal sewer lines will need to arrange for their waste water

Figure 5.13 Spring release tap nozzle on hand-wash stations used by Latitude Festival in the UK. The foam in the trough is from the Ecover hand-wash supplied, which is environmentally sound and not harmful to the land

Source: Festival Republic

to be pumped into tankers and taken by road to sewage treatment plants, or to work out a way to dispose of it on site.

Local government and environmental agency regulations will place a restriction on how close grey water collection, sources of grey water creation and grey water disposal points can be to waterways.

The area that acts as an interface between dry land and a stream or river is called the riparian zone. Protecting this very sensitive ecosystem is vital. The plants that live in this zone protect soil erosion, holding banks in place.

Assuming you're not going to send your grey water direct to the sewage treatment plant, you have two options for your grey water:

- Soakaway and surface run-off.
- Grey water treatment and water re-use.

Let's now look at the basics behind these options. As you are dealing with direct emissions to land and water, it's advisable to get expert assistance in setting up your grey water treatment systems. Each region will have different regulations on what level of treatment is necessary and how you can use the resulting recycled water.

Soakaways and Run-Off

Soakaways are basically a big hole dug in the ground which fills up with waste water, and naturally drains away back into the water table. For situations where you have minimal water flow from taps and showers, and you are assured of no chemical contamination to the grey water, you can simply pipe your water away and let it run off, naturally soaking from the surface back into the ground.

Figure 5.14 This system uses a soakaway to drain away the water

Source: Meegan Jones

Soakaways and natural run-offs need to be positioned away from waterways. The soil acts as a natural filter, and as the water drains away, any residue that was in the water will be left in the soil. In using this system for water disposal, it's very important that no chemicals or other contaminants are in the water.

If rather than send your water directly back to nature you re-use it on your land, you will need to store, treat and then re-store it. Treated grey water can be used to flush toilets, for dust suppression or irrigation. Let's look at a couple of ways to treat grey water at your event.

Grey Water Treatment

Grey water treatment processes can use a completely natural system such as a reed bed, or a system of chambers and filters. I have included an overview of reed beds below as I kind of like the idea of them, being so natural. Depending on volumes, consistency of use, etc., a more technical grey water treatment set-up may be the way you end up going. Temporary events that are getting volumes of water at once, need to treat it and get it used, even if it's to give the event grounds a good old watering over a couple of weeks. Of most importance is that you get any solid matter out of the water before it needs to be pumped and filtered.

At **Peats Ridge Festival** in Australia, fresh water is delivered to shower blocks via an underground irrigation pipe system. The fresh water is sourced from a natural groundwater spring under the property. It's pumped into a tank and fed down into the pipe system. Grey water is removed directly from shower blocks and initially stored in 1000-litre pallet tanks. It's then pumped into the underground grey water line to 25,000-litre storage tanks.

Reed Beds

If you have the opportunity to build a reed bed filtration system, you get top marks. In this system reeds (water plants) are planted in a pond with a bed of crushed volcanic stone. Grey water is sent into the pond (once solid matter like ends of carrots have been filtered out or allowed to fall as sediment in a septic tank or preliminary holding tank or pond). The reeds' roots send oxygen back into the pond bed, and the contaminants in the water settle down there and get eaten up by the micro-organisms which thrive on a diet of both. A lovely film grows on the bottom of the reed bed pond. If the combination of the reeds, the micro-organisms and the specially prepared pond bottom of rocks do their job, the result will be lovely clear clean water which can flow out the other end of the pond and into a reserve tank ready to be used for irrigation, flushing loos or other recycled water purposes.

> **Box 5.6**
>
> # At your Event: Water Management
>
> Sustainable water management for your event should include:
>
> ## Chemical-free cleaning products
> - Ensure waste water is chemical free.
> - Food outlets to use chemical-free cleaning products to ensure waste water is not polluted.
> - Chemical-free cleaning products and disinfectants will be used for toilet cleaning.
>
> ## Protection of waterways
> - Set up a grey water catchment system.
> - Arrange the storage and treatment of grey water so it can be recycled and used again at your event site.
> - Ensure the supply of adequate toilets to avoid urination on land and waterways.
> - Gravity feed water where possible to reduce the need for powered water pumps.

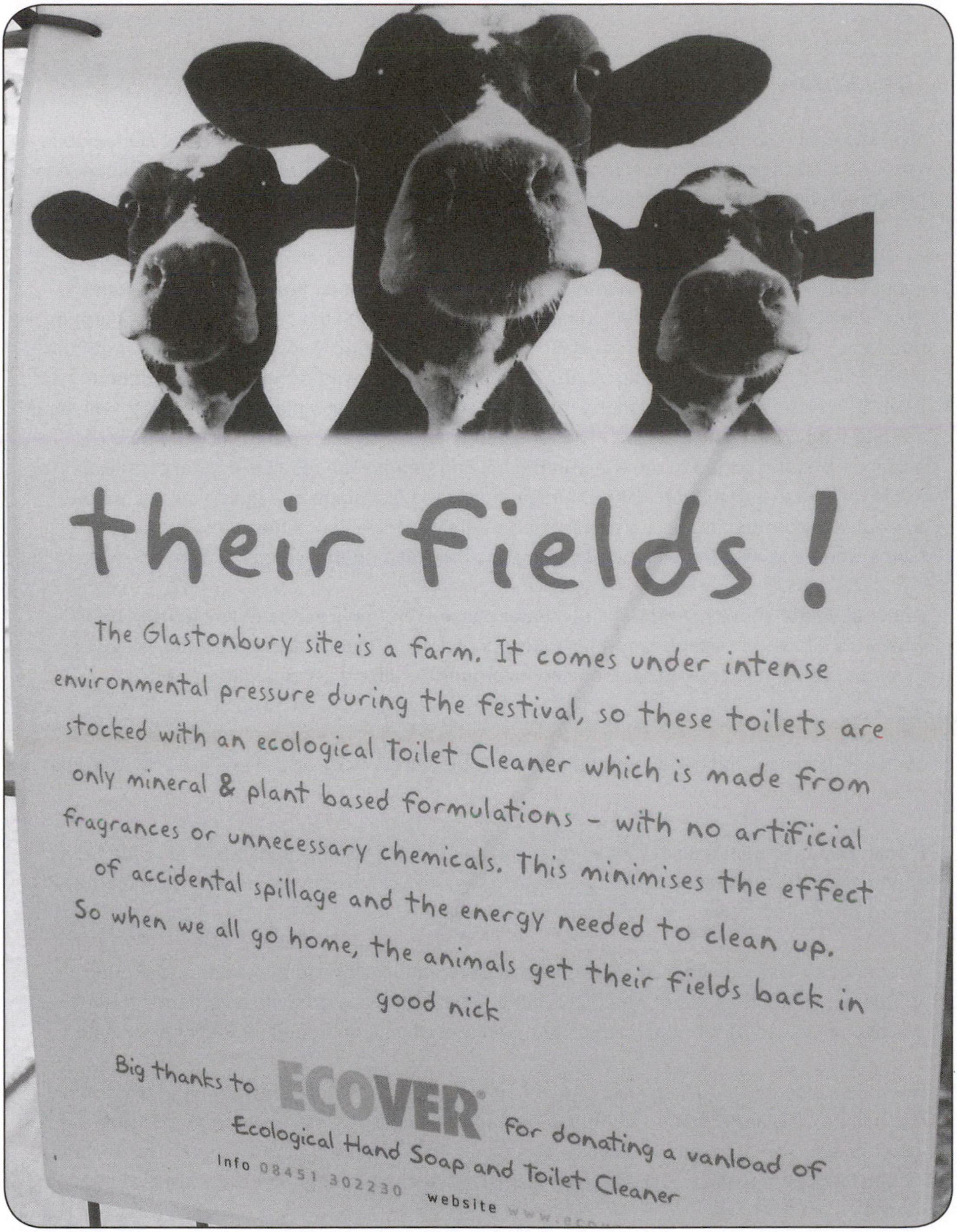

Figure 5.15 Ecover supplies body wash and cleaning products to events in the UK. This partnership helps ensure minimal chemicals hit the grey water and also act as a promotional opportunity for the brand's range of consumer cleaning products

Source: Glastonbury Festival

Box 5.7

Grey Water Management, Boom Festival, Portugal

Over the years Boom has distinguished itself through activities in environmental sustainability. Through a partnership with the Ecocentro IPEC of Brazil, Boom started worldwide pioneering projects to deal with sensitive areas inherent to large-scale events.

At Boom there are biological control and treatment facilities for all residual water. This includes all water from the restaurants, showers and kitchens at the festival. Used water from showers, sinks and all washing can create serious problems of pollution if discharged untreated into the lake. Grey water at Boom is treated through 'evapotranspiration', with the addition of minerals and aquatic plants – a technology that was developed by Ecocentro IPEC. The water passes through the root zone of several aquatic plants where most pollutants are digested by micro-organisms. The remaining minerals are absorbed with the help of enzymes that are added to the water in the holding ponds. The result is crystal clear water ready for re-use in irrigation. Evapotranspiration is the last stage of a biological treatment system. Evapotranspiration is a natural part of the water cycle. It's the sum of natural evaporation and also transpiration by plants as they take up the water.

After use in the showers and sinks the water passes through a series of wet garden beds where it's allowed to evaporate while the roots of aquatic plants clean the water, removing minerals. Later these plants can be used as organic fertilizers on agricultural fields.

The remaining water is stored in a retaining pond specially constructed to allow biological cycles to develop. To speed the process up, a number of micro-organisms are added to the pond water.

Floating aquatic plants also work in digesting some of the excess minerals that come from soaps and other chemicals used by people in the showers. Boom provides environmentally sound products for use in the showers to minimize this.

After enough time has passed, a complete ecosystem develops in the water and around it. This is the natural state of water, providing habitat for many animals and plants, thus sustaining life. No further treatment is required and all environmental regulations are met.

Boom has also installed water saving taps and showers to reduce the amount of water used and still provide appropriate sanitation. The taps are the first step on being responsible for water usage. The complete shower system generates a flux of 50 litres/minute. This means 72,000 litres of grey water per day. All this water is passed through the evapotranspiration system.

By controlling what ends up in grey water, through the use of non-hazardous products, Boom Festival can be certain that the management and disposal of their grey water is not harmful to the delicate arid landscape where the event is held.

Ecocentro IPEC has developed a bespoke solution at Boom Festival taking these natural processes and tailoring a system for the environment of the site.

www.boomfestival.com

Figure 5.16 The lake on the Boom Festival site is well protected by organisers and respected by patrons.

Souce: Jakob Kolar

www.ecocentro.org

Source: Information in this case study has been supplied by Dr André Soares, Ecocentro and Boom Festival

Figure 5.17 Rows of portaloos awaiting custom

Source: Meegan Jones

Toilets

We all have our own toilet horror stories, travelling overseas or at a rock concert. Some people have even been rolled down a hill trapped inside a portable toilet! Toilets at any event with large numbers of people invariably end up in a terrible state and cause untold trauma to those that have experienced the horror face on.

Apart from the personal experiences of all that have crossed the threshold of a stinking sweaty plastic bubble of hell and survived, there are other areas of interest when sustainability comes into play. These are:

- Water use.
- Chemical use.
- Transport of kit and sewage.
- Treatment of sewage.
- Emissions, both methane and CO_2.

If you're an event organizer who is involved in toilet wrangling, it's highly recommended you stop reading now and go out and hire the Australian movie *Kenny*. It will offer you some comic relief, and also a sense of perspective before you delve into the depths of toilet technology.

At indoor events, you won't need to worry too much about toilets. You can request certain products to be used in cleaning them, for the duration of your event, or even go as far as influencing the ongoing products used. You can enquire whether low-flush toilets are used, and what the situation is with urinals.

For outdoor events, we are in a whole different universe. There are many portable toilet options including:

- Portaloos.
- Cabin toilets.
- Long drops.
- Urinals.
- Compost toilets.

Before discussing the different types of toilets in more detail, let's look into the key impact areas for most loos.

Water Use

I am sure you are aware that flushing toilets with unnecessarily large volumes of water, and water that's of drinking quality, is wasteful. Solutions to reducing the impact of the flush at home can include putting a brick or a full bottle of water in the cistern so that it lowers the flush volume. People pee in their gardens, or make home-made nitrogen rich fertilizer. The old 'if it's yellow, let it mellow' is a technique used to reduce flushing volumes in many a hippy household. However none of these solutions is really practical for a large-scale event that needs additional toilets hired in.

The only solution to reducing the volume of water used at your event due to overzealous flushing of water down the loo is to ensure you use:

- Low volume flushing toilets.
- Waterless toilets (composters).
- Waterless urinals.

Chemical Use

Sewage treatment plants use natural biological methods to treat sewage. Large amounts of disinfectant or chemicals in the effluent you send impair the ability of these systems to work. So if your event produces large amounts of sewage that will be taken to a local and relatively small treatment plant, care should be taken to treat your toilets with appropriate products. Check with the local sewage treatment plant if there is any effect your 'deposit' will have on their operations.

The function of the chemicals used in portable toilets is primarily odour masking. It's not always necessary for your toilet supplier to use harsh toxic chemical treatments in their loos. They may have a preference for using a particular product because it's tried and tested, but there are many non-harmful and yet very effective biological alternatives. These include products such as **BioBlue**, **BioGreen** and **Bac to Nature**. Do research to see what options are available for the temporary treatment of toilets. It must be noted, if biological treatments are used, that excessive use of disinfectants to clean the toilets will negate the effectiveness of these natural products.

Another problem in the use of chemical treatment products is health and safety for the toilet workers and cleaners. In the rush of a high pressure event, safe handling of chemicals may not always happen. You need to minimize the risk of accidents, spills and splashes.

Figure 5.18 WaterAid's 'Love Your Loo' campaign at Glastonbury Festival had the twin goals of informing people about worldwide water and sanitation issues, while also getting people to focus on toilet etiquette, and not peeing in the streams and bushes. It also fitted in with the overall campaign for the festival in 2008, which was 'Love the Farm. Leave No Trace'

Source: WaterAid

Transport of Toilets and Sewage

The transport of sewage to treatment plants can have a significant environmental impact. Trucking thousands, sometimes millions of litres of liquid waste from your event to the nearest treatment plant or sewer line access point will add significantly to your overall transport emissions.

Apart from the waste, of course the actual portable toilets must be moved to the event, further adding to the transport emissions impact. You can reduce the transport impact of toilets and sewage by:

- Reducing water for flushing – which significantly reduces transportable sewage waste volumes.
- Choosing portable toilets which fit the largest number of cubicles per lorry.

GHG Emissions

The treatment of sewage has its own recognized emissions factors. This takes into account both the methane which is naturally emitted, along with energy needed to run the processing plants. Information on this is included at the end of this chapter.

Let's now look at the various options for temporary toilets at your event.

Portaloos

Portaloos come in flushing, chemical and (top of my personal 'disgusting' list) the 'recirc' where a urine and chemical cocktail is used as the flushing liquid. Straight chemical loos are like a pit toilet, where a shallow level of chemical

and water is in the holding tank, and no flushing involved. These are the ones that have the rich blue liquid at the bottom and have that distinct smell that wafts over all that pass by. These are also the type where you get the famed mountains of 'bangers and mash' as it were. (If you're not from the UK or Australia, please ignore the previous sentence.)

There are some innovations happening with portaloos such as solar power to provide lighting and power for pumps. The portaloo will probably always be a familiar site at outdoor events as they are cheap to hire, offer an easy solution for the event organizer, and if managed and emptied on time, are generally hassle free. However, sustainable they are not. They take up a lot of space on the back of a truck, thus the transport impact of moving them about is significant. They generally use a chemical toilet 'blue' for odour masking and sanitizing. The waste needs to be evacuated from the holding tank and transported to the sewage treatment plant and the sight of a great gurgling hose straight down the toilet bowl can be kind of off-putting. I've seen these suck trucks accidentally press blow, rather than suck, to the dismay of all around.

Long Drops

The long drops are something developed at UK festivals. This is a large volume self-standing or permanently installed pit toilet, with a massive holding tank, which services a dozen or more individual toilet cubicles. The tank has a shallow level of chemical and water to attempt to mask the smell. They generally are roofless which helps with the stinkiness level. They need emptying at least once a day depending on how hard they are hit.

They are quite large as stand-alone units and thus if they need to be transported from show to show, the impact can be significant. However they are a great solution for large volume capacity. The size of the holding tank means emptying is not needed as frequently as portaloos. They do have the unfortunate feature of someone having to get inside them with a pressure hose to clean them at the end of the show … (A note of acknowledgement to Dean the dunny man at this moment. Dean, well done, but please don't keep coming into the site office mid-job.) They use minimal water as there is no flushing. As they are used, the level of the tank contents rises until it gets to high tide mark, and they are then emptied. The most important thing to remember when using these toilets is 'don't look down'.

Cabin Toilets

Cabin toilets are the swankiest of the lot and come in a variety of options and luxury levels. They are hitched onto the back of a truck and towed to your event. They can be full flushing toilets like you'd have at home, a recirc system as per the portaloos described above, or a low-flush chemical. They have a holding tank at the bottom of the cabin and depending on the length of the event and the usage rate, these will need emptying during the day, or could have enough holding capacity to get through your event.

Urinals

Waterless urinals are a great way of keeping the guys out of the cubicle toilets, keeping the urine separated from the solid waste (when using composting loos) and reducing water consumption if you have flush loos. You should also plan to back up your cubicles with waterless urinals to reduce line-ups at the loos.

Figure 5.19 Long Drop toilets awaiting delivery
Source: Meegan Jones

Compost Toilets

Compost toilets are environmentally friendly alternatives to water or chemical intensive toilets. Essentially a dry toilet, they are chemical free, odour free and if operated at their best, reduce transportable waste by 80–90 per cent.

This reduction in transport of sewage is achieved if the waste is composted on site at your event. That is not as scary as it seems. The sewage is collected in individual tanks under each toilet. The liquid waste (urine) is drained away. Depending on volume, lay of the land, soil type, proximity to waterways, etc., this urine can actually be piped into the ground and left to soak away with no damage to the natural environment, but usually it would be collected in holding tanks and taken away by a sewage truck.

The remaining solid waste (poo, sawdust shavings and toilet paper) stays in the container (generally a wheelie bin or other solid container that's sealable). It is seeded with microbes and worms/worm eggs and sealed shut. The system is aerobic, and there is other hardware

Figure 5.20 Composting toilets at the Falls Festival
Source: Mik la Vage

and expertise needed to get the composting happening, so don't just try and replicate what I have explained above. This is a basic explanation and each type of compost toilet operator uses a slightly different set-up.

Depending on weather conditions, clean compost is available in three to twelve months. For an event that's repeated annually, this is perfect as the bins can be emptied of compost and used in gardens on the event grounds. The empty bins are then ready for use at the next event. The compost that's produced is 'faecal content' free and the process includes testing the final product to prove it's safe for use.

There are a several options in the marketplace to hire in compost loos, and it's likely more toilet operators or enterprising businesses will develop their own solutions as they are just so fantastic. Events that own their own land should seriously consider permanent installation of these units.

Comfy Crappers in the UK have developed a 'pay-to-poo' powder room style toilet set-up. A great solution for events wanting to showcase composting toilets and to offer a boutique toilet experience for their patrons. The whole area is kept spotlessly clean and is a toilet oasis in what is usually a sea of toilet misery. They also set up a precinct which has info about how compost loos work.
www.comfycrappers.com
My favourite for making a real impact on the sustainability of your event are those created by **Natural Event.** This excellent option for outdoor events was developed, tested and perfected in Australia, at mainstream music festivals,

psychedelic trance festivals, ute musters and even at 2007's Live Earth at the Sydney Cricket Ground. They flat-pack, so that there are further savings in transport to the event. They can fit 80 toilets on the same sized truck as 16 portaloos. They operate in Australia, the UK and Europe. www.naturalevent.com.au

These loos have been permanently installed at the **Falls Festival** in Australia. They are flush free and waterless, which saves well over 50,000 litres of fresh drinking water at each event (enough to fill 150,000 beer bottles). By treating and composting the waste onsite, there is no need for transporting and dealing with it in a treatment plant, and it doesn't get pumped out into the ocean. Falls Festival were the first large event to put in this loo technology permanently, and credit must be given to Buzz and the crew for supporting it. This has enabled the mobile version to become a viable option, now expanding around the world.

Box 5.8

At your Event: Toilets

- Use low flushing toilets.
- Use water-free toilets (compost loos).
- Use biological treatments rather than chemical products.
- Compost your sewage waste on site to minimize transport impact of the waste.
- Use the resulting compost to fertilize the land your event is held on.

Figure 5.21 Comfy Crappers toilets are housed in a wooden hut with two toilets back to back. The unit pictured is servicing market stall traders back of house. The capacity in the holding tank means it doesn't need emptying during the show

Source: Meegan Jones

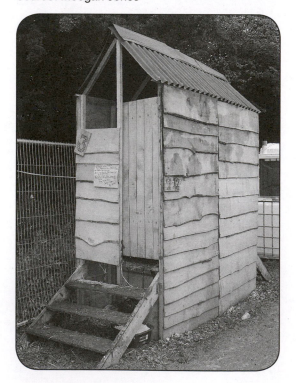

Figure 5.22 The mobile compost toilets are flat-packed and constructed on site. This maximizes the number of toilets that can be transported to the event on one truck
Source: Peats Ridge Festival

Figure 5.23 Filled wheelie bins waiting to be sealed at Meredith Festival in Australia. The bins contain food waste from traders as well as sewage
Source: Natural Event

Box 5.9

Compost Toilets at Boom Festival, Portugal

Boom Festival in Portugal is held in an arid landscape, yet it is by a lake. Water conservation and grey water management are very important. To reduce water use and to produce life-giving compost for the festival's gardens, Boom festival has developed composting toilets.

When a conventional toilet is used, approximately 20 litres of potable water are wasted in discharge. Composting toilets don't use water to flush down the drain. Instead, the waste falls into composting chambers located in the bottom part of the construction, where the biological process solves what would have otherwise been a problem for the festival to dispose of and also for the environment.

After using the toilet, a bit of dry organic matter such as sawdust is added. The mixture of human waste and sawdust initiates the process of composting, responsible for eliminating all of the pathogenic micro-organisms (which can cause diseases).

The process of composting occurs in containers that are sealed with metal, as it retains solar heat. This way, the inner temperature reaches 60 degrees Celsius, enough to guarantee complete elimination of pathogenic micro-organisms. The gases released in this process exit via a central exhaust piping that leaves the air inside the toilet free of odours.

The next step in the system of human waste recycling is to take the compost from the containers to a worm farm so that worms transform the compost into humus. In this digestion process the worm completes the treatment of the compost, making it adequate for use from a vegetable garden to fruit trees.

www.boomfestival.com
www.ecocentro.org

boom festival 08

Source: Information in this case study has been supplied by Dr André Soares, Ecocentro and Boom Festival

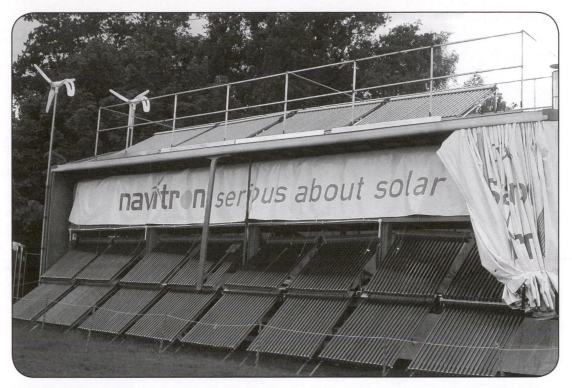

Figure 5.24 Solar heated showers by Navitron
Source: Meegan Jones

Showers

Events that provide showers to their patrons have the dual challenges of water supply and waste water management. Influencing users to reduce water consumption (take short showers) and to use only natural and non-harmful personal products are key.

The main areas that will impact the sustainable management of showers are:

- Devising ways to reduce water consumption.
- Managing grey water.
- Water heating methods.
- User messaging.

In the following pages we look at various options, and also hear from events and contractors which have come up with some fantastic answers to the shower challenge.

Water Heating

It's reported by the UK's **Waterwise** that heating water is responsible for 25 per cent of domestic CO_2 emissions.[3] It makes sense to think that at a commercial level, although maybe not 25 per cent, that water heating (through electricity or gas) will be a significant contributor to CO_2 emissions. If you reduce volume of water consumed for showers, you will reduce the energy needed to heat the water, and consequently the CO_2 emissions.

Options to reduce the impact of water heating for permanent and temporary showers are:

- Coin operated systems so hot water is only available on demand.
- Solar heating.
- Wood pellet heating.
- Instantaneous gas heating.

Permanent Showers

At permanent venues, showers, water supply and waste water systems are likely already in place and event organizers that don't own the venue won't have an opportunity to influence these installations.

Those events held at venues with permanent showering facilities such as sports stadiums, exhibition centres, hotels, conference centres, etc., will need to concentrate on user messaging to encourage reduced water use.

If you're an owner/operator, such as owning the sports field or exhibition centre and also run events there, or an outdoor festival that owns the land, you should be looking to retrofit your water systems. There are many resources available, including websites, books, manuals and of course consultants, to advise you on the best system for your situation. The main points you need to consider are:

Fresh Water Harvesting and Storage

Rainwater tanks should be installed to capture rain from roofs. This water can be used for irrigation, in showers and toilets, and depending on quality, for drinking. Reducing reliance on water supplied through the mains will reduce costs, as well as reduce carbon emissions. Energy is required to capture, store, treat and transport water through municipal supply. Reduce your consumption of mains water, and you reduce your environmental impact.

Water Reduction Mechanisms

Ways to do this are to reduce water pressure, install low-flow shower heads, and put timers on showers. You can use taps which are press and release. These run the shower for about 30 seconds and the user needs to keep pressing the button to re-activate the shower. A fantastic way to reduce demand for a long hot steamy shower.

Grey Water Capture, Treatment and Recycling

Put in a waste water drainage system so grey water doesn't end up with your toilet waste. Capture, store and treat this water, before using it for irrigation, dust suppression or to flush toilets.

Temporary Showers

Things become trickier, and yet much more exciting opportunities present themselves, when you have an event where you must bring in temporary showers. If you own the land your event is on and wish to install permanent showers, water capture and waste water recycling, the options become really interesting and there are even greater opportunities to showcase a model system at work.

Like permanent showers, water supply, water conservation, water heating and waste water management are going to be your main areas of concern.

The options you have are:

- Single unit port-a-showers (look like the loos).
- Cabin showers.
- Shower tents.
- Solar showers.
- Passive solar showers.

Single units, cabin showers and shower tents are all straightforward, mainstream hire-in products. The water is heated by gas or diesel generators supplying electricity to heaters.

The best ways to reduce the impact of these are:

- No hot water.
- Low-flow showerheads.
- Short shower policy.
- Press & release taps.

We move from run of the mill shower solutions to more environmentally conscientious showers when we look to the sun. Solar water heating is available for domestic use and operators (boutique or solar installers) are setting up alternatives for event organizers to use the power of the sun to heat their water.

Navitron Solar Showers are pictured in Figure 5.24. They market domestic solar water heating solutions, along with solar and wind energy products. They have come up with this system to jointly offer events an alternative shower option while also promoting their solar hot water products for the home. Pictured is the heating mechanism. Behind this unit is a shower tent. www.navitron.org.uk

Truly passive water heating can also be used for smaller needs. Any black receptacle such as piping or bladders left lying in the sun will heat water. Get creative and come up with ways to heat water in a DIY fashion. We hear from **Spiral Sun Solar Showers** coming up, who have taken this idea and perfected it for hire to events.

But for now, let's read about the wonderful shower and toilet solution that Greg Peele, self-confessed frustrated wannabe architect, has created for **Meredith Music Festival** and **Golden Plains**, held in a drought affected area in rural Victoria, Australia.

Box 5.10

Water Saving Toilets and Showers at Meredith Music Festival and Golden Plains, Victoria, Australia

Meredith Music Festival and Golden Plains are two annual events held on the same site in rural, semi-cleared bushland, 90km west of Melbourne, in Victoria, Australia in December and March. The venue is a spectacular permanent site, set up specifically for both events, owned and managed by the festival producers. It has been purpose built and continually refined using 18 years of collective know-how to provide a premium experience for performers and patrons.

The festivals both run over two days, with most people camping. Meredith has an audience of 10,000 and Golden Plains 8000. There are many sustainable initiatives at the festivals such as on-site composting of waste, energy efficient lighting and retrofitting underway, and on-site solar powered kitchen with rainwater capture. The focus of this case study however is:

- Permanent composting toilets.
- Harvested water sustainable shower blocks.

The problem

Toilets and showers have long been the bane of the festival goer's generally happy existence. In order to address this and the many operational issues associated with water-based toilets and showers, the festival management decided to build their own on-site permanent infrastructure that's far superior to standard hire-in options. This has improved the comfort and overall experience for festival goers and makes the festival itself easier, cheaper (in the long run) and more enjoyable to operate for management and staff.

Also of consideration is that the Meredith site is in an agricultural and farming area of regional/rural Victoria that gets very little rain. The region is feeling the effects of the ongoing drought and is on stage-four water restrictions. In February 2009, the Meredith site got around 2.5mm of rain compared to the average monthly rainfall of around 8mm. Water is a very valuable and diminishing commodity that people in the area rely on to support their livelihoods. It's therefore vital for the festival to play its role in the community and utilize resources in a manner that's befitting the values of the community. Similarly, it could be said that if the festival was using water unwisely to facilitate the activities of people outside the close community (festival goers), it could create tensions within other members of the community who might resent resources being used for such activities at the cost of their farms and livestock. However, as the festival has implemented best practice examples of water use, there can be no reason for the festival to get anything but support from the community.

Pre-production planning

Greg Peele, the festival's co-director and site manager, essentially did the planning and design of the toilets and showers. Greg is a builder and self-described frustrated 'wannabe' architect. He conceived and designed the units and called on the festival crew to come on site at various times of year to work on the projects and build them.

Prior to the build, relevant authorities were contacted for planning and regulatory approval. Given the long history of the festival, its excellent management record and support for local organizations, the local council is generally receptive and willing to work with the event on projects of this nature.

The new showers are completely private, sheltered, eco-friendly installations, and provide steaming hot water (or cold if it's hot) from low-flow yet good pressure shower heads.

Figure 5.25 The showers

Toilets

The composting toilets are a permanent version of the mobile solution for events developed by Natural Event (www.naturalevent.com.au). The major difference between these composting toilets and those at other events using the same system is that they are permanent site infrastructure. Generally, Natural Event flat-packs the toilet infrastructure and transports it to the next event, but leaving the full bins of waste to compost on site. Although the toilet infrastructure is permanent, the waste is still captured in the same bins as the mobile version and composted by worms and mixed with food waste from the event. Once this has processed for a year, the end product can be used as compost on the festival land. The wheelie bins which capture the waste sit under the toilet platform, and need to be changed over only once over the course of the two-day event. Once the first wheelie bin is full, it's moved to another area on site where the liquid is drained and the remaining solid waste material is left for composting.

There are currently about 100 of these private, waterless, odourless composting beauties at the festival, built permanently into two separate areas either side of the amphitheatre.

Figure 5.26 The compost loos

Results

The water used in the toilets is around 45,000 litres per event. This is down markedly on the 250,000 litres that used to be used on the portable water consuming toilets hired and transported to the site. The water previously had to be harvested on site, used in the toilets and then taken by trucks off site to a depot for processing. Now, the festival organizers save huge amounts of water that can be then used and re-used on site through showers and grey water systems, not to mention the reductions in transport emissions as the waste does not have to be transported off site.

Set up is also easier. The event doesn't have trucks coming to and from the event, reducing congestion and traffic management on site during the show.

The cost of the toilets will be recouped in around four years. Initially when management considered building the toilets, they thought the payback would be around ten years. However, more analysis of costs beyond just the toilet hire which looked at waste disposal, labour to clean and manage the toilets, trucks, management of installations and delivery, plumbers and electricians created an estimated payback on the investment in the toilets of around four years.

In addition to the business case, the composting toilets receive a very favourable response from punters, create a compost product that can be used on the festival land and they are a lot easier to manage and clean. More toilets will be built in the coming years so no water-based toilets will need to be used at the event again.

Showers

There are two shower blocks, with each block containing 16 showers. All of the water for the showers is harvested on site and the grey water produced is re-used on site. They use instantaneous gas hot water heaters, with one water heater for four showers. The showers are relatively self-sufficient and are coin operated with punters paying a dollar a minute for a shower. There are attendants on site who distribute tokens and ensure they are used in an orderly manner and give out biodegradable soaps and shampoos which help the waste water re-enter the earth with a minimum of fuss.

Results

Water from the roof of the shower blocks is captured in 22,000-litre water tanks next to each block throughout the year. When these fill up the water is then pumped to a 180,000-litre central water tank up a hill.

When events are on, the larger tank gravity feeds into the smaller ones for use. The shower waste water feeds into a grey-water system and is used for irrigation on site. Water from the tanks is also used for the taps for punters to wash their hands.

The use of rainwater for the showers and handwashing saves around 70,000 litres of water per event per shower block.

Initial figures put the payback on the showers at around 12 years. However, given how well the showers have been received, people are more inclined to take a shower as they are a lot more inviting than portable units.

Tips and hints for new players

Greg Peele encourages people to 'get in and do it'. Once you've started and are in there getting the job done and making progress, things aren't as hard as they may have seemed from the outset. Do research and study as much as you can before you act. There's help out there when you need it, look around and ask others.

Look at the overall cost of what you want to do, it might seem expensive, but when you look at all of the expenses that constitute an event, it makes good business sense to plan and build for the long term and be sustainable with your resources.

www.mmf.com.au

www.goldenplains.com.au

Source: Information for this case study provided by Greg Peele (Meredith Music Festival Director) and Liam O'Keefe (Creative Environment Enterprises (CEE). CEE are Sustainability Consultants to the Meredith crew). Photos: Mik la Vage

Box 5.11

Spiral Sun Solar Showers

Spiral Sun Solar Showers have been built specifically for the outdoor festival market as a way of providing hot showers to campers without having gas heating or diesel generators powering hot water heaters.

They use passive solar water heating systems to provide the hot water. The showers have a central cubicle which sits inside a tipi and acts like a greenhouse. The passive solar collectors are spirals of black plastic pipe (as pictured below) sitting between the interior shower cubicle and the exterior tipi. The sun heats the water in the pipes, which snake their way up to the top of the tipi and out of the shower. Each solar shower head is controlled by a hot and cold mixer valve so water temperature can be adjusted to desired levels.

Part of the aim of Spiral Sun Solar Showers is to help raise public awareness of the potential for alternative technologies by providing attractive facilities they can use and complementing any similar eco-friendly messages event organizers wish to convey.

Each solar shower unit services two cubicles; a solar collector tent with an inner cubicle and an attached outdoor cubicle. The inner cubicle provides a draught-free warm environment and a reassuring sense of seclusion. The outer cubicle provides for the pleasant experience of showering in fresh air. Both cubicles can be used at the same time. Spiral Sun Solar Shower performance in sunny weather is comparable to gas powered trailer/ electric powered portaloo types. In poor weather or early mornings the solar showers use a wood fired water heating system to compensate for the lack of sunshine.

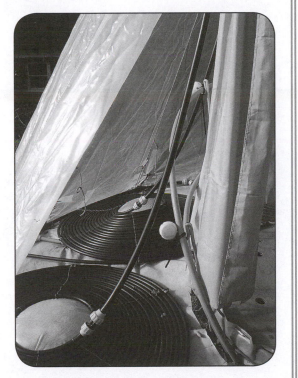

Figure 5.27 Coiled pipe heating water

www.spiralsun.co.uk

Source: Information and photos supplied by David Wick of Spiral Sun Solar Showers.

Figure 5.28 Spiral Sun Solar Showers

Key Sustainability Indicators

To measure your performance and set Key Sustainability Indicators for water management, you need to measure:

- Volume of water used in m³.
- Volume of sewage produced in m³.
- Volume of grey water produced in m³.
- GHG emissions from water production.
- GHG emissions from sewage treatment.
- GHG emissions from water heating.

You can also measure:

- Transport impact of sewage cartage.
- Transport impact of fresh water delivered by tanker.

Water Volume

Getting this figure should be straightforward. Ask for a meter reading by the venue owner before and after your event. If you have an outdoor site with plumbing contractors on the job, make sure you pre-warn them that you want this information post event.

Sewage Volume

Measuring sewage volume at indoor events with flushing toilets won't really be possible. If you want, you can get general estimate figures of how many times a day someone goes to the loo multiplied by the volume of each flush of the toilet.

For events that need cartage of sewage, this will be an easy figure to obtain from your contractor. If you are using composting toilets, you should do a comparison on how much would have been sent to the sewage treatment plant if you had normal loos.

Grey Water

If your waste water ends up with your sewage, down the drain or into a suck truck for haulage, the explanation above fits. However, if you are capturing grey water, treating and recycling it, you should take accurate measures of volume so you can report on energy and transport saved in treatment if sent with sewage. Also report on its re-use, and replacing the need to use fresh water.

CO_2 Emissions

It's a relatively simple process to calculate CO_2 emissions as a result of water production, heating and sewage treatment. Take the figures in m³ and multiply them by the emissions factor below, or use diesel, gas or mains power used to heat the water.

Water and Sewage Emissions Factors

Water (production)

0.2710kg CO_2 per m^3 water production

Sewage (treatment)

0.4760kg CO_2 per m^3 sewage treatment

Note: there are a thousand litres in a cubic metre.

Source: Water UK Sustainability Indicators 2006–2007

Notes

1   The **Food and Agriculture Organization** (FAO) of the United Nations reports that water usage has been growing at more than twice the rate of population increase in the last century and that by 2025, 1.8 billion people will be living in countries or regions with absolute water scarcity and two-thirds of the world population could be under stress conditions. FAO, www.fao.org/nr/water/issues/scarcity.html, accessed January 2009.

2   FAO, www.fao.org/nr/water/issues/scarcity.html, accessed January 2009.

3   Waterwise UK, www.waterwise.org.uk, accessed January 2009.

Figure 6.1 Installation by Tracey Shough part of the Green Way at Glastonbury Festival.

Source: Reproduced with the permission of Tracey and Glastonbury Festival

chapter 6

Purchasing and Resource Use

Purchasing and resource use are two powerful players in the overall and eventual sustainability of an event. A mountain of 'stuff' is needed to run most events, much with a once-only use. Purchase decisions are made every day in the pre-production phase, and the right choices need to be made to reduce the impacts of consumption.

Events can play their part in resource conservation, reducing consumption, and product redesign, and I hope to inspire you to take these issues on board at your event. Using recyclable materials, re-use and closing the loop are all ways to reduce the environmental consequences of your purchasing. Choosing organic, buying fair trade, buying locally and using products with low carbon footprints are all steps along the sustainable procurement path.

This chapter discusses purchasing and the way your decisions can be altered to make a more sustainable future for your event and for the Earth. We look at ways to green your supply chain, at the impacts of consumption, and environmental, ethical and socially responsible purchasing. Also discussed is the climate impact of purchasing. We'll look at the full life cycle impact of products and materials. Eco-labelling is demystified to help you use these programmes to inform your purchase decisions.

The questions you need to ask when deciding to buy something are:

- Where did the product come from?
- Who made the product?
- What is it made of?
- What does it come packaged in?
- How will it be disposed of or could it be used again?

Let's now look at how this can be put into practice at your event.

Impact of Consumption

The materials and supplies we use to produce our events, especially those products with a one-way and short-lived life span, affect the potential for a sustainable future and deplete resources. Most events are for enjoyment, for entertainment, for celebration. Some are hedonistic in nature, and could be viewed as indulgent. Of course without celebration, an opportunity for release, expression and creativity, to share ideas, participate in sporting achievements or promote new concepts, what would we have? No matter the reason for your event, there is a responsibility that should be carried by event managers to purchase with sustainability in mind. When making purchase decisions, be mindful of the impact on the environment and community. This is through:

- The product's life cycle right from the extraction or growing of raw materials.
- The impact on community and neighbours of growing and production.
- The distance raw materials and products travel.
- How workers are treated and growers paid.
- Whether your purchase decisions add to the depletion of natural resources and pollution.

We're using more than our planet can give us, we're eating into our capital investment, earning no interest and our nest egg is shrinking. The amount of stuff we personally buy in our lives, let alone in association with putting on events, is causing depleted resources, polluting waterways and contributing to climate change. The by-product of all of this consumption is waste. And waste equals climate change. The climate change potential of a one-way system of resource use, manufacture, transport, product consumption and disposal is immense. Every step along the way is causing greenhouse gas (GHG) emissions and the depletion of non-renewable resources. The demand for more stuff means more mining, more transport and more land clearing, all of which are contributors to climate change. As discussed in Chapter 7 on waste and climate change impact, the end product and its actual disposal is just the tip of the iceberg. Behind every product lies a story of resource extraction, toxic waste, energy consumed and fuel burnt, snowballing waste at every step, and possibly a large number of underpaid workers, displaced communities and destroyed ecosystems. Unless you dig into this shady history of the lovely fresh box of what-have-yous that you've ordered in for your event, you can very easily close your eyes to the likely consequence of your purchase decisions. It's hidden from you, hidden from view, and unless you question their origin and impacts, you'll never know. It's easy not to ask these questions. But it's your responsibility to ask them.

Please, ask questions. And then act.

If you're ready to ask, I'm sorry but it's very possible you won't like the answers. Putting it into a personal perspective, it's easy to buy a lamb chop on a plastic tray from the supermarket, but if you had to look the lamb in the eye and slaughter it, could you?

Similarly, would you like to watch the back-breaking work of indentured labour in cocoa plantations, while snacking on a chocolate bar made from the product produced from their hard labour? If you had to go to the river and watch the toxic chemicals flow from a manufacturing plant, causing chaos downstream to ecosystems and human health, would you enjoy that? Could you stand in a factory amongst underpaid workers watching them produce the products you screwed your supplier down to his 'best price' for?

Apart from discovering the potentially shady past of the products you may purchase, you need to consider the future of them as well. Some of the questions you'll need to ask are:

- Is the product re-usable or more durable?
- Is it made from recycled materials or sustainably produced materials?
- What is the end-of-life plan for the product?
- Can it be recycled, re-used, composted or returned to the manufacturer?
- Will mountains of landfill be created, or will your 'waste' become valuable resources, closing the loop?
- Is any special handling in the disposal necessary?
- Does the product conserve energy or water?
- Does the product meet the relevant eco-labelling certification?

We can vote with our dollars, buying responsibly produced products, ones that are sustainable, considerate of the environment, that look after their workers, and pay a fair price to producers. We can buy products made from recyclable materials and that are also recyclable. We can ensure they are in fact recycled. We can reduce consumption by re-using and repairing.

The incessant search for material comforts and their multiplication is such an evil, and I make bold to say that the Europeans themselves will have to remodel their outlook, if they are not to perish under the weight of the comforts to which they are becoming slaves.

Mahatma Gandhi, 1931

Box 6.1

Responsible Purchasing Checklist

Create a purchasing policy including:

- Sustainably grown.
- Locally produced.
- Recycled content.
- Re-used materials.
- Certified organic.
- Fair wear.
- Fair labour.
- Fair trade.
- Chemical free.

Identify the items likely to be used at your event that can be ethically sourced and/or the most environmentally preferable, including:

- Foods – e.g. tea, coffee, sugar, chocolate, rice, bananas.
- Timber.
- Paper.
- Fabric.
- Garments.
- Merchandise.
- Paint.
- Cleaning products.
- Handicrafts.
- Electronics.
- Consumer products.

Go organic, fair trade, environmentally sound, ethical

- Make a commitment within your event's production office to environmentally and ethically preferable purchasing.
- Make a commitment for all food and merchandise traders to go organic, fair trade and/or ethically produced.
- Make a commitment with contractors that they will also embrace these policies.

Buy Less

Buying the most environmentally and socially responsible products for your event is all well and good. But we must also consider just how much stuff is needed.

- Do you need to have new fencing scrim every year?
- Do you need to hand out an additional 100,000 promotional flyers creating more litter, when different advertising opportunities are available?
- Do you need to have stalls selling useless crappy items?
- With some extra organization and people power, can you salvage, store and re-use materials from your event breakdown?
- Can you divert materials from landfill by pre-identifying potential waste streams and redirecting them to salvage for another off-site use?

Look seriously at your purchasing habits. It's very easy to detach from the reality of purchasing when you are using someone else's money, and the only thing between you and the production of thousands of dollars worth of materials is a purchase order sent down the fax machine. Understand that every 'OK' on a purchase order means the mining up of resources, transport and manufacture, energy consumed, GHG emissions and waste.

Conscious Consumption

Making conscience purchasing decisions is so very important. Take time to think through and investigate the upstream impacts of your intended purchases, along with the consequential end-of-life disposal.

- Are the activities at your event promoting needless consumption to your audience?
- Do the product placement or sponsorship deals you make promote less than responsible brands?
- Are your activities buying into the one-way flow of resource use, consumption and disposal?
- Can you come up with a better model?

Boom Festival in Portugal is a logo-free consumption environment. This encourages a culture of change, conscience and responsibility. The food establishments at the festival are rigorously selected in order to provide the best quality and diversity, but above all, healthy choices. A great part of the Boom economy is based on human creativity and the concept of bioregionalism, which also strengthens the local economy.

Burning Man is money free. Everything works on gifting. Almost like the pay-it-forward concept. Everyone comes armed with the 'stuff' they are willing to gift. Strangers are invited to share food, and no money changes hands. You give to someone and another person gives to you. Food, jewellery, bikes. Beautiful.

Purchasing Policy

Establishing a written purchasing policy highlighting all the likely purchasing categories and impact areas is a useful process. For one-off events, it may be as simple as putting a sign up on the wall reminding everyone to purchase FSC timber, recycled paper, eco paint, green cleaning products, etc.

For those of you with multiple events, and large and continual year-round purchasing, a more thorough policy should be established. Here's what to consider in your policy:

Commitment and Overall Goals

- State your commitment to sustainable purchasing, list the stakeholders and decision makers.
- Highlight any quantifiable goals.
- Detail any specific elements particular to your situation.
- Include your intentions on buying re-usable, refillable, durable and repairable goods.

Energy and Emissions

- Technology and electronic equipment. including energy star ratings.
- Vehicle choices – purchasing and hire.
- Travel policy and offsetting.
- Lighting, low energy.
- Heating and cooling.

Water

- Low-flow and efficient products.

Toxins and Pollutants

- Cleaning products.
- Paints and varnishes.
- Printing inks.
- Pest control.

Forest Conservation

- Timber.
- Paper products.
- Coffee, tea and other rainforest crops.

Recycling and Re-Use

- Choose products and packaging made from recycled materials.
- Choose products that can be recycled at end of life.
- Actively source salvaged products for creative re-use.
- Send your used products for re-use.

Biodegradability

- Consumables.
- Food.
- Waste management.

Local Supply and Product Miles

- Buy local first.
- Buy products made in your country from materials grown, mined or created in your country.

Fair Trade and Fair Production

- Buy products which pay a fair wage/price.
- Buy products manufactured under fair labour conditions.

Greenwashing

When deciding to 'go green' in your purchasing you need to be aware of greenwashing. It's where companies appropriate terms such as 'eco', 'natural', 'green', 'biological', but don't have any substance to back up their claims. Scrutinize the claims and ask questions if they are vague or have no certification apparent.

In an effort to describe, understand and quantify the growth of greenwashing, **TerraChoice** conducted a survey of six category-leading stores. They identified 1018 consumer products bearing 1753 environmental claims, and all but one made claims that are demonstrably false or misleading. As at result, they put together the Six Sins of Greenwashing. They are reproduced in the following box.

Life Cycle Impact

The bedrock of any sustainable purchasing policy has to be consideration for product life cycle impact. Every product leaves its mark on the environment from extraction of raw materials and their transport and processing, to the manufacturing, distribution, sale and use of the product, and of course its ultimate disposal or return to the manufacturing system through recycling. To move towards sustainable management, it's essential to consider the full life cycle environmental impact of the products you choose to use to produce your event, or indeed those you sell to your audience at the event.

It may be daunting to consider this kind of research into the products used; however, in these pioneering days of sustainable event management, the questioning and consideration of the full life cycle impact of purchase decisions by event producers is essential. Looking at the products you use or sell at your event, the materials they're made from, the impact of their manufacture and the welfare of those that grow and manufacture the goods, is essential to making informed and environmentally considerate purchase decisions.

You'll be helping to grow the market for sustainable alternatives and hopefully push those that are not, out.

Product Life Cycle Assessment

A life cycle assessment (LCA) is a technique used to assess the environmental aspects and potential impacts associated with a product. You can use this increasingly popular assessment method to find out what the impact of a product or material you propose to use is. You don't need to actually run the research yourself, as a quick search on the internet should reveal reports on the product you're interested in. The basic idea behind an LCA is to look at the energy, materials used and resulting emissions and by-products to land, air and water. An LCA evaluates the potential environmental impacts of the resource use and emissions or by-products, and then interprets the results to make a final assessment and recommendation.

There's an international standard on LCA technique in the ISO 14000 series – ISO 14040 – which regulates the assessment technique for those undergoing an LCA.[1] A full LCA is generally lengthy and technical, such as the one on PVC by the **European Commission**.[2] But you will also be able to find extracts, summaries and interpretations, which should provide you with adequate information to make an informed purchase decision. Of course you do need to be aware that some organizations may have a vested interest in providing a favourable LCA, so do check the source of the study. Depending on your product you may need to see if an LCA has been done on the product itself or also the materials it's made of.

Luckily there is legislation in most countries that regulates manufacture of certain products, the allowable emissions and use of certain materials and substances. You do still need to do your own diligent investigation into products you think may be of concern or whose use could go against the policies and goals you have put in place for your event. Helpfully, carbon 'labels' are starting to appear. Just like ingredients or calories, the label states the carbon footprint of the product's manufacture. Look out for the UK Carbon Trust's new 'Carbon Label'. More on this coming up.

Ecological Footprinting

Footprinting is a popular concept. It allows you to visualize in physical proportions, the impact of a particular activity by a given measure. A carbon footprint is expressed in kilograms or tonnes of CO_2. Gas is a hard thing to think of in terms of weight, so for illustrative purposes, it's often then reinterpreted into something that's easy to comprehend. **C Change**[3] has a great way of explaining the weight — by elephants. The 'Face your Elephant' concept explains that in the UK 6 million tonnes of CO_2 are emitted annually, which is the equivalent weight of 2 million elephants. C Change's Face your Elephant interactive display tours festivals in the UK and talks to young people about facing their elephant. It's a great way of reinterpreting a scientific concept into one that's easy to comprehend by most people.

Whereas a carbon footprint refers to CO_2 emissions which result from various human activities, the concept of sustainable development as a holistic approach has its own footprinting concept — the ecological footprint. Calculating an ecological footprint gives an insight into how our consumption of stuff and consequential natural resource use relates to the biological productivity potential of the Earth. The Earth can only produce so much and an ecological footprint shows how much of the Earth and its potential for creating natural resources is required to carry out the production of a particular activity or industry, or to support a country's demands, or in fact the entire world population. It ends up with how many hectares per person are needed to support our current lifestyle. An ecological footprint is of course a symbolic concept. Land and sea won't be carved up per person, but it's a fantastic tool to get a snapshot of where we are headed and an indicator of the impacts of sustainability programmes.

If you're considering assessing your personal or event's ecological footprint, there are many consultancies and agencies, tools and resources you can look at. The **Global Footprint Network**[4] is working towards regulating ecological footprinting methodologies so that comparing results across industries is possible. If various methodologies and measures are used, then the tool becomes significantly weakened.

The 'Living Planet Report'[5] produced by **WWF** and **Global Footprint Network** lists all the biologically productive land on the planet. They have assessed that the Earth's capacity for biological production (biocapacity) is 11.3 billion global hectares, which is only about 22 per cent of the Earth's surface. The rest is non-arable land such as the desert, or places where biological productivity for human use doesn't occur such as in high mountains and the deep ocean. Of course some of the land potential needs to remain untouched to support the Earth's biodiversity, and the report suggests 10 per cent for this, leaving total global hectares of potentially biologically productive land and sea at 10.17 billion. That's all we've got. So being sensitive to what share of this finite resource the activities you're involved in use up should become part of your thinking. It's simple maths really. How much could the Earth supply, how many people are there, and how much stuff do they need to be produced to survive. A very important part of this maths formula is time. How long do we want to keep using stuff and how long does it take for the Earth to replenish the stuff we drag out of it? If we use too much, too soon, we're either going to run out in our lifetime, or our inheritance to our children and grandchildren will be depleted resources and an empty planet. Lovely.

When calculating an ecological footprint, matters such as direct energy used, materials usage and resulting waste, transport impact and water usage are taken into account. Although we have these potential 10.17 billion global hectares to play with, it's further split into land that is built on, land that is used to produce energy (mines, wind farms, power facilities, etc.), and finally land and sea capable of biological productivity.

Just like a farmer knows how many head of cattle or sheep a hectare of land can sustain, the Living Planet Report has assessed, based on our current rate of consumption, what land and sea mass is needed to sustain us, given our current population and consumption rates. In 2001 it was sitting at 1.21. That's 1.21 times the amount of available biological productive land and sea we currently have. Clearly not a sustainable scenario. We're logging forests, burning fossil fuel reserves, depleting oceans, over-farming land, mining up minerals, etc. to feed our demand, and we are doing this by dipping into our capital, rather than living off the interest.

The **One Planet Living** (OPL) initiative, developed by **WWF** and **Bioregional**,[6] offers practical solutions to living within our fair share of the planet's resources. Ecological footprint studies tell us that if everyone on the planet lived like those in the US, we'd need five planets to support us and that overall, humanity consumes 30 per cent more than the planet's biocapacity. WWF have created guidelines following the OPL principles of sustainability (developed jointly with Bioregional Development Group) to help events organizers to reduce events' ecological footprint.

Read their objectives, reprinted with the kind permission of WWF in Table 6.1. Access their tips on www.panda.org/opl/events.

Event Ecological Footprinting

It may be outside the scope of most live events to calculate their ecological footprint, though impressively, this is exactly what Radiohead commissioned for their 2003 amphitheatre tour and their 2006 theatre tour. It can be viewed at the following address: www.radiohead.com/radiohead_bff.zip.

The team that did this, **Best Foot Forward**, based in the UK, have developed an online footprinting tool for events. For those event organizers who feel they need to establish a footprint, perhaps to report to a client or to consider offsetting, this can be a useful tool.
www.event.footprinter.com

More on the footprinting and its relevance to events in the section in Chapter 1.

Table 6.1 One Planet Living Events

ONE PLANET LIVING EVENTS		
GLOBAL CHALLENGE	**ONE PLANET LIVING PRINCIPLE**	**ONE PLANET LIVING GOAL FOR EVENTS**
Climate change due to human-induced build up of carbon dioxide (CO_2) and other greenhouse gases in the atmosphere	**Zero Carbon**	**Achieve zero net CO_2 emissions** All energy demand (infrastructure, lighting, music, IT, etc.) is supplied from on-site renewable sources, topped up by new off-site renewable supply where necessary
Waste from discarded products and packaging creates a huge disposal challenge while squandering valuable resources	**Zero Waste**	**Eliminate waste flows to landfill and for incineration** Reduce waste generation through careful products offer at the event. Encourage re-use, recycling and composting; generate energy from waste cleanly; eliminate the concept of waste as part of a resource -efficient society
Travel by car and airplane can cause climate change, air and noise pollution, and congestion	**Sustainable Transport**	**Reduce reliance on private vehicles and achieve major reductions of CO2 emissions from transport** Provide transport systems and infrastructure that reduce dependence on fossil fuel use, e.g., by cars and airplanes. Offset unavoidable carbon emissions from air travel and perhaps car travel
Destructive patterns of resource exploitation and use of non-local materials in construction and manufacture increase environmental harm and reduce gains to the local economy	**Local and Sustainable Materials**	**Transform materials supply to the point where it has a net positive impact on the environment and local economy** Where possible, use local, reclaimed, renewable and recycled materials in construction and products, which minimizes transport emissions, spurs investment in local natural resource stocks and boosts the local economy and reduces transport impacts
Industrial agriculture produces food of uncertain quality and harms local ecosystems, while consumption of non-local food imposes high transport impacts	**Local and Sustainable Food**	**Transform food supply to the point where it has a net positive impact on the environment, local economy and peoples' well-being** Prefer local and low-impact food production that provides healthy, quality food while boosting the local economy in an environmentally beneficial manner; showcase examples of low-impact packaging, processing and disposal; highlight benefits of a low-impact diet

ONE PLANET LIVING EVENTS		
GLOBAL CHALLENGE	**ONE PLANET LIVING PRINCIPLE**	**ONE PLANET LIVING GOAL FOR EVENTS**
Local supplies of fresh water are often insufficient to meet human needs due to pollution, disruption of hydrological cycles and depletion of existing stocks	**Sustainable Water**	**Achieve a positive impact on local water resources and supply** Implement water use efficiency measures, re-use and recycling; minimize water extraction and pollution; foster sustainable water and sewage management in the landscape; restore natural water cycles.
Loss of biodiversity and habitats due to development in natural areas and overexploitation of natural resources	**Natural Habitats and Wildlife**	**Regenerate degraded environments and halt biodiversity loss** Protect or regenerate existing natural environments and the habitats they provide for fauna and flora; create new habitats. Ensure that outdoor events do not impact negatively on local biodiversity.
Local cultural heritage is being lost throughout the world due to globalization, resulting in a loss of local identity and wisdom	**Culture and Heritage**	**Protect and build on local cultural heritage and diversity** Celebrate and revive cultural heritage and the sense of local and regional identity; choose structures and systems that build on this heritage; foster a new culture of sustainability.
Investment in new communities is often not targeted at local economic development and does not maximize the use of local resources	**Equity and Fair Trade**	**Ensure that the event has positive economic links with the wider local and global community** Prefer local production and supply of goods for the event. Promote equity and fair trading relationships to ensure the event has a beneficial impact on other communities both locally and globally, notably disadvantaged communities.
Rising wealth and greater health and happiness increasingly diverge, raising questions about the true basis of well-being and contentment	**Health and Happiness**	**Increase health and well-being of all event participants/attendants and others** Promote healthy lifestyles and physical, mental & spiritual well-being through well designed structures and community engagement measures, as well as by delivering on social and environmental targets.

Visit www.panda.org/opl/events for more details, tips for event organizers and updates on WWF's One Planet Living Initiative.

Source: Reproduced with the permission of WWF

 **Product Redesign**

The products that currently exist only in the minds of cutting edge designers will soon be available for us to use. The vision for sustainable design is products that are completely recyclable, that don't hurt the environment, are free of toxic substances, perform better, and last longer, rather than being designed for obsolescence.

Only through drastic changes in the design and manufacture of stuff can we see a future of sustainable resource use. There are simply too many people in this world who want to buy stuff, and we just don't have enough natural resources to feed this demand. We have to get smarter. We have only one planet, no spare. We need to close our loops, setting up resource and product systems that feed each other in endless cycles.

You can do your bit right now to help us move to this sustainable future through purchasing ethically, socially and environmentally responsible products. By doing this, you're adding to demand for these products and helping to create healthy and viable markets for this new and necessary generation of product redesign. Look for opportunities to trial a newly designed product, or even solicit the development of a product to suit your purpose. By voting with your dollars you are showing there is a market for these new sustainable solutions.

Cradle to Cradle^{sm}

The **Cradle to Cradle**^{SM} (C2C) approach looks to reorient the design of products and systems so that one feeds into the other. Products are designed with their eventual end-of-life purpose in mind so materials can flow in continual closed loops. An important part of the design process is ensuring the product's component parts and materials can be easily disassembled and separated from each other so extraction of valuable secondary resources is possible and cost effective.

C2C design was developed by William McDonough and Michael Braungart through their company **MBDC**. They have also developed a 'C2C Certification' that 'provides a company with a means to tangibly, credibly measure achievement in environmentally-intelligent design and helps customers purchase and specify products that are pursuing a broader definition of quality'.

McDonough and Braungart envisage a paradigm shift to the 'Next Industrial Revolution' in which products and services are designed based on patterns found in nature, eliminating the concept of waste entirely and creating an abundance that's healthy and sustaining. 'Eco-effectiveness' is MBDC's design strategy for realizing these results by optimizing materials to be food either for nature's ecosystems or for humans' industrial systems – perpetually circulating in closed systems that create value and are inherently healthy and safe.

Cradle to Cradle certification means:

- Using environmentally safe and healthy materials.
- Design for material reutilization, such as recycling or composting.
- The use of renewable energy and energy efficiency.
- Efficient use of water, and maximum water quality associated with production.
- Instituting strategies for social responsibility.

www.c2ccertified.com

Figure 6.2 Cradle to Cradle CertifiedCM is a certification mark of MBDC

Cradle-to-Cradle Concept at Events?

Embrace the concept of the closed loop:

- Keep an eye on the ever increasing number of C2C certified products.
- Envisage the next life the materials used at your event could have and set in play the means to make it happen.

For example:

- Can your banners be recycled?
- Is the material that masks your fencing able to be recycled?
- Can you request metal banding rather than nylon on palletized deliveries of fencing so that it can be put straight into the metals skip?
- Work with your supply chain to design-in end-of-life intent and get them thinking about closing their production loops.

Whenever a purchase is made, consider its final disposal and whether it's designed for a very short single use and then to be sent straight to landfill. Rather, if to be used for a single purpose and then would be discarded, is the product made of an optimum material and in such a way that it can be easily broken down into its component parts and recycled, returning to the manufacturing cycle as valuable secondary materials?

Figure 6.3: Organic cotton production in India
Source: Continental Clothing. www.continentalclothing.com

Environmentally Responsible Purchasing

Choosing products that have been manufactured with care for the environment is imperative to meet your sustainable event management objectives.

In the following pages we look at how to reduce the environmental impact of your purchasing, including eco-labelling, organics, local procurement, sustainable agriculture and the climate impact of purchasing.

For a product to be environmentally responsible you need to consider the following:

- The immediate environmental impact of the extraction or growing production of raw materials.
- Pollution and emissions from materials production and product manufacture.

These impacts can be countered through:

- Minimizing toxic materials used.
- Minimizing waste.
- Conservation of energy and water.
- Ensuring the use of renewable resources and consideration for the depletion of natural resources.

- Using materials that can be recycled and contain recycled content.

There are many tools that you can use to ensure the purchase decisions are the most environmentally sensitive possible. Eco-labelling is one such tool. This certification system addresses the above issues and is a great short cut to ensure you're buying products and materials produced and manufactured with the environment in mind.

Eco-Labelling

A labelling system is in place in many countries making purchase decisions easier for the consumer. **Global Ecolabelling Network** (GEN) is the association of certifying organizations from various countries and is an overarching body regulating the labelling programmes.[7] The common goal of the eco-labelling organizations from each country is to establish third party environmental performance recognition, certification and labelling. Many products have 'green' symbols or 'claim statements' developed by the manufacturers themselves, often misleading consumers. In contrast, third party certifying processes award eco-labels so making buying environmentally preferable products all the easier. The range of product categories that are covered by eco-labelling includes:

- Batteries.
- Burners/boilers.
- Cleaning.
- Clothing/textile.
- Construction/building.
- Home appliances.

- Home care products.
- Lights.
- Office equipment/furniture.
- Office supplies (not paper specific).
- Packaging/containers.
- Paper products/inks.
- Personal care products.
- Services.
- Solar-energy.
- Vehicles/fuels.
- Water-saving.
- Food, plants.
- Adhesives.

Examples of eco-labels include:

Australia   EU

USA   Nordic

North America   India

Table 6.2 Eco-Labelling

Eco-Labelling

Here is a selection of Eco-labels from around the world. If your country is not listed check the Global Ecolabelling Network website to see if you have a national Eco-label. www.globalecolabelling.net

Australia – Good Environmental Choice Australia – www.geca.org.au
A fantastic resource that has been developed by Good Environmental Choice Australia and the Australian Green Procurement Network is the Australian Green Procurement Database. www.greenprocurement.org.au This database is a free resource of environmentally preferable products and services available in Australia.

New Zealand – Environmental Choice – www.enviro-choice.org.nz

Brazil – Brazilian Ecolabelling www.abnt.org.br

European Union – EU Ecolabelling, including Denmark, France, Italy, Spain, Greece, Sweden, Portugal, Germany, Belgium, The Netherlands, UK, Finland, Ireland, Austria, Luxembourg, Norway, Iceland, Liechtenstein. ec.europa.eu/environment/ecolabel

Nordic Countries – Nordic Swan – www.svanen.nu Includes Denmark, Iceland, Finland, Norway, Sweden

Sweden – Green Label – www.sec.org.sg

Germany – Blue Angel – www.blauer-engel.de

Czech Republic – Environmental Choice – www.ekoznacka.cz

Ukraine – Living Planet – www.ecolabel.org.ua

Hong Kong – Green Label Scheme – www.greencouncil.org

India – Ecomark - www.enufor.nic.in/cpcd/ecomark/ecomark.html

Indonesia – Indonesian Eco-Label Programme

Japan – Eco Mark – www.ecomark.jp

Korea – Environmental Labelling – www.koeco.or.kr

Taiwan – Green Mark – greenliving.epa.gov.tw

Thailand – Thai Green Label – www.tei.or.th

Canada and USA – EcoLogo – www.ecologo.org

USA – Green Seal – www.greenseal.org

Organic Food

Organically produced food fits perfectly into the sustainability model. It's grown without the help of synthetic fertilizers or pesticides, without genetic modification, it's not irradiated and animals grown organically do so without antibiotics or steroids. Organic agricultural production is sensitive to nature conservation and biodiversity preservation, its processes ensure ongoing soil fertility, and water use is reduced. Seeds, farmers, food processors, retailers and restaurants can all gain organic certification. This certification is sometimes overseen by national governments, sometimes by state governments, independent agricultural region associations, or non-governmental organizations.

Organic labelling is a minefield and it's generally a case of buyer beware. Brands are appropriating the language of organics to infer organic production and certification. Conversely, many organic certification systems are so strict that it pushes small producers out of the running. Some small and often local producers are in the transition stage, and particularly for fresh local produce, should be supported on their journey to full certification, through your patronage.

But of course certified organic produce and food is a very good thing to stand by. There are literally hundreds of certifying organizations around the world. **The International Federation of Organic Agricultural Movements** (IFOAM) has 750 member organizations and it ensures equivalency of standards in over 100 countries.[8] IFOAM doesn't undertake certification activities but the standards it sets form the basis for many nations' organic standards.

Other Organic Products

Food isn't the only thing that's grown organically. There is a huge variety of products which have organic production. If you're looking for a particular product and wonder if there is an organic alternative, check out the **Organic Trade Association's** 'Organic Pages Online'. It's an excellent resource to find almost anything you want. It's based in the US, but most other countries have a similar online resource. www.theorganicpages.com

Sustainable Agriculture

Agriculture uses a large proportion of the Earth's arable land. Agriculture on an industrial scale is a massive polluter, using chemical fertilizers and pesticides, which contaminate land and water systems and endanger the health of workers. Industrial agriculture is also a huge consumer of water.

Choose produce and meat that has been grown or raised sustainably. Organic or eco labelling is a great indicator that the produce you are buying has been farmed sustainably.

With increasing world population, pressure to convert forests to farmlands is on the rise. The **Rainforest Alliance** has recognized that current agricultural practices will only continue to accelerate the cycle of poverty experienced by most farmers, especially in and around our planet's most sensitive and unique ecosystems which are under threat from the continuing march of the fields into the forests. In response they have introduced a certification system for farms within

Table 6.3 Organic labelling

Organic labelling

There are hundreds of organic labelling systems around the world. Some are nationwide, and others are limited to smaller geographic and sometimes agricultural regions. Here are some of the main certifiers:

US

USDA Organic | www.usda.gov

Their requirements are strict, including: no irradiation; no GM; no sewer sludge fertilizers; no synthetic pesticides or fertilizers; and no antibiotics or hormones in meat.

Also in the US are these labels:

Farm Verified Organic and **Organic Crop Improvement Association**.

UK

The Soil Association | www.soilassociation.org

This logo is found on about 70 per cent of organic food produced in the UK.

Organic Farmers and Growers Ltd.

CANADA

Organic Agriculture Centre of Canada | www.organicagcentre.ca

Certified Organic Associations of British Columbia (COABC) and **Alberta Organic Producers Association**.

AUSTRALIA

Australian Certified Organic | www.australianorganic.com.au
Biological Farmers of Australia | www.bfa.com.au

Australian Certified Organic is Australia's largest certifier for organic and biodynamic produce and has over 1500 operators within its certification system. ACO is a fully owned subsidiary of Biological Farmers of Australia.

EUROPE/SCANDINAVIA

Switzerland has the '**bud**' or '**knopse**' logo.

France runs the '**AB**' logo.

Italian organic products often have the '**bio agri cert**' label.

Denmark has the '**Stats-kontrolleret okologisk**' logo.

Source: Information and logos reproduced with permission of the owners

Box 6.3

Organic Food at Peats Ridge Festival

Peats Ridge Festival has an organic and local produce policy. Local growers and organic fruit and vegetable wholesalers, an organic dry goods supplier, an organic dairy and an organic butcher service the event's food stalls.

Each stall has to be a minimum of 50 per cent organic. (They started with a goal of 100 per cent and realized quickly this was not feasible at the time.) Signs are placed on each stall so the audience can tell what level the stall is at. Some had X per cent across all ingredients on their menus, while others had X per cent of their menus 100 per cent organic and then X per cent non-organic. The festival has an organics coordinator who works with the food traders to ease the progression to organic for those that have not previously ventured down this road. Stalls pay an 'organics' bond, which is returned when they produce A$2000 worth of receipts for organic purchases.

There's also an organic fruit and vege store, along with displays from organic community gardens and an organic vegetable box buying cooperative. No Coke or other such brands are sold, only a range of organic soft drinks, and only organic wine is available.

Source: www.peatsridgefestival.com.au

rainforests. These 'Rainforest Alliance Certified' farms have reduced environmental footprints, are good neighbours to human and wild communities and are often integral parts of regional conservation initiatives. They protect wildlife, soils, waterways and the rights and welfare of workers, their families and communities.

Sustainable farms are managed in ways that are environmentally sound, socially equitable and economically viable. Rainforest Alliance Certified™ farms meet the standards of the **Sustainable Agriculture Network,** a coalition of leading conservation groups that determine good agricultural practices.

Rainforest Alliance Certified™ means:

- Less water pollution;
- Less soil erosion;
- Reduced threats to the environment and human health;
- Wildlife habitat is protected;
- Less waste as by-products are used for organic fertilizer;
- Less water used;
- More efficient farm management;
- Improved conditions for farm workers;
- Improved profitability and competitiveness for farmers;
- More collaboration between farmers and conservationists.

www.rainforest-alliance.org

Meat, Fish, Eggs, Dairy

The production of meat and animal products is also something that should be considered. The main concerns are:

- Climate change impact.
- Animal welfare.
- Free range and organic.
- Hormone free.

Meat and Climate Change

The UN's **Food and Agriculture Organization** (FAO) has estimated that meat production accounts for nearly 20 per cent of global GHG emissions.[9] This is produced through clearing of forests for grazing and growing feed crops, and through methane emissions from the cattle. The FAO has also stated that meat consumption is set to double by the middle of the century. I am not suggesting you ban meat at your events, but do keep an eye on global thinking around meat production and climate change.

Animal Welfare

Live animal transport is an important area of animal welfare. Many animals die from heat exhaustion, crush injuries, thirst and suffocation when being transported. The long-distance transport of live animals for slaughter is protested by animal cruelty activists. For more information visit the **Handle with Care** website. This is a group of animal welfare charities which have formed an alliance to focus on long distance animal transport.
www.handlewithcare.tv

One of the main concerns with wool production is 'mulesing'. This is where the skin is cut away from under the sheep's tail so that no wool grows there, thus preventing them from getting 'fly strike'. Many are protesting this practice (primarily done in Australia), with bans by many European retail chains from using Australian merino wool. The industry has pledged to ban the practice as of 2010.

Feedlotting is a concern in beef production. Those cattle raised in factory farms may not have the best of lives. By going 'organic' or 'grass fed' you will have some assurance at least that the cattle haven't spent their lives in pens, knee deep in shit.

Figure 6.4 Organic food at Organic Islands Festival

Source: www.organicislands.ca

Figure 6.5 Rainforest Alliance Certified cocoa in Ecuador

Source: Robert Goodier / Rainforest Alliance

Seafood

Unsustainable fishing practices are pushing our fish stocks and oceans to crisis point. Overfishing and by-catch (species not targeted in long line and net fishing, but caught and killed anyway) are the main concerns. Make sure the seafood served are species which are thriving, which are sustainably caught, and whose harvest doesn't endanger other threatened species. 'Dolphin Free' is just one common claim, but there are many other species that get caught up in by-catch. Ask food vendors selling fish as a main product to prove they are using only sustainably caught seafood.

Free Range, Organic, Hormone Free

Free range chickens are happy chickens. They aren't locked in tiny cages, their necks rubbed bare. If you choose free range eggs, make sure it's from a company that doesn't also sell caged hen eggs, because that's a tad hypocritical.

Going organic for meat and chicken means the cattle, sheep, , goats, chickens and pigs are roaming free (or happy in their homes), and are grazed on pastures grown without chemical fertilizers and pesticides. If hand fed, the food they are given has also been cropped without chemical assistance and is not genetically modified.

Animals raised organically are also free of added hormones or other 'additives' injected into their bodies, or added to their feed.

UTZ Certified

UTZ Certified is one of the leading certification programmes in the world. Its vision is to achieve sustainable agricultural supply chains where farmers are professionals implementing good practices which lead to better businesses, where the food industry takes responsibility by demanding and rewarding sustainably grown products, and where consumers buy products that meet their standard for social and environmental responsibility. UTZ Certified started in 2002 with coffee. Currently it's working on a certification and traceability programme for cocoa and tea and was contracted by the Round Table on Sustainable Palm Oil to develop and implement the traceability system for sustainable palm oil.

www.utzcertified.org

Climate Impact of Purchasing

The purchasing of stuff produces emissions up and down the supply chain from the moment the raw material is extracted or grown to its final consumption and eventual disposal, through electricity use and transport. The fact that consumption of 'stuff' has an impact on the environment, and on climate change is a given. How much an impact one product has compared to another is a much greyer area.

As a general rule, you can reduce the climate impact of your purchasing through:

- Buying local, to reduce transport impact.
- Buying products which have been produced with energy efficient methods.
- Buying less stuff.

As well as buying locally, the theory goes that by choosing products made from raw materials sourced locally and then manufactured locally, you will reduce product miles and consequentially emissions.

The amount of energy used to produce a product is being measured by an increasing number of manufacturers and they are using this information as part of their sales pitch. Low carbon footprint products are hitting the shelves.

It must be noted that as the measurement of total life cycle carbon emission impact of products becomes more sophisticated and detailed, and the results for competing options are compared, we may discover that something as simple as 'buying locally' is not the answer. For example does producing agricultural products organically without chemical fertiliser and pesticides and then shipping across the world produce fewer carbon emissions than the same being grown or raised where chemicals are used?

Several tools are now available to make it easier to choose climate-friendly products such as the **Greenhouse Friendly** logo in Australia, or the **Carbon Trust**'s 'Carbon Reduction' label. These tell you the emissions profile of a product or ensure that the product has taken reduction steps and/or offsets its emissions. Look out for a programme in your country.

Box 6.4

Environmentally Responsible Purchasing Checklist ☑

Use certified products

☐ Choose products that are certified by an eco-label or are certified organic.

'Go' organic

☐ Consider 'going organic' and embracing and promoting the consumption of organic foods.

Source local produce

☐ Consider food miles. Buying local should be a major part of your procurement policy. Support the community that supports your event.

Sustainable agriculture

☐ Use Rainforest Alliance or UTZ Certified produce in your catering and encourage food traders and stalls to do the same.

☐ Use organic, free range, hormone-free meat and animal products

☐ Choose animal products only from those that have been raised free of cruelty.

☐ Use only sustainably harvested seafood products.

Carbon Labelling

The Greenhouse Friendly logo tells you that a product or service meets the standards set by the Department of Climate Change. You're assured their emissions have been offset, or balanced out by other activities to reduce GHG emissions.

www.climatechange.gov.au/greenhousefriendly

The Carbon Reduction Label has been developed by the Carbon Trust, the UK's leading authority on carbon reduction. The label is printed on products to help you understand the carbon footprints of products and services.

www.carbon-label.com

Figure 6.6 Thinking about food miles

Source: Courtesy of Tracey Shough

Figure 6.7 Garment workers produce t-shirts under International Labour Organizations standards for Ethical Threads

Source: Ethical Threads

Ethically and Socially Responsible Purchasing

The US Federal Government's **Environmental Protection Agency** has a programme called 'Environmentally Preferred Purchasing'. A huge amount of information and resources are available on their website. Produced for government departments, it's also a great tool for directing your own purchase decisions.

www.epa.gov/epp

Sustainability, as a definition, looks at the triad of economic, environmental and social concerns. As well as an environmental focus, ensuring ethically and socially responsible purchasing in association with your event is essential for it to meet your sustainability goals.

It's likely you've heard of the fair trade concept, and have seen various symbols on products on your supermarket shelf. Goods such as tea, coffee, sugar, bananas, honey, cotton and rice are the prominent product ranges that are part of fair trade producer schemes. The concept of fair trade expands further than primary agricultural production and also includes handicrafts, clothing and goods made by artisans in the developing world. Organizations can also receive Fair Trade Organization certification through the **World Fair Trade Organization** (WFTO).[10]

The various labelling and certification systems around the world are generally overseen by the **International Social and Environmental Accreditation and Labelling Alliance** (ISEAL) whose vision is to create a world where environmental sustainability and social justice are the normal conditions of business.[11]

A fair trade label on products lets consumers know that the farmers and workers who supplied the raw materials are getting a better deal. Fair trade supports the payment of a fair price for a wide variety of goods produced in developing countries and sold to developed countries. It protects producers from the whims of the commodity market where they can be left empty handed at the end of a gruelling year of work, if prices fall.

The guarantee of a fair price paid creates opportunities for economically disadvantaged producers or those marginalized by the conventional trading system, and empowers them to economic self-sufficiency, becoming stakeholders in their own enterprises. Apart from these economic considerations the movement promotes sustainability and environmental sensitivity, fair work conditions, ensures women's work is properly valued and rewarded and makes sure participating organizations respect the UN Convention on the Rights of the Child.

The overarching body for fair trade is the WFTO. Membership covers the entire fair trade supply chain from production to sale. In order to receive the FTO Mark, organizations must pass through their monitoring system which embeds the '10 Standards of Fair Trade' – including all the elements mentioned under the Fairtrade product label (printed on the following pages).

There are many fair trade labelling organizations including TransFair, the Max Havelaar label. There are also several umbrella network fair trade organizations that also work towards fair trade goals. These include Network of European Worldshops and European Fair Trade Association.

Fairtrade Label

The Fairtrade label, is a product label, and an initiative of **Fairtrade Labelling Organization International**.[12] They report sales of certified fair trade products at approximately €2.3 billion in 2007, with a 47 per cent year-to-year increase. This volume of sales is only a fraction of world trade, but fair trade products account for up to 20 per cent of sales in their categories in Europe and North America, which is remarkable. In 2007 there were 637 certified producing organizations around the world, encompassing an estimated 1.5 million workers.[13]

Figure 6.8

Buy Fair Trade

There are many products events need which are regulated by the concept of fair trade, and you can help to grow the profile and market for fairly traded and responsibly produced products by using them at events. Do this by insisting traders use and sell them at your event, and through promoting the concept out to the audience.

Apart from raw materials such as cotton produced under fair trade certification there are many more people along the manufacturing process, particularly in the garment industry, who also need some protection and support. If you purchase clothing and other fabric-based merchandise, or have stalls selling such goods, look to the ethical production of the garments back up the supply chain. Organizations such as **Fair Wear** and **Clean Clothes Campaign** work for and protect the rights of garment workers worldwide, particularly in developing nations. We discuss fair labour conditions in factories coming up.

Box 6.5

Ethical purchasing checklist ☑

Choose fairly traded and ethically produced products

☐ Have a policy to purchase and use fair trade certified goods, such as tea, coffee, chocolate, sugar, rice and fruit.

Insist on market stalls doing the same

☐ Those events with food traders can have this requirement contracted into their participation agreement.

Ethical merchandise

☐ Produce t-shirts and other merch from organic cotton, or alternative fibres, from factories with fair labour practices.

Ethical markets

☐ If you are having market stalls with 'world crafts' as a major product category, look at having only Fairtrade certified handicrafts or those that can be tracked back directly to the artisan.

Promote to your audience

☐ Contact local fair trade and organic organizations to arrange promotional material to let your audience know that your event is selling and using fair trade goods.

Figure 6.9 Fairtrade wine produced for Roskilde Festival in tetrapaks

Source: Roskilde Festival

Box 6.6

The Ten Standards of Fair Trade

The World Fair Trade Association prescribes ten standards that fair trade organizations must follow in their day-to-day work and carries out continuous monitoring to ensure these standards are upheld:

Creating Opportunities for Economically Disadvantaged Producers

Fair trade is a strategy for poverty alleviation and sustainable development. Its purpose is to create opportunities for producers who have been economically disadvantaged or marginalized by the conventional trading system.

Transparency and Accountability

Fair trade involves transparent management and commercial relations to deal fairly and respectfully with trading partners.

Capacity Building

Fair trade is a means to develop producers' independence. Fair trade relationships provide continuity, during which producers and their marketing organizations can improve their management skills and their access to new markets.

Promoting Fair Trade

Fair trade organizations raise awareness of fair trade and the possibility of greater justice in world trade. They provide their customers with information about the organization and the products, and in what conditions they are made. They use honest advertising and marketing techniques and aim for the highest standards in product quality and packing.

Payment of a Fair Price

A fair price in the regional or local context is one that has been agreed through dialogue and participation. It covers not only the costs of production but also enables production that is socially just and environmentally sound. It provides fair pay to the producers and takes into account the principle of equal pay for equal work by women and men. Fair traders ensure prompt payment to their partners and, whenever possible, help producers with access to pre-harvest or pre-production financing.

Gender equity

Fair trade means that women's work is properly valued and rewarded. Women are always paid for their contribution to the production process and are empowered in their organizations.

Working conditions

Fair trade means a safe and healthy working environment for producers. The participation of children (if any) does not adversely affect their well-being, security, educational requirements and need for play and conforms to the UN Convention on the Rights of the Child as well as the law and norms in the local context.

Child Labour

Fair trade organizations respect the UN Convention on the Rights of the Child, as well as local laws and social norms in order to ensure that the participation of children in production processes of fairly traded articles (if any) does not adversely affect their well-being, security, educational requirements and need for play. Organizations working directly with informally organized producers disclose the involvement of children in production.

The Environment

Fair trade actively encourages better environmental practices and the application of responsible methods of production.

Trade Relations

Fair trade organizations trade with concern for the social, economic and environmental well-being of marginalized small producers and do not maximize profit at their expense. They maintain long-term relationships based on solidarity, trust and mutual respect that contribute to the promotion and growth of fair trade. An interest-free pre-payment of at least 50 per cent is made if requested.

www.wfto.com

Source: Reprinted with the permission of World Fair Trade Organization

Fair Production

Apart from the environmentally friendly cultivation or production of materials, the fair treatment of farm workers and a fair price paid to farmers, you need also to consider the working conditions in manufacturing factories.

There are several certifying and activist associations in existence to regulate and monitor the working conditions of the world's factories, some industry specific and others overarching all manufacturing.

Worldwide Responsible Accredited Production (WRAP)

WRAP is an independent, non-profit organization dedicated to the certification of lawful, humane and ethical manufacturing throughout the world.

WRAP has been working since 2006 with a group of retailers, buyers and interested stakeholders to develop the new 'Universal Code of Ethical Conduct' (UCEC). UCEC is a modification of the existing WRAP principles to allow inclusion of all labour-intensive consumer products such as home furnishings, pottery, glassware, furniture, electronics and even agricultural products.

Several non-apparel companies in the toys, plastics, physical exercise equipment and housewares businesses have applied and had their factories certified to the existing WRAP standard. In studying a broad range of labour-intensive consumer products, it was noticed that all such businesses are virtually the same in their process and manufacturing organization in that raw materials are converted to finished goods. The only processes that vary are the actual assembly or conversion process, but the functional areas within the company – purchasing, receiving, production, quality control, human resources etc. – are all the same.

Information supplied by WRAP.
www.wrapapparel.org

Fair Wear Foundation

The Fair Wear Foundation supports and promotes good labour conditions in garment production. The foundation was set up by various organizations, NGOs and trade unions related to the fashion industry. Fair Wear Foundation verifies whether companies comply with the Code of Labour Practices.

www.fairwear.org

In the West we like to wear beautiful and, if possible, inexpensive clothes. These clothes often originate from factories lacking proper workers' conditions.

Erica van Doorn,
Director Fair Wear Foundation

International Labour Organization (ILO)

No piece on fair working conditions would be complete without profiling the **International Labour Organization**. The ILO is devoted to advancing opportunities for women and men to obtain decent and productive work in conditions of freedom, equity, security and human dignity. Its main aims are to promote rights at work, encourage decent employment opportunities, enhance social protection and strengthen dialogue in handling work-related issues. www.ilo.org

Figure 6.10 Workers in a Fair Wear Foundation certified garment factory.

Source: Fair Wear

Clean Clothes Campaign

The **Clean Clothes Campaign** (CCC) takes action on specific issues related to unfair labour conditions. As workers producing clothes for brands and retailers around the world struggle to organize and improve their own conditions, so consumers, trade unionists and activists worldwide can join together to exert pressure at all levels of supply chains. The CCC brings together consumers, trade unions, campaign groups and other diverse organizations to do just that, calling on those with the power in global supply chains to take responsibility for workers' rights. National CCCs target companies in their countries, pushing them to take action. They also work as part of the international CCC network – including partners in countries where garments are made – to join together for coordinated international campaigns such as the 'Play Fair 2008' campaign. Information supplied by Clean Clothes Campaign. www.cleanclothes.org

Box 6.7

Fair Labour Checklist ☑

Buy products produced under fair labour conditions

☐ When choosing your products and merchandise, the sustainable choice includes consideration for the working conditions of those that have manufactured them.

☐ If you care where your t-shirts and uniforms are made, look out for labels which regulate and certify the industry.

Box 6.8

Ethical Threads

Ethical merchandise

Ethical Threads is a fair trade company based in the UK and supplies t-shirts and other merchandise to the live events industry. They are committed to ensuring their products are sourced from manufacturers who comply with the core ILO conventions.

The Ethical Threads story began when Billy Bragg approached the London Region of Britain's general trade union the GMB and asked if they would be able to source non-sweated t-shirts and merchandise for his tour. GMB, together with Battersea and Wandsworth Trades Council used their union connections to seek out workplaces in the UK and abroad that met international conventions on workers' rights to supply Billy's shirts. Once the word was out that there was a guaranteed source of ethically made t-shirts available the orders started pouring in. And so Ethical Threads was born. They now supply shirts to many other artists, campaign groups, venues, festivals, unions and NGOs. Customers include Amnesty International, the National Film Theatre and Glastonbury Festival.

Ethical is a very broad term and initially their main concern was the fair treatment of workers all the way through the supply chain. Though this is very much still the case, they have broadened the policy to include environmental and health concerns and now intend to phase-in entirely organic cotton stock. Ethical Threads are determined to use fair trade certified cotton, where possible, so that the farmers who toil in the fields receive a fair price for their part.

The team personally inspect the factories where their garments are made, speak to the workers without management present, and ensure that employers adhere to the core ILO conventions.

The Ethical Threads manifesto:

- No forced labour.

- No child labour.

- Freedom of association: the workforce is free to join a trade union. Our suppliers must allow access for local trade unions to talk to staff about joining a union and to verify employment practices.

- All health, hygiene and safety requirements are met by the company and can be independently verified.

- Decent shift patterns and regular breaks for staff.

- Decent pay to the workforce and compliance with all minimum wage requirements.

- Equality of opportunity for all staff.

- Paid holidays, paid sickness leave and paid maternity leave for staff.

- Suppliers to comply with environmental standards and to meet Oeko-Tex standard 100.

www.ethicalthreads.co.uk

Balancing Environmental, Ethical and Climate Change Issues

When making product purchasing decisions, you may need to choose between going for fairly traded products, completely organic materials, or just buying locally to support your community and also to reduce the transport impact of your purchasing. You may not always get all three in the one product, but if you do, you win the gold star.

Reducing food miles versus supporting sustainably produced products and materials from the developing world is something to think about. If you're in a country where products such as tea, coffee, chocolate, rice, sugar, bananas and cotton are grown, you may wish to support local production over fair trade. This is a reasonable option; however, look into the farming practices used, as the extra food miles and social benefits may outweigh potentially chemical heavy and destructive farming methods used locally.

Furthermore it is estimated that 45 per cent of certified fair trade producers are also organic and that this figure is continually growing.[14] It generally holds that organic production also has fair wages and good labour conditions. So you can't lose really.

Figure 6.11 Factory floor

Source: Ethical Threads

Box 6.9

Roskilde Festival's Purchasing Checklist

Ethical purchasing

Roskilde Festival has put environmentally and socially responsible purchasing through their market stalls and catering. Here's what they've achieved so far, and it includes using 2689kg of fair trade coffee!

- Organic and/or fair trade tea and coffee.
- Fair trade sugar.
- Fair trade wine.
- Organic dairy products in collaboration with Naturmælk.
- Fair trade and organic drinks, juices and smoothies are available.
- 100 per cent organic fruit and vegetables via Grøn Fokus.
- In collaboration with Eco Lab, environmentally sound cleaning products.

www.roskilde-festival.dk

Figure 6.12 Printed material at Peats Ridge Festival is made from non-tree paper

Source: Peats Ridge Festival

Products

With 2009 the UN International Year of Natural Fibres, the Earth's abundant supply of sustainable materials is in the spotlight. Let's choose to use these products. Let's also redesign with end of life in mind. Let's close production and disposal loops and reduce the pressure on the Earth to endlessly feed our appetite for more and more.

Products made sustainably and from alternative materials are available for many event procurement needs. Choose them and you push demand and encourage their continued development. Products with recyclable components, made from sustainable materials and whose processes close loops are the end goal. Use timber from sustainably managed forests. PVC and non-organic cotton should be avoided. Your paper can even be tree free. Cleaning products shouldn't poison waterways.

Let's take a look at how we can use our purchasing decisions to help lighten the load.

Timber Products

Events use timber for building and construction, set design, décor, fencing, staging, signage, outdoor furniture, and woodchip on the ground. This timber is sourced from the world's forests. The problem with timber is, once logged and moved from its original forest, it's difficult to identify not only whether it was sustainably produced, but also whether it was legally logged.

Illegal logging is a massive business, but due to its illegal nature, its size can't really be accurately estimated. The only way to be sure that the timber or timber products you are using aren't from old-growth virgin forests and possibly logged illegally is to purchase certified forest products. Illegal or poorly managed forests ruin ecosystems, deplete biodiversity and displace communities preventing the self-sufficiency of indigenous people depending on the forest for their survival.

Greenpeace reports that an estimated 80 per cent of the world's forests have already been either destroyed or degraded, and half of that has been in the last 30 years.[15] The world needs forests to survive. Its lungs are being chopped out by our insatiable desire for timber products, copy paper, toilet paper, new furniture. I haven't even mentioned climate change yet. Nor have I mentioned extinctions of species on a grand scale.

The point is, without getting too emotional (although I do feel a little so right now), if it keeps going at the same rate, every last bit of old-growth forest could be lost. **In our lifetime.** We're talking a football field every two seconds.

We're going to run out of old-growth forest if we don't urgently do something to stop the demand for illegal forest products. Once it's cut down and on its way to Europe or the US, the horse has bolted. If you buy timber products without any certification, you are adding to the problem. Please don't.

There are other issues that feed demand for timber. Forests are being cut down at a wholesale rate, but the timber is just a bonus. Palm oil plantations are going in their place to feed our lust for supermarket products. Not to mention the demand for palm oil from the biofuel industry, or soya bean farms going in place of forests and churning out the feed for chickens that in turn feed our fast food appetite.

Forest Certification

There are many certification systems around the world, but the main and most respected is the **Forest Stewardship Council** (FSC).

Approximately 100 million hectares of forest in over 79 countries were certified to FSC standards in April 2008. This represents 7 per cent of the world's managed forest. FSC estimates the value of products labelled with the FSC mark at over US$20 billion.[16]

It's possible for your event to have FSC certification. An FSC representative can visit your event and complete an application audit including the specifications, quantity and total cost of the wood material or products used. An audit of wood sourcing includes invoices, a purchasing log and proof of the FSC certified status of the purchases. So basically they need a visual audit of the timber on site, the purchasing documentation and the FSC certifications from your supplier.

Other certification programmes include the **Sustainable Forestry Initiative**, Canada's Standards Association's **National Standard for Sustainable Forest Management**, **Programme for the Endorsement of Forest Certification** (PEFC) and the **Rainforest Alliance**.

The timber from these forests is certified with the appropriate label, as are products made from them. This branding assures purchasers that the timber or product they are buying comes from sustainably managed forests that meet social, economic and environmental goals.

Figure 6.13 All the timber at the Greenpeace field at Glastonbury Festival is FSC

Souce: Meegan Jones

Figure 6.14 Smart Ply is an example of a brand of FSC certified timber

Souce: Meegan Jones

Use Sustainable Paper

Most paper is manufactured from pulped forest products (um, trees). If you're reading this book, then it's very likely that you're well aware of the existence of recycled paper. It's also likely your offices use it, and your printed material is made from recycled paper. I'm not telling you anything new here.

It may be worth doing a review of the stationery order and a report on the last year of print jobs, just so you can be sure. You may find that the paper you've been using isn't all it makes out to be. When choosing your recycled paper you should be careful of 'recycled' claims as most people think of 'recycled' paper being made from the paper you put back into the recycling system. There are actually three categories of paper that can be used as feedstock for making recycled paper.

Post-consumer recycled paper is made from paper discarded after use, from the home and office, the standard recycling you think of when you think of paper recycling.

Next we have pre-consumer wastepaper, which is produced from paper discarded before it reaches homes and offices, such as print over-runs, misprints, damaged or unsold stock, etc.

Lastly is what's known as mill broke, paper trimmings and scrap from the actual manufacture of paper, and this is recycled internally within the mill, but sometimes branded as 'recycled'.

Many papers are blends of virgin paper and recycled content, and that's OK as it must be

remembered that paper can't be recycled indefinitely. The general thinking is that virgin paper can be recycled four to seven times, as the fibres are weakened and shortened with each reprocessing. Make sure the virgin pulp used in your mixed sources paper is sustainably sourced, and choosing FSC certified paper is a way of doing this. We discussed FSC and other certified forest products in the previous section.

Recycling paper is a market driven concept. It's generally a little more expensive than virgin pulp paper to buy a ream made from a high percentage of recycled sources. But with increased demand that should even out. People who have a concern for the environment do still baulk at coughing

Figure 6.15 Evolve Papers use 100 per cent post-consumer recycled paper pulp

Source: www.evolve-papers.com

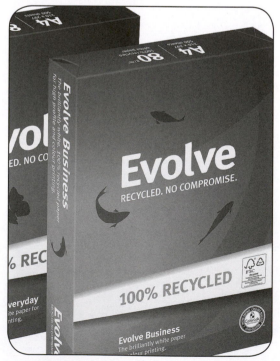

up the extra dollars for the most environmentally responsible product. They'll go to a monster office supplies store owned by a huge corporation and buy a cheap ream of brilliant white virgin pulp paper – products that support multinational timber companies and chlorine bleaching. A few big players control the retail paper market, cheaper paper is demanded by customers, and to keep the competitive edge, retailers pressure paper manufacturers to supply cheap paper. Cheap paper means the cheapest form of fibre (new trees) and cheap processing means using chlorine or chlorine derivative bleaching (bad) as opposed to oxygen bleaching (good).

So Does Recycling Paper Save Trees?

It's difficult to quantify as demand is growing with population growth and trees are used for many non-paper purposes. However, recycling does extend the life of the total yield of each tree, and that's a good thing. As discussed in Chapter 7, one of the main benefits of recycling paper and using recycled paper is to reduce the volume of waste sent to landfill or to incineration. It reduces GHG emissions potential. By reducing the demand for virgin pulp, recycling also reduces the energy and fossil fuels needed in planting and maintaining forests, harvesting, transport and milling. It takes the pressure off forests.

The Recycled Mark

In the absence of formal regulation, some country's paper associations have developed 'recycled marks' which inform the consumer about the percentage of recycled paper content.

In the UK the National Association of Paper Merchants (NAPM) has a recycled mark that informs the purchaser of 50, 75 or 100% recycled content.

It doesn't stipulate between pre-consumer or post-consumer feedstock papers but doesn't allow 'mill broke' to be included in the recycled paper content calculation.
Look for the recycled mark in your country and choose to use 100%.

www.napm.org.uk

Other Paper-Based Products

Other paper products used as your event could include toilet paper, napkins, paper towels, table-cloths, notepads, packaging, folders, cups and food packaging. All should be sourced from recycled content or certified sustainable forests. We go through options for food packaging coming up.

Paper Bleaching

Another consideration in choosing a paper is how it's bleached. Wide-scale bleaching using chlor-ine decreased in the 1980s and 1990s when it was discovered that a by-product of this bleaching was the production of 'dioxin', a highly toxic and carcinogenic substance.

Elemental Chlorine Free (ECF)

Regulations on dioxin levels in waste-water effluent from paper mills were consequently introduced, and elemental chlorine free (ECF) bleaching came into vogue. ECF papers are made from pulp that has been bleached using deriva-tives of chlorine such as chlorine dioxide or other chemicals, but in the absence of pure chlor-ine. The chlorine derivatives used in ECF papers, while less harmful than elemental chlorine, still produce toxic compounds such as chloroform, and these are released into waterways to do their damage.

Totally Chlorine Free (TCF)

If using a virgin pulp paper, totally chlorine free (TCF) is what you want your paper to be, with it either oxygen bleached or not bleached at all (as well as being FSC certified of course).

Processed Chlorine Free (PCF)

As recycled paper is produced from all sorts of recycled content, some which could have origin-ally been chlorine or ECF bleached papers, they can't be called TCF. Recycled papers from mixed sources, bleached in the absence of chlorine or its derivatives are known as processed chlorine free (PCF).

TCF or PCF are the most environmentally prefer-able alternative for paper bleaching, depending on whether you are buying paper made from virgin or recycled pulp.

Unbleached

Alternatively, you can make a strong point in your communications material and use unbleached stock. **Ecocern** has a fantastic unbleached 100 per cent PCW paper with a natural brown colour. It's available in Australia but there may be similar products in your country.
www.ecocern.com.au

Chlorine Free Products Association

This organization offers TCF and PCF certifica-tion for papers. Look out for the logo on papers.

www.chlorinefreeproducts.org

Tree Free Papers

Trees are not the only thing that paper can be made from. The relatively lower fibre content and higher lignin content of wood pulp is reputed to make this a less efficient option than many other quick growing crops. Until the mid-1800s all paper was produced with agricultural fibres, not wood. This included rags and fabric scraps along with purpose-grown crops and agricultural waste by-products. Even today much of the paper produced in China and India is made from crops such as wheat straw, rice straw and sugar cane bagasse.

Paper can be made from cotton, a similar plant kenaf, from hemp, recycled sugar cane fibre, and many other fibres used in the speciality paper market such as tobacco, coffee and even elephant poo.

As some tree-free alternatives are cropped and need land allocated for their growth, the environmentally preferable option is the use of agricultural waste and residues as source fibre. These pulps can be combined with recycled paper fibres or with sustainable virgin wood pulp to make conventional papers such as photocopy paper, coated papers for magazines and programmes, as well as newsprint or high-end speciality papers.

However, a tree's longer growth cycle creates biodiversity, sequesters carbon and uses fewer chemical fertilizers. Deciding on which is the most environmentally preferable option is a difficult decision. It's one of those grey areas and one to keep an eye on as the industry progresses.

Sugar Cane/Bagasse Paper

Bagasse is the fibrous residue left over after sugar cane has been crushed and the sugar removed. It's an agricultural by-product which would otherwise probably be burnt. It's used widely and is the world's most popular non-tree fibre. In India, the nation's primary paper producer, **Tamil Nadu Newsprint and Paper Company**, uses paper primarily from bagasse using as little wood as possible.
www.tnpl.com

Kimberly Clark is a major producer of bagasse paper, primarily for paper towels and tissues. Their Orizaba, Mexico mill produces 300,000 tons of paper products per year. **Staples**, the massive office supplies chain, uses bagasse in their EcoEasy range of notepads.

Raleigh Paper makes a bagasse paper product 'Harvest Recycled'. It's made from 60 per cent recycled sugar cane waste. The remaining 40 per cent of paper is softwood fibre sourced from internationally certified forests (PEFC, FSC, SFI, CSA). This paper is used by Peats Ridge Festival for all printed material (posters, flyers, programme.)
www.raleighpaper.com.au

Cotton Fibre Paper

The benefit of using cotton for paper is that the fibres are almost pure cellulose, compared with tree fibres which are only 50 per cent cellulose. Fewer chemicals are needed to produce cotton paper – but of course, cotton farming is a chemical and water intensive agricultural process and that needs to be considered when looking at full life cycle impact. **Crane Paper**, a supplier of boutique papers, sources its cotton not from the fields but from scraps left from the manufacture of cotton garments such as jeans and t-shirts, making it all the more environmentally preferable as these scraps would otherwise be sent to landfill.
www.crane.com

Kenaf Paper

Kenaf is a plant related to cotton and okra and originated in Africa. Its fibres are similar to wood fibres. It's fast growing, pulping requires less energy, heat and time than wood pulp and it's easily bleached with chlorine-free processes. Keep an eye out for this as a non-tree paper alternative.

Hemp and Flax Papers

Hemp fibre is a popular alternative fibre not only for paper but for fabrics. It's fast growing, has a natural resistance to pests and out-competes weeds, so there is the dual reduction in necessity for herbicides and pesticides, which is a very good thing. Its high fibre yield as compared to wood means its pulping is less energy intensive. The length and strength of flax fibres also make it a great paper feedstock.

Greenfield Paper in the US has a range of hemp papers from a mix of PCW and hemp grown in the States. www.greenfieldpaper.com. **Eco 21** is another North American hemp paper, made from 40 per cent hemp, 40 per cent flax, 20 per cent cotton. The **Living Tree Paper Co** also has a range of flax/hemp pulp blended papers. www.livingtreepaper.com. Ask your printer what hemp or flax fibre papers are available.

Bamboo Paper

Bamboo is a sustainable and renewable resource. It's fast growing, doesn't use pesticides or fertilizers, and needs little water for growth. It's still a speciality paper and not widely available; however, one to watch.

Wheat Sheet

Paper made from wheat straw pulp is produced mainly in China and India. However, countries such as Canada, the US and Australia are

Box 6.11

Designer Resource

Lovely as a tree
This website offers advice on paper choices tailored with the graphic designer in mind. Encourage your graphic designer or print job coordinator to look through this site to get clued up on what's what in sustainable paper choices.

www.lovelyasatree.com

all producing massive amounts of wheat straw which could be used for paper making. It will be interesting to see if a commercial market develops for this product in these countries. The *Canadian Geographic* in 2008 printed its magazine using wheat sheet as a demonstration of what is possible with tree-free papers.

Using tree-free papers for your event's promotional printing and stationery will make a strong environmental statement.

Box 6.12

At your Event: Paper Purchasing

Printing

- Use 100 per cent post-consumer recycled paper where appropriate, or if a blend, ensure virgin pulp is FSC certified.
- Any laminate used on printing should be biodegradable or recyclable.
- Any varnishes used on print jobs should be low VOC and vegetable or water based.
- Your printing company should use soy or vegetable-based inks.
- The ink clean-up process your printing company uses should be solvent free.
- Your printing company should have environmentally friendly waste ink disposal methods in place.
- Choose a printer who is ISO 14001 certified.[17]

Paper

- Use paper with a high level of PCW, preferably 100 per cent post-consumer recycled paper.
- Ensure if it says it's from recycled paper that it isn't made from 'mill broke'.
- If from a mix of virgin and recycled pulp, check that the virgin pulp is FSC certified and at most 25 per cent virgin and 75 per cent recycled.
- Use tree-free paper.

Paper bleaching

- Choose only chlorine-free bleached paper.
- PCF if recycled and TCF if from virgin pulp or mixed.
- Go for unbleached stock and make a statement with your printed material.

Where's the source?

- Choose a paper manufactured in your country, from recycled paper also from your country to reduce product miles.
- Check that your supplier of office paper has a distribution centre close by and that paper isn't being shipped around the country before coming to you.

Use Sustainable Food and Beverage Packaging

Serving drinks and food is a major activity of most events. Unless at a formal set-up, where tables and chairs are in a restaurant format, it's likely food will be served in takeaway containers. The most sustainable option is washable and re-usable cups, crockery and cutlery, but at many events this is not a practical option.

Let's now look at the myriad sustainably produced disposable food packaging options available to you. We will look at how to deal with the consequential waste stream you create by using them in Chapter 7.

First off I need to make a point and that point is: there is absolutely no reason why polystyrene products need to be used while there are fantastic completely sustainable options available. If you do one thing … BAN POLYSTYRENE. Let's take a moment. Breathe. And let's repeat.

BAN POLYSTYRENE

I would prefer to go hungry than accept a meal on this horrible product. I have done so many times, leaving a perplexed and confused kebab seller after an anti-polystyrene berating by me. I've really got to get my spiel a little less confused and a little more informing. But I just can't help myself. It hurts like a stab in the heart every time I see one of those foamy evil things lying in the gutter.

Polystyrene is a plastic, made from petroleum, which as we know is a non-renewable resource. It can look like 'normal' plastic, such as inside CD jewel cases, or be 'foamy' like the ubiquitous coffee cup or hamburger container (expanded polystyrene). This foamy material is a significant pollution problem as it's light and blows in the wind and floats on water. It's also difficult to recycle, and barely any kerb-side recycling pickups take it. It will be very unlikely that adequate recycling facilities will exist in your area to process it and your event really shouldn't be endorsing a product made of non-renewable resources that's made for a minute on the lips and a lifetime in the tip.

There are some manufacturers of this product that are taking on the responsibility of recycling it. At an industrial level, polystyrene is a plastic that has some value and so advances are being made in its recapture and recycling. However this isn't likely to make its way to the domestic takeaway container any time soon.

You may already have a ban on polystyrene food packaging in your state or city. Many across the US are passing laws at local or state government level to this effect.

So no to plastic or polystyrene, then what are the alternatives? The answer is for your food packaging to be made from sustainable materials and to be biodegradable.

Bagasse

Bagasse is the by-product of sugar cane production. It's the fibrous pulp left after the juice has been extracted from the cane. It's used to make paper products, including copy and printing paper, as discussed earlier in this chapter. It's also used widely to make excellent takeaway food containers.

The products available include plates, bowls, cups, trays and lunch boxes. They are heat resistant, chlorine-free bleached, and sustainably produced. They are made in just about every country that sugar cane is manufactured. Your standard food packaging supplier should be able to source the product for you. Just make sure you check its origin too in case it's done several trips around the globe before it reaches you. If your only option is to use imported stock, consider a product transport offset to counteract the transport emissions.

Bulrush

Bulrush grows wild in the low mountain areas and marsh lands in southeastern China. The bulrush is harvested sustainably once a year from wild crops rather than from cultivated plants. Bulrush is robust and grows rapidly making it a great raw material fibre for producing paper-like products. Bulrush packaging has received Cradle to Cradle[SM] certification.

Palm Leaf Plates

These wonderful plates are usually made in India but have found markets far and wide across the globe. They are made simply from fallen palm leaves. The areca palm is the tree of choice and the manufacturing process uses no chemicals or bleaches, no glues or resins. It's manufactured by soaking the leaf in water and pressing into shape.

It's a truly sustainable product which uses a waste product that would otherwise be burnt or left to degrade naturally. I encourage you to use them. Again, ask your food service packaging supplier to source them, or go directly to the companies set up in just about every country that imports this terrific product. The knock-on social benefits are also wonderful, with the reputable companies that manufacture and supply areca

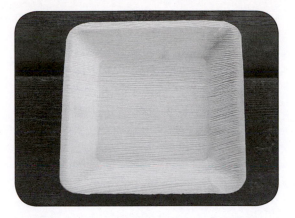

Figure 6.16 Areca palm plate available through the Whole Leaf Co based in the UK
Source: www.thewholeleafco.com

palm plates also integrating fair trade concepts in the sourcing and manufacturing of the products. Look back up the supply chain and make sure the palm plates you choose also benefit the communities they are sourced from.

Potato Plates

Potatoes are another great source of starch and this starch can be used to make packaging. In this method, the starch is extracted from the waste water of potato product manufacture, like when they chop up potatoes for frozen chips and wedges. **Splore Festival** in New Zealand uses potato plates. Find them here:
www.potatoplates.com

PLA Products

PLA or polylactic acid is a resin developed by Cargill and Teijin Limited of Japan under the banner of **Natureworks LLC** (www.natureworksllc.com). PLA uses the carbon stored in starch plants such as corn, which break down into sugars. A fermentation process changes these natural sugars into a plastic look-alike material. Its popular use is for cups and straws, but it is also used as a coating for paper products. PLA biodegrades in four to six months. According to Natureworks LLC it 'uses 65% less fossil fuel resources to produce, and reduces greenhouse gas emissions by 80–90% compared to traditional petroleum-based polymers'. (Plastic to you and me.) The raw material, the proprietary PLA, is marketed as Ingeo™ which is sold on to remanufacturers of packaging products. There are also a handful of minor manufacturers who produce PLA for their own product lines.

The big problem with this seemingly sustainable product is that it can corrupt existing recycling systems and the emergence of PLA look-alike 'plastic' bottles is potentially a big problem. These get thrown into recycling bins with PET and other plastics and contaminate the recycling. The industry is tackling this problem and technology is available to accurately separate PLA bottles from plastics. However, every region's Materials Recovery Facilities (MRFs) operate in slightly different ways and you need to check if your MRF can separate PLA from plastic bottles. Furthermore, in-vessel compost facilities can't take bulk PLA waste, as their processes usually turn out the end product in a week or two, and PLA just can't biodegrade in that time, no matter the intensity of the process. The only real home for PLA products is in long-term windrow compost set-ups, the kind that take months to process. That's not a problem, windrow composting is a very effective method. But in this situation, a great load of PLA bottles, containers or cups are not going to compost by themselves. They need wet organic waste in a healthy ratio to the amount of PLA, in order to commence the decomposition process.

You certainly don't want to send these items to landfill. They need oxygen to breakdown, and in a closed landfill, it's likely they will just sit there in their current form.

Coated paper products could be a better solution than 100 per cent PLA, if you don't have a system in place to capture the PLA products separately. These would be paper products coated with PLA to make them waterproof, but will biodegrade quicker.

The benefits of PLA are dual. They don't use fossil fuels as a source material, and they are biodegradable. If you use PLA cups or food containers, please make sure you also have an appropriate disposal method to benefit from using them – that they will be collected separately and composted, rather than accidentally confused for recycling, or worse – ending up in landfill.

Extended Producer Responsibility

Now might be the time to drop in this little gem. For some time there has been pressure on companies such as beverage bottlers to take responsibility for the packaging that their products come in. We can see this taken in hand in countries where bottle deposits are the norm. You will notice however, as you move from country to country, that the same multinational companies have different systems in different countries. It's not so much their heart-felt environmentalism that leads them to recycling and re-using bottles, but the laws of that country.

The concept of Extended Producer Responsibility is something we are seeing increasingly written

Box 6.13

Eco-Friendly Packaging

Southbound Festival's aim is to use as little packaging as possible – and where packaging is used to ensure that it's biodegradable and compostable.

The event has an Environmental Packaging Policy for Stallholders and they must use biodegradable and compostable packaging, including biodegradable pseudo-plastic. They have endorsed a preferred supplier, Dzolv, who have a range of EFGLO (environmentally friendly greener living options) products which are 100 per cent biodegradable and 100 per cent compostable and include cutlery, plates, straws, cups, etc. The products are made from certified forest product paper and coated with PLA. This means the products have the sturdiness necessary to take liquid, but as the coating is biodegradable, it can be composted along with the left-over food. All beverages served in cups purchased from any of the bars at the festival, as well as all recycling bags, have been provided by Dzolv.

All the plates, food boxes and cutlery are compostable and biodegradable and are combined with food waste and locally sourced green waste before being mulched and composted.

www.dzolv.com.au,
www.sunsetevents.com.au

into laws. It's designed to promote the integration of environmental costs associated with full product life cycle impact. Manufacturers must guarantee physical or financial responsibility for final disposal. It's particularly relevant for packaging as this is the part of the product that has almost immediate redundancy built into its design.

An excellent example is that of TetraPak's work in India. They have teamed up with an NGO to get waste pickers allocated to schools, working with the children to recycle the thousands of milk cartons consumed every day across the city. The children flatten their packs after drinking and they are picked up by the waste pickers and taken to a central recycling plant. The waste pickers who collect the tetrapaks are given a guaranteed price per kilogram by the recycler, guaranteed by TetraPak.

PVC Banners

Vinyl banners play a big part in the stable of signage for most events. They are convenient, easy to handle, durable, weather resistant, relatively inexpensive and quick to produce. It's a quick fix for many event organizers when they need to produce a sign. But what of the costs to the environment? Vinyl banners are made from PVC (polyvinyl chloride), a material many describe as a 'poison plastic'.

US based **Centre for Health, Environment and Justice** has a campaign specifically around consumer awareness of the hazards of PVC manufacture and use. It describes PVC as 'one of the most hazardous consumer products ever created'.[18]

Greenpeace campaigned hard against PVC in the 1990s including being involved in ensuring the Sydney Olympics 2000 were PVC free.

Smells can ignite memories, and one of my earliest memories is triggered by the smell of PVC. We used to go on weekend excursions to the 'rubber' and outdoors store as my dad would pick up bits and pieces for the fishing boat or our latest camping expedition. The store's intoxicating (how true) smell reminded me of exciting Christmas mornings unwrapping presents and breathing in deeply the delightful smell of new blow-up toys to take to the beach. Now a whiff of PVC brings me back to those days picking out my new blow-up toy, or unwrapping it Christmas morning and running to try it out in the backyard pool. I am sure you have similar memories. To me, the smell of PVC means Christmas. That is a little worrisome.

Rather than the smell of summer and the smell of Christmas, I was breathing in PVC's process of off-gassing. Off-gassing is the evaporation of volatile chemicals at normal atmospheric pressure. Think of all those products which have a lingering 'smell'; the interior of a new car, paints, varnishes, stains, carpet, insulation, linoleum flooring, kitchen countertops, paint strippers. These products are all off-gassing volatile organic compounds (VOCs), a GHG, and you're breathing them in, and if you don't catch them up your nostrils, off they go, up into the atmosphere, playing their part in our man-made atmospheric delights.

PVC is hazardous during its entire product lifecycle. Its production process is chemical heavy, toxin rich and dioxin emitting. When in use it 'off-gases'. When disposed of, burning causes more dioxins and toxic gases to be released, and if landfilled its eventual breakdown can cause the cocktail of nasties it was made from to leach into the ground and waterways.

PVC can't be recycled easily or cost effectively, so that's not really an option. If mixed with other plastics it's going to contaminate the recyclate. Interestingly, bottles or other hardened PVC products are sometimes printed with the universal recycling symbol with the three arrows and a '3' inside. This symbol was developed by the plastics industry to identify each type of plastic, not to indicate if it's recyclable. So, if you see the '3' in a recycle symbol on any products, don't throw it in the recycling as your MRF probably won't be able to handle it. Certainly, PVC banners can't be recycled. The only option is to turn them into other things, such as the wonderful bags pioneered by **Freitag** (www.freitag.ch) and now copied by companies salvaging vinyl advertising banners around the world, or to be used for waterproofing and temporary covers. Or turn them over and use the other side for another banner.

At events, PVC in banners is the most common, but PVC is also used in many construction materials, household products and office supplies. It is likely to make an appearance in plumber's water and waste-water piping, cables, floor coverings, shower curtains, furniture, binders, folder and pens. They are all likely to be made of PVC.

So, what we're really saying here is PVC isn't the most environmentally preferable product and if you can find alternatives, you are encouraged to use them. **FortiBanner**™ is an example of the new generation of PVC alternative banner materials. It's made from **low density polyethylene** (LDPE) coated polypropylene and is 100 per cent recyclable.

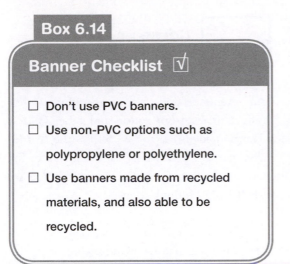

Box 6.14

Banner Checklist ☑

- ☐ Don't use PVC banners.
- ☐ Use non-PVC options such as polypropylene or polyethylene.
- ☐ Use banners made from recycled materials, and also able to be recycled.

Bottles into Banners

Ecophab™ is a PVC alternative material for banners. It's made from 100 per cent post-consumer soda pop bottles.

A fine example of up-cycling, the plastic bottles are taken through the recycling process, and spun into fibre which is then woven into fabric. This process produces the Ecophab fabric.

Banner Creations in the US uses Ecophab to produce a huge range of products including banners, table covers, table runners, point of purchase displays, backdrops, flags and a range of bags.

www.bannercreations.com

Sustainable Printing

Printing for an event can include promotional posters and flyers, event programme booklet, tickets, vehicle passes, on-site newspapers and publications, plus various forms and documents. Many participating organizations may also print specific things in association with your event.

Vegetable-Based Inks

Printing inks are made up of pigment for colour, liquid that carries the pigment, which evaporates, and other resins and polymers which make it stick to the paper. The problem with traditional inks is the emission of volatile organic compounds (VOCs) and the toxicity of the residue in the clean-up process. The liquid used in inks is generally petroleum based, a non-renewable resource. Vegetable-based inks use vegetable oil instead. It drastically reduces the VOCs and the clean-up process can be done with water, rather than more solvents, which would emit further VOCs. Some of the pigments used in some colours are quite toxic. It's best to avoid metallic or fluorescent colours as they comprise toxic compounds, and if they eventually end up in landfill, these may leach into the water table.

Biodegradable Laminate

In printing there is often a gloss finish. This is called gloss OPP (oriented polypropylene) lamination. Traditionally this gloss finish is made from petrochemicals, and as it's a 'plastic' it will not readily biodegrade. The use of a gloss finish, of course, is often an important part of the finished job, but now there are gloss 'laminate' finishes which are able to be recycled with the rest of the paper, and also will biodegrade if sent for composting. The benefit for you is the production of printed material without using non-renewable resources, and you can be confident that when ready to be thrown away, your posters, flyers and programmes can be composted or recycled effectively. The benefit to your printing company is that any trim that comes off finished jobs can be kept with the rest of the paper scraps and not contaminate their in-house recycling systems. **CelloGreen** is a wood-based laminate, developed by UK company Celloglas. www.celloglas.co.uk

Low VOC varnish

Varnishes offer a gloss or matt finish and are usually applied to print jobs that need extra durability or longevity. They coat the paper and protect it from scratches, finger prints, scuff marks etc. Varnishes are applied during the printing process just like ink, and are generally solvent based and thus emit VOCs. The most environmentally friendly option is to use a vegetable-based or water-based varnish. If you've found a printer who will use vegetable inks, then asking for a vegetable- or water-based varnish should be no problem.

Box 6.21

Printing Checklist ☑

☐ **Use vegetable-based inks.**

☐ **Use biodegradable laminate.**

☐ **Use low VOC varnishes.**

☐ **Choose an FSC certified printer.**

Garment Production

Many events produce t-shirts and merchandise products made from cotton and other fabrics, manufactured in factories across the world. When purchasing clothing for event staff or for merchandise to sell to your audience, there are several things to think about:

- Made from sustainable materials.
- Fair trade grown raw materials.
- Fair conditions for the factory workers that manufacture your garments.
- Final product toxic substance free.

That's quite a lot to deal with when just wanting to order a humble t-shirt. Let's look at some facts to keep you in the loop and make your purchasing decisions easier.

Organic Cotton

Cotton farming is water, pesticide and fertilizer heavy. Moving to organic cotton eliminates most of the bad elements of cotton production. No chemicals means better health for workers in the field, no pollution of toxins to the land and waterways, and an end product you'd feel safer using. Cotton farming is an intensive agricultural practice and takes its toll on the land and conventional cotton is one of the most chemically dependent agricultural crops.

Now the crux of the problem, apart from these chemicals remaining with the cotton all the way along the manufacturing chain until they are clothes on your back, is that a fair amount of these chemicals will make their way back into our ecosystem. They wash down off the plants into the soil, into the water table and on their merry way to our streams and rivers, wreaking havoc as they travel. These chemicals are also doing damage to the health of workers on the farms and those who are dependent on the surrounding natural environment, let alone the poor fish in the rivers. (Let's all pay homage to Rachel Carson's work at this moment. See the end of this section for details on her ground-breaking work.)

The **Organic Exchange** produces the *Organic Cotton Farm and Fibre Report* and according to it, the amount of organic cotton farmers grew worldwide in 2007/2008, increased by 152 per cent to 145,872 metric tons (668,581 bales) grown on 161,000 hectares in 22 countries worldwide.[19] The top ten countries, in order of volume produced are India, Syria, Turkey, China, Tanzania, US, Uganda, Peru, Egypt and Burkina Faso.
www.organicexchange.org

Ironically, when working on events in India recently, I found it difficult to source organic cotton for domestic use. India supplies just over 50 per cent of the world's organic cotton, but is growing for the export market with supply contracts in place. There has been a whopping 292 per cent increase in organic cotton production in India from 2006/2007 to 2007/2008.[20] A move away from chemical fertilizer because of its cost has in part driven this demand.

Cotton (whether organic or conventional) is India's largest agricultural crop and its produc-tion continues to poison the environment. There is a massive domestic cotton market in India but there seems to be little consumer awareness about organic cotton in this country. India's land and water systems are being polluted by conventional cotton production. If consumer demand for organic cotton within India increases, this could push production of organic cotton even further. Perhaps organic cotton is hitting the shelves but it just isn't being marketed as such.

As an indicator of where things are heading with organic cotton in other parts of the world (and other sustainable fabrics), you can now walk into the major supermarket chain Tesco in the UK and choose an organic, fair trade or recycled (PET) fabric school uniform for your child. Tesco has extended its Corporate Social Responsibility (CSR) even further through offering a 'buy one, give one free' deal. For every pair of 'Save the Children' school trousers purchased, they donate one to a child in Kenya enabling them to have a uniform to attend school.

Cleaner Cotton™

An alternative to organic cotton which has appeared in the US is 'Cleaner Cotton'. This is a brand and campaign developed by the **Sustainable Cotton Project**. They are a group that helps farmers develop a working knowledge of chemical-use reduction practices that can be successfully and economically applied to cotton. They have come to the realization that in the US, cotton grown in California is not economic-ally viable to be produced organically as the consumer is not willing to pay the premium.

By getting many farmers using these production methods, the cumulative reduction in chemical use is impressive. They report that in 2007 there were 22 cleaner cotton farmers growing 2000 acres reducing chemicals by about 2000 pounds. This compares to their estimate that two organic farmers grew 240 acres of organic cotton reducing chemicals by 500 pounds.[20]

They have developed the brand and the Cleaner Cotton Campaign to help manufacturers develop strategies to incorporate Cleaner Cotton and organic cotton fibres into existing products. Manufacturer demand is essential to increasing market opportunities for farmers growing Cleaner Cotton and organic cotton. www.sustainablecotton.org

Soy Silk™

Soy Silk is a trademark of Southwest Trading Company Yarns. It's an environmentally friendly fibre made from tofu manufacturing waste. Soy protein is liquefied and then extruded into long, continuous fibres that are then cut and processed like any other spinning fibre. The texture of this yarn feels like a cross between cotton and linen.

PET Bottle Fabrics

We've all heard about 'polarfleece' made from PET bottles. The official title is Fortrel EcoSpun™, a polyester fibre made out of recycled plastic bottles which can be made into fleece. Manufacturing these fibres is preferable to creating new petroleum-based fibres and, given the sheer amount of plastic bottles in existence, makes this fabric a no-brainer. ROTHBURY Festival's green volunteers' t-shirts are made from this, as are the t-shirts given as souvenirs to runners at the London Marathon.

Modal

Modal is a processed bio-based textile made from reconstituted cellulose from the beech tree. It's very soft and popular for both clothing and household textiles such as bedding, upholstery and towels.

Box 6.16

Chemical-Free Fabric and Clothing

Fabric standard

The Oeko-Tex® Standard 100 was introduced in the early 1990s as a response to the needs of consumers and for textiles that posed no risk to health. The demands we make of modern textile products cannot be realized without the use of specific chemical substances. Fashionable colours, easy-care properties, a long life span and many other functional properties are now demanded of textiles, and are essential in some cases, depending on the intended use. The label allows consumers to assess the human ecological quality of textiles and it gives a uniform safety standard for textile and clothing companies.

CONFIDENCE IN TEXTILES
Tested for harmful substances
according to Oeko-Tex Standard 100
No. 00000000   Institut

www.oeko-tex.com

Hemp

Hemp is one of the longest, strongest natural fibres on Earth, said to have double or triple the strength of cotton. It grows in just about any climate and, with the proper cultivation and rotation practices, without the need for chemical pesticides, herbicides, fungicides and fertilizers. It's a great fabric option for t-shirts and buttoned shirts. Look for a merchandise range made from hemp in your country.

Lyocell

Lyocell is a fabric better known by its brand name **Tencel®**. It has a soft finish, packs light and is made from cellulose (vegetable matter), or wood pulp, typically a mix of hardwood trees like oak and birch. This makes it a natural fabric, and it's noted for its durability and strength, in addition to its eco-friendly manufacturing techniques.

Bamboo Fabric

Bamboo is fast growing and its cultivation is sustainable using no pesticides or fertilizers. As a natural fibre, it's also completely biodegradable.

Wool

Wool is a wonderful natural fibre, but the size of this industry has caused some less than preferable practices. 'Mulesing' is highly controversial, and is carried out in Australia on merino sheep. We discussed this earlier. Bleaching wool has all the problems associated with bleaching cotton or paper. However, all of these issues can

> **Box 6.17**
>
> ### Fabric Checklist ☑
>
> **Choose alternative fabrics**
> ☐ If you are using fabric for set design or décor, or to be used to manufacture clothing, consider the use of alternative and sustainable materials.
>
> **Choose chemical-free fabrics**
> ☐ Insist on Oeko-Tex Standard 100 certified products.
>
> **Choose sustainable cotton**
> Help grow the demand for more sustainably cultivated cotton through choosing merchandise, t-shirts and uniforms made from organic cotton, or if available in your region, Cleaner Cotton™.

be overcome and environmentally friendly and sheep-friendly wool growing is out there. If you're purchasing woollen uniforms or merch, you may wish to consider the source of your wool.

Ingeo™

Ingeo is a synthetic biopolymer or PLA made by NatureWorks LLC. PLA is generally used for food packaging as a plastic alternative, made from plant starch. It mimics the properties of 'plastic' but is not made from oil as are traditional plastics. The PLA is woven with cotton or wool to make a fabric which is used in garment production.

Box 6.18

At your Event: Production and Contractor Purchasing

Production and contractor purchasing policy
- Make a commitment within your event's production office to purchase environmentally and ethically preferable products.
- Make a commitment with contractors that they will also embrace these policies. Include this in their agreements.
- Make a commitment to use only ethically produced and environmentally responsible event merchandise.

Fair labour products
- Garments.
- Merchandise.
- Fabric.
- Electronics.
- Consumer products.

Environmentally preferable products
- Timber.
- Paint.
- Stationery and office supplies.
- Printed promotional materials.
- Cleaning and sanitation products.

Cleaning and sanitation products
- Phosphate and solvent free.
- Completely biodegradable.
- Natural ingredients, fragrances.
- Toilet treatment products to be biological rather than chemical.

Merchandise
- Raw materials sustainably produced, with fair labour agreements and a fair price paid to farmers.
- Garments and other merchandise manufactured in a fair labour environment and with appropriate certification.
- Reduced packaging.
- Offset transport of merchandise if sourced overseas.

Construction and sets
- Timber to be sustainably sourced and certified.
- Paint to be non-toxic, water wash-up, solvent free and low or zero VOC.

Cleaning Products

As you can imagine, conventional cleaning products are a fantastic cocktail of chemical compounds, solvents, bleach, artificial fragrances and the like. They may cut through grease, decontaminate and leave a room lemon fresh, but at what cost? We clean to protect our health; ironically, while conventional cleaning products may kill germs, they are also adding toxins and poisons into our environment and into our bodies. Apart from the direct health impact on people, the black marks against conventional cleaning products also include:

X They Use Non-Renewable Resources

The bulk of raw materials are made from petroleum. As we know, this is a non-renewable resource, and the impact on our planet through its extraction and processing is considerable.

X They Emit Greenhouse Gases

Due to the solvents and other chemical compounds we get abundant VOC emissions from conventional cleaning products with consequential climate change impacts.

X They Poison Waterways and Aquatic Life

And the final black mark is that the cocktail of nasties is flushed away down sinks and drains, onto land and into streams, poisoning waterways and wreaking havoc on aquatic life.

Green cleaning should protect health without harming the environment. And so what do we look for in a green cleaning product?

√ They Use Renewable Resources

Environmentally sound cleaning products have raw materials sourced from vegetable and mineral resources. They are renewable, able to be grown again or replenished.

√ They are 100 Per Cent Biodegradable

Certified environmentally sound cleaning products will be 100 per cent biodegradable. This means that all components of the product will biodegrade, with all that remains being water, CO_2 and minerals.

√ Non-Toxic

Green cleaning products are non-toxic to aquatic life, safe for septic systems (and therefore your sewage treatment plant) and free from chlorine bleach, synthetic dyes and artificial fragrances.

√ Solvent Free

If it does not contain solvents, you are likely also looking at a VOC-free product. This means it's not off-gassing harmful GHGs.

√ Phosphate Free

Phosphates were a popular cleaning product ingredient as they are the bit that removes dirt and grease. Many countries have banned or limited phosphates in most cleaning products; however, it's still a prime ingredient in dishwashing powder. When phosphates hit the waterways they disrupt the natural balance in lakes and streams, allowing abnormally high algae growth.

√ Meet Government Standards

In applying environmentally sound cleaning products to commercial cleaning you should look into your country's government standards for cleaning products and, of course, the actual product performance.

If your existing cleaning company hasn't considered these issues get them on the case and reporting back to you on the state of environmentally sound cleaning products and practices.

Federal, state and local government may place controls on products used for cleaning public places. These are generally based around food handling and washroom hygiene concerns. Historically these regulations have been to the exclusion of 'green' products, with only chemical heavy products meeting stringent demands. However, we are seeing environmentally sound cleaning products benefiting from Environmental Preferential Purchasing (EPP) policies being implemented on a wide scale through government.

Where this isn't the case, 'green' cleaning products are finding workarounds by using science to ensure their products meet the exacting standards of the likes of council food inspectors. Products are being developed that tick all the boxes of bureaucracy, while also meeting the goals of environmental sensitivity. They are also, of course, lobbying against the dangers of chemical laden products through inhalation, skin contact and also the build up of these chemicals in our environment.

Your cleaners may insist on using certain products under the assumption that these are the only ones that can be used. Old habits die hard and you may need to put some strategies in place to coax them to using a different product. Instead of forcing them to change, work with them on a trial of a cleaning product with a view to rolling it out full scale in the future. What you want to aim for is to encourage your cleaning contractors to permanently switch to environmentally sound cleaning products.

Figure 6.17 At Leeds Festival in the UK, Ecover sponsors the event through product placement in the showers

Source: Festival Republic

The **GreenClean** product range was developed after a specific request to an event's consumables supplier for an environmentally sound cleaning product that meets the government requirements in the UK for public hygiene and cleaning standards. It was developed with the specific cleaning needs of outdoor events. The supplier, **Concept Products**, markets it directly to the festival's cleaning contractors and the festival organizers request that their cleaning contractors use this product or any other that meets the same standards. This product has been taken on by the cleaning companies to be used at their other events.

Eco-Certification

With the huge increase in demand for green cleaning in offices, schools and homes, certification systems are appearing to regulate the industry. This is really necessary as there are so many cleaning products out there that are not a green clean but a greenwash.

Also appearing are training and certification systems for janitors/cleaning staff. Your green cleaning is only going to be as good as the people doing the job and those staff that have for years used conventional cleaning products will need to be convinced to use the new products with enthusiasm and effectively. You may benefit from this as the cleaning companies likely to be used for your event will have contracts with offices, buildings and schools.

from the chemical and solvent mix that paint is made from. The carcinogens and neurotoxins in paints include benzene, formaldehyde, kerosene, ammonia, toluene and xylene. (Those last two are solvents.)

Using water based-paints and varnishes means you aren't using further solvents for clean-up and you aren't using up even more precious mineral oil.

Paints that are water based will still contain pigments and chemicals and you need to also consider the wash-up and waste-water disposal. More in Chapter 5.

Paints and Varnishes

Many events will use paint for signage, sets, décor and to preserve permanent infrastructure. To purchase the most environmentally friendly products, you need to look for paint and varnish that are VOC free and water based.

You can go one step further and use paints that have non-toxic pigments. Look for 'eco paints' – there are many on the market.

You remember that lovely freshly painted smell? That's the paint off-gassing. Luckily, in most events the painted structures are outdoors so you won't have the problems of indoor air pollution. However those VOCs are still setting sail off into the atmosphere. The VOCs come

Figure 6.18 Glastonbury Festival, low VOC paint is policy. The seats, festoon lighting poles and rubbish bins are all creatively painted and make up a major part of the overall festival décor. They also use paint provided by Community RePaint (see boxed text)

Source: Glastonbury Festival

Box 6.19

Community RePaint

Community RePaint, based in the UK, is a redistribution hub for unused paint.

They estimate that up to 56 million litres of unused paint lies stored in homes, garages or just thrown away. They take donations of unused paint and redistribute it to community groups, charities, voluntary organizations and people in social need.

www.communityrepaint.org

Green your Supply Chain

All this work you're doing in sourcing the best products can be helped along immensely by greening your supply chain. If you recruit your contractors, product suppliers and third parties to get in on the green act with you, your job will almost be done. You want to get to the point where your suppliers and contractors are presenting you with the most sustainable choices as a matter of course. With enough continual reinforcement of what you want them to supply, eventually you'll be batting them off with a stick.

By going through every area of procurement, and back-tracking up the supply chain, you can make a massive impact. Understanding that the cheap cotton t-shirt you buy and have screen printed for your event has a big environmental price tag, and then taking some action to change, is the ultimate in effective green purchasing.

Rather than simply swapping to a new supplier, work your existing contacts. For example, get them to investigate organic cotton, to report to you on the welfare of the workers in garment factories, and to understand the climate impact of transporting goods around the world.

Roskilde Festival in Denmark did just this. For the past few years they have been working with their merchandise partner to make a shift towards fair trade and environmentally friendly products. Instead of changing to another partner, they encouraged their current supplier to change their collection. After checking the supply chain, last year they succeeded in having a certified fair trade t-shirt as the crew t-shirt and official 2008 t-shirt. In 2009 the official t-shirt was additionally made from organic cotton and eco-labelled.

You can also create bespoke products for your event which may inspire a permanent new range. In 2008 **Roskilde Festival** also changed to fair trade wine. Needing to be glass free, they collaborated with TetraPak and their wine merchant to produce a custom made cardboard carton for fair trade wine. This also allowed them to print the logo and the refund instructions, ensuring the cartons were returned for recycling.

As was illustrated in the example with the GreenClean product range developed for festivals in the UK, your impact can cast a much wider net as other events and businesses benefit from the new products you have helped along the way.

Box 6.20

Cleaning and Painting Checklist ☑

Use environmentally sound cleaning products

☐ Identify the cleaning products used and seek out the most environmentally sound alternatives.

☐ Engage your cleaners, staff, food stalls, caterers and any other person who may have a mop and bucket or spray bottle and cloth and get them committed to cleaning green.

☐ Contract into cleaning agreements the use of your chosen cleaning products or that meet the same specifications.

☐ Supply handwash, bodywash, shampoo, etc., for your audience.

☐ Use zero or low VOC paint and varnish.

☐ Use paint with non-toxic pigment.

☐ Donate unused paint for re-use.

☐ Use donated paint.

☐ Manage water run-off in the wash-up.

Box 6.21

At your Event: Ethical Market Stalls

Organic, fair trade, environmentally sound, ethical traders
Make a commitment for all food and non-food traders to go organic, fair trade and/or ethically sourced.

Food Stalls

- Make contact with wholesalers to ensure that supply is available in your area, and broker a deal between them and the markets or coordinator of the markets for supply at a competitive price.
- Discuss the requirement of ethical and environmentally responsible products with market stall traders, before insisting they use them.
- Give traders adequate notice, as traders are likely to order stock well in advance, or have stock carry over from previous events.
- Instigate a requirement for all food traders and/or caterers to use ethical and environmentally responsible products and contract this in.
- Make contact with the fair trade and organics organizations in your country, region or city to establish a relationship and potential for support or promotion of your conversion to these products.
- Put together a strategy to promote the use of fair trade, organic, local, etc. products on site such as signage or posters at every stall using the goods.
- If you have branded cups for beverages, arrange to have the appropriate certification logo printed on takeaway coffee cups.

Ethical Market Stalls

- Work with your market stall coordinator to ensure active recruitment of traders selling fair trade, environmentally preferable and ethically sourced goods.
- Include a policy of being able to track the production of the goods back to the artisan or craftsperson, and that funds flow directly back. There are some amazing organizations doing this. Search them out and invite participation.
- Include 'locally made' or 'direct from producer' products as part of your market stalls, to promote the work of local artisans, craftspeople and growers.
- Set up a theme or promotional campaign to communicate your 'ethical' markets.
- Ensure the message is communicated prior to the event, as well as clearly at the event.

Figure 6.19 All material for décor at Peats Ridge Festival is from re-used and salvaged materials

Source: Meegan Jones

Re-Use and Repurposing

Conventional re-use is a pretty basic concept: using an item again for the same function. In new life re-use or repurposing we use an item again but for another purpose. We can get a bit more adventurous here, by actively seeking out second-hand materials from other sources for creative re-use at your event, or conceiving secondary uses for items at your event which would otherwise become waste.

If your event is repeated each year, each month, each quarter – don't throw away the stuff you use to produce it. Store and re-use. It seems a simple principle but it doesn't happen enough.

By taking useful products and re-using them either for the original intent or creative repurposing, we are saving energy, money, time and resources. Reducing consumption and saving resources ticks my boxes.

On a large scale, activating re-use through scrap stores and re-use centres creates businesses and jobs while also being a positive environmental activity.

Re-use is a tool of old, before the environment was even considered as part of the motivation. Financial necessity along with difficulty and expense in delivering new goods meant that re-use and repurposing was the status quo. In the developing world it's still very much a part of everyday life. Countries with huge populations from the global south are the most ingenious and inspiring re-users of the discards and disposables of the modern world.

Due to environmental pressures and an awareness of these issues amongst consumers, we are seeing attitudes change and regulations coming into play to move back to re-use. As discussed in Chapter 7, refillable bottles for soft drinks and milk are an example of re-use schemes that have never gone away in some countries and are experiencing a renaissance in others.

Pallet exchange, plastic crates for bread and fruit and vegetables, retreading tyres, etc. are all functional re-use schemes which are working on a wide scale. We need to upgrade this concept to include more materials, products and processes.

By keeping materials and products as functioning items, we are making savings in energy and raw materials consumption as replacing many single use products with a re-usable one reduces the amount that need to be manufactured from scratch. In re-use we also have the dual waste management benefits of reduced disposal costs and reduction of volume to landfill.

Of course there are some challenges to re-using or repurposing products and materials. The main issues are time for sorting and handling, cleaning, storage, redistribution and the consequential human labour costs involved. You may not also get exactly what you need, and so must be a little flexible in your expectations.

Figures 6.20 and 6.21 Structures in 'The Park' at Glastonbury are all made from salvaged materials and reassembled each year

Source: Glastonbury Festival

Re-Use Centres and Virtual Exchanges

Re-use centres are the scrapyard of the new millennium. For ages past, the humble scrapyard has been the cornerstone of the re-use concept. Lumber and building materials yards, car parts and spares yards, the second-hand shop attached to a charity, and the local dump have always been and will always be.

But now we see the emergence of re-use centres which mine industry, commerce and households for their discards and redistribute and sell them. Columns in theatre props were once the cores of massive rolls of vinyl. Once shapes have been cut out of foam, plastic and vinyl, the left-overs are put to creative re-use. Fabric scraps, old promotional banners, plastic drums, overruns and misprints all make their ways to these Aladdin's caves of creative delight.

The next step on from re-use centres are online virtual exchanges. These websites, either self-moderated or with staff to facilitate the process, match those people with surplus and those that are looking for goods.

The **California Materials Exchange** (CalMAX) is an initiative of the California Integrated Waste Management Board. Operating under the premise that one business's trash is another business's treasure, the website has searchable functionality enabling the user to find or get rid of almost anything. The **New York Waste Match** is a similar service.

www.wastematch.org
www.ciwmb.ca.gov/calMAX

The **Freecycle Network™** is made up of 4670 groups with 6,340,000 members across the globe. It's a grassroots and entirely non-profit movement of people who are giving (and getting) stuff for free in their own towns. It's all about re-use and keeping good stuff out of land-fills. Each local group is moderated by a local volunteer. Membership is free.

www.freecycle.org

Box 6.22

Re-Use Centres

The fantastic Addison Road Centre is right in the middle of Sydney, Australia, and is home to several re-use initiatives. Reverse Garbage is a re-use centre that collects over 8000 cubic metres of re-usable off-cuts, over-runs and rejected material annually. The City of Sydney street flags, which get changed over regularly, are a much sought after décor item for events and fairs, being cut up and repurposed to make bunting and new flags.

Next door is The Bower, 'Traders of the Lost Artefact'. They collect, resell and repair goods diverted from municipal landfill sites. They also do prop hire, with some amazing found objects which are great for décor.

www.addisonrdcentre.com.au

Operating on a similar concept but as a worldwide matching service is **Global Hand**. This matches excess materials and goods from industry and business with those in need throughout the world, distributed via charity. Even the transportation of the goods is gifted by freighting companies. In 2007 more than 10,000 items of camping gear donated by festival goers at the UK's Reading and Leeds Festival was redistributed through the Global Hand network. www.globalhand.org

If you need inspiration on what to do with your left-over materials and how to re-use them at your event, hit the internet for some ideas: there are plenty of creative re-use sites out there.

The **Re-Use Development Organization** or 'ReDo' promotes re-use as an environmentally sound, socially beneficial and economical means for managing surplus and discarded items. www.redo.org

All the building materials used at **Boom Festival** in Portugal are recycled from other festivals. The two main ones that Boom has established a relationship with are the **Festival Internacional de Banda Desenhada da Amadora** (International Comic Book Fair / Amadora) and **Rock in Rio Lisboa**. Instead of being trashed and thrown away, the materials from these events are re-used at Boom.

Figure 6.22 Peats Ridge Festival makes its signs from salvaged materials including old banners

Source: Peats Ridge Festival

Box 6.23

Salvage Checklist ☑

☐ **Use salvaged materials**
You can do better than trawl through your local scrap store or re-use centre to get your materials for set building and décor.

☐ **Salvage at your Event**
Your event can contribute to the re-use and repurposing economy by donating the valuable detritus from your event for re-use.

☐ **Salvage and Reuse your Own Materials**
Identify items from your own event that can be repurposed at future events.

Sponsor and Partner Opportunities

Partnering with environmentally responsible products and companies at your event can add value. Here are some ideas:

- Offer product exclusivity deals to environmentally and socially responsibly produced products.
- Strike a deal with a cleaning product range to sponsor your event and/or to provide cleaning products in exchange for exposure.
- Choose brands that have both consumer and commercial ranges so they can be used to produce your event as well as to show the audience choices they can make.
- Align with a local farmers' market and have them 'clip in' a version of their market at your event.
- Invite activist groups whose themes are environmental issues and social justice to have a presence at your event.
- Invite lobby or industry associations working in organics, sustainable agriculture and fair labour to be at your event.
- Set up an 'ethical' market and invite all the above brands and organizations to participate.
- Invite re-use centres and community recycling organizations to do your event's décor and signage from re-used and salvaged material, promoting their services and activities at the same time.

Figure 6.22 Signs being made by volunteers from recycled materials at Peats Ridge Festival, Australia

Source: Glastonbury Festival

Watch | Read | Visit

WorldChanging
A Users Guide for the 21st Century

Edited by Alex Steffen

(Harry N. Abrams, Inc 2006)

This book is a groundbreaking compendium of the most innovative solutions, ideas and inventions emerging today for building a sustainable, liveable, prosperous future. From consumer consciousness to a new vision for industry; nontoxic homes to refugee shelters; microfinance to effective philanthropy; socially responsible investing to starting a green business; citizen media to human rights; ecological economics to climate change, this is the most comprehensive, cutting edge overview to date of what's possible in the near future – if we decide to make it so. www.worldchanging.com

Silent Spring

Rachel Carson and Edward O. Wilson

First published by Houghton Mifflin in 1962, *Silent Spring* alerted a huge number of people to the dangers of wide-scale pesticide spraying. Her work ignited changes in laws concerning the environment. It's a depressing and infuriating read. Full of example after example of the stupidity of the human species not learning their lessons, even when it's slapped in their face with birds literally falling out of the sky, and causing the title of the book, a silent spring. Many editions of this book exist.

The Story of Stuff

Annie Leonard

The Story of Stuff by Annie Leonard is a fantastic short film that illustrates the compounding impacts of resource depletion, consumption and disposal. Watch it here:

www.storyofstuff.com

Cradle to Cradle^{SM}
Remaking the Way We Make Things

William McDonough and Michael Braungart (North Point Press, 2002)

William McDonough's book, written with his colleague, the German chemist Michael Braungart, is a manifesto calling for the transformation of human industry through ecologically intelligent design.

Through historical sketches on the roots of the industrial revolution; commentary on science, nature and society; descriptions of key design principles; and compelling examples of innovative products and business strategies already reshaping the marketplace, McDonough and Braungart make the case that an industrial system that 'takes, makes and wastes' can become a creator of goods and services that generate ecological, social and economic value.

www.mcdonough.com/cradle_to_cradle.htm

Responsible Purchasing Network

RPN is an international network of buyers dedicated to socially and environmentally sustainable purchasing.

www.responsiblepurchasing.org

Notes

1 ISO 14040: 2006 Environmental Management, Life Cycle Assessment, Principles and framework, www.iso.org.

2 European Commission's LCA on PVC, ec.europa.eu/enterprise/chemicals/sustdev/pvc-final_report_lca.pdf, accessed 10 November 2008.

3 C-Change, www.switchonswitchoff.org.

4 Global Footprint Network, www.footprint-network.org.

5 Living Planet Report, www.panda.org/about_our_earth/all_publications/living_planet_report, accessed December 2008.

6 One Planet Living, www.oneplanetliving.org; Bioregional www.bioregional.com; WWF, www.panda.org.

7 Global Ecolabelling Network, www.global-ecolabelling.net.

8 International Federation of Organic Agricultural Movements, www.ifoam.org.

9 Food and Agriculture Organization, www.fao.org.

10 World Fair Trade Organization, www.wfto.com.

11 International Social and Environmental Accreditation and Labelling Alliance, www.isealalliance.org.

12 Fairtrade Label, www.fairtrade.net.

13 Fairtrade Labelling Organizations International Annual Report 2007, www.fairtrade.net/uploads/media/FLO_AR2007_low_res_01.pdf, accessed November 2008.

14 Fair Trade Association of Australia and New Zealand, www.fta.org.au/?q=node/159, accessed October 2008.

15 Greenpeace, www.greenpeace.org.uk/forests, accessed November 2008.

16 Forest Stewardship Council, www.fsc.org, accessed November 2008.

17 ISO 14001 Environmental Management – ISO 14001 specifies the actual requirements for an environmental management system. It applies to those environmental aspects that the organization has control of and over which it can be expected to have an influence, www.iso14000-iso14001-environmental-management.com/iso14001.htm.

18 Center for Health, Environment and Justice, www.besafenet.com/pvc, accessed December 2008.

19 'Organic Cotton Farm and Fibre Report', Organic Exchange, www.organicexchange.org, accessed December 2008.

20 Sustainable Cotton Project, www.sustainablecotton.org.

Source: Festival Republic

chapter 7

Waste

Events create waste. People buy stuff, eat stuff, throw stuff away. How you manage this waste, and influencing whether it's produced in the first place, will have an effect on the overall sustainability of your event.

In the following pages we look at the creation of event waste and how to limit what's thrown in a hole in the ground or goes up in smoke at the end of your show. No matter the event size, waste management strategies are similar. towards zero waste is the goal. Along with guiding principles, suggestions, tips and examples of successful operations, to put it all in context we'll also look at developments in waste management technology and take a peek at the changing face of attitudes to re-use, recycling and waste reduction and how your event can help move this along.

Of incredible importance is the understanding that waste occurs at every step along the one-way road of resource consumption, production, use and disposal. By reducing the amount we use or responsibly sourcing the products we sell and consume, we will in turn be reducing waste back up the supply chain. For every tonne of end-of-life-cycle waste, approximately 71 tonnes of waste are produced during the original product's journey from raw material to manufacturing, distribution and sale.[1]

To manufacture the products events use and dispose of, a constant flow of resources needs to be dug up, manufactured, transported, distributed, purchased, used, and then if not responsibly recycled, composted, re-used or repurposed, finally buried or incinerated at the local garbage facility.

As you read about waste management in the following pages and develop solutions for your event, keep in mind the additional volume of waste produced as the single use products you need come into creation, not just what you put in bins at the end of the show. If you purchase and consume irresponsibly, you're contributing to the problem of compounding waste generation and potential destructive exploitation of primary resources. A bit gloomy really.

Of course consumption is what keeps the money wheel ticking over at many shows. You don't want to reduce the sale of stuff so much your event is no longer financially viable. You want your audience to eat and drink, buy a programme, get a souvenir t-shirt, spend money at the market stalls, participate, enjoy themselves. But you can make good decisions on what you sell, what useless stuff is given away for free, how things are packaged, etc. These decisions will have a massive impact on the waste volumes at the end of your event and on the upstream impact of waste creation.

Considerations such as ethical purchasing, product miles and buying products made from recycled and sustainable materials are just some of the ways you can help reduce waste production. These are discussed in greater detail in Chapter 6.

If you have a large event you'll invariably have a waste management company on board to plan and conduct waste operations. You need to know your way around garbage so you can work with them to achieve the best result. This chapter gives you a tune up on waste management know-how, taking you through each type of recyclable material likely at your event, logistics on how to do waste separation and pre-treatment on site, plus the different types of waste processing off site including recyclable and biodegradable materials. If you're running the waste yourself, you'll find the content of this chapter most useful.

We look at ideas from events around the world on how they have tackled waste challenges and also engaged their audiences in their recycling and composting projects.

There are several questions you need to consider when starting to plan your waste management strategies:

- What waste treatment facilities are in your region and what processes do they use?
- What types of waste will be generated at your event?
- How can you influence or regulate the types of waste generated?
- How can you manage the waste at your event to move it towards zero waste given the answers to the above three questions?

Read through the checklist in Box 7.1 and get ready to dive into the garbage pit.

Box 7.1

Waste Management Checklist ☑

☐ **What Waste in your Community?**
- What is your audience's waste personality? Are they used to separating their waste and understand the concepts?
- What facilities are there for processing waste in your region and what can be recycled?
- Are there composting or biogas facilities locally to process your biodegradable waste?

☐ **Minimize Waste**
- Identify what waste could be produced at your event and come up with alternatives so it's not produced in the first place.
- Put restrictions on traders and contractors likely to generate waste. Even on the audience!
- Consider re-usable food serviceware. If you have to go disposable, make it biodegradable.

☐ **Zero Waste and Closed Loop Concepts**
- Audit the areas of production likely to produce waste, and ruthlessly wrangle the big hitters.
- Don't overorder supplies or overcater for food.
- Envisage the end life of everything you purchase to produce the event and all the products you sell there. Where could the waste end up, and how can you ensure it's sent back into the system as recyclate, compost or repurposed materials?

☐ **Waste Separation: Audience Participation**
- Set up at-event separation and get your audience involved in actively separating waste.
- Make the bin signage easy to understand and bin stations positioned for ease of access and convenience.
- Offer incentives or rewards for recycling.
- Put deposits on cups or bottles, and refund when returned.
- Have recycling volunteers promoting your programme and standing guard over the bins.

☐ **Waste Processing**
- Set up a waste processing facility on site to decontaminate bins and maximize success rates of recycling before you send it onwards for processing.
- If you own the land event is held on, consider composting biodegradable waste on site.

☐ **Production Waste**
- Pre-plan what production waste will be generated prior to, during and post event build.
- Place appropriate bins and skips for timber, metal, film plastic, etc. in production areas.
- Get your teams involved in minimizing waste production. Set targets and offer incentives.

☐ **Salvage, Re-use and Repurposing**
- Pack up, store and re-use everything possible.
- Identify what could be salvaged for re-use at your event or by someone else as is or repurposed.
- Set up a salvage yard and have a team work towards collecting everything salvageable.

☐ **Key Sustainability Indicators**
- Percentage of waste recycled, composted, salvaged, landfilled/incinerated.
- Total volume and tonnage of each.
- Measure the CO_2 impact of waste disposal (landfill).

Figure 7.1

Source: iStock photos

Waste Management in your Community

To make the best decisions for your event, you need to understand the various waste treatment processes. The frustrating thing about managing waste from event to event is in each location, town, city, municipal government area, etc., recycling is handled differently and some areas don't have facilities to treat biodegradable waste.

How you set up to manage waste will depend on what facilities are available nearby for onward

processing. You may also find the venue you choose, or the waste management service you engage, already has contracts with a particular waste haulage firm, who in turn may be connected to a treatment facility. You need to know these details to effectively manage what waste is generated and how you manage it on site to minimize volume to landfill.

It may also be possible to separate your waste into single recycling streams and to deal with each of the recycling reprocessors directly, bypassing the Materials Recovery Facility (MRF; see explanation in the following pages). Most recyclate is worth money, and depending on volumes you could be looking at a profit or conversely your haulage fees may bring you to break even.

Fundamental to the direction you take will be the overall waste strategy of your country and the waste habit of its citizens. What's your country's recycling habit?

Europe is leading the way in waste management, and their way is away from landfill. Across Europe countries are recognizing landfill as the last resort for waste and as a result have introduced restrictions on the landfilling of biodegradable waste and recyclable materials. Everything must go through treatment to maximize recycling, and minimize landfill.

In analysing its own position on sending biodegradable waste to landfill the UK's **Department for Environment, Food and Rural Affairs** (Defra) is looking across the channel to Europe as a guiding light.

As Defra has reported, the following European countries are leagues ahead:[2]

- **Austria**: Restrictions on landfill (2004).
- **Denmark**: Ban on combustible wastes suitable for incineration going to landfill (1997).
- **France**: Ban on landfilling non-residual wastes (2002).
- **Germany**: Ban on non-treated wastes to landfill (1993); ban on combustible waste to landfill (2001). No landfilling after 2015.
- **Netherlands**: Ban on all wastes that can be re-used or recovered (1995).

- **Sweden**: Ban on non-treated municipal solid wastes to landfill (1996); ban on combustible wastes to landfill (2002); ban on organic wastes to landfill (2005).

European countries are the masters of recycling with figures unheard of in other Western and developed nations. Recycling is part of a European citizen's everyday life. Recycling on the go in public places the norm. So if you're putting on an event in a European country, chances are the mindset of your audience, the resources available to put your systems in place and the treatment facilities available to send your waste to, will be leagues ahead.

Let's now look at the basic treatment methods for recycling, biodegradable waste and general waste. We'll also discuss the concept of zero waste, before looking at what waste will be generated and how to deal with it.

Recycling

Recycling paper, cardboard, plastic, glass, metals, timber and aluminium is common practice. Residential and commercial recycling services are available in most developed nations and through necessity developing nations seem to do a good job of taking anything of value and recycling or re-using it. The best place for any recyclable material is the recycling plant or being re-used or repurposed, and not in a landfill site or incinerator.

Figures 7.2 and 7.3 Cardboard beer cups are compacted and baled at Reading Festival before being sent for recycling. Once baled, they need to be placed onto pallets so they can be fork lifted or hand trollied, as the weight of a bale is too heavy to hand lift.

Source: Festival Republic

Materials Recovery Facility (MRF)

In most circumstances mixed recycled materials will be taken to what's known as a Materials Recovery Facility (MRF, pronounced MERF). MRFs are ingenious places and you're encouraged to find out how the MRF your waste will go to operates. There are suckers and blowers, magnets and conveyor belts, lines of people, and things that whizz and whirr. Each type of recyclable material is sent shooting off in a different direction, contaminants pulled out each step along the way. Some MRFs are council run, others are private concerns and the technology and investment in infrastructure varies, which impacts on what can and can't be recycled. Some will take plastic drink bottles, but not milk bottles. Only some can take tetrapak (cardboard cartons lined with aluminium). Some need glass separated by colour. Some MRFs are able to take a wide range of plastics and others just clean plastic bottles of one type such as PET. They may need the plastic bottles to be uncrushed as the technology used may look for cylindrical objects when separating plastic bottles and crushed ones will get missed.

Most MRFs don't want plastic bags, and what's more, require all their waste coming in loose rather than bagged – so if your system is to bag and tie all your waste, you may need to put an additional process in to slash and empty bags into skips or trucks.

Your waste manager needs to know what the MRF will accept and how they want it presented to optimize the final recycling results. Don't just collect the waste, think you're doing an awesome job, close your eyes, hold your breath and hope everything will be OK once you wave goodbye to the recycling truck at the back gate.

Have the MRF, recycling processor, local council, waste contractor or waste manager supply you with a list of items they will recycle so you can work backwards in making your purchasing decisions and managing what waste will be generated in the first place. You can then put in the most appropriate regulations to traders and participants, prepare the best way to present bin stations and signage, and work out the on-site treatment and separation of waste.

What if There's No MRF?

In countries such as India where there is a massive population and massive rubbish problem, waste is a big business. There aren't many automated MRFs, and to the casual onlooker the streets may seem dirty and to have no organized waste system. But if you take a closer look, you'll discover a magical world of recycling and resource recovery. Anything of value is quickly snapped up and taken on a terrific journey from a pile on the street, into a 'rag picker's' sack, through a network of scrap dealers and brokers and eventually to a recycling processor. Anything with a recycling or re-use value makes its way through many pairs of hands, but rather than any concern for the environment, this system happens through financial necessity.

In Dharavi Slum in Mumbai, India lies the recycling heart of this huge city. Completely unofficial and practically unrecognized by the municipal council, millions of people make their living, often in terrible working conditions, from the recycling precinct in the slum. They scrape out a living by scouring the streets, bins, rubbish trucks and rubbish dumps and collect every last thing of value, which is then processed by hand in a labyrinth of micro processing plants in the slums. I recommend a visit to see it in action if you are ever in Mumbai; it is at once amazing, inspiring and heartbreaking. To find out more of how this system works, go to www.dharavi-project.org.

Figure 7.4 Electronics awaiting deconstruction and recycling in Mumbai's Dharavi Slum's recycling precinct

Source: Parasher Baruah

As well as waste pickers scavenging recyclable material, in place of mechanized MRFs India has the 'Kabadi Walla' system. Collectors (Kabadi Wallas) move through the streets calling for cardboard and other recycling. Caretakers and cleaners at housing estates collect anything of value and they sell them to these dealers.

If you're running an event in a country that has no mechanized MRF or any formal recycling separation facilities but has an 'underground' recycling industry, seek out organizations that work with and support people who earn their existence off the stuff other people throw away.

Have waste separation at your event so your audience to has an appreciation of the value of recycling and an understanding of the importance of what they throw away. Then get

organizations that support waste pickers to come and collect your recycling, offering them a valuable income stream and helping to improve the working conditions of the people that provide cities throughout the developing world with this essential yet unrecognized sanitation service.

An example is the fantastic organization Stree Mukti Sanghatana (SMS). They train women waste pickers on safe handling practices, assist in transport of collected items and help broker a good price and guaranteed outlet for the recycling they collect.
www.streemuktisanghatana.org

Biodegradable Waste

The only real way to prevent the negative impacts of sending biodegradable waste to landfill (creating methane emissions) or for incineration (CO_2) is to stop it from entering them. Alternatives to landfill or incineration are composting and anaerobic digestion (AD). Methane created at landfill sites can be harvested; however, the success rates of this method vary significantly. Energy from waste is created at incineration plants, but this is a controversial option. We discuss the massive impact waste has on climate change potential at the end of this chapter.

Composting

Collecting biodegradable waste separately and sending it to the closest processing facility, whether an in-vessel composting site, windrow set-up or even composting on the land where

Figure 7.5 Child rag pickers in India sort through waste for valuable recycling. By supporting NGOs working with waste pickers you can be sure workers receive fair prices for their collections, and only adult labour is used. Thanks to this young girl who allowed me to take her photo

Source: Meegan Jones

your event is held, is an important step to reducing the landfill footprint and consequential production of methane emissions. Uncontaminated biodegradable waste can enter an in-vessel compost system and be out the other side as life-giving compost within a week or two.

At **Latitude Festival** in the UK, an audit of waste generated in the arena showed ten bags of compostables to two bags of recycling to one bag of landfill. The majority of waste produced was takeaway food packaging and food scraps. By capturing this waste separately, the event was able to prevent a major proportion of arena waste from hitting the local landfill site.

So what of compost itself? What is it good for? Compost adds organic matter to soil, improving plant growth, offering a natural fertilizer. Modern agricultural techniques deplete organic carbon levels in soil, making it less stable, less able to hold water and contributing to erosion and salinity. Compost also has a wonderful benefit of sequestering carbon, keeping it in the soil, where eventually it will be taken up by plants and returned to the natural carbon cycle. It also reduces the amount of chemical fertilizer that needs to be manufactured.

Anaerobic Digestion and Biogas

Anaerobic digestion (AD) is used all over the world, particularly on a small scale in agriculture in nations such as India and Thailand, and is also used widely in Europe. AD is composting biodegradable material in the absence of oxygen. The result is biogas (a mixture of methane and CO_2), used to generate electricity and heat, and digestate, the solids/liquids left at the end of the decomposition process. This digestate can

---

Box 7.2

Composting On Site at Woodford Folk Festival

Woodford Folk Festival in Queensland, Australia is held on land owned by the Queensland Folk Federation, who also run the event. It has continuing sustainable development of the land as an underlying feature of the event and site operations, and composting the biodegradable waste is part of this.

Organic waste is collected from the Festival Village and camping areas in 120-litre bins and transported to the on-site processing location. An effort is made to manually remove non-organic contaminants from the collected waste. The level of this contamination is the weakest point in the process. The site the composting takes place on is graded hard stand, and has its own leachate dam. This is where rainwater run-off goes. The dam is mechanically drained to on-site 'black water' systems.

The raw festival waste is blended with a carbon rich waste stream and placed in a windrow on the hardstand. The windrow dimensions are governed by the composition of the two waste streams. Post festival the heap is covered with waste hessian to deter animal interference and aid moisture retention.

The heap is left to the elements and natural life forms to break it down to compost which will be less than 10 per cent of the volume of the original material. It's anticipated, after stick picking the remnants of biodegradable cutlery and shredding them for mulch or discarding them, this product will be used to activate the fresh waste collected at the next festival.

www.woodfordfolkfestival.com

Source: Information supplied by Queensland Folk Federation

be used as agricultural fertilizer or additionally treated in a traditional composting operation.

Defra's *Waste Strategy for England*, published in 2007 strongly supports AD to treat food waste.[2] The UK government is now encouraging local authorities and businesses to use AD. Keep an eye on whether there are AD facilities in your local area that your compostable waste could be directed to.

Incineration

Incineration is often the final method of waste disposal chosen in Europe, but it must be noted this is only after the maximum amount of recycling and compostables has been salvaged. Incineration can undermine recycling projects in nations not predisposed to the recycling habit. Most European countries have moved to the point of maximizing recycling opportunities

and send to incineration only the waste that can't be salvaged as a secondary raw material.

Some countries have leapfrogged the recycling habit and send stuff straight for incineration opting for the 'Energy from Waste' (EfW) process. Waste is 'burnt' in the absence of oxygen through a process called pyrolysis, and 'syngas' produced. This gas then fuels energy generation. Although some federal governments are jumping straight to incineration as an answer to their waste challenges, as a result of pressure from the people against incineration at a municipal level, cities and local government are pushing back against this recycling deterrent by putting in their own recycling and composting schemes to prevent non-treated waste from making its way to incinerators.

Landfill

Landfill is the end of a one-way road for our habit of buying, using and discarding. The by-product of consumption, our dirty little secret. Well maybe not so secret, and definitely not so little. Shall we just call it dirty?

Massive lost opportunities lie in the heart of a landfill. Tonnes of valuable recyclable material sit buried while fresh resources are extracted and created in factories to replace what we have discarded. Tonnes of biodegradable waste lies rotting, sending up methane, when it could have become fertilizer if composted, or energy if used as feedstock for biogas or gasification plants.

Beyond methane emissions and lost resources, landfill holds the potential for the escape of

Figure 7.6 Bagged and separated waste awaiting transport

Source: Meegan Jones

leachates, causing soil and ground water pollution. In some areas we are simply running out of landfill space. Enter stage right landfill mining. Sites are being up-turned to pull out recyclables, deal with toxicity issues, take out the soil which has now combined with rotting biodegradable waste, and also to free up landfill space to put more stuff back in.

Zero Waste

In nature, systems are cyclical, producing no waste, one thing feeding into the next. Earth, water, air and solar energy continually exchange, create, regenerate. The only species in nature that creates un used waste is human beings.

The zero waste movement has an overall vision for the future where we are working within closed loops, producing no waste at all. The idea is to see any waste as a residual product or potential resource and to develop systems to optimize this. The goal is to design-in waste prevention through processing techniques, component design, materials choice, minimizing packaging, eliminating hazardous processes and materials, and forward planning uses for residual products.

The goal of moving an event towards zero waste is to identify every type of waste that could be generated, and plan in advance to eliminate its creation or target its recycling, composting, re-use, salvage or repurposing. By doing this we'll be reducing waste management costs, reducing purchasing and potentially moving to profit making from the sale or re-use of 'waste'.

> **Box 7.3**
>
> ## Zero Waste Checklist ☑
>
> ☐ Are you producing too many posters and flyers?
>
> ☐ Are you ordering too much merchandise?
>
> ☐ Do you throw out boxes of programmes at the end of the show?
>
> ☐ Do you overcater food service?
>
> ☐ Do you have too many stalls for your event's capacity?
>
> ☐ Do you overorder bulk materials and supplies?
>
> ☐ Do you use materials just once, where instead, with a commitment to re-use and some human resources, you could clean, pack and store for future use?

Inefficiencies and overproduction are big waste creators and something you should review.

The Closed Loop

The entire life cycle of a product's journey from extraction of resources, through manufacturing, transport, use and disposal is a one-way system for many products. We need to imitate nature and close our loops, creating continuous cycles of resource creation and use, so our waste re-enters the manufacturing system as valuable secondary materials. A product, its components, packaging and manufacturing by-products all have the potential to become the materials from which new products are made.

'Up-cycling' is the ultimate, where new and valuable products are made, keeping the resources out of landfill or incinerators, rather than 'down-cycling' where lower and lower grade products are made from recycled materials, only putting off for a little while longer their eventual home in the ground.

Upcycling, keeping materials in a constant flow, being recycled, or being used in or as a product is a concept known at 'the closed loop'. Paper recycling is virtually a closed loop system, though virgin pulp does need to be introduced into the cycle as paper can only be recycled four to seven times before its fibre length is too short to be useful. Plastic recycling has traditionally down-cycled, with each cycle of re-use producing lower grade material. However technological advancements are seeing plastics being re-used for their original purpose. Aluminium and glass both have near perfect closed loop recycling potential.

Box 7.4

Burning Man's MOOP map

Matter out of place
Any look at Burning Man's sustainability starts with its standing as the world's largest 'Leave No Trace' event. No garbage cans are provided.

Participants must remove from the event site any matter out of place, known as 'MOOP', whether cigarette butts, boa feathers or even substances otherwise considered natural.

Black Rock City at Burning Man is laid out into a systematic labyrinth of themed camps. At the end of the show Burning Man officials prowl the playa with GPS devices to identify camps that neglected their trash, ready to make public maps of shame. A MOOP map is produced and camps are identified by red, green or yellow, depending on how well they cleaned up after themselves. Have a look at the MOOP maps from previous years on the Burning Man's website. Search for 'After Burn Reports'.

www.burningman.com

Figure 7.7 Once people get into the swing of separating their waste, they would prefer to overflow the correct bin rather than put their waste in the wrong one. Can you see what doesn't belong in these compost bins? They've done a pretty good job

Souce: Meegan Jones

What Waste at your Event?

When you go step by step through your event, you will be able to identify what rubbish will be created and where. You'll then be able to plan for recycling separation, composting, salvage and re-use.

Waste will be generated in the pre-production phase, the building or creation of your site or event, activities such as workshops, food stalls, display booths and of course by the audience at the show. Significantly also, the aftermath of the event, the exodus and the pull-down is a big one. What's discarded by all that have participated is often a troublesome and high volume waste stream.

In the next pages we'll look at waste produced from planning to pull-out, created by your audience, production and traders, and techniques to prevent waste from being created in the first place.

Production Waste

Back of house production areas will generate recyclable and biodegradable waste every day as staff, crew and other people go about their work. But there are also unique waste streams from production work. As each event is different, the list could be endless, but here are examples of some of the waste that could be created:

- Timber offcuts.
- Metal strips from pallet deliveries.
- Cling wrap from pallet deliveries.
- Cardboard boxes.
- Scrap metal.
- Plastic piping from plumbing.
- Electrical cabling offcuts.
- Batteries.
- Plastic and cardboard packaging.
- Plastic sheeting/scrim for fences.
- Fabric drops used to mask backstage areas.
- Blown light globes and fluoro tubes.
- Packaging material such as polystyrene balls (aaagghh!) And bubble wrap.
- Paint tins, fuel tins and other receptacles of liquids.
- Waste cooking oil or machinery oil.
- Compostable catering waste.
- Damaged equipment and goods.

Wave Rock Weekender Festival in Western Australia issues a challenge to their staff – the no gaffa tape and no cable ties challenge! This is so all their production set-ups are either compostable or re-usable. Even the roadies enjoy the challenge and before the event they share ideas about different ways to hang or stick things around the site. The answer ends up being a good stock of clamps, clips, twine and u-bolts.

Figure 7.8 Production waste contains many items that can be recycled or salvaged for re-use by the event or for donation to community groups or re-use centres. Put a programme in place to monitor what is thrown out by traders and other participants and establish a salvage programme

Source: Meegan Jones

Box 7.5

Production Waste Checklist ☑

☐ Identify what can be recycled back of house and set up bins or skips with good signage at convenient locations, to collect recyclables and those materials identified for salvage.

☐ Consider setting up a 'salvage yard' and encourage contractors to bring stuff there that they think might be good for re-use.

☐ Put a motivated volunteer who knows their scrap to be the salvage yard steward. Or if you have pre-identified which organization will be the recipient of the salvaged items, have them post someone at the salvage yard. This is so it doesn't become a dumping ground for any useless piece of trash.

Figure 7.9 Latitude Festival in the UK had a comprehensive back of house salvage campaign, collecting about a tonne of stuff that would otherwise have hit the tip

Source: Festival Republic

Audience Waste

By controlling what food and drink is sold, restricting what people can bring, and managing the interface between exhibitors and the audience, you'll also manage the creation of waste. At many events, waste streams from audience participation could be as follows:

- Aluminium cans.
- Plastic bottles.
- Glass bottles.
- Newspapers, magazines and flyers.
- Plastic shopping bags.
- Food packaging and drink cups.
- Incidental items such as abandoned gear, packaging from merchandise purchases, and things the audience bring along.

You should also identify any areas of waste generation specific to your event:

- Are sponsors bringing in unique items?
- Is a particular activity planned likely to produce more waste of a certain type than others?
- Are promo flyers handed out only to be dropped moments later?
- Is there a free drinks station at a sports event generating loads of disposable cups or bottles?

7.10 A 10p deposit on all beer cups sold in the arena at Reading Festival UK encourages recycling

Source: Festival Republic

Waste Prevention

Can you control what waste is generated at your event? If you're in a position to restrict what people bring inside your gates or doors and to control what is sold inside your event, you have a massive head start over those whose have no control over what wanders into their event in the audience's hands. Let's take a look at ways to reduce waste creation.

Printing and Paper

By reducing the amount of printed material you produce you'll save resources, money and the eventual waste when it's inevitably all thrown away. This may be created at your event or on the streets (when you have distribution companies handing out your flyers or doing letterbox drops).

- Commit to paperless ticketing.
- Reduce the volumes of promotional flyers and posters printed and distributed.
- Be frugal in producing your printed programme and other material. Don't overorder.

Production and Infrastructure

Hiring site infrastructure, production, décor and other gear such as carpeting, rather than purchasing, is the most obvious way to reduce waste creation on the build for your event. It has the added benefits of the gear being re-used and the reduction of the necessity to manufacture new products – and all the environmental impact that comes with this.

Giveaways

Promotional items, samples, resource notes, goodies bags, merchandise freebies. These are all creators of vast amounts of rubbish. Expos are the biggest culprits. Who hasn't been to a travel expo or 'sustainable living fair' only to be weighed down under all the stuff thrown at you? Encourage your participants to come up with creative ways of 'activating' their brand or business at your event, rather than blindly handing out samples and promotional leaflets, all neatly wrapped in plastic and then popped in a plastic bag. Experiential promotion is the name of the game. Get those that want to 'hand things out' to create an interactive set-up which will offer both entertainment and a chance for them to promote their message or product.

Audience Waste

The bottles, cans and cups that drinks come in will make up a huge proportion of waste at many events. By controlling the sale of the drinks you can control the waste, as you can decide if you sell in re-usable cups, if you put a container deposit in place or other incentive to encourage recycling. Events that don't have control over either the sales of products or what people can turn up with in their bags will need to use psychology and persuasion to influence their audience's waste habits.

Depending on how draconian you wish to be, you can restrict all beverages and food from entering your event and consequently completely control what waste will be generated on site. This may not be suitable for your event; however, if it is and you decide to go with this option, you'll know exactly what waste will be produced and will be able to plan your waste management in response.

Food Service

It's likely at most events, indoor or out, people are going to eat. They may purchase food, or you may provide it as part of the deal, but either way people will eat and waste will be created. In either case, you have the power to influence what waste is generated and how it's dealt with.

Re-Usable Crockery and Cutlery

This is a no-brainer for indoor events with kitchens and restaurants using plates, cups and cutlery that are rewashed. Things get a little trickier in an outdoor greenfield environment, and more so as your event numbers swell into the tens of thousands. Rather than handing out food on disposable albeit biodegradable plates, implementing re-usable and rewashed plates, bowls and cutlery can drastically reduce the total volume of waste produced. As every event, audience type and event site is so different this won't be a solution for all. However, if a service is available in your area, you think your audience will respond, you have adequate waste water disposal options, staff to service the set-up, and willing food stalls, this is something that could put a massive dent in your overall waste volumes.

Local government food handling regulations need to be checked to make sure what the rules are for water temperature, grey water disposal, etc. If re-usable crockery is too complicated you can opt for the easier solution of just having re-usable cups for coffee, tea and beers.

Figure 7.11 PLA cups are used at ROTHBURY Festival. 'Please Compost' is printed on them to make sure they go in the compost bin rather than the recycling bin as they are plastic 'look-a-likes'

Source: The Spitfire Agency, ROTHBURY's greening consultant

Disposables Decision

The mountains of used plates, cups, containers and bowls people have eaten out of, only to be thrown out a moment later, is a massive waste creator. If you're serving food on disposable packaging, you really should make sure it's always compostable and biodegradable. There's no use selling food in recyclable plastic packaging as most reprocessors want clean plastics.

Make sure your food takeaway eco 'plastics' are **biodegradable** and not just **degradable** or **photo-degradable** like those plastic shopping bags, which, whoops, will only degrade if exposed to the sun. Not the case when it's covered by a compost heap.

The biodegradable food packaging should also be made from sustainable sources, and/or recycled/waste material. Biodegradable food packaging can be made from straight paper/cardboard, or could be made from some of the wonderful non-paper options such as palm leaves and sugar cane waste. Cutlery can be made from potato starch or timber. We look at the options for sustainable food packaging in Chapter 6.

Figure 7.12 ROTHBURY Festival doesn't hide their waste, they highlight it. By colour coding bins and installing 8ft tall overhead signs to match, the trash just might have been the most prominent item at the festival

Source: The Spitfire Agency

Figure 7.13 Re-usable beer cups used at Latitude Festival in the UK

Source: Festival Republic

Beverages

The obvious way to reduce waste volume from bars is to sell drinks poured from kegs and post mix machines into re-usable cups. The cups would be collected by staff, or have a deposit on them to entice the audience to bring them back for a refund. Selling single-serve drinks in disposable containers, either cups, bottles or cans, is going to generate a lot of waste. Certainly pouring single-serve drinks from bottles and cans into disposable cups is the most prolific waste creating option. Drinking is a big one for most events, and coming up with methods to produce the least amount of waste in the first place is a good goal to have.

Bottled Water

Ban bottled water and you reduce the amount of plastic bottle waste. If you have water standpipes (taps) available and the water is of good drinking quality, consider giving up the profit you earn from selling bottled water and give it away for free. It's possible the money you drop on water sales may end up similar to the cleaning and waste removal costs of all those empty plastic bottles.

You'll need to:

- Make sure the water is 'potable' (suitable for drinking); have it tested and promote the results of the test to reassure your patrons what they're drinking is healthy.
- Put water filters on taps if there is any doubt or psychological barriers to drinking it.

Box 7.6

Mug Jugglers, National Folk Festival, Australia

Rather than throw out, recycle or compost thousands of cups, the National Folk Festival in Canberra, Australia has developed the 'Mug Jugglers' programme.

The Mug Jugglers supply, collect, wash and then resupply green mugs that have become synonymous with the festival. This service means nearly 30,000 polystyrene or cardboard mugs are not put into the festival's waste streams.

Once the audience has used the mug, they are asked to place it into white wire baskets with the 'Mug Juggler' sign on. The baskets are then collected, properly washed, and redistributed.

As a lovely example of community spirit, the National Folk Festival loans their green mugs to Peats Ridge Festival to use so they don't need to use more resources by buying a whole extra set of cups to use just once a year.

www.folkfestival.asn.au

Box 7.7

Re-Usable Cups at Latitude Festival

Workers Beer Company in association with the Cup Concept and Latitude Festival piloted a re-usable pint cup at Latitude in 2007.

Washable and re-usable plastic cups were used for beer rather than disposable paper or plastic cups. In addition to the unprinted cups, which are the property of Cup Concept, 30,000 Latitude branded cups were produced, 16,000 of which were retained as souvenirs.

Customers were charged a £2 refundable cup deposit. If they came back to the bar with an empty, they just exchanged it for a clean and filled cup of beer, not needing to pay the £2 again. When they finished drinking for the day, or if they didn't want to carry the empty cup around, they brought it back to the bar to get the £2 refund.

Considerable investment in specialized washing facilities is needed in this project as the plastic cups can't go in a standard dishwasher. This system is used widely throughout Europe as a standard set-up, and it's hoped this also becomes the case in the UK off the back of these pilots.

www.latitudefestival.com

- Pre-promote to the audience that they should bring their own bottles for refilling.
- Double check the health and safety regulations with regards to 'spit transfer' from tap nozzle to bottle opening.
- Have refillable bottles for sale.
- Adequately signpost the water points.

At **Peats Ridge Festival** in Australia, they aimed to reduce plastic water bottle waste through offering free drinking water and also bulk dispensing by the water sponsor, a local mineral water bottler from Peats Ridge, into refillable bottles. Empty refillable water bottles were also sold. The water tank was supplied free of charge by sponsor NECO, who is a retailer of sustainable living solutions for the home and promotes water tank sales. Standpipes were also placed around the festival arena and campgrounds so everyone had constant access to free potable drinking water.

Refillable Bottles

Re-using glass bottles is the most environmentally preferable option. Refillable bottles are used in many European countries, North America, Latin America and India. It was also part of my childhood memories in Australia, but sadly now only an option in South Australia.

The US has quite a few states with bottle deposits laws with a number with public campaigns underway to bring refillable bottles in. Denmark is a winner yet again, requiring all domestically produced soft drinks and beer to be sold only in refillable bottles and placing deposits on cans. They also enforce the deposit/refund on imported brands. Norway has pioneered the reverse vending machine. The bottles are taken to vending machines and the customer puts

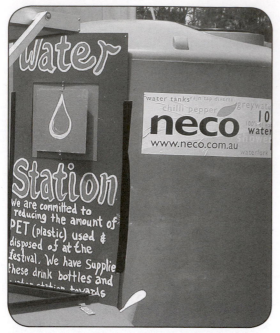

Figure 7.14 Water station at Peats Ridge Festival

their empty can or bottle in, and receives a token or coin refund.

Laws on container deposit, or 'Bottle Bills' as it's known by the lobby group of the same name, are what drive refillable bottle programmes.[3] If your country doesn't have this in place, there's nothing stopping you doing your own container deposit system, as illustrated by the examples in this section. You could also team up with Bottle Bill activists in your region to help push the example of how effective bottle deposits can be in getting maximum recyclable bottles collected.

If you want to understand how bottle deposits work or to find out whether there is currently any move towards introducing container deposits in your country or state, the Bottle Bill website gives up to the minute information. www.bottlebill.org

Figure 7.15 Re-usable bottles ready for collection. In India and Brazil the realities of costs to remanufacture new bottles has created a highly effective bottle return culture. There isn't a deposit, but it's ingrained in the consumer and retailer that drinking from glass automatically means you hang around the shop and return the bottle immediately

Source: Meegan Jones

ROTHBURY Recycling Record

ROTHBURY Festival's commitment to reducing disposable items being used on site and ensuring all food packaging and cups are biodegradable has resulted in record-breaking waste diversion rates.

Estimates are as follows for inside the festival arena:

- Recycling 70 per cent
- Compost 23 per cent
- Landfill 6 per cent
- Other 1 per cent (charity donations, scrap metal etc.)

Because Michigan is the highest deposit state around (10c per bottle and can), it's difficult to assess the true diversion rate outside of the festival areas, in the campsites. Attendees were given bright blue Anheuser Busch Recycling bags so they could collect and take home their own recycling, and get refunds on the products once home. However, ROTHBURY did re-sort the camping waste and ended up with approx 30 per cent recycling and 70 per cent trash from what was left behind.

www.rothburyfestival.com

Figure 7.16 Broken metal camping chairs were stripped of fabric and sent for metal recycling

Source: Spitfire Agency

Box 7.8

Water Bottle-Free Bioneers

Bioneers is an annual conference held in San Rafael, California. It's a conference and networking event which focuses on sharing the practical solutions for environmental sustainability and social justice. In 2007 they aimed to be a bottled water-free conference. The event provided only tap water to its attendees.

Tap water was available inside the buildings and outside where tented venues are set up; a reverse osmosis filtration system was used. Bioneers staff refilled big jugs of water from the water filter and distributed them to all the tented venues.

Bioneers encouraged everyone to bring their own re-usable water bottle. Stainless steel bottles were also available for sale at a booth set up next to the water filter, and another vendor sold re-usable plastic bottles. Bioneers also provided compostable cups at the water stations.

To pre-promote to the audience, Bioneers sent out notices to all registered participants, starting four months ahead of the event, explaining it was going to be a bottled water-free event. The organization maintained regular communication about the event being bottled water-free to help remind people to bring their own re-usable bottle.

Tips from the organizers: ensure you talk to all vendors to ask them not to provide bottled water. It may take several conversations for them to understand you do not want any bottled water at the event. They advise you plan the water distribution carefully to ensure water and containers are easy to access. They also suggest you take the opportunity to educate your audience about the problems associated with using bottled water.

www.bioneers.com

BIONEERS
Revolution from the Heart of Nature

Source: Information in this case study was provided by Food and Water Watch and Bioneers.

Box 7.9

At your Event: Waste Prevention

You must anticipate what products, and therefore waste-in-waiting, will end up at your event. Some regulations you can put in place include:

Hire don't buy
- Hire rather than purchase wherever possible, unless you're able to store and re-use your materials each year.

No polystyrene
- Ban polystyrene takeaway food packaging and require all such product packaging material to be taken away by the trader at bump out.

No plastic bags
- Put a No Plastic Bag policy in place and encourage traders to sell or give away re-usable shopping bags.

Say No to bottled water
- Ban bottled water and use refillable cups and bottles only.

No single-serve sachets
- Ban single-serve sachets and straws, and discourage individually pre-wrapped food items (muffins in plastic wraps, pre-made sandwiches in plastic wedges, etc).

Biodegradable food packaging only
- Ban pizza boxes, polystyrene coffee cups, plastic plates, stirrers and spoons. Send it all for composting.

Limit handouts and freebies
- Restrict handouts of brochures, showbags, sample sizes and freebie promotional items.

Electronic and Bluetooth
- If your event is one at which presentation notes or resource pages would normally be handed out to participants, consider supplying material on a thumb drive, rather than printed out copies.
- Send programmes via Bluetooth as participants enter your event.

Paperless ticketing
- Establish a system with your ticketing provider to go paperless rather than printing and mailing thousands of tickets out.

Vendor and sponsor contracts
- Write the above restrictions into all vendor, sponsor and contractor agreements to ensure they adhere to these points.
- Include clean pitch bonds, refundable post event.

Figure 7.17 Put a programme in place to capture every last aluminium and metal can. Don't let any go to landfill

Source: Meegan Jones

Waste Management

Before we discuss the different types of waste at your event, let's look at the most fundamental element of getting your systems to work and your audience involved – separation of the waste by your audience at the source, and the signage and visual communication tools you use to get them to successfully participate. Then we'll move on to tips and tools for maximizing collection.

The first thing to think about is your audience and event personality and what will best suit your situation. There are practicalities to bear in mind when going for public place waste separation. As well as considering which items you will separate through your waste systems, think about the vibe your event will have and ask the following questions;

- Will the event be congested and busy, hustling and bustling, or will it be more like a relaxed day in the park?
- Will people be able to get to the bins and have a moment to sort their rubbish into the right bin?
- Will people be seated when they eat and drink, or will they be walking around?
- What shade of green are they and how into getting it right will they be?
- Will your event audience be distracted and likely to chuck their rubbish in whichever bin is closest, or will they have the head space to put some thought into their rubbish disposal?
- Will your audience litter onto the ground, or hold onto waste until they come across the next bin?
- Do they need to be rewarded, bribed, penalized or encouraged to participate?

Some of the answers to these questions will inform the separation decisions you make, the style of signage on your bins, and also give insight into the overall waste management system you should operate.

Figure 7.18 Detailed waste separation is undertaken at Big Green Gathering in the UK. The audience is practised at recycling and composting and this predisposition to getting it right transfers to the festival and the waste etiquette there

Source: Greensweep

Bin Quantity and Placement

We will assume you have decided to separate waste into recycling, compostables and general waste.

Once defining things such as audience profile, event personality, audience density, access to bins and other logistical concerns you'll be able to make some basic waste management decisions.

Remember a full to overflowing bin may lead to the immediate disintegration of your well thought out recycling plan. As soon as a bin starts to overflow bin etiquette sometimes goes out the window. So make sure you have enough bin volume and enough staff to empty them. To achieve this you need to accurately plan:

- Number of bins.
- Volume/size of bins.
- Placement of bins.
- Access for emptying.
- Frequency of emptying.

The site layout and access will be major factors in this decision, along with budget for waste staff.

If you have to do the waste planning yourself the quantity of bins and their size or volume capacity is really just a numbers game. Included in the calculation needs to be: audience numbers; types of waste; size and layout of your event site; entry and exit points, etc. Walk your event, either in your mind, or on the ground with a site map in hand, and work out what will be necessary. Be ready to be flexible and to react to the need for rearranging the location of your bins once show day's here and the event takes on a life of its own.

Figure 7.19 Bins are always in clusters of three or six at Glastonbury Festival in the UK. The colour coded plastic bin 'shrouds' fit over the top of a 44 gallon oil drum. The holes in the top are cut to suit the shape of the rubbish that's to go in each

Source: Glastonbury Festival

Sign It Right

Getting the right look to your bins will go a long way towards successful waste separation by your audience. You may find in your state, territory, country or council district pre-existing colour coding or symbols are used to identify various recyclables. It may be foolish to try and reinvent this if recognition already exists for this recycling branding. Research your area's government recycling board, as they're likely to have resources you can use.

If there's no local branding create your own easy to understand theme. Colour coding is a good way to go. No matter what your bin sign design will be, the wording must be as simple and straightforward as possible. It needs to be at eye level or on top of the bin, rather than on the front where it will be blocked by people's legs.

Have several people look at your proposed signs before you commit, as you may miss the obvious. This was evident at a **very green** fair I went to in a park in London that really does have excellent recycling separation, including stewards at some of the bins. However, one small word 'FOOD' made their recycling bins become terribly contaminated. The bin they had for drink cans had 'Food Tins & Drink Cans' written on the sign. The idea was for metal cans (drink cans) to be collected, but at this one-day fair in a park, no one would be opening up a can of baked beans. The inclusion of the word 'Food' in the first line of the sign resulted in food plates in the bin meant for aluminium drink cans. The logo was taken straight from the WRAP artwork toolbox, and if they had used the one that just said Aluminium Cans it may have been a better result.

Figure 7.20 Bin tops developed by Leisure Support Services in the UK

Source: Leisure Support Services

One way to place signage at your bins is to use the very effective bin top, rather than a sticker on the front (not at eye level) or a flat sign standing behind the bin. The bin top is a cap that goes on the top of the bin. It restricts the size of the hole into the bin (preventing traders from putting cardboard boxes in), as well as offering an excellent eye level signage location. It also reduces copycat contamination where, rather than reading any signs, a person peers in the bin and follows the lead of what's already been thrown in. So if the previous people have contaminated the bin, more is likely to happen in an open topped bin.

Without someone standing guard over your bins to make sure everything is put in the right bin, copycat contamination is likely to be one of your biggest obstacles.

Contamination may not be too big a problem for recycling bins if you're running your waste through a MRF after the event, or if you have your own mini MRF back of house. However, if you're trying to collect compostables separately, contamination is your enemy. Too much plastic or metal (or possibly any at all) may result in your composting load being rejected. Every biodegradable item in the wrong bin will add to your landfill figure. If you use a dry MRF, too many food plates and food scraps in with your plastic bottles, cans and cardboard, and your load of recycling could also be rejected.

Box 7.11

Bin Signage Checklist ☑

Group your bins

☐ If you have waste separation make sure you always have each bin option available.

Use bin tops

☐ Cover the top of the bin with a lid, plastic shroud with a hole, or bin cap. This offers a spot for signs and also reduces copycat contamination.

Eye level and overhead signs

☐ Signs on the front of bins may look great when you're sticking them on, but once there's a crowd, who can see them?

☐ Place signs at eye level and/or overhead so they can be seen from afar and over the crowd.

Box 7.12

WRAP Recycling Logos

WRAP (Waste and Resources Action Programme) helps individuals, businesses and local authorities to reduce waste and recycle more, making better use of resources and helping to tackle climate change.

The 'Recycle Now' brand and resource www.recyclenowpartners.org.uk offers assistance, logos and signage.

Using the highly recognizable recycling symbols promoted by WRAP at a UK event is encouraged.

www.wrap.org.uk

Figure 7.21 Peats Ridge bin tops are a standard bin top produced by SULO in Australia. They fit straight onto the top of a 240-litre wheeled bin. The festival has purchased these bin tops, but some waste management contractors offer them as part of their services. Also some government waste programmes lend bin tops out for free

Source: Peats Ridge Festival

Figure 7.22 An example of Network Recycling bin tops. They have taken the UK's nationally recognized Recycle Now symbols and made them into their own designs

Source: Network Recycling

Figure 7.23 This image is printed on the back of the hand-held map given out at ROTHBURY Festival in the US. It's also reproduced as a large sign and placed strategically around the festival

Source: The Spitfire Agency

Source Separation

To get the most effective recycling and composting rates and to ensure none of your loads are rejected by the waste reprocessor, you need to put strategies in place to achieve clean waste separation. Your options include:

- Pre-treatment or a mini mrf onsite.
- Planning volume, quantity and placement of bins.
- Volunteer bin stewards.
- Audience incentives.

Mini MRF On Site

Waste can be pre-treated and re-sorted before it goes off in the trucks or skips. This can be done through setting up a conveyer belt system where bins are tipped on and either recyclate or food packaging picked out or contaminants picked out, depending which bin the waste is coming from. If you don't hire in conveyor belts you can also set up big tables where waste is tipped and sorted.

Alternatively you could put a very simple pre-sort in place. As vehicles arrive with either bins or bin bags, staff are armed with a litter picking stick (or hands and gloves) and contaminants or recyclate are picked out before or as it's tipped into the skip.

Figure 7.24 Hands on in the Trash Palace sorting centre on site at Splore Festival in New Zealand

Source: Splore Festival

Box 7.13

On Site Materials Recovery Facility, Glastonbury Festival

Glastonbury Festival in the UK has an incredible quantity of waste created due to the sheer size and duration of the event. Running for almost 40 years, this festival is a grandmother event and has had time to fine-tune and re-jig its systems until the best processes for the very unique set of circumstances have been found including doing a pre-sort of recyclable materials on site.

Due to the congestion with the huge numbers of people, vehicle movement is difficult. Add to this a fairly high likelihood of knee-deep mud in some places, and you have a challenging waste removal process. The main vehicle movement on site during the show days is the waste trucks, and they have come up with an incredible method to get them around the site. Because of the size of the site and the difficulty in movement, volume of bins is the answer. At last count there were upwards of 20,000 barrel bins. Old 44-gallon oil drums are stockpiled, painted, repainted and replaced over the years – these colourful bins have become part of the festival décor, but they also serve a very important purpose. They provide sufficient (almost) holding capacity for the waste on the festival grounds to give the waste team time to get around the site and empty them. A combo of tractors hauling long trailers, and garbage trucks with bins emptied straight in the back is used.

There are no bin bags in the bins, the contents are emptied loose. The bins are colour-coded with a plastic printed cover with a different shaped hole. Empty barrel bins are brought around on trucks and immediately swapped with full bins. These are then transported back to the waste area and the contents of the recycling bins go to the on site mini MRF and are tipped onto conveyor belts where contaminates are picked out.

Bin bags are also provided to campers, green ones for recycling. These are also brought to the MRF on site for decontamination before sending for reprocessing.

www.glastonburyfestivals.com

Figure 7.25 Conveyor belts are used to pick out contaminants from recycling bin contents

Source: Glastonbury Festival

Waste Stewards

A great way of reducing contamination and offering a point of interaction and eco-education is having waste stewards stationed at sets of bins (volunteer eco-warriors). It will work wonders in minimizing contamination rates. If you have access to a labour force (volunteer or paid) you should consider this as you'll immediately increase the quality of your separation and almost guarantee no contamination of the various waste streams.

They can be armed with gloves and a litter picking stick, and they can pull out anything chucked in the wrong bin, offering a quick pre-treatment solution at the coal face. These stewards can also work as a back up to your waste team. If bins start to get close to full, the steward can swap over the bin liner.

Figure 7.26 Green Messenger steward at Latitude Festival, UK. These volunteers are stationed at every set of bins and ensure the audience places the right rubbish in the correct bin. Results included zero contamination of compost bins, and four tonnes of biodegradable waste sent for composting

Source: Festival Republic

Recycle Stations and Incentives

A great way to ensure you get your recycling returned by the audience rather than it ending up on the ground or in the wrong bin, is to have an incentive to encourage the audience to be bothered handing it in. You can do this by charging a deposit on bottles, cans and cups of drinks sold, the 'incentive' being to receive their deposit back. The other option is to offer rewards such as vouchers or merchandise in return for bags of recycling. Set up recycle 'exchanges' or stations throughout your event for people to bring back their booty to collect their bounty.

Reading Festival in the UK charges a 10p deposit on all drinks sold in cups over the bars, along with beer cup trays. They report a 94 per cent redemption rate. Anyone who has been to this festival over the past 20 years will know the norm was previously ankle-deep beer cups in the arena. The festival also has an incentive to bring back a bagful of cans in exchange for a free beer.

Splendour in the Grass in Australia has a recycling initiative where they give away a $3 drink voucher for every five empty cans or bottles returned to their recycling centres. They received 180,000 cans and bottles back at the 2008 event. For a show with just 17,500 people, that's some serious recycling statistics. Of course this also means 36,000 drinks being given away. However all drinks are sold on site and profits flow through the festival. So if you run your bars and control the wholesale sales of soft drinks and water to your traders, an increase in price along the chain should cover the cost of this campaign.

Box 7.14

Recycle Incentive, Roskilde Festival

At Roskilde Festival in Denmark, they have the benefit of the Danish refillable bottle deposit scheme. As a result they run a highly successful recycling programme where the majority of bottles and cans are returned and refunds given out.

However, as the audience travels from across Europe to the event, and can bring any food and drinks they want into the campsites, the festival ends up with many bottles and cans on site that were sourced from outside the Danish refund scheme.

Roskilde Festival honours a refund for any bottle or can, whether it was part of the original countrywide deposit system or not. They cover the cost of these extra refunds. It also ensures the cans, plastic and glass bottles are kept separate, and then they sell them to recyclers to help recoup some of the costs.

Also, all drinks sold inside the arena come in cups and a one Danish Krone deposit is charged, which is refunded when the cups are returned.

www.roskilde-festival.dk

Box 7.15

Recycle Incentive, Electric Picnic

The 'Bin Your Empties' campaign at Electric Picnic in Ireland encourages people to be more conscientious about their litter and to help make it easy for them.

B.Y.E. teams greet people on arrival with recycling bags and guidelines and tips for easy and efficient waste management for the weekend. The teams circulate the main arena and campsites each day distributing more bags where needed and reporting black spots to the waste management teams in instances where rubbish bins are overflowing, or if busy areas need servicing.

They also staff smaller Recycling Centres around the site for those who find themselves too far from the larger Recycling Stations. These are serviced regularly and brightened up with colourful art installations to make waste disposal a more cheerful experience than usual.

www.electricpicnic.ie

Box 7.17

Recycle Incentive, TRASHed Recycle Store

Since the first Coachella, the promoters have had difficulty with waste management, the trash problem so bad people were literally wading through it. There was no front of house recycling programme in place and it was apparent a system needed to be installed to encourage festival attendees to help with trash maintenance. Global Inheritance were charged with the challenge of coming up with fun ways for people to recognize the roles they could play as recyclers.

10-For-1 Bottle Exchange

The 10-For-1 Bottle Exchange allows festival attendees to trade in ten recyclable water bottles for one new bottle of water. In the arid heat of the desert, this is quite a popular programme. It's also cost effective for festival attendees, as some events charge guests up to US$4 for a bottle of water. This programme encourages people to take an active part in helping keep the venue clean. People get excited about the prospect of turning their trash into valuable currency.

TRASHed

The waste station concept has been taken a step further with the TRASHed Recycle Store, a one-stop recycling incentive shop. Born in 2004, the TRASHed Recycling Store is an interactive recycling centre powered by motivated people who recycle their empty plastic bottles/cans in exchange for free merchandise. Based on the value of the merchandise, people are able to purchase items ranging in cost (number of bottles/cans). They have given away everything from autographed beastie Boys skateboard decks and Smith sunglasses to Motorola RAZR phones and DJ kits. By offering an enjoyable recycling experience, the simplicity of recycling and how to play a part in solving the problem of excess waste is easily learned, and as a bonus, event grounds are picked clean of empties.

Figure 7.27 Recycle store tent
www.globalinheritance.org

TRASHed has now been featured at events ranging from Virgin Festival Toronto to the AFI Film Festival in Los Angeles, and has developed experiences unique to each event.

Source: Information in this case study has been provided by Genna Eyrich of Global Inheritance

Personal Waste Kits

If you have a camping festival or an event where people will be picnicking or generating rubbish without really wanting to get up and walk to the nearest bin straight away (outdoor cinema for example) providing their own set of bin bags is a good option. Be aware people are often excited about getting to an event, so at the entrance many not be the best place to hand out the bags. Have people roving around the campsites or those seated with their picnics, etc., and hand out the bin bags. The bags should match your waste system. For example a black bin bag for general rubbish (make it a small one), a nice big green bag for recycling, and a clear or bio-degradable bag for compostables. (So when they return them you can check out the contents to make sure the compost isn't contaminated.) You can print the instructions on them too.

I have yet to try out the method I am going to suggest next, but if you do, and it's successful, please let me know. The ubiquitous and trouble-some plastic shopping bag is a constant problem for anyone wanting to manage waste. At shows such as camping events where people go shopping before they come, plastic shopping bags make up a large volume of the waste. I'd like to see a project where rather than handing out yet another plastic bag we encourage the audience to re-use the plastic shopping bags just like they do at home. I've come up with 'Three Bags Full'. Bring three bags full and you'll get XYZ reward (a beer, a meal voucher, festival dollars, what-have-you). Let me know if it works will you?

Recycle Incentive, Southbound Festival

Southbound Festival in Western Australia has introduced 'Green Money' – the festival's DIY recycling programme that rewards for recycling.

Patrons simply need to drop by the Recycling Stations or Campsite Pods and grab a biodegradable recycling bag, then fill it with crushed empty cans or water bottles. They bring it back and in return receive a clear conscience and a A$5 Green Money voucher to spend at the festival. The cost of these green money vouchers is covered by the event.

www.sunsetevents.com.au

Figure 7.28

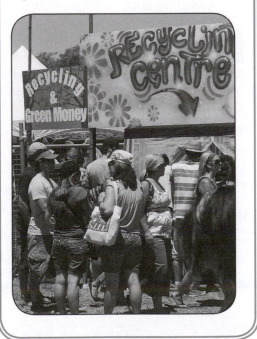

Cigarette Butts

It has been estimated that globally 4.3 trillion cigarette butts are littered every day.[4] If people drop butts at the same rate at events as they do the rest of the year, a massive number of butts could hit the ground over a multi-day event. It can take up to 12 years for a cigarette butt to break down and it can leach poisonous chemicals such as cadmium, lead and arsenic within an hour of contact with water. So at a wet or muddy event, this contamination is happening en masse.

Let's do some figuring. It's estimated that in the UK 23 billion butts are dropped a year. With a population of around 61 million, that's 377 butts per person per year. Let's say one ciggie butt a day per person give or take. So it's pretty simple to work out your butt drop numbers:

Days of event × number of people = butt drop potential.

Figure 7.29 Ubiquitous cigarette waste as seen on the ground in every country in the world, except those with exceptional littering laws such as Singapore!

Source: CSR Solutions

A three-day event with 50,000 people, you're looking at 150,000 butts. A one-day event with 10,000 people – 10,000 butts. **Glastonbury Festival** in the UK has 177,500 people on site for potentially five days. That could mean more than 880,000 butts. The Glastonbury 'Green Police' use fantastically effective theatrical interventions on butt flickers, but at the same time also nicely encourage behaviour change giving

Figure 7.30 The new no-smoking law in the UK has caused clusters of smokers outside venues (including tented venues with less than three sides open). Glastonbury Festival places these bins around the site. Ingenious but simply made: chicken wire stretched over the top of a drum with some sand in the bottom. Painted white, they stand out as all other bins at the festival are colourfully and artfully painted

Source: Glastonbury Festival

them a portable ashtray (film canister) to help correct their dirty habit. The festival also believes many people roll their own at this event, given its audience profile, so they may not experience the drastic figure in the example above. No matter, the Green Police are still out there trying to encourage a more responsible behaviour by smokers, which is a very good thing.

Production areas, back of house, outside catering tents, outside dressing rooms (or inside), outside offices, and loading docks behind stages are all likely areas where smokers will congregate. Make sure you place ashtrays or butt bins in these hot spots to capture back of house cigarette litter.

CSR Solutions are leading experts on how to reduce cigarette litter and they have launched the 'ButtsOut' personal ashtray into the UK retail market (see www.buttsout.biz). Their objective is to establish personal ashtrays in the public psyche and to change what smokers do with their litter 'so we can all work together towards a cleaner local environment'.

Many events hand out portable ashtrays. There are a number of options on the market, from the cute little ButtsOut containers that look like Tic Tac packages, through to awesome flat ones made of recycled material. Some see these as possibly causing yet another waste problem. It really does depend on the predisposition for butt littering by your audience. Handing a portable ashtray to a smoker who has an auto response to flick it on the ground, and getting them to change their habit as a result, would be a wonderful result.

In the following pages we will look at collecting and managing biodegradable waste and hear from events that have done this successfully.

www.csrsolutions.co.uk

Figure 7.31 Southbound Festival distributes thousands of free personal ashtrays made from recycled film canisters. Smokers are urged to take one from the Info Point, Base Camp or Eco Village and dispose of their cigarette butts in a responsible way

Figure 7.32 Waste is composted on site at Peats Ridge Festival. All biodegradable waste is put through a shredder and composted in a series of 'pens' made out of pallets. The resulting compost is then used on the festival land, Glenworth Valley, which year round is a farm and horse riding facility

Biodegradable Waste

If there's a lot of takeaway food service at your event, there is also the potential of a large volume of biodegradable material being generated. This will be maximized if you insist on the use of biodegradable takeaway packaging by vendors.

Apart from plates, bowls, cutlery and cups, the main waste of the compostable variety will be catering waste and food scraps. (Oh, and also poo, but we talk about that in Chapter 5.)

Now you're going to have all this biodegradable material, what to do with it? You may be feeling pretty happy you have no plastic food packaging going into landfill. You're not using up fossil fuels to produce this plastic. But unless you put in a third set of bins to capture it, all that compostable food packaging, food scraps and catering waste could end up in landfill, rot down and create methane, a potent greenhouse gas (GHG). It's your responsibility to ensure you track the full journey of potentially one of your biggest waste streams. You may find your landfill site harvests methane, and if this is the case, you could make a decision to send your compostables into the general bins and then into the ground.

If methane harvesting isn't carried out at your landfill site, or if you prefer to create compost rather than energy from your waste, then only through separation of the biodegradable waste, are you going to be able to compost it. Your options for onward processing are:

- Commercial in-vessel composting.
- Commercial windrow composting.
- Processing into biogas through anaerobic digestion.
- Composting on your event site through windrow, heap or compartment composting.

Don't just leave it to your waste contractor to work out where your biodegradable waste will end up, especially if they're a little rough and ready with the details. Insist on knowing where your biodegradable waste will be processed, what level of contamination is acceptable, what actual process the waste will go through, and what will be done with the compost on completion.

Let's now look at the mechanics of collecting and handling biodegradable waste, and then we'll hear from events that have successfully put composting operations in place.

Collecting Biodegradable Waste

If you're producing large volumes of biodegradable waste then you'll need to put an additional waste collection and handling system in place across your event. This handling system will include:

- Audience bins.
- Back of house or trader/vendor waste.
- On-site waste collection.
- Bulk storage and processing on site.
- Transport off site.

Figure 7.33 Bins at Latitude Festival are separated into Recycling, Composting and General Waste. Previously bins were labelled 'Compost', 'Recycle' and 'Landfill'. However it was discovered that people weren't sure what was in fact compostable, so 'Plates & Food Scraps' was used as the main heading for compostable material, and 'Plastic Bottles' for the recycling sign as this was the main recyclable item which found its way into the arena

Source: Festival Republic

If your event is large enough to have a contracted cleaning company managing the waste, and the event has been around for sometime you may get some resistance by the contractor to changing the way they usually operate. They may need to make considerable adjustments to their routine to cater for this additional waste stream.

However, events with a lot of takeaway food sales will find the bulk of the audience waste will be made up of biodegradable rubbish and this really does end up being the main material to be dealt with and therefore should be given maximum attention. Put incentives and bonuses, to reach compostable and recycling percentages and minimize landfill tonnage, in your contract with the company.

Next we look at how to effectively manage the collection of biodegradables. If you're not using a waste contractor, the following information will be especially helpful to planning an in-house system.

Audience Bins

You'll need at least a triple separation system to keep biodegradable waste away from recyclables and rubbish for landfill. It needs to be clearly signed with a description of what can go in the bin.

Ensuring that the audience put nothing but biodegradable material in your bins allocated for compostables is the first step you need to take. Minimizing contamination at this first step is important to the success of the whole operation and will mean your volunteers or staff won't need to pick through bags of last night's dinner to get out cans or straws thrown in.

Waste stewards, volunteers or staff standing by the bins is always a great way of minimizing the contamination levels.

Figure 7.34 Near zero contaminate was achieved at Latitude Festival

Source: Bioganix

Figure 7.35 Compost from Latitude Festival breaks down within a week using the in-vessel composting system

Source: Bioganix

Back of House and Trader Waste

The theory is that food traders should organize themselves so that they are throwing out minimal food during and at the end of the show. Food stalls doing a lot of preparation at the event such as chopping up vegetables will produce compostable waste during the show. Fruit juice stalls are also prime targets. Caterers for staff and crew, guests and performers will also be doing a lot of kitchen prep. Pre-identify which vendors will need to have bins allocated to them to collect biodegradable waste. The clincher in getting this system to work will be what they do inside their food units, tents and kitchens at their prep benches. They'll need their own bin system inside their operation so their staff can easily separate food scraps into a bin which is then tipped into the larger bin that the event will provide.

It's a good idea to have a dedicated member of the waste team to act as a communications, service and quality control coordinator for food stalls' compost waste collection, particularly if you have a large number of vendors.

Post event is another matter altogether. The best case scenario is your food operators sliding into home plate with little more than a bread roll and a carrot in their kitchens, but this isn't likely. Traders with perishable stock will need to throw food out at the end of the show. Be prepared for this potential. Work out when they will pack down, and have a clear process for them to leave their perishable food waste for collection.

Although cardboard is also biodegradable it's best to just keep it to food scraps. If you feel they won't empty boxes of bread rolls and bags of chopped onions into compost bins without a fuss, let them put it all out in one pile still packaged and have a team of your people go around and de-pack the cartons and bags.

Compost Bins, Big Green Gathering

The Big Green Gathering has up to eight separate bins at their waste stations. Their audience is deep green and needs little instruction on what to put in each bin.

The bins are clearly labelled and it's a simple case of the person being conscientious enough to separate correctly. The separation even includes two biodegradable bins, one for wet waste such as food scraps, and one for dry such as cups and plates.

The waste system was devised by the brilliant Shane Collins and his team at Green Sweep. He has made bespoke bin frames, which are collapsible. These hold a clear bag and signage. The detailed separation and vast numbers of small bins at Big Green Gathering results in a very low volume of waste to landfill, making this festival well on its way to becoming a Zero Waste Event.

www.big-green-gathering.com

Figure 7.36

Collection, Storage and Transport

If you have a small venue you should be able to do all your collections by hand, and if outdoors, then with the assistance of a wheelbarrow or trolley. However, large outdoor events or those with many venues on a campus such as at an expo centre, will need to move waste with a bit of mechanical assistance: golf buggies, horse and cart, pushbikes with trailers, utes or pickup trucks, vans and trailers or rubbish trucks.

Depending on how your other waste streams are collected, you could empty and collect the contents of your biodegradables bin at the same time as the other waste, or separately.

One thing's for sure, you're going to need to use bin liners so you don't get smelly and fly-attracting bins.

Depending on whether there will be a lot of wet waste in your compost bin, or whether it will be mainly empty biodegradable food containers

and cups, will make a difference to the style of bin liner you use. Wet waste is quite heavy and will need sturdy strong bags to move the waste about. You also need to think about the size of the bin as pulling bags out of 240-litre wheely bins will be very difficult if filled with wet waste.

If you feel you'll get minimal or zero contamination in the bins at audience level, then using a biodegradable bin liner is a good option. These are generally opaque. The top can be tied shut and the whole neat package put in a skip or truck. However, if you need to do a visual contamination check, then a sturdy clear plastic bag will be the best option. Make sure they have been made from recycled plastic. Beware of bin liners promoted as 'degradable'. This means photo-degradable, not biodegradable. They need sunlight to breakdown, which is not going to happen in a compost heap or in-vessel composting facility.

All your waste will need to make its way back to a central storage location. Things can get pretty stinky if left in an open rubbish skip for more than a few days. Plan the skip size and removal timing so this doesn't occur. It can also attract vermin and birds. Over the course of a few days you can also get eruptions of previously unseen insect numbers as they find a juicy home to reproduce in your skip.

Waste staff should know what is a bag of compostable waste and what is a bag of recycling or landfill, but this isn't necessarily so. Remember you're likely dealing with large numbers of staff or volunteers and they won't all be as motivated as you are to see an uncontaminated skip full of precious compostables leave your event. You may need to put some dumb-arse signage on your bulk collection bins, or actually roster someone to stand guard over them. One or two bags of

Figure 7.37 Trader waste left out for composting at Latitude Festival

Source: Festival Republic

general waste or recycling thrown up and over the top of a skip can muck up all your good work.

You'll get a lot more into a skip if you empty the bags out rather than throw in whole (even if using biodegradable bags). This second stage of handling will offer an opportunity to pick out any cans, bottles or other foreign objects.

Figure 7.38 A 40-yard skip holding biodegradable waste full to the brim. It's important no other waste gets thrown in, so label your bulk waste bins as well

Source: Festival Republic

Processing Biodegradable Waste

Once your biodegradable waste is collected, you can send it off site for processing into compost or biogas, or keep it at your event and compost it on site.

If you have a smaller event with consequently smaller waste volumes, you could partner with a local community garden, allotment, or other organization interested in small scale composting, and deliver your waste to them. They would then use a windrow or compost heap, or shred it and build a worm farm, to process the waste into life-giving fertile compost for their gardens.

Stomp Festival in Newcastle NSW did just this. Bins were given to Figtree Community Garden whose volunteers painted them up. They were then brought to the event, filled up with biodegradable waste, and returned to the gardens for composting and use there.

If your event owns the land it's held on, such as a sports ground, school, club or outdoor festival, or if you have an agreeable landowner, you may wish to compost your waste on site as at **Bonnaroo Festival** in the US. Their case study coming up describes how they manage their compost. You can also read about **ExCeL Centre's** in-house wormery in the following pages. Read about **Meredith Festival's** on site composting in Chapter 5. They mix the food waste in with their compost toilet waste to produce beautiful compost for the land the event is held on.

Figures 7.39 and 7.40 At Peats Ridge Festival in Australia, biodegradable waste is shredded on site and then placed in bins made of old pallets

Source: Peats Ridge Festival

Box 7.19

Composting at Rothbury Festival

ROTHBURY decided early on that if it's disposable they would rather not have it on site at all.

The biggest impact made was by swapping all food service items to compostables. Cups and cutlery were made from corn starch, plates from sugar cane and napkins were made from recycled paper.

To enforce the disposables policy they contracted with all staff, sponsors and even food vendors not to hand out potential trash items at the festival.

All 30 tons of compost were pulped on site at ROTHBURY by Michigan's Morbark Industries. It was then brought to Spurt Industries in Grand Rapids, where it was processed for three months into lush, rich soil for the local community.

www.rothburyfestival.com

Figure 7.41 The Corral at Golden Plains Festival in Australia. Compostable waste is placed in this structure which becomes a giant worm farm

Source: Mik la Vage

Figure 7.42 The biodegradable waste is mulched on site at ROTHBURY Festival before being taken off site for composting

Source: The Spitfire Agency

Box 7.20

Composting Pad at Bonnaroo Festival Case Study

Bonnaroo is a four-day camping festival held on rural farmland for 80,000 people, on the second weekend each June, in Manchester, Tennessee, US.

The largest and most revered music and camping event in the US, Bonnaroo has elevated the American rock festival to an unprecedented level. As the only round-the-clock major US music festival, Bonnaroo packs an unparalleled amount of entertainment options into its four days.

The event offers attendees the amenities and community spirit of a small city, with 24 hours of activities including a comedy theatre, cinema festival, jazz club, silent disco, arcade, internet cafés, restaurants, yoga classes and hundreds of high quality craft vendors.

The festival promoters own the site, allowing them to explore permanent infrastructure options. This year Bonnaroo installed permanent electricity, tying them into the electrical grid and eliminating many of the generators used.

The challenge

Bonnaroo began composting six years ago. They collect waste from patrons and vendors. All vendors are required to use compostable wares. Every year Bonnaroo has been hauling the waste to regional compost facilities. Because of the amount of waste produced in such a short amount of time the regional facilities have had difficulties processing it. In 2008 Bonnaroo couldn't find anyone to accept the compostable waste because the tonnage would have put the facilities at capacity, so they undertook a very quick turnaround project to design and construct a system to process compostable material collected at the festival, on the land where the event is held.

Objectives of the project

The objective of the project was to create a system to allow on site composting of biodegradable festival waste. Of most importance was to assess permissions, design the best model, and to get the compost pad built properly given the time frame (three weeks before the festival began). They achieved their goals and now the pad is built the goals are to increase the amount of materials collected and find ways to use the waste on site.

About the project

The project consisted of installing a gravel pad at the proper slope and to design and install the treatment cell for run-off from the pile. When it rains excess water must run off to allow the compost heap to remain at a functioning level of moisture. Too wet or too dry and the composting process won't happen properly. Bonnaroo created a system for gathering and dumping the waste and properly mixing the collected waste with bulking material during the festival. A compost thermometer was installed to guide turning at correct intervals throughout the year in order to ensure the waste breaks down as efficiently as possible.

Pre-production planning

Before delving into the composting project, permitting issues were researched with the festival's lawyer and the state environmental department to make sure composting on site would be allowed. After it was established that having composting onsite would be permitted, the organizers worked with composting expert Buzz Ferver to design the pad and treatment cell system. The festival operations team worked with the composting expert to determine the best location on site for the pad to be permanently installed.

Stakeholders

As a vital part of the ongoing site operations it was important the composting initiative wasn't an add-on 'sustainability' project, but was seen by all relevant festival staff as part of the permanent festival infrastructure. Operations and waste management staff participation was actively engaged in order to get the project completed. Festival management worked with waste and operations areas to devise a system for collection, turning, hauling, etc. so any disruption to the work they have to do during the festival was at a minimum and the success of the project wouldn't be hindered by potential sidelining during the pressure of the show. A communications programme was also put in place with other key staff to educate them on the benefits and process of composting in order for them to be engaged in making the pile successful. This mainly consisted of face-to-face discussions and emailing.

Figure 7.43 The compost heap steaming and rays of sun shining down

Source: Bonnaroo Festival

Resources
- Purchases required for the compost pad project were: gravel, Filtrexx treatment cell, mulch.
- The actual construction of the compost pad including the building of a sloping pad, and installation of the Filtrexx treatment cell.
- Team of volunteers staffing collection areas and unloading on the pad.

Operations logistics
Approval from the state was given, as it was established a permit was not required as long as the compost material originated and stayed on the site. The compost expert drew up the actual design, where the waste would be dumped on the pad, where the bulking material would go, etc.

The gravel was packed and the Filtrexx treatment cell installed. It was important the pad and gravel were constructed in such a way all water run-off when it rains would be properly filtered. The treatment cell is an organic treatment process for run-off.

Once the pad was set up (two days before they opened the doors for the festival!) it was ready to go. While the pad was under construction the head of waste management company Clean Vibes was brought in to make sure that once they dumped the collected waste the grounds keeper would come and fold in mulching material. Thanks to the great team of volunteers everything went smoothly during the festival. Throughout the year the grounds keeper turns the pile, once it reaches the proper temperature.

Tips for new players
The key to this project is owning the festival property land or having permission from the landowner. The great thing about composting on site is you really are closing the loop on your waste. Even if you rent your festival property the compost can benefit the landowner throughout the year.

Results
- Ten tons of compostable waste were collected and composted.
- Transport of waste impact was reduced.
- Valuable compost was made available to use on the festival grounds.

www.bonnaroo.com

Source: Information in this case study provided by Laura Sohn of Bonnaroo Festival

Box 7.21

Wormery at ExCeL Case Study

ExCeL London is an international exhibition and conference centre situated on the Thames in the heart of London's Royal Docks. They have also installed the UK's largest – and only commercial – wormery.

The venue is part of a 100-acre campus, including three on-site train stations, easy access to the London underground tube line and London City Airport, parking for 4000 cars, five on-site hotels and numerous on-site bars and restaurants.

In July 2008, ExCeL installed a MRF on site and colour coded bins for all events and the ExCeL campus, including on-site partners and hotels. The MRF is able to recycle paper, cardboard, plastic, wood and glass. The wormery holds 300,000 worms capable of eating at least two times their body weight a day. Earthworms are the ultimate recycling machine. All types of food waste can naturally be recycled into productive, nutrient rich soil. Food waste is collected from the kitchens and preparation areas and delivered to the wormery. It's processed through a macerator into a pulp which is fed to the worms. The pulping makes the food easily consumable for the worms, removing the need for rotting to break it down. The worms digest the waste and convert it into rich worm cast. Environmental benefits of the wormery (which has scope for expansion, if needed) include:

- Reduction of carbon emitted from transporting waste, taking lorries off the road.
- Reduction in landfill – volumes reduced by approximately 90 per cent.
- Production of valuable soil additive which can be used around the excel campus.
- No smell or liquid run-off.
- Minimal power usage.

www.excel-london.co.uk

Figure 7.44 The wormery in action

Source: ExCeL

An ADNEC Group Company
Source: Information in this case study provided by Gemma Parkhouse of ExCeL

Box 7.22

At your Event: Waste Management

Is source separation right for your event?
- Is your audience used to recycling, or will you be teaching them about it for the first time?
- Will they actively participate in the recycling – do they have the time, access and inclination?
- Does your audience need convincing to participate – rewards, penalties or bribes?

Identify your recyclate and biodegradable material
- What waste will be produced that can be recycled or is biodegradable?
- What are the likely volumes of each type of material?

Treatment methods
- What recycling and biodegradable treatment facilities are available locally?
- Determine if you will collect co-mingled recycling, single source, or a mix.

Bin style and signage
- Does your waste contractor supply bins and signs or bin tops?
- Design stickers or signs for bin tops, or bin signs.
- Investigate existing recycling messaging and campaigns by local government or recycling agencies or materials specialists such as plastics or aluminium associations.

Create a recycling image and programme
- Create incentives for recycling to be maximized.
- Consider placing a refundable deposit on bottles, cans and cups sold at the event.
- Work with sponsors and your merchandising department to create recycling incentives.
- Consider including theatre in your waste. Set up recycling stations, interactive displays, recycling centres, etc.
- Develop a theme, slogan, image or brand, in order to have continuity in your communication.

Operations logistics and internal communications
- Set targets with your waste management contractor.
- Ensure you have adequate budget to achieve your goals if likely to be labour or infrastructure heavy.
- Work with all your key waste producers (staff, crew, contractors, stallholders, caterers, etc.) to make sure they understand your goals and to engage them to actively participate in your programme. Discuss logistics with them to work out the best way to suit their operations on show days.
- Make sure you have appropriate back of house production signage and skips/bins/waste/salvage depots ready.

Audience communications

- Include info in all pre-event communications on what waste facilities will be available and how they can participate.
- This can include website, newsletters, printed letters and brochures with tickets, along with media releases.
- Develop an at-event communications programme, including signage, information in programmes, briefing volunteers, announcements and video messages.
- Engage volunteer stewards to be stationed at your bins to help the audience put the right thing in the right bin.
- If you have a 'Green Zone' make sure you have a section on recycling, composting, biogas, etc.
- Engage local zero waste groups to be part of your campaign.

Figure 7.45 Recycle Exchanges at Reading and Leeds Festivals are the point to bring back bags of cans for recycling and to receive a beer token in exchange. They also act as the drop-off points for donated camping gear

Source: Festival Republic

Figure 7.46 Back of house waste display at Peats Ridge Festival. Pictured is Ilka Nelson of The Last Tree who created the on-site communications of the green initiatives. www.thelasttree.net

Source: Peats Ridge Festival

Recycle

Separating waste at your event by the audience, and getting it right, is the ultimate goal. By doing this dual objectives are achieved: ensuring a good proportion of waste will be recycled and encouraging participation by your audience, getting them into the recycling habit.

Don't be put off by the prospect of the wrong thing going in the wrong bins if you don't quite get it right. I have a habit of peering in bins around the world to see what the contamination levels are like, and unless you have someone standing next to a bin directing people, you'll always have people putting things in the wrong bin. Well maybe not in Germany, but everywhere else. By putting recycling separation in place the mere fact you've given it a go, your audience has participated, and you have learnt from your mistakes, makes you one step closer to getting it right next time.

Just about every event should have the ability to undertake some kind of recycling. Those that can't for whatever reason should look to send the whole contents of their bins to a 'dirty' MRF where recyclate is separated from general rubbish and then different recyclable material streams are separated out from each other. But if you collect all the rubbish at the event into one bin and send it straight to a MRF without any separation at your event, you aren't helping your audience to become more aware of their dirty habits and to get into recycling on the go. You may also find that an audience used to separating recycling at home and at work, may find it odd you don't also do this at the event, negatively impacting on your reputation.

 ## Plastics

It takes hundreds of years for a piece of plastic to decompose. Every piece of plastic ever produced, since it first was developed in the 1950s, is still with us today. And it isn't going anywhere fast.

Plastics are an obvious material to target for recycling. Plastic bottles will be used for water, soft drinks and possibly for alcoholic drinks, and are made of PET (polyethylene terephthalate). However there are many other materials which are used at events, which are made of plastic and can also be recycled.

There are many types of plastics which can be recycled. High density polyethylene (HDPE), low density polyethylene (LDPE), linear low density polyethylene (LLDPE) and polypropylene (PP) are the other plastics to look out for. Make sure you check that your MRF or recycling facility can take all the plastics you intend to collect, as otherwise it will end up in landfill anyway.

If, for whatever reason, your MRF won't take a certain type of plastic (like film plastic) and you'll produce a lot of it, then search out a reprocessor you can send it to directly. You may have transport costs to pay, but this shouldn't be more than your landfill per tonne fee you'll have to pay. What's more, depending on the market at the time of your event, for plastics, you may be paid for your recycling.

The demand for plastics does fluctuate, as much of it's shipped to China for reprocessing, and the demand by China had decreased significantly at the time of writing, causing an oversupply of recycling, and the requirement for storage of plastics until the market bounces back. Watch what plastics recycling is doing so you can ensure yours doesn't end up in landfill.

Bottles, shopping bags, piping and playground equipment, etc. are made from HDPE. At an event, you may have left-over water piping or hose from bars, damaged plastic furniture, etc. It's possible you could put any HDPE product in with your mixed recycling to be picked out at the MRF as you'll probably have small quantities of it.

LDPE is often used for shopping bags (the ones that make a loud scratchy noise), detergent bottles and plastic containers. LLDPE is the stretchy film plastic such as cling wrap and bubble wrap. More detail in the section on production waste.

Figure 7.47 At Reading Festival a 20p deposit is placed on all bottled water sold on site to encourage bottle returns

Source: Festival Republic

Figure 7.48 Plastic shopping bags are a big waste problem at many events

Source: Meegan Jones

Recycle Incentive, Peats Ridge Festival

Australia's Peats Ridge Festival sells its beer in cans. In order to capture as many cans as possible for recycling, they charge an A$0.50 container deposit on every can sold.

This is extended to every drink sold, plastic bottles, non-alcoholic drinks included. The container deposit encourages the audience to collect cans and bring them back for recycling, and leads to close to 100 per cent recycling of them.

This event is an example of getting very close to zero waste. One year's waste audit of the event showed less than 200 grams of waste going to landfill per person. Many regular events would be hitting the multiple kilograms per person. The festival also created 'KNOW YOUR WASTE' stations. In the arena at every set of bins, a pop-up marquee is erected with a 'KNOW YOUR WASTE' sign. A volunteer is stationed in the tent and they talk to people about recycling and make sure everything goes into the right bin.

www.peatsridgefestival.com.au

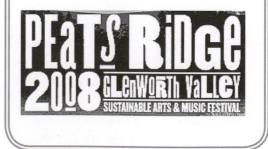

Aluminium Cans

Aluminium has the potential for indefinite closed loop recycling. Compared to paper and most plastics recycling, which generally lose quality with each recycling loop, aluminium retains its integrity. The high cost and energy needed to create aluminium from scratch compared with the efficiency of recycling it, makes aluminium an excellent target for events' recycling programmes.

An aluminium can recycled today could be back on the shelf within six weeks doing its job as a can again. The recycling of aluminium yields excellent GHG benefits, as to create an aluminium can from recycled material takes just 5 per cent of energy, against 95 per cent used to create it from scratch.[5] For each tonne of aluminium recycled, rather than produced from raw materials, 11 tonnes of CO_2 are saved.[6]

Read about the aluminium can recycling project, 'Your Cans Count', run by **Reading Festival** in the Appendix.

Figure 7.49

Glass

If you're in a country or state with refillable glass bottles, you'll need glass recycling as well. Most high-energy events ban glass from their shows for safety reasons. However, glass will turn up no matter if it's banned and it needs to be dealt with. Having glass confiscation bins, which collect only glass, to in turn send for recycling is a good formula. If you ban glass from your event, and have confiscation in place, putting out other bins in the general event area with 'glass bottles' signage on them may be at cross purposes. But you will need a system so the inevitable contraband that gets in can be recycled. This could be done through briefing bin stewards and recycling point staff to accept glass, and setting up a process to ensure its separate handling. Sure we're probably not going to run out of sand to make glass soon, and really re-using glass bottles is the better option, but if all else fails, recycling glass still has positive environmental benefits.

TetraPak

TetraPak produce beverage cartons, most popularly used to hold juice and milk. They are made of cardboard, coated with polyethylene and lined with aluminium. They are completely recyclable, but not all MRFs have the technology to sort them from other recyclate. Also recycling processors are needed to recycle the cartons back out into their component parts. Find out if yours will take Tetrapak.

The reprocessing of Tetrapak is really quite ingenious. They take the cardboard back out as pulp, which can then go for onward recycling. The plastic coating, polyethylene and the aluminium are then combined to form a composite product. This is used for roofing or wall cladding. A further option is available to end up with separated polyethylene and aluminium which can then be individually recycled.

Production Recycling

Back of house you'll produce various rubbish, a lot of which can be recycled. The following are some waste streams you may need to set up recycling systems for:

Figure 7.51 Production recycling

 **Timber**

Timber used for construction and set design, if it's not going to be re-used, should be recycled. Set up a separate skip for this and work with your production team to ensure that during the breakdown all scrap timber makes its way into this skip for recycling. The recycling of timber is really just salvage. It will make its way to a scrap timber merchant where it will be used again. The biggest hurdle will be getting your crew to be diligent in putting all scrap timber in the right skip, and not contaminating it with other materials. Work with them to make sure they understand what you're trying to do – to prevent valuable resources from going into landfill or

Figure 7.50 TetraPak's Poly-Al sheets are created from recycled beverage cartons

Source: TetraPak India

incineration. This will prevent CO_2 emissions as well as sequestering carbon, and reducing the need to harvest more trees.

If you have a need for woodchip, and you produce a good quantity of scrap timber, you may wish to hire in a woodchipper and turn all your scrap timber into a resource for your next event. Alternatively you could use your own scrap timber for décor, set design and construction in the following years.

Metal

Scrap metal is quite a valuable resource and can be continuously recycled. What's more, it's possible, depending on your volumes, you could be paid for the scrap metal, rather than having to pay for its removal. At a minimum, a scrap metal merchant should supply you the rubbish skip and its delivery and removal, in exchange for the metal you put in it. One motivator for ensuring you get the maximum metal in the skip is to come up with a deal with your site crew that they will get the proceeds of the metal recycling money, to use for beer at their end of show party. This has proven to be an excellent recycling motivator.

Figure 7.52 Scrap timber is used to construct the bars at Latitude Festival

Source: Festival Republic

Figure 7.53 Scrap timber used to make an installation at Big Green Gathering

Source: Meegan Jones

Figure 7.54 Broken chairs are discarded by campers at Reading Festival in the UK. These are stripped of cloth and sent for recycling. It's a labour-intensive operation, but comes out just about break-even after the scrap metal payout is received. Included in this calculation is the cost of transport and dumping fees if this was to be sent to landfill

Source: Festival Republic

Film Plastic

Cardboard

Film plastic materials are thin, pliable sheets or collapsible tubes made of LDPE. Items such as builder's sacks, shade cloths, etc. are LDPE and should be recycled. The cling wrap plastic that comes wrapped around just about every pallet of goods delivered to an event is also a form of film plastic. It's designed to stretch and stick and called LLDPE (linear LDPE). Bubble wrap is also LLDPE and can be recycled.

But finding a MRF or recycler that will take it could be a problem. There is absolutely no problem in recycling it; however, the hassle comes in whether it's all mixed up with other stuff, making it troublesome to separate. So often a MRF or recycler won't take it due to handling issues. The best thing you can do is to ensure it's all bundled up together, bagged if necessary, so it's easily handled at the MRF or reprocessor.

One thing to watch out for, when separating out LDPE or LLDPE from other plastics, is to not mix in shopping bags, which are often made from HDPE. HDPE is usually not see-through and has a more crinkly feel (less soft than LDPE). Don't mix these plastic bags in with your LDPE or LLDPE. Keep them separate.

Film plastic includes:

- Cling wrap.
- Bubble wrap.
- Builder's sacks.
- Plastic bags.
- Fencing 'scrim' – plastic sheeting.

All plastics apart from PVC can be recycled. More on PVC in Chapter 6.

Cardboard is invariably produced wherever food and beverages are provided. The massive stash of cardboard that accrues behind food traders is a ubiquitous scene.

If you have enough volume, collect cardboard separately, keep it in a compacting skip, or bale it, and send it directly for recycling.

As anyone that has worked at a supermarket during their high school years knows, flattening boxes makes the whole process a lot easier.

Figure 7.55 The author's attempt to demonstrate how much LLPDE (film plastic) came out of the back of two bars

Source: Meegan Jones

Sponsor and Partner Opportunities

- Engage your beverage suppliers to be active participants in your recycling operations.
- Invite local recycling groups to be part of your operations and to set up information stalls.
- Engage local government, state or national recycling and composting programmes to be part of your campaign to promote recycling at your event.
- Take on any existing recycling or composting branding, logos or messaging from your region, to strengthen your messaging.
- Invite a brand, beverage or otherwise, to sponsor recycling and composting.
- Include their branding on bins or signs, logos on waste staff uniforms, etc.
- Create a partnership with community gardens or other groups which promote composting, and possibly have them as the recipient of the finished compost.
- Bring on board a re-use centre, scrap store or other group that promotes re-use and repurposing to create your décor.
- Partner with scouts, welfare agencies, charity shops, etc., to be recipients of any left, donated or salvaged items from your event's audience and production operations, including food from catering.

Box 7.24

At your Event: Production Recycling

Flatten and bundle cardboard

- Contract into agreements with those who will be the big cardboard waste producers that they must flatten and bundle cardboard.

Collect and recycle film plastic

- Food traders, bars and caterers will be the big producers of film plastic.
- Create a campaign to help them understand that film plastic can be recycled, to allow them to identify what sorts of film plastic to separate out, and to set up systems to make it easy to do.

Set up a scrap metal yard

- Encourage your crew to separate and save all scrap metal. Offer them the proceeds of the scrap payment to encourage them to do this.

Collect scrap timber

- Send for recycling or wood chip it and re-use it on site.

The Recycle Symbol

Back in the day (around 1970) a paper company put on a competition to create a symbol to promote the recycled content in their products. A Uni student won the competition, the company did some slight alterations and the resulting three chasing arrows recycle logo was born. This symbol has been appropriated by many since then and has become a universal, if somewhat overused design. The plastics industry put their system of numbers inside the recycle symbol to identify the type of plastic. Unfortunately many people take that chasing arrows symbol with a number inside to mean the item is recyclable. It still depends on what your local facilities will take. There is even one for PS, which is polystyrene. Forgive me if I'm wrong, but I am still to discover a recycling facility that genuinely processes polystyrene with a viable use for the resulting recycled material.

The recycle symbol isn't trademarked and can be used by anyone. In various countries and states, government has put restrictions on its use to ensure misrepresentation of recycled content does not occur. In the UK, a '%' can be placed inside the symbol to indicate the percentage recycled content.

Box 7.25

Recycling Codes

1 – PET (often soft drink/soda bottles)
2 – HDPE (bottles, shopping bags, piping, playground equipment)
3 – PVC (banners, non-food bottles, pipe)
4 – LDPE (plastic bags, containers, detergent bottles)
5 – PP (auto parts, industrial fibres, food containers, dishware)
6 – PS (insulation, packaging, expanded polystyrene 'Styrofoam')
7 – OTHER (acrylic, fibreglass, nylon and other plastics)
20, 21, 22, 23 – cardboard, mixed paper, paper, paperboard
40, 41 – steel, aluminium
50, 51 – wood, cork
60, 61, 62 to 69 – cotton, jute, other textiles
70, 71, 72, 73 to 79 – mixed glass, clear glass, green glass

Key Sustainability Indicators

To understand your waste management performance, you'll need to audit the volumes of waste produced. The climate impact of waste generation can also be measured, using CO_2 emissions factors for waste treatment. This figure can be fed into your total carbon audit. Key Sustainability Indicators are:

- Percentage of waste recycled, composted and sent to landfill or incineration, or salvaged.
- Landfill waste – tonnage/volume.
- Recycling – tonnage/volume.
- Biodegradable waste – tonnage/volume.
- Salvage – tonnage/volume.
- Ghg emissions from landfill waste.

You can also measure transport impact of waste haulage by converting total mileage to CO_2 emissions. (More info on calculating this in Chapter 4.)

Landfill waste treatment emissions: 0.112kg CH_4 (methane) per kg waste.
Multiply by 23 to get CO_2 equivalence (IPCC, 2001).

e.g.: 1000 tonne waste $\times 0.012 \times 23 = CO_2$kg

Recycling and composting are allocated zero emissions impact.

Source: Defra, UK Landfill Methane Emissions 2005 and Estimated Emissions of CH_4 by IPCC Source Category 2006

Waste Audit

If you're sending co-mingled recycling to a MRF for further separation you won't know your true recycling figures unless you do a waste audit on site before sending your rubbish away. (Unless you have a massive event which will take over the MRF for a number of days.) Once your co-mingled recycling hits the MRF, it will be added to all the other waste coming in and it will be impossible to work out what the contamination rate was, let alone the percentages of different recyclable materials such as plastics, aluminium, glass, etc.

So if you want to gauge your true recycling rates, you'll need to have someone monitoring the bags of waste as they come from the bins before landing in the skip or waste truck. You don't need to do this for every bag of rubbish, but select sample bags across the course of the event to scrutinize. Have them opened up and the various waste streams in each bag counted: plastics, aluminium, metal, glass, cardboard/paper, tetrapak, general waste contamination, biodegradable waste contamination. On completion of a good sample size you will have percentages of recycling categories which you can then apply to the total recycling tonnage you are provided by your MRF.

Tonnage versus Volume

You can look at your waste by tonnage or by volume. As each material has a different weight, sometimes tonnage can be deceiving.

Figure 7.56 Builder's sacks were used to collect salvaged gear at Reading Festival

Source: Festival Republic

Salvage

The purchase and use of 'stuff' to produce your event creates volumes of waste, GHG emissions, and uses up fossil fuels and non-renewable resources. Introduce salvage, re-use, and repurposing into your event planning and make a positive impact on your event's sustainability and on the environment. Fewer new materials will need to be purchased and produced, along with less waste, both of which are money savers and Earth savers.

Scavenger, Tatter, Salvager?

Salvaging materials at events is a favourite of mine. I have fond childhood memories of scavenging at the local tip for crazy bits and pieces to make billy carts out of (and other awesome finds). My mum and dad thought of it as a family outing (!). When a teenager I looked back horrified at the thought that they took us to the tip, but now I realize it's engrained and I proudly say yes, I have tatting in my blood. So the joy that beholds me finding homes for all the items left behind at big music festivals is truly a paradise found. I am continually working to come up with an effective way of reducing the massive volume of stuff overprivileged and drunken young people seem to think it is their right to use and discard at music festivals … but I think this is a bigger one than I can tackle alone. Nonetheless, I have taken to the concept of salvage with open arms, and am very proud of the dent we have made in the landfill footprint of some of the world's largest festivals. So, to get salvage operations happening at events, look at the following:

Find your Stuff a Home

The most important thing, apart from identifying what can be salvaged, is establishing a home for these goods. You need to have worked out who could possibly use the ice cream containers or bread crates left at your event, before you start diligently gathering them up. The first place to look is for creative re-use centres. These marvellous facilities take industrial waste to be used for arts, commercial, décor and design use. Look in your local area to find a scrap store or re-use centre. If there's none in your area, investigate whether there is a recycling organization, community organization or theatre group that may need a particular item you feel you will have in excess, such as banners, set design pieces, décor, light bulbs, etc. You may even find you could kick start a salvage or re-use centre business. Other groups that love to get hold of stuff are charity shops, school flea markets, scouts and guides, pre-schools and holiday camps (for craft). I have even had a dog's home come and take blankets. Get creative in thinking who can get creative with your salvage.

Buried Treasure

If you have a multi-day event with camping, it's likely there will be some really good things left by your audience which can be re-used for their original purpose. Salvageable stuff from the production or event activity areas is also likely to be abundant and this can be harvested and re-used creatively by someone else. Go through each section of potential waste and identify what could be re-used.

Operation Salvage

After working out what will be available to salvage, and working out where it will go once salvaged, you will need to concentrate on who will actually do the salvaging. Its a hands-on job and many hands are needed. Set up salvage bays to make it easy for the process to happen during your event build. After is a different story. You need to work salvage operations in with waste operations so you aren't in a situation of racing against the bin trucks.

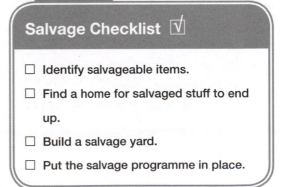

Box 7.26

Salvage Checklist ☑

- ☐ Identify salvageable items.
- ☐ Find a home for salvaged stuff to end up.
- ☐ Build a salvage yard.
- ☐ Put the salvage programme in place.

Box 7.27

At your Event: Salvage

Behind the scenes there is likely to be a goldmine of quirky items that can be re-used as is or repurposed for another use, rather than being thrown in the rubbish skip and sent to landfill.

Food and merchandise stalls
- Buckets and lids (that things such as mayonnaise, ice cream, sauces come in).
- Plastic and wooden crates (bread, fruit and veg).
- Hessian and fabric sacks (potatoes, rice, flour).
- Cooking oil (to make biodiesel).
- Over-runs of event specific stock – merchandise, giveaways, promo items, printed materials.
- Banners and signs.
- Flags, bunting, fabric, tablecloths, shade cloth.
- Printed cups and containers.

Of course, they also produce perishable items at the end of the show which need to be composted, loads of cardboard for recycling, and of course mountains of cling wrap from palletized stock.

Site infrastructure
- Plumbers piping (makes great props).
- Cabling and tubing from bars (can be re-used as hose, or for props).
- Electrical cabling.
- Carpet offcuts.
- Timber and metal offcuts.
- Cable wheels (make great tables).

Décor and set design
- Banners and signs.
- Fabric, flags and bunting.
- Stage flats, props and design pieces.
- Left-over paint.
- Timber, metal, aluminium offcuts.

Box 7.28

Salvage at Reading Festival

Each year thousands of tents are discarded by festival goers. A salvage campaign has been held at Reading and Leeds Festivals since 2006 to attempt to divert as much of this abandoned gear as possible, along with encouraging the audience to pack it up and take it home.

Objectives:

The objectives of the Reading and Leeds Festival Tent Salvage campaign are:

- To reduce the number of tents going to landfill (taking them home or packing down and donating).
- To encourage campers to pack up and hand in tents and camping gear for re-use by charity.
- To shift attitudes away from viewing festival camping gear as disposable items.

Communications

The objectives are achieved through raising awareness amongst campers of the option to donate unwanted tents and camping gear. This is done through communicating the 'pack it up – hand it in' and 'don't trash it' message through a variety of ways in the lead-up to the festival and during show days.

Pre-Festival: Online, media release, seeding of info into forums, included in ticket wallet and ticket letter.

At Festival: 'Green Messenger' stewards promote the message face to face, posters, banners and tent donation points, internal communications to other festival departments, arena screening of video promo, inclusion in the programme and the programme laminate.

On-site operations

Green Messengers are put in teams, one for each campsite zone, under the direction of a paid supervisor. Green Messengers arrived Wednesday afternoon and worked 24 hours over Thursday, Monday and Tuesday.

Reading Festival

Their duties included:

- Handing out recycling bin bags and talking to people about the recycling project.
- Talking to campers about taking their tents home or donating their gear, specifically packing it up and handing it in.
- Working post festival on tent pack up duties including tent sorting.

Green Messengers set up the Tent Donation Points. These are eight builders' bags with signs on for each of the following items: tents, sleeping bags, roll mats, chairs, wellies, food, pots n pans, clothes. Approximately 30 of these are set up at key points in the campgrounds, including the Recycle Exchanges and Zone Control Caravans. They are each staffed by two stewards; the remaining stewards spread the pack-it-down and hand-it-in message to the campers as they are leaving the campgrounds.

Vehicles go around to the Tent Donation Points and Recycle Exchanges where massive

Figure 7.57 Tent donation point

volumes of gear have been donated and bring it back to a central sorting shed.

Tips for new players

- It's recommended that most pre-sorting of gear is done out in the campgrounds, to avoid double handling in the sorting shed.
- The staff doing the salvage, or staffing the donation points need to be really well briefed and diligent in not taking broken, unusable or unsuitable items.
- Pre-determine who is going to be the recipient of your salvaged items.
- Consider the transport impact of salvaged gear to make sure you're not transporting salvaged goods across the country or around the world.

www.readingfestival.com   www.leedsfestival.com

READING   **LEEDS**

Figure 7.58 Mountains of chairs are donated or discarded

Figure 7.59 Discarded camping gear at UK festivals is a massive problem and an incredible waste of resources. Creating ways to discourage campers from abandoning or trashing their gear, to set up salvage programmes and to find a home for this abandoned stuff is a challenge event managers in the UK must address urgently

Waste and Climate Change

From the production of waste-in-waiting (stuff), through to its ultimate disposal in landfill or by incineration – waste, my friends, equals climate change. In mining, manufacturing, distribution and retail of goods, at every step along the way, energy is used and GHGs are huffed and puffed. How we manage the eventual volume of waste created at our events plays its part in climate change.

As discussed in Chapter 6, if we send our end-of-lifecycle-products on a one-way trip to landfill rather than being composted or recycled, we must continually extract new resources to replace those materials buried or burned. Waste management strategies such as recycling and composting not only reduce the use of non-renewable primary resources, but there's also a reduction in climate change potential by putting secondary raw materials back into the manufacturing cycle or creating natural fertilizers through compost.

Methane is created in landfills, as biodegradable waste breaks down in the absence of oxygen. Methane is a powerful GHG, anywhere from 25 to 75 times more potent than CO_2, depending on the life span measurement considered. In the UK **Defra** reports that 40 per cent of methane emissions in the country come from landfill alone.[7] Combine this with the study from the UK's **Waste and Resources Action Programme** (WRAP) that claims 6.7 million tonnes of food in the UK is thrown out annually, amounting to about one-third of all food purchased. Astoundingly 60 per cent of the food thrown out has never even been touched.[8] How much uneaten food ends up in the bins at your event?

Incineration and CO_2

If compostables and recyclables end up in an incinerator to be burnt, the CO_2 emissions as a result go out at a rate higher than from a coal fuelled power station.[9] Energy from Waste plants that generate power through burning waste are seen by some as no more than poorly disguised incinerators. This is a controversial subject and one that's hotting up, as it were.

Having an option for waste disposal such as energy generation from incineration, can encourage guilt-free single use and a throw away mentality. In Europe, where years of the recycling and composting habit are ingrained in citizens, this is not so much a problem. However in countries where it's not the national norm to separate compostables and recyclables in the home, in public spaces and in business, having this easy alternative could seriously impact on keeping valuable compostable and recyclable resources from their highest purpose and do nothing to encourage frugal consumption.

The thirst these incinerators have for timber and paper products is immense. When built, local authorities are contracted to supply them a minimum amount of materials to burn. Targets need to be met and this obviously goes against pushing recycling and composting programmes.

Through incineration, timber and paper products are lost from the recycling process and virgin material now needs to enter the system. More trees are being felled (carbon no longer sequestered), trucks are transporting timber to the mills (pumping out fumes), and additional energy is being used to bring the timber to pulp.

However, there are always two sides to the coin. As incineration is not going away in a hurry and urgent solutions to sequestering (stopping carbon from re-entering the carbon cycle) are required, a new use for its residue by-product – biochar – is being found. The concept of adding charcoal to soil to offer fertilizing properties is ages old. Projects are now being set up to take the biochar resulting from pyrolysis incineration processes, and put it into soil, offering the dual benefit of improving soil fertility and the sequestration of carbon. See www.biochar-international.org for more information on biochar and its climate change mitigation benefits. I haven't expanded too much on biochar here, but it really is an exciting area of development. I encourage you, for your own interest, to read up more on it.

It must be noted that incinerator supporters see the burning of food waste, green waste, paper and wood as carbon neutral as it's considered part of the natural carbon cycle, and therefore they don't include emissions from these sources in their data. But because there is a much higher purpose for recyclables and compostables, I choose not to ignore CO_2 that comes out of an incinerator's smoke stack. If we get to a point where pyrolysis is being used on a grand scale in industrial agriculture and municipal waste and we are sequestering massive amounts of carbon through biochar, then I'll be on the other side of the fence. But right now, I choose to compost and recycle.

You need to decide where you sit with these varying opinions.

Landfill Gas

Landfill owners, waste treatment companies and the like are rolling out investment heavy technology and infrastructure to capture the energy potential of methane generation from landfill – Energy from Waste (EfW). In the US there are EfW landfill gas harvesting landfill sites in every state. But, and this is a BUT-with-a-capital B, having these EfW sites can also encourage guilt-free trashing and destruction of resources.

Methane is generally accepted to be between 23 and 27 times more potent a GHG than CO_2, but there is some debate over this figure. In order to come up with a standard set of measures to place the various GHGs on an even keel, CO_2 is used as the base, with a 100-year life span. But methane's average life span is just 12 years. When you consider the actual short-term potency of methane, it's far more than 23 times that of CO_2

– possibly really 75 times as powerful. We're dealing with a very effective GHG here, and every time we throw something compostable into the bin to make its way to landfill, we're contributing to the problem in quite a big way.

The solution? Do not send biodegradable materials to landfill. This means paper, timber, green waste from gardening and agriculture, food scraps or anything else that can 'rot'.

What does this mean for events? Do not send biodegradable materials to landfill. This means paper, timber, green waste from gardening and agriculture, food scraps or anything else that can 'rot'.

Imagine the impact, both immediate and from an educational point of view, if all the events in the world were to start separating food and other biodegradable waste. Imagine if all events get their recycling sorted to such a degree that just about everything that can be recycled, is. By playing our part in keeping biodegradable and recyclable materials out of landfill and incinerators, events can help to significantly reduce methane emissions from landfill and CO_2 from incineration and the knock-on climate impacts.

So once again we come to the fact that, as an event manager you have the power to implement change. Use every item in your arsenal to move your event towards zero waste, to reduce the pressure of resource extraction on our precious planet and to reduce the climate change impact of our activities within the live event industry.

Watch | Read | Visit

Eco-Cycle

Eco-Cycle is a non-profit zero waste organization based in Boulder County, Colorado. They provide zero waste services for local events of all sizes, including recycling and compost collection in uniquely created zero waste stations. They also offer volunteer recruitment and training, along with supplying compostable single use food packaging products. They feature a do-it-your-self zero waste kit for smaller events as well as an online training package for organizers wanting to create zero waste event programmes in their communities.
www.ecocycle.org

Waste Wise Events Guide

This guide has been developed by the NSW Department for Environment and Climate Change. It's targeted at councils, landowners and managers, and event organizers. Waste Wise Events is a well recognized campaign in Australia and events that are held in this country are encouraged to take on the ideas set out in the guide and become a Waste Wise Event. The guide is set out in three stages: before, during and after your event. Each stage has a checklist and useful tools such as sample planning documents, surveys and media releases. Events can also apply to be an accredited Waste Wise Event. Each state in Australia's waste board or similar manages the local version of the programme. Download the guide here:
www.environment.nsw.gov.au/warr/WWE_Home.htm

Respect your Festival

'Outs' Festivals and punters not doing well.
www.respectyourfestival.com

Gone Tomorrow: The Hidden Life of Garbage

Heather Rogers (New Press, 2005)

'In the U.S. 95% of all plastic, two-thirds of all glass containers, 50% of all aluminium beverage cans, and half of all paper are never recycled; instead they get burned or buried.

Eat a take-out meal, buy a pair or shoes, or read a newspaper and you're soon faced with a bewildering amount of rubbish. The United States is the planet's number one producer of trash; each American throws out 4.5 pounds daily. How did we end up with this much waste, and where does it all go?

By excavating the history of rubbish handling from the 1800s — an era of garbage-grazing urban hobs and dump-dwelling rag pickers — to the present, with its high tech "mega-fills" operated by multi-billion-dollar garbage corporations. Rogers answers these questions offering a potent argument for change.'
www.gonetomorrow.org

Stop Trashing the Climate

Read the amazing report 'Stop Trashing the Climate'. If you're interested in how waste impacts climate change, download the report; it's excellent reading.
www.stoptrashingtheclimate.org

Festival Salvage

Make contact with those who specialize in 'mining the festival landscape'.
www.festivalsalvage.com

Notes

1   B. Platt, D. Ciplat, K.M. Bailey, and E. Lombardi (2008) *Stop Trashing the Climate*, p4, www.stoptrashingtheclimate.org, accessed October 2008. Originally sourced from Brenda Platt and Neil Seldman, Institute for Local Self-Reliance (2000), *Wasting and Recycling in the U.S. 2000*, GrassRoots Recycling Network, Cotati, CA, p13. Based on data reported in Office of Technology Assessment, Managing Industrial Solid Wastes from manufacturing, mining, oil, and gas production, and utility coal combustion (OTA-BP-O-82), February 1992, pp7, 10, accessed December 2008.

2   Defra (2007) *Waste Strategy for England 2007*, www.defra.gov.uk/environment/waste/strategy/strategy07/pdf/waste07-strategy.pdf, accessed September 2008.

3   The Bottle Bill, www.bottlebill.org, accessed September 2008

4   Butts Out, www.buttsout.net/litter_stats, accessed September 2008.

5   International Aluminium Institute, www.world-aluminum.org, accessed September 2008.

6   Defra (2007) *Waste Strategy for England 2007*, www.defra.gov.uk/environment/waste/strategy/strategy07/pdf/waste07-strategy.pdf, accessed September 2008.

7   Defra (2007) *Waste Strategy for England 2007*, www.defra.gov.uk/environment/waste/strategy/strategy07/pdf/waste07-strategy.pdf, accessed September 2008.

8   WRAP (2008) *The Food We Waste*, www.wrap.org.uk/downloads/The_Food_We_Waste_v2__2_.0e2b7c17.5635.pdf, accessed September 2008.

9   Information sourced from *Stop Trashing the Climate*, www.stoptrashingtheclimate.org, accessed November 2008. Originally sourced from *How Does Electricity Affect the Environment*, www.epa.gov/cleanenergy/energy-and-you/affect/air-emissions.html, accessed September 2008.

Appendix

Box A.1

2008 Democratic Convention Greening Case Study

The Democratic National Convention was held in Denver, Colorado, US, 25–28 August 2008. It was held over four days with a total attendance of 85,000 people across four venues. For the first time in history, the Democratic National Convention Committee (DNCC) hired staff focused on implementing sustainability principles into the planning of the Convention and reducing the overall carbon footprint of the event on the host city.

Efforts to make the 2008 Democratic National Convention a sustainably produced event were a success – from wind and solar power being used to support Convention venues to an extensive waste diversion and recycling effort supported by more than 1000 volunteers. These results provide a valuable benchmark for future events in Denver and Democratic National Conventions for years to come. The carbon footprint of the event was calculated. Delegates were encouraged to sign up to be a 'Green Delegate' by offsetting their travel to the Convention.

Venues

The Hyatt Regency Denver was the official headquarters hotel for the Convention. The Colorado Convention Center was occupied on all four days of the event and featured breakfasts, caucus meetings, receptions and a public area for attendees to gather and interact.

The Pepsi Center was the official Convention venue for the sessions running from Monday, 25 August to Wednesday, 27 August. Invesco Field was the official Convention venue for the fourth night – President Obama's acceptance speech in front of 85,000.

Objectives

The mission was to produce the most environmentally sustainable political convention in modern American history. The organizers initiated the comprehensive greening plan a year before the Convention and incorporated sustainability principles in all aspects of planning and restoration. Programmes ranged from minimizing waste at resource recovery stations to measuring the Convention's carbon footprint. The goal was to holistically design-in environmental sustainability measures in every possible way, take responsibility for the impact on the climate and create a lasting environmental legacy for the Democratic Party and the City of Denver.

Pre-production planning

The choice of Denver as the host city was influenced by the fact that the City of Denver expressed their support for implementing strategies for greening the Convention which would remain in place on a permanent basis. The first major decision was to locate the DNCC Denver offices in an Energy Star building at the hub of the city's mass transit lines.

The Green Team interns worked for months in advance of the Convention researching various items from compostable cups to environmentally friendly signage options. They were also responsible for recruiting and building the volunteer corps of 1008 greening volunteers to assist with the waste diversion effort over the four-day event

Stakeholders

The greening initiatives involved the support and participation of all internal department heads as well as the support from the host city of Denver and the Convention venues. The success of the programmes relied heavily on the buy-in from these key stakeholders. The Convention's logistics and operational teams were asked for the first time in history to retool their plans in order to reduce the environmental impact of their activities. The changes varied from subtle to significant such as requesting the transportation department to order hybrid, flex-fuel and biodiesel vehicles, or converting the housing process into an online system to reduce paper use. These achievements were possible because of the support of the various members of the Convention planning team.

Carbon

A convention first, the carbon footprint of the Convention was comprehensively calculated. Camco was the Official Carbon Advisor, and this organization ran the audit. The goal was in the first instance to reduce greenhouse gas (GHG) emissions, and where emissions were unavoidable, to offset through verified carbon offset programmes, focused on American renewable energy and agricultural and landfill methane capture projects.

DNCC offices

Because of the central downtown location, more than 65 per cent of DNCC employees walked or took public transit to work. The office layout was such that daylight was maximized and motion-sensor light switches controlled energy efficient T8 fluorescent bulbs. The walls were painted with low VOC paints and the cubicles were designed with repurposed and recycled materials. Appliances used were locally produced compostable bioware utensils in the kitchen and non-toxic cleaners in the restrooms.

The office featured a successful single-stream (all recyclable items in one bin) recycling programme. With the assistance of the IT staff, energy efficient computers were ordered, double-sided printing was set as the default on all printers, which were fed with 100 per cent post-consumer recycled paper, and a system was in place to recycle all used ink cartridges. For the first time ever, the DNCC housing process was handled entirely online which resulted in savings of an estimated 50,000 to 100,000 sheets of paper.

Figure A.1 Inside the Invesco Field venue where 85,000 people gathered to hear the acceptance speech by President Obama

Source: Jaime Nack

Resources and sponsors

Several official providers were brought on board and these companies were also required to join in on sustainability initiatives. Coca-Cola Recycling was the Official Recycling Provider for the Democratic Convention and they supported the waste diversion efforts. Without this sponsorship and partnership the recycling and composting results would not have been achieved. The Official Vehicle Provider, General Motors, provided a variety of low emission transportation options.

Energy

The majority of venues were connected to the grid. For the Pepsi Center, the Convention Center and Hyatt Regency Headquarters Hotel, 100 per cent of the power was powered by wind energy through Green-e certified renewable energy credits. Energy conservation measures were also incorporated into planning for all official Convention venues. At the Pepsi Center, high-efficiency lighting systems, including compact fluorescent, LED and solar powered, were used where possible. Both the Pepsi Center and the Convention Center had been working independently to institute long-term sustainability measures on site. They have both installed permanent solar power systems.

Waste diversion

The Convention aimed to reduce the amount of waste sent to landfill from Convention activities and implemented a comprehensive recycling, composting and waste minimization programme with the assistance of hundreds of DNCC Green Team volunteers. All organic materials (food scraps, napkins, paper towels, etc.) were composted. The goal was to not only lower the waste impact for the Convention but also implement a long-term legacy of recycling, composting and sourcing recyclable materials at these venues. At official Convention venues, attendees had the experience of using three-bin recycling stations where they were able to place waste in various receptacles – designed for recycling, compost or landfill.

The waste minimization effort from Convention week resulted in more than 82 tons of waste being diverted from landfill or incineration. At the Pepsi Center and the Colorado Convention Center, guests diverted more than 70 per cent (nearly 62 tons) of waste from landfill through a comprehensive recycling and composting system. At INVESCO Field at Mile High, more than 50 per cent (more than 20 tons) of waste was diverted from landfill through a single-stream recycling effort. These are the highest waste diversion rates experienced for any event of this type to date.

Sustainable materials and production

Choosing sustainable materials was at the heart of the greening plan for the 2008 Democratic Convention. Sustainable sourcing, re-use and reduction of all materials were considerations for every facet of Convention planning and production. All contractors and subcontractors were chosen in part because of their demonstrated commitment to sustainable planning principles, and many agreed to participate in the carbon tracking programme.

Sustainably harvested wood products and rented or re-used materials were used everywhere possible. Materials used were measured, tracked and wherever possible re-used or donated to community organizations at the conclusion of the Convention.

Figure A.2 Recycling Centre set up at the DNCC
Source: Adam Griff PhD

The DNCC production team was committed to implementing environmentally aware procedures throughout the design and build of the stage and podium that would showcase the nominee during his acceptance speech. These measures included using innovative technologies to replace disposable set pieces, low-energy alternatives in lighting, re-usable and/or recyclable staging materials such as rental decking, and environmentally sustainable construction materials, such as recycled and/or recyclable carpeting, non-toxic adhesives and low VOC paints.

Transportation

The Pepsi Center, Convention Center, DNCC Headquarters Hotel and the DNCC offices were all located within walking distance of either the Regional Transportation District (RTD) light rail or the 16th Street mall shuttle, which runs hybrid (electric/natural gas) buses. A majority of delegation hotels were also accessible from these public transportation systems.

Figure A.3 Bike parking for delegates

Source: Ryan Ozimek

The buses used to transport delegates and media from the hotels to the Pepsi Center were either the hybrid shuttles or buses fuelled with biodiesel. The city's 'Engines Off' anti-idling programme kept taxi, shuttle and bus idling to a minimum to reduce air pollution.

The Official Vehicle Provider, General Motors, worked with the DNCC's transportation team to offer hybrid, E-85 and high fuel efficiency vehicles to support the fleet needs. All DNCC vehicles and bus miles were tracked and included in the carbon footprint calculations.

Green community service and education

Giving back to the community of Denver was a top priority for the DNCC. The 'DNCC Service Days' campaign focused on three areas of importance to the Denver area community: youth, environmental projects and the combined issues of homelessness and hunger. Local river clean-ups, tree-plantings and tree care events were part of how the DNCC created an environmental legacy in Denver and the surrounding communities. Colorado provided the ideal backdrop for the greening efforts as it is the home of the National Renewable Energy Lab, the National Center for Atmospheric Research and many of the recent Nobel Prize winning scientists who shared the 2007 prize with Vice President Al Gore.

Legacy of sustainability

The DNCC was devoted to leaving behind a strong legacy of sustainability and environmental stewardship both in Denver and for future Democratic Conventions. The DNCC believed they had a responsibility to not only green the 2008 Convention but also educate all who attended, as well as those who watch from their living rooms around the world. Many of the recycling and composting systems remained in place after the Convention. The staff and volunteer training helped to create a corps of trained individuals for future greening efforts.

For more information on the 2008 Democratic National Convention Greening Program: www.demconvention.com/greening

Source: Case Study information was provided by the 2008 DNCC's Director of Sustainability and Greening Operations – Jaime Nack, President, Three Squares Inc (www.threesquaresinc.com)

Box A.2

Sustainability Policy, Bluesfest, Byron Bay, Australia

The following is Bluesfest, Byron Bay, Australia's sustainability policy. It is an extraordinarily thorough treatment on all sustainability issues and is a great example of what to strive for in putting together such a document and programme of objectives.

Commitment to Sustainability

We are committed to improving and developing our sustainability (including environmental, social and governance) initiatives for our future Bluesfests. Our strategies and initiatives are aimed at lowering our festival's footprints and introducing proactive sustainability features that will position the festival as a global leader in this area. Our sustainability strategy is underpinned by six Strategic Goals, each backed up by a series of Management Objectives and Key Actions.

Strategic Goal 1: Building Institutional Capacity

We have engaged a Sustainability Coordinator/Partner with a view to:

- Reducing sustainability related risks, facilitating appropriate responses to sustainability related issues and challenges as and when they arise, demonstrating Bluesfest Management's commitment to achieving a legitimately sustainable festival (reducing the risk of 'greenwashing').
- Building on Bluesfest's success in winning the international Greener Festival award for Australia 2007.

Strategic Goal 2: A Culturally Relevant Festival

Bluesfest management in consultation with Arakwal Aboriginal Corporation Byron Bay and the Bundjalung Elders Council Aboriginal Corporation (or whomever the two organizations agree is appropriate) will develop an implementation plan to achieve the five key recommendations of the Preliminary Cultural Heritage Statement. A working group will be formed to manage the process prior to any redevelopment of site with agreed terms of reference in writing.

Continued consultation will occur with relevant stakeholders leading up to each year's event. The festival will develop an ongoing celebration of Aboriginal culture as the core contribution into each year's programme, building on previous years' experience.

Local Aboriginal elders will be invited to bless and open/close each year's festival.

Strategic Goal 3: A Festival that Respects, Transforms and Grows Local Community

Traffic, emergency response, music volume and other community impact management and mitigation measures will be built in to the management plan submitted to Council prior to each year's event, starting in 2009.

- By committing to a permanent site the Bluesfest management realizes the opportunity of building-in attributes such as belonging, being locally relevant and contributing to local economic stability. A value added statement will be published following the 2009 event and for each year thereafter. The statement will highlight new local suppliers and report on why non-Northern Rivers suppliers were used over local suppliers. The statement will be prepared in consultation with local industry groups (including Northern Rivers Tourism Inc).
- We will develop an employment policy that includes an obligation to proactively employ Aboriginal people to the extent where Aboriginality is a requirement for effective service in some aspects of the event. An annual statement will be published detailing the extent of local hiring following the 2009 event and beyond.
- The festival will continue to facilitate the special needs of people with disabilities and their carers. This includes provision of access for children with disabilities. A management plan will be developed for improved access for people with disabilities and the frail aged.
- Bluesfest has a proud record of giving back in terms of donations and other forms of support for a wide range of Northern Rivers based NGOs. The Bluesfest management will re-evaluate its corporate social responsibility (CSR) policies and practices leading up to the 2009 event with the view to improving the positive impacts related to this giving. An annual statement will be published detailing the corporate social responsibility spend and resultant positive impacts to our society.
- Bluesfest management will engage with artists and involve them more in Bluesfest sustainability initiatives. Artists' travel-related emissions will be offset. A review of transportation offset options will form part of the carbon footprint analysis currently underway. The Bluesfest management will communicate these efforts prior to each year's event, so that artists can promote these efforts during their shows.
- The Bluesfest management will build on past efforts where volunteer 'green police' roam the site removing waste for recycling and engaging with our audience around environmental issues. It will also improve 'green ticket' options that offset transport related emissions available to our audience.
- The Bluesfest management will introduce a sustainable procurement policy for suppliers, and will introduce annual 'Responsible Trader' awards to recognize traders who stand out in terms of lowering their ecological footprints.
- Each year's festival will be used to raise awareness of social/environmental causes and to showcase sustainability solutions. In particular the Bluesfest management will initiate and develop environmental sustainability showcase area/s. Demonstration installations will deal with waste, water conservation, energy conservation and renewable energy and sustainable land management. A number of selected projects/initiatives will be piloted in 2009.
- The Bluesfest management will build in these sustainability aspects as core attributes of the Bluesfest brand.

Strategic Goal 4: A Zero Waste Festival

The Bluesfest management will conduct a strategic review of waste streams at the annual festival, with the aim of building on the successful increasingly high levels of recycling achieved over the last seven years. The review will take a fresh look at waste streams, identify alternatives to materials used and explore waste management opportunities and challenges related to managing a permanent site for the first time. The findings of the review will feed into and inform the further actions discussed below.

- The Bluesfest management will continue its policy of supplying only 100% recyclable food and beverage containers and utensils (plates, bowls, cups, wraps, eating utensils etc.) made from renewable and sustainable produced sources, preferably Australian. Bluesfest has been a leader in waste management in Australia for ten years. This leadership has been recognized by numerous green organizations, most notably with Bluesfest receiving the International 'A Greener Festival' award in 2007.
- The Bluesfest policy of composting all organic solid (food) waste will continue. Bluesfest management will complete a feasibility study regarding onsite organic composting as part of the waste management review discussed above. If organic waste cannot be composted onsite for legal or technical reasons the requirement for organic waste composting (offsite) will be included as a condition of the waste management contract.
- The Bluesfest management will continue its current policy of conducting ongoing reviews of key materials used in Bluesfest with the view to identifying practical and affordable (possibly cost saving) sustainable materials as alternatives to those currently being used. This would include packaging materials, promotional materials, structural elements, tent and stall materials, containers, onsite vehicles, IT infrastructure, etc. Continued implementation of these initiatives will occur at Festival 2009 and will be reviewed in advance of subsequent festivals.
- As an alternative to relying on chemical toilets, the Bluesfest management will conduct a feasibility study to investigate installation of permanent onsite wastewater treatment systems (such as grey water systems, bioactive wastewater systems – e.g. Biolytix systems) that could reduce the need for less sustainable offsite wastewater treatment. The study will investigate alternative high volume systems to improve the current treatment process. Steps will be taken to develop demonstration installations in partnership with organic wastewater solution providers, commencing with the aim to have at least one demonstration installation available at Festival 2009 and if successful will be introduced onsite within five years.
- Bluesfest management will conduct a study in 2008 to investigate the opportunities to reduce the demand on potable water supplies and to increase water use efficiency onsite.

Strategic Goal 5: Carbon Neutral Initiatives

Bluesfest management aims to complete its Carbon Footprint Report on the festival by August each year. The current study is analysing emissions from waste generation (methane from landfill), electricity usage, the burning of fossil fuels (petrol, diesel) and road and air travel emissions directly related to the festival and will develop guidelines for measuring and monitoring GHG emissions for the Tyagarah site.

- The Bluesfest management will investigate the feasibility of solar and wind power with solar water heating as an option for all permanent and non-permanent structures onsite. The study will be completed by February 2010.
- The Bluesfest management will purchase renewable energy for all direct electricity needs that cannot be met by onsite generation, with the aim of achieving 100% renewable energy by Festival 2012.
- The Bluesfest management will introduce initiatives to: encourage onsite campers to stay onsite throughout the event, e.g. promote 'residency' of site campers; facilitate onsite mobility; provide onsite activities (e.g. in the mornings before shows start); provide bus transport to and from Byron Bay, nearby towns, beaches and local attractions; and provide attractive amenities for campers. Acoustic artist performances will also be held on the evenings before and after the Bluesfest officially opens to encourage some festival goers to arrive early and leave later. This should aid in reducing traffic congestion and peak traffic flow densities.
- The Bluesfest management will investigate and implement cost effective and resource efficient options for improved public transport between key existing transport nodes in Byron Shire and the festival site during festival periods, commencing with a pilot project in 2009.
- The feasibility of introducing a limited train service between Byron Bay and the festival site during festival periods will also be investigated.
- The Bluesfest management will investigate the opportunities to use a proportion of sustainably sourced biodiesel for some of the onsite generators required to run the festival.
- Commencing in 2009, all permanent structures will be progressively designed, renovated and constructed to maximize energy and water efficiency. All existing structures onsite will be refurbished and renovated to comply with NSW government building sustainability index (BASIX).
- The Bluesfest management will investigate annual offset projects and initiatives that are, where possible, local, auditable and sustainable. Following the completion of the current GHG emissions report an aggressive but realistic target will be established in terms of percentage carbon footprint offset for the 2009 event, identify 2009 offset project/s and commence engagement with offset partners to realize targets set. Commit to a 60–80 per cent emissions reduction by 2050, consistent with EU policies and exceeding current Australian targets.

Strategic Goal 6: A Festival Site that is a functioning, Healthy Natural Ecosystem

Previously cleared land within the site will be utilized for the festival activities, with the remaining vegetation being retained and conserved within a vegetation protection area (VPA). The Bluesfest management will implement the Vegetation Management Plan, the Ecological Site Management Plan and the Koala Plan of Management prepared for the Development Application (DA) process, to protect and enhance the site's natural ecosystem functioning. Invasive and exotic flora and fauna will be managed on an ongoing basis to improve conditions for native plants and animals to survive and flourish.

- The Bluesfest management will use the information provided in the suite of ecological reports completed for the DA to develop interpretive material (e.g. signs, posters, brochures, etc.) for the festival site that educate and celebrate the site's natural biodiversity features.
- Bush Fire Asset Protection Zones nominated in the DA bush fire report will be implemented and maintained.
- All onsite chemical and petrochemical fuel storage will be constructed in full compliance with applicable health, safety and environment (HSE) laws and bylaws, and with adequate secondary containment (e.g. bunding) and spill response plans in place.
- All roads will be constructed in such a way that soil erosion is reduced. Appropriate vegetation will be planted to further reduce soil erosion.
- The Bluesfest management will rapidly phase out the use of inorganic agrichemicals and investigate the feasibility of obtaining organic certification for the site's agricultural operations and product.

www.bluesfest.com.au

Source: Reproduced with the kind permission of Bluesfest.

Box A.3

A Sustainable History, Boom Festival, Portugal

It was decided in 2004 that Boom would be a sustainable festival. To diminish the impact of thousands of people on the event's natural environment, a protocol with IPEC Ecocentre was established to reformulate drainage, energy and waste management.

2002
- Beginning of garbage recycling.
- 12,000 portable ashtrays distributed freely to avoid polluting nature.
- 50 people cleaning the event 24 hours a day.

2004
- 15,000 pocket ashtrays distributed freely.
- Plastic, metal, paper and glass recycling.
- 100-member team (Eco Team) permanently cleaning the festival site.
- Conferences on sustainability practices.
- Introduction of solar panels in camping and caravan areas.

2006
- Setting up of chemical-free biological toilets.
- Composting of residues made biological fertilizer that was returned to farmers in the region of Idanha-a-Nova – technology credited by IPEC Ecocentre.
- Usage of showers with biotechnological treatment of water through plants and evaporation – technology credited by IPEC Ecocentre.
- Free distribution of biological soaps and shampoos.
- 18,000 pocket ashtrays provided freely.
- 150-person Eco Team taking care of the environment daily.
- Internal garbage sorting central depot that filtered the residues before being headed to the waste transfer station.
- Conference area, info stand and World Music stage run on solar power.
- Re-usage of abandoned and burned wood for building infrastructures.

2008
- All of the above plus the recycling of materials from other festivals for use at Boom.
  www.boomfestival.com

boom festival 08

Source: Information in this box provided by Dr André Soares of Eco Centro and Boom Festival

Box A.4

Sample Website Hierarchy

WHAT YOU CAN DO

Getting here	Public transport	
	Driving	
	Walking and cycling	
	Lift share and car pooling	
	Impacts of travelling to the event	
Getting ready	What to bring/Buying stuff	
	Take it home/Love me don't leave me	
	Impacts of what you buy	
When you're here	Setting up camp	Campers' waste kits
		Recycle exchanges
	Rubbish	Recycling
		Composting
		Re-use, salvage and donation
		Recycling rewards
		Impacts of what you throw away
	Showers and toilets	Compost loos
		Toilet paper
		Don't take the piss (wee in streams!)
		Eco-showers
		Environmentally sound shower gel
		Grey water recycling
	Food and drink	Fairtrade, organic and local
		Food packaging and composting
		Container deposit/refund
	Markets	Ethical and fair trade
		Merchandise
	Eco-entertainment	The Green Zone
		Workshops and panels
	Partners	Green Sponsor 1
		NGO 1
Going home	Clean campsites	Donate and salvage

BEHIND THE SCENES

Products	FSC timber
	Eco paint
	Cleaning products
	Signage and banners, materials
	Suppliers
	Environmentally Preferable Purchasing Policy
Printing and promo	Tickets
	Programme
	Posters and flyers
	Merchandise
Site production	Powering the event
	Lighting
	Salvage and re-use
	On-site transport
	Sustainable Transport Policy
	Contractors
Stage Production	Lighting
	Sound
	Transport of kit
Catering	Fair trade, local and organic
	Composting and recycling
	Refillable water bottles
	Re-usable crockery and cutlery
Staff, crew, performers and participants	Uniforms
	Transport
	Accommodation
	Clean campsite policy
	Communications
Waste	On-site separation of recyclables
	Dual litter picking
	Salvage
	Wood chipping
	On-site composting

Box A.5

Magnificent Revolution, Pedal Power and Business Ethics

A magnificent contractor

Let's hear from a new generation of contractors and what drives MAGNIFICENT REVOLUTION. In their own words...

As a small not-for-profit organization, it is our principles that drive us. We try to maintain a holistic approach to both our internal organization and the running of our events; from who funds our ventures, to the food we eat. We feel that if we expect people to be willing to make a difference as a result of our work, we have to set a good example and practise what we preach. As one can imagine, this ideology brings with it a whole host of different challenges, as the infrastructure for sustainable event management has yet to be fully developed. This is how we have responded to these challenges...

Transport

A recent Julie's Bicycle study has pointed out that one of the great contributors to greenhouse gas emissions in the music industry is the transport of people, artists, staff and equipment to gigs and festivals.

In the past, when we've attended festivals locally, we attempted to get most of our crew and gear to the site using trailers and bicycles. It is a good option, but can only work when the distances we have to cover are short, for example getting from Cambridge to the Secret Garden Party festival site that was 18 miles away. We certainly can't reasonably expect our crew to take three days off to cycle from London to The Big Chill Festival site at Eastnor Castle on the border of England and Wales. There is always the option of using the train, together with our bicycles and trailers. However, there are limits on travel times and how many bicycles can board a train at one time. We've also subsequently learnt that trailers are not allowed on some trains, making this option rather impractical.

For longer distances we've been forced to use a van. We are aware that burning fossil fuels to transport pedal power gear around is contradictory to our ethos and so is something we have subsequently needed to address. What were our choices? Not to do events that we can't cycle to or find a source of alternative fuels for our van. We went with the latter option and became involved with a project at the Hackney City Farm to manufacture our own bio-fuel from local waste cooking oil.

In 2008, we were invited to Greece to put on a pedal powered cinema at the Thessaloniki International Film Festival. Flying simply wasn't an option, as it would clearly go against the grain of our ideals. Shipping our gear separately and leaving the crew to take the train would have cost an extortionate amount, so we decided to travel by train, and personally deliver our pedal power kit. We agreed to obtain all other audio-visual equipment from the festival's suppliers. It took us three days to travel from London to Greece, and as result we had to add six extra days onto this particular job, something that not all people may be able or can afford to do. To the casual observer, taking pedal power gear on a train all the way to Greece may seem like a ludicrous idea, but in order to stand by our ideals this was our only option. However, the insight gained from that journey with regards to the challenges we face in transporting our equipment whilst maintaining a reduced impact was invaluable.

Sponsorship

Another challenge that we face is where the cash for our work comes from. We know that this is a topic that could perhaps take up the majority of this book and all organizations have their own policies on this topic. It is an issue that MR is continuously struggling with as a small organization. Our principles focus our funding options to companies who share our ethical ideals and whose work we respect in relation to issues such as climate change.

We've previously been asked to do work sponsored by a major power company and the answer was a defiant 'NO'. Hypocrisy is not a good way to set an example for our audiences. Everyone, especially large energy companies, seems to be eager to jump on the renewable energy bandwagon and our work would in some cases serve as a great greenwashing campaign. We've had instances in the past when corporations and other large companies, who weren't even directly funding us, wanted to use our event as a feature of their company's PR campaigns, seemingly forgetting that they were actually only doing the bare minimum in tackling their company's environmental impact.

On the positive side, through our diligence we've managed to open up healthy dialogues with festivals' fundraisers to highlight issues surrounding the mismatch of sustainable events with companies that don't necessarily share the same ideals. Even though obtaining funds from companies that we're not 100 per cent certain about will be unavoidable if we wish to continue to do our work, opening up dialogues about our concerns with these funding bodies brings these issues to the table and will hopefully propel future change.

The bigger, the better: Fact or fiction?

Our next challenge is the music and film industry's trend towards the belief that the louder the sound or the bigger the screen then the better the experience. MR believes that this is not the case and we feel that we have never compromised the quality of our events by using low powered audio and visual equipment.

A situation arose where we were unable to power a venue's sound system with our generators. The problem wasn't simply that we couldn't generate enough power but that a 100 person capacity tent with a 1000W (3000W rated) sound system is simply unnecessary. Consuming more energy does not necessarily lead to better sound quality or a better listening experience. A multitude of factors contribute to this experience. Just to prove our point, on this occasion we ended up running our own small pedal powered tent with a 200W sound system. Our event was an immense success and is now a feature of this festival every year. Another example has been our use of 3000W projectors over 5000W projectors with a reduction in ambient light in the area to compensate.

We believe that changing the current infrastructure for how festivals are run and funded will be a challenge and clearly can't become reality without effort and vision. MR hope to inspire festival organizers and attendees to see the sustainable transformation of their events not just as a set of necessary compromises, but as an opportunity for creativity within the industry.

www.magnificentrevolution.org

Source: Words by Lucy of Magnificent Revolution

Box A.6

Water Statistics, WaterAid

The following water statistics were compiled by WaterAid:

- 884 million people in the world do not have access to safe water. This is roughly one in eight of the world's population.
- 1.8 million children die every year as a result of diseases caused by unclean water and poor sanitation. This amounts to around 5000 deaths a day.
- For every $1 invested in sanitation, $9 is returned in increased productivity and a reduced burden of healthcare (UN Development Programme (UNDP)).
- The weight of water that women in Africa and Asia carry on their heads is commonly 20kg, the same as the average UK airport luggage allowance.
- In the UK the expansion of water and sanitation infrastructure in the 1880s contributed to a 15-year increase in life expectancy in the following four decades.
- In the developing world as a whole, around 90 per cent of sewage is discharged untreated into rivers, polluting them and affecting plant and aquatic life (UN).
- An old lavatory uses at least nine litres of water a flush; a low-flush model uses as little as three litres. Each household in the UK uses about 50 litres a person a day for flushing – 35 per cent of domestic water use (Environment Agency).
- Agriculture accounts for over 80 per cent of the world's water consumption (UN Environment Programme (UNEP)).
- The average amount of water needed to produce one kilogram of potatoes is 1000 litres, wheat is 1450 litres and rice is 3450 litres (Gleick, 2001).
- 97.5 per cent of the Earth's water is saltwater. If the world's water fitted into a bucket, only one teaspoonful would be drinkable.

WaterAid

Source: Unless otherwise stated, figures were taken from the Human Development Report 2006

Box A.7

Aluminium Recycling Programme Case Study, Reading Festival, UK

Reading Festival is an iconic UK rock festival, which has been running for more than 20 years. A grandfather event, this five-day camping festival is held in a peri-urban location on a greenfield site close to a major public transport hub. The capacity is 80,000 and it's held on the August Bank Holiday weekend each year in Reading, Berkshire, UK.

The Challenge

At Reading Festival cans are banned from the arena, but campers are allowed to bring reasonable amounts of beer into the campgrounds. This usually rounds out at about a case of beer per person, with a good amount also sold from the can bars in the campgrounds. A conservative estimate would be 500,000 cans, but if the case per person figure is correct, that's almost 2 million cans. At 62,000 cans per tonne, there could be a whopping 30 tonnes of cans to potentially recycle.

Unfortunately several brands of beer still sell in steel, which makes source separation slightly more complex. Compounding this is the camping culture at this festival. Traditionally quite a rowdy campground environment, cleaning up after oneself is not the social norm. Festival goers seem happy to create colourful chaos in their campsites, which includes loads of rubbish. The audience profile is predominately 18 to 25 year olds, most likely still living at home, in shared houses or university dorms.

Objectives of the project

The objective was to devise a way to maximize the number of aluminium and steel cans recycled and sent directly to a metal merchant. A twin objective was to come up with the best method to encourage participation by the audience, getting them into the act of recycling and understanding the benefits, without taking on a preaching tone or taking the fun out of the festival.

About the project

Unlike the 10p deposit on paper pint cups sold in the arena, the campers have no financial incentive to return beer cans for recycling. Instead a bribe tactic was employed.

Campers are encouraged to bring back a bagful of cans and in return they receive a beer voucher for another can of beer. A printed bag was handed out at wristband exchange and also available at recycle exchanges, campground headquarters and handed out by roving recycling stewards (Green Messengers).

Pre-production planning

As this recycling initiative is an overlay programme, alongside the standard waste management on site, a team was required who were motivated to run the initiative on the ground to ensure its success.

As there is a good profit potential for aluminium recyclate (up to £650 a tonne), a community-based recycling group was engaged with the promise of all funds raised from the can recycling project to go to their organization

Stakeholders

Research was undertaken to assess the situation for recycling on the go in the UK to determine if there were any projects or messaging programmes in existence or about to be launched. Contact was made with Alupro, the aluminium can manufacturers' association in the UK. They were in the process of devising a new campaign 'Your Cans Count', for recycling on the go. Alupro were brought in as support partners to the programme. They brokered a deal on behalf of Reading Festival with a local metal recycler, and offered assistance to the festival and to the community recycling group engaged for the project – Bright Green (www.brightgreen.org.uk).

Bright Green, of course, were primary stakeholders as they were the group that would be running the project on the ground and who would reap the financial benefit of the can recycling payout.

Figure A.4

Figure A.5

The waste contractor for the event was included in planning as there was a requirement for them to provide separate space for a dedicated aluminium skip, to ensure their staff didn't accidentally contaminate it, and also to transport collected cans from the recycle exchanges to the processing area.

Campground managers, precinct managers and campground stewards are also key to this campaign's success through continual reinforcement of the Bring Back a Bagful and Your Cans Count message.

Resources

Eight recycle exchanges were set up, one in each campground area. These were built out of temporary fencing panels, with scaff infrastructure to support signage. A pop-up marquee was placed beside each compound so that weather protection for workers was available.

Bin bags were printed with the can recycling message and handed out to campers. Bright Green allocated staff to each recycle exchange, and the festival also allocated four volunteer stewards to each.

Space for a skip dedicated to aluminium cans and one for steel was required. Space for hand sorting aluminium from steel cans was also set up.

Operations logistics

The first step was to plan the locations of the recycle exchanges. Visibility to campers, accessibility by them and also importantly by waste removal vehicles was of high importance. The psychology of walking away from the arena was considered, as people are most likely to bring their bag of cans to a recycle exchange when they are on their journey from their campsite to the arena. Siting of skips, changeover planning and location of the sorting area was planned. As there is a much higher value for pure aluminium, separating the steel cans from the aluminium was done on site with each type sent for recycling in different skips.

The confiscation area at the arena entrance was identified as a primary target for can collection. Cans or opened plastic bottles are not allowed in the arena and a system is set up for cans and bottles to be dropped in bins at the arena entrance. Usually this is just managed by waste staff with bin contents and rakings piled into bags and put in the mixed recycling skips. Recycling stewards were tucked in next to bins in the arena entrance and kitted up with clear bin bags held open by 'handy hoops'. The stewards then verbally called for cans to be placed into the bags rather than the bins. Any cross contamination was dealt with by the steward using a litter picking stick.

These bags were taken straight to the sorting centre and aluminium was sorted from steel. Mid-way through the show, because of the huge volumes of cans still hitting the ground in the arena entrance bins and also dropped on the ground at arena entrance and raked, it was decided to move these 'rakings' and bin bags to the sorting area to salvage aluminium and steel also. It is estimated that one-third of all cans collected came from the arena entrance confiscation system.

Back at the recycle exchanges, one tonne builders bags were set up. These bags are 1m² with handles. Campers returned a plastic bag of cans and were given their beer ticket and then recycling stewards hand sorted the aluminium and steel into the builders bags. These builders bags were collected by the waste team, and if pre-separated, taken directly to the aluminium or steel skip, and if mixed, to the sorting area.

Promoting the message

As the project requires voluntary participation, getting the word out was very important. Promotion methods included:

- mention in ticket letter;
- website;
- electronic newsletters to audience and stakeholders;
- prominent signage on recycle exchanges:
- advertisement in festival programme;
- page included in audience programme laminate lanyard;
- on-screen messages between bands on main stages;
- project specific bin bags printed with Bring Back a Bagful and Get a Free Beer message.

Figure A.6

Figure A.7

Tips for new players:

- Consider where your likely areas of can waste will be generated and the best way to collect, sort and transport.
- Have an appropriate system in place to transport the bags as they can become quite heavy.
- Think about the liquid waste from unfinished cans, particularly in confiscation areas.
- If you will have a high level of steel cans mixed with aluminium, your cash-in rate will be reduced by about one-third. Decide if it is worth separating metal from aluminium considering your volumes, the need for more hands to sort on site, and the lower price for mixed metal.
- Ensure you have people 'working' the project to maximize the potential yield. Give ownership.

Results

- Four tonnes of aluminium cans and one tonne of steel cans were collected.
- Money raised for Bright Green.
- Project participation increases from 2007 to 2008.

Conclusions

Although only a small percentage of potential cans were returned voluntarily, the participation by the audience was highly visible. Massive mountains of bags of cans were collected and the message about recycling certainly was taken up. It is hoped that as this campaign is refined, improved and repeated in coming years, further increases will be experienced.

www.readingfestival.com

Source: Information in this case study supplied by Festival Republic

Case Study: Live Earth

On 7 July 2007, Live Earth brought together 150 music artists with almost two billion fans, in person and through the media, for a 24-hour, seven-continent concert series that was broadcast around the world.

Live Earth was the beginning of a multi-year campaign to increase awareness of global warming and its causes and risks, and to help motivate individuals around the world to take action in their personal lives – and to prompt corporations and governments to do likewise. The ultimate in both including an environmental message and producing the event sustainably.

Official concerts were staged at Giants Stadium in New York; Wembley Stadium in London; Aussie Stadium in Sydney; Copacabana Beach in Rio de Janeiro; the Coca-Cola Dome in Johannesburg; Makuhari Messe in Tokyo; the Oriental Pearl Tower in Shanghai; and HSH Nordbank Arena in Hamburg.

From the moment they started planning the concert events for 7 July 2007, they aimed to bring them as close to the ideal of 'zero net impact' as they possibly could. Projections on energy and resource use were carried out, and they developed a plan to mitigate impacts.

In the end, Live Earth achieved more than they ever thought possible. But only did they measure the concert's impacts, they produced a report available publicly which also shows the reader how they did what they did.
Live Earth's objective was to limit the amount of energy consumed, and to substitute renewable for non-renewable energy sources wherever possible, while working within the real constraints imposed by each concert site and its location.

ENERGY: Live Earth's objective was to limit the amount of energy consumed, and to substitute renewable for non-renewable energy sources wherever possible, while working within the real constraints imposed by each concert site and its location. The single most important decision that was made was to hold most Live Earth concert events during daylight hours, which probably reduced emissions by hundreds of tons by reducing the need for illumination. Stage lighting used energy-efficient discharge and LED lights, stadiums adjusted their energy management systems to eliminate unnecessary lighting. At venues in Japan, Brazil, the United States, England and Australia, generators that powered the stage and broadcasts were fueled with neat (100 per cent) or blended biodiesel. Green electricity was sourced directly from the grid where available; where it was not, renewable energy certificates were purchased to offset our consumption through the production of cleaner energy.

WASTE: Due to aggressive efforts to reduce the amount of physical resources consumed and to procure low-impact alternatives, the concerts generated only 97 tons of waste, a fraction of what was originally projected. Through concerted recycling and composting efforts, including at the venues on the concert day, it is estimated that 81 per cent of all waste was diverted from landfills on concert day, with Tokyo reaching 99 per cent.

TRANSPORT: Audience ground travel was a significant source of emissions, and Live Earth worked hard to mitigate those emissions by encouraging lower-impact alternatives such as mass transit and carpooling. Of course many venues were in the heart of the city and good public transport uptake occurred. Public transport was free in Hamburg and Sydney to the concerts. In Shanghai and Tokyo 75 per cent of the audience used public transport. Even in New York an unprecedented 23 per cent travelled to the Giants Stadium by mass transit. While only a small percentage of concertgoers flew to the Live Earth concerts, air travel is such a heavy contributor to emissions that audience travel by air accounted for a significant portion (80 per cent) of audience transportation emissions. Approximately 8 per cent of the London and New York audiences travelled by air to the concerts.

To reduce artist air travel, Live Earth undertook to recruit artists who were already on tour or who were based near their Live Earth venue. In addition, the vast majority of artists flew with commercial airlines rather than private charters.

Figure: Live Earth Hamburg

Source: Live Earth

Information in this case study was reproduced with the kind permission of Live Earth and is from the Live Earth 2007 Carbon Report which can be viewed in full on the website: liveearth.org.

Index